Writing Talk
Paragraphs and Short Essays
with Readings

Second Edition

Anthony C. Winkler

Jo Ray McCuen

Glendale Community College

PRENTICE HALL Upper Saddle River, New Jersey 07458

Library of Congress Cataloging-in-Publication Data

Winkler, Anthony C.
    Writing talk: Paragraphs and short essays with readings / Anthony
C. Winkler, Jo Ray McCuen. — 2nd ed.
        p.   cm.
    Includes index.
    ISBN 0-13-099697-1
    1. English language—Paragraphs—Problems, exercises, etc.
2. English language—Rhetoric—Problems, exercises, etc. 3. English
language—Grammar—Problems, exercises, etc. 4. Report writing—
Problems, exercises, etc. 5. College readers. I. McCuen, Jo Ray,
1929–   . II. Title. III. Title: Paragraphs and short essays with
readings.
PE1439.W55   2000   99-13318
808′.0427—dc21   CIP

Editorial Director: Charlyce Jones-Owen
Editor-in-Chief: Leah Jewell
Senior Acquisitions Editor: Maggie Barbieri
Editorial Assistant: Joan Polk
Developmental Editor: Harriett Prentiss
Director of Production and Manufacturing: Barbara Kittle
Senior Managing Editor: Bonnie Biller
Project Liaison: Fran Russello
Manufacturing Manager: Nick Sklitsis
Prepress and Manufacturing Buyer: Mary Ann Gloriande
Creative Design Director: Leslie Osher
Art Director: Anne Bonanno Nieglos
Cover Designer: Maria Lange
Cover Image: Barry Scharf/SIS, Inc.
Marketing Director: Gina Sluss
Marketing Manager: Sue Brekka

This book was set in 11/13 New Century Schoolbook by
Publications Development Company of Texas
and printed and bound by Press of Ohio.
The cover was printed by Press of Ohio.

Reprinted with corrections February, 2000
© 2000, 1997 by Prentice-Hall, Inc.
Upper Saddle River, NJ 07458

Printed in the United States of America

10   9   8   7   6   5   4   3

ISBN 0-13-099697-1

Prentice-Hall International (UK) Limited, *London*
Prentice-Hall of Australia Pty. Limited, *Sydney*
Prentice-Hall Canada Inc., *Toronto*
Prentice-Hall Hispanoamericana, S.A., *Mexico*
Prentice-Hall of India Private Limited, *New Delhi*
Prentice-Hall of Japan, Inc., *Tokyo*
Pearson Education Asia Pte. Ltd., *Singapore*
Editora Prentice-Hall do Brasil, Ltda., *Rio de Janeiro*

Contents

Basic Philosophy of Writing Talk

Have you ever asked your students to read something out loud to see if it sounds right? *Writing Talk* takes a traditional skills approach to teach basic writing, while weaving throughout a strategy that calls on students to use skills they already possess—talking and listening—to help them become better writers. By incorporating skills students already possess, *Writing Talk* offers a less intimidating environment for students to develop their writing skills. This supportive approach is reinforced by the coverage of the writing process and other features such as:

- A chapter dispelling some of the common and discouraging myths students have about writing.
- A section on rhetorical strategies.
- A section on the 20 most common sentence errors.
- Hundreds of exercises and quizzes help students master the material in the chapter.

Key Pedagogical Features

NEW! Talk Write Assignments give students practice in translating real world speaking into its formal written equivalent. The Talk column on the left side of the page presents imagined dialogue that might be overheard in an informal discussion. The goal of the exercises, found at the end of every chapter, is to help the student understand how to convert nonstandard phrases into their Standard English equivalents. These new assignments are organized around a single unifying theme, with every sentence contributing either another opinion or an additional observation to the subject under discussion.

UNIT TALK WRITE ASSIGNMENT

In this exercise a student expresses his opinion on animal cruelty. In the process, he makes several errors in subject-verb agreement. You have two assignments: First, correct all subject-verb agreement errors found in the *Talk* column. Second, using the sentences in the *Talk* column as your starting point, create a Standard English paragraph in the *Write* column, beginning with a discussible point and proving it with sufficient details.

TALK	WRITE
1. I know a man who don't care about animals and always treat them cruelly.	
2. Each of his dogs are dying for affection. Maybe you don't think that's important, but I promise you it is.	
3. There is lots of violent criminals who who starts out being mean to cats and dogs in the neighborhood. I saw a television program that said criminals was often pet-abusers as children.	
4. One of my cousins are that way, too, always being mean to her pets.	
5. Where is the rewards of being mean to an animal who haven't a chance to complain about bad treatment?	
6. Nobody make these mean people stop mistreating animals because they don't want to interfere. Well, interfere.	
7. Often, neither the mother nor the father seem to care if their child tease an animal.	
8. Some people say, "Aw, animal abuse—that's not a real crime." But the TV show said it is a crime in many states. Moreover, both a scientist and a doctor on the show says it is a proven fact that abusing animals lead to abusing humans.	
9. One of those guys who just get a tongue lashing for being mean to a pet might be the next serial rapist or killer.	
10. The bottom line is this: Everyone of us need to do our best to stop cruelty to all living creatures if we want to be moral people.	

Photo Writing Assignments offer a change of pace by asking students to write on a topic suggested by a photograph. These assignments appear at the end of every chapter along with numerous other writing activities and a unit test.

PHOTO WRITING ASSIGNMENT

This photo is a still from *Shane*, a classic western. Westerns (sometimes called "oaters," used to be very popular but have lately given way to other kinds of movies, such as disaster epics, action stories, and so-called "buddy films." Which kinds of movies do you particularly like? What are some of your favorite films? Write a paragraph giving your views on movies. Check that you have punctuated your sentences correctly. Use the Revising Checklist to revise.

UNIT TALKING ASSIGNMENT

A. Read the following sentences aloud, asking a partner to spell the words in italics. Confirm that the spelling is right or correct it.

1. Jane's *past* work has always been excellent.
2. I have had *quite* enough trouble from you.
3. We had cookies for *dessert*.
4. *They're* over *their* limit of credit.
5. You have a hole in the *sole* of your shoe.
6. She has red hair, and she is *awkward*.
7. Lately the weather has been *changeable*.

Unit Talking Assignments at the end of every chapter are tips to guide the students in using oral communication skills to develop their writing skills.

Ear Alerts appear as a guide when your ear may mislead you when writing. First, the formal rule is explained. Then the text shows how the practice in everyday speech varies from the rule. Finally, the "Ear Alert" label and distinctive icon in the margin warn students that this is a point of grammar on which the ear cannot be trusted.

If you do not know which pronoun to use in a sentence, simply try the pronoun by itself. Your ear will tell you if you've used the correct form. For example:

I mentioned the problem to (she, her) and the landlady.

Test: I mentioned the problem to she.
I mentioned the problem to her.

Your ear will tell you that *her* is correct.

The preposition that probably gives the most trouble with pronoun use is *between*. How many times in everyday speech have you heard these incorrect forms?

Incorrect	**Correct**
between you and I	between you and me
between John and he	between John and him
between Mary and she	between Mary and her
between you and he	between you and him
between they and the police	between them and the police
between he and she	between him and her

Because the incorrect form is so common in everyday speech, this is one usage where you simply cannot trust your ear. Just remember that *between* is a preposition, and an object pronoun must be used after a preposition. You must observe this ironclad rule of grammar in your writing and should learn to use it in speaking.

Ear Alert

If one subject joined by *either/or* or *neither/nor* is singular and one is plural, the verb should agree with the nearer subject. Here are some examples:

Incorrect: Either the rats or the raccoon were here.
Correct: Either the rats or the raccoon was here.

Incorrect: Either the raccoon or the rats was here.
Correct: Either the raccoon or the rats were here.

In a Nutshell

Each, *every*, *either/or*, and *neither/nor* take singular verbs except when they join two subjects, one singular and one plural, in which case the verb agrees with the nearer subject.

In a Nutshell summarizes key concepts, providing students with an easy way to review important material.

UNIT TEST

1. Write a simple sentence with modifiers about the clothing you are wearing today.

   _____

   _____

2. Write a compound sentence by connecting two simple sentences with "but."

   _____

   _____

3. Write a complex sentence beginning with "Although." Be sure to place a comma following the dependent clause.

   _____

   _____

4. Use the pattern of the following sentence, but change the words to create your own sentence on any topic of your choice: "I will never forget my Aunt Stella, because she was my favorite relative." What kind of sentence is this?

   _____

   _____

Identify each of the following sentences as simple, compound, or complex.

1. When John entered his astronomy class, he was embarrassed to find everyone staring at him. _____

2. Let's follow the instructions carefully, and then we'll compare what we've done with the picture. _____

3. If you hurry, you can probably catch her. _____

Unit Tests are provided in addition to the hundreds of exercises to help test students' mastery of the skills in a particular unit of the book.

Revising Checklists in every chapter help students focus on the practical goal of revising their writing.

Key Supplements

 NEW! Companion Website for *Writing Talk,* second edition, www.prenhall.com /winkler, is free to every student using the text. Prentice Hall's exclusive *Companion Website*™ that accompanies *Writing Talk,* second edition, offers unique tools and support that make it easy for students and instructors to integrate this online diagnostic tool with the text. The site is a comprehensive resource that is organized according to the chapters within the text and features a variety of learning and teaching modules:

For students:

■ **Diagnostic Modules** that contain a variety of exercises and features designed to help students with self-study. These modules include:

—*chapter objectives* that help students organize key concepts to be learned

—*essay questions* that help strengthen critical thinking skills

—*quizzes* with multiple-choice, true/false, and fill-in questions that supply instant scoring and feedback on student mastery of core material

—*built-in e-mail* routing option that gives students the ability to forward essay responses and graded quizzes to their instructors.

■ **Reference Modules** contain *Web Destinations* and *Net Search* options that provide the opportunity to expand upon the information presented in the text. Through a directory of websites relevant to the subject matter of a chapter, this reference feature enables students to quickly reach related information on the web.

■ **Communication Modules** include tools such as *Live Chat* and *Message Boards* to facilitate online collaboration and communication.

■ **Personalization Modules** include our enhanced **Help** feature that contains a test page for browsers and plug-ins.

For instructors:

■ **The Faculty Module** includes resources for teaching. This includes Lecture Hints, and Class Activities, all coordinated to each chapter. This module is accessed via a password provided by your local Prentice Hall representative.

■ **Syllabus Manager**™ tool provides an easy-to-follow process for creating, posting, and revising a syllabus online that is accessible from any point within the companion website. This resource allows instructors and students to communicate both inside and outside of the classroom at the click of a button.

The Companion Website™ makes integrating the Internet into your course exciting and easy. Join us online at the address above and enter a new world of teaching and learning possibilities and opportunities.

■ **Instructors Manual** includes additional exercises with answers, answers to all exercises in the book, teaching tips, how to use the book with ESL students, CLAST and TASP correlations, and much more.

■ **NEW! Transition Notes** are available for select titles to help you make the transition from your current book to the *Writing Talk* series. Ask your local Prentice Hall representative for details.

■ **Diagnostic Tests** include pre- and post-test to assess students' level and judge students' progress. Answers to test items are keyed to the appropriate sections of the text.

■ **Writer's Solution** is an interactive writing program that helps students improve their writing skills. Basic writing and grammar skills for effective writing are covered through the use of video, fine art, animations, and other multimedia. There are two separate CD ROMs: *The Language Lab* and *The Writing Lab*.

 The Language Lab CD ROM provides activity-based lessons that build grammar, usage, and mechanics skills for better writing. Features include: lessons organized around high-interest themes relating to cross-curricular topics; paragraphs and sentence level exercises; interactive video and audio that lead the student through the program; and coverage of developing writing style and shaping language skills. *The Language Lab* CD is available to school labs free upon quantity adoption. See your local Prentice Hall representative for details.

 The Writing Lab CD ROM focuses on the writing process by presenting ideas that inspire students to think creatively. Features include: guided lessons in major types of writing; media to lead students through each stage of the writing process; and interviews and writing of professional writers. The program works well for individual study, small groups, or in class. *The Writing Lab* CD ROM is available to school labs free upon quantity adoption. See your local Prentice Hall representative for details.

■ **Writer's Toolkit** is a collection of writing tools and activities found in *Writer's Solution*. Topics include choosing and narrowing a topic, considering audience and purpose, gathering and organizing details, drafting, revising and editing, and proofreading.

 Writer's Toolkit is ideal for those who do not require instruction on particular modes of writing, but need only tools, activities, or writing ideas. This CD ROM provides all of these tools in one place.

 The *Writer's Toolkit* CD ROM can be packaged with any Prentice Hall English text at a discount price. Please contact your local representative for more details.

About the Authors

Anthony C. Winkler was born in Kingston, Jamaica, and educated at Mt. Alvernia Academy and Cornwall College in Montego Bay, Jamaica. In 1962, he came to the United States to attend school, and received an A.A. from Citrus College, and a B.A. and M.A. from California State University at Los Angeles.

For seven years, he taught as a part-time evening college instructor while working full time as a book representative first for Appleton Century Crofts, and then for Scott, Foresman.

Winkler began collaborating with Jo Ray McCuen in 1973, and became a fulltime freelance writer in 1976. He is the author of numerous textbooks, trade books (including *Bob Marley: An Intimate Portrait by His Mother*) and screenplays (including *The Lunatic,* based on his second novel). He lives in Atlanta with his wife and two children.

Jo Ray McCuen was born in Belgium and grew up in Europe, coming to the United States for her college education. She received her B.A. from Pacific Union College and her M.A. and Ph.D. from the University of Southern California. While working on her doctorate, McCuen was hired to teach English at Glendale Community College, from which she retired in 1996.

A chance meeting in 1973 with Tony Winkler, who was a college textbook sales representative, led to a partnership that has produced fifteen coauthored textbooks used at colleges and universities across the country. "I have reached the place," says McCuen, "where I have difficulty remembering what I've said in what book."

McCuen has one son, David Cotton, a perinatologist at Wayne State University. When not revising her textbooks and writing new ones, Jo Ray enjoys traveling, reading, opera, snow skiing, and tennis.

Preface to the Second Edition

The second edition of *Writing Talk: Paragraphs and Short Essays with Readings,* like the first, takes as its starting point the assumption that grammar for the native speaker is a built-in skill, not an added-on one, and that the best sense for grammar in the native speaker is the ear. This is not a radical idea. In fact, it is almost self-evident. People speak the language they hear spoken around them from birth. An English infant raised in a genteel drawing room will emerge from it speaking like an Englishman raised in a genteel drawing room. Transplant that same infant to an urban area like Brooklyn, and he will grow up to speak like someone raised in Brooklyn. We have never seen an exception to this observation. The fact is that we learn to speak our mother tongue not from a book, but from using our ears.

Yet as English teachers, we know that many of our students neither speak nor write what we have been trained to call "good grammar." Students use fragments; they punctuate badly; they misplace modifiers and garble sentences; they speak and write slang. How can we say that a speaker's ear for grammar is so absolute when all around us we have evidence to the contrary?

The answer is simple: These are not errors of bad grammar; instead, they are errors of inappropriate usage. If you are raised using *ain't* as an everyday verb, you will grow up to speak and write *ain't*. But since *ain't* is regarded today as nonstandard and unacceptable usage in formal writing, it is our job as English teachers to wean students off that word when the circumstances demand the formality of standard English.

Usage variations aside, it is still a fact that all native speakers as well as those who have spoken the language for years have within them an ear for grammar that foreign speakers do not share: That is the prime assumption behind the pedagogy of this book.

Our title, *Writing Talk,* is a deliberate play on words. On the one hand, we talk about writing; on the other hand, we write about talk. It is our intention to treat writing as an extension of speech, to encourage students in the belief that if they can "talk" English they can learn to write it, and that when they write English, they should always draw on their speaker's ear.

But there are occasions when the ear is utterly at odds with the formal rule and of no help whatsoever in deciding what is right and appropriate. A case in point is the infamous *between you and I*. Although used by a surprising array of prominent men and women in the media, this construction is incorrect. In fact, the formal rule indicates *between you and me* to be the right form. A unique feature of *Writing Talk* series is the *Ear Alert* warnings provided in such instances. We first explain the formal rule; we then show how its practice in everyday speech varies from the rule. Finally, the *Ear Alert* label and distinctive icon in the margin warn that this is a point of grammar on which the ear simply cannot be trusted.

When it was originally published, *Writing Talk* appeared in four versions: *Writing Talk: Sentences and Paragraphs; Writing Talk: Sentences and Paragraphs with Readings; Writing Talk: Paragraphs and Short Essays; Writing Talk: Paragraphs and Short Essays with Readings*. Based on feedback from users, we decided to revise only the two versions of this book with readings. *Writing Talk: Paragraphs and Short Essays with Readings* is now the second book in a series of two, and it has the following features:

- *Common Myths and Standard Written English.* We begin by dispelling some common and discouraging myths that students believe about writing. Writing is hard for everybody (no doubt rare exceptions exist, but we can't think of any offhand). We also know that the fumbling and revision that goes with writing is not a sign of ineptness, but a universal condition of the discipline. Many students do not understand how difficult writing is and tend to misinterpret the normal tedium of composing as a sign that they cannot write.

- *Paragraph Writing.* We break down the paragraph into its principal parts, discussing at length the topic sentence and supporting details. We then discuss the importance of sticking to the point and linking sentences for coherence. A unique feature of this book, and one in keeping with its rationale, is its discussion of the paragraph and talking, where we show how a spoken paragraph differs from a written one and encourage students to use their "ear for language" to help their writing.

- *Rhetorical Strategies.* Each discussion of rhetorical strategy is presented under three headings: "What Am I Trying to Do?" "How Can I Do It?" and "What Do I Need to Look Out For?" To counter the negative attitude that students sometimes have regarding the practicality of English writing assignments, every unit in this section begins with an example of how the particular rhetorical strategy might be used in the real world.

- *The Whole Essay.* Here we present the essay as a template, showing students exactly how an essay is written by breaking it down into three major parts—the introduction, the body, and the conclusion—with specific advice on the writing of each part regardless of the topic.

- *The 20 Most Common Sentence Errors.* This section reviews the errors we've seen students make most frequently in their writing—from fragments and run-ons to unnecessary commas and misspelled words. Our explanation of grammar in this section of the book (1) emphasizes functional problems, not descriptive grammar; (2) uses a minimum of terminology; (3) gives short, pointed explanations with a light touch; (4) is followed by immediate practice; and (5) includes abundant exercises.

New to This Edition

The new edition continues these features and adds one more unique wrinkle: a *Talk Write Assignment* that gives students practice in translating oral dialogue into its written formal equivalent. Each assignment presents a dialogue that might be overheard in an informal discussion and then asks students to write the equivalent in a more formal style. The new edition ends most chapters with the following four types of exercises:

■ A *Unit Talk Write Assignment* that reinforces the difference between spoken and written language.
■ A *Unit Test* that tests mastery of the chapter. (All the chapters in Part Five and Part Six of this book have a unit test. The others do not.)
■ A *Unit Talking Assignment* that gives students an opportunity to interact in group sessions and put their ear to use in practicing the contents of the chapter.
■ A *Unit Writing Assignment* that gives students a chance to apply the writing principles they have just learned.
■ A *Photo Writing Assignment* that asks students to write on a topic suggested by a photograph.

We have made other changes and improvements as well. The biggest change was in removing the overlap of exercises and examples that formerly existed in the early chapters of the *Sentences and Paragraphs* and the *Paragraphs and Short Essays* books. In the first edition, some chapters of the two books were nearly identical, with examples and exercises repeated between them. This is not the case in this second edition. We have entirely re-written all the exercises and examples in the second book, *Writing Talk: Paragraphs and Short Essays*. All the exercises and examples in this book are now unique to it.

In addition, we have added more exercises throughout the book, but selectively, based upon feedback from users. Every teacher knows that exercises and drills walk a fine line between usefulness and tedium. To simply pile on more exercises whether or not they are necessary is to confirm every ugly misconception students have about English classes. So we've added more exercises only when we think they are useful and necessary.

We've also made some changes, although minor, to the actual textual explanations. Always, we've tried to be simpler and more direct, and where the opportunity presents itself, to add a dollop of humor to what might otherwise seem to the student to be typically grim exposition of grammatical principles. Teaching grammar is a serious enterprise, but is does not deserve the graveyard sobriety of tone it is so often given.

Teachers have asked us to make our exercises more contextual, to make the individual sentences more about one thing rather than just scattershot examples. Where possible, we have done exactly that. The new *Talk Write Assignments* are all organized around a single unifying theme, with every sentence contributing either another opinion or an additional observation to the subject under discussion.

The readings in this second book, *Writing Talk: Paragraphs and Short Essays with Readings,* unlike the first, are arranged rhetorically to give students authentic examples of how writers use the strategies in their workaday world. Grouped under the eight rhetorical strategies taught in the book—"Narrating," "Describing," "Illustrating," "Explaining a Process," "Defining," "Classifying," "Comparing and Contrasting," and "Arguing," the readings are, as before, multicultural and multi-ethnic. This section begins with an introduction, "Help for Your Reading," giving practical, nuts-and-bolts advice on the techniques of reading. The readings range from a funny process piece, "How I Was Bathed" by Sri Lankan writer Michael Ondaatje to "Daddy Tucked the Blanket," a wrenching narration by an African-American writer who observed the painful unraveling of his parents' marriage.

Each essay is prefaced by a headnote and followed by comprehension questions *(Understanding What You Have Read)* and thought-provoking questions *(Thinking About What You Have Read)*. Finally, two *Writing Assignments* are included for each reading.

Throughout both books, we have tried hard to make our explanations deft and light, to explain everything step-by-step, to provide exercises immediately after explaining any rule or principle, and to respect and encourage the student's innate "ear" for grammar.

Our thanks to Maggie Barbieri, former senior acquisitions editor at Prentice Hall, who encouraged our efforts every step of the way, and to the production and manufacturing staff at Prentice Hall: Bonnie Biller, Senior Managing Editor; Fran Russello, Project Manager; and Mary Ann Gloriande, Senior Buyer.

We would also like to thank the following reviewers: Keith Coplin, Colby Community College; Bonnie Hilton, Broward Community College; and Deborah Marrott, Utah Valley State College.

In every enterprise of this kind, there lurks in the background one indispensable person who has had a significant and influential part in the outcome. Usually, this person is a freelance editor hired by the publisher to prod the writers into doing their utmost. In our case, the unsung hero who played this role was freelancer Harriett Prentiss. She goaded; she prodded; she corrected, edited, influenced, rewrote, and encouraged. She occasionally drove us mad; but she made us do more than our utmost. She made us do our best both in the first edition and in this, the second. Thanks, Harriett.

Anthony C. Winkler
Jo Ray McCuen

Preparing to Write

In this part of *Writing Talk*, you will learn some common myths about the writing process that, if believed, can affect your confidence as a writer. You will also learn the three major purposes behind most writing and the relationship between audience and writer. You will learn how to tailor your writing to a particular audience by asking some basic questions. Finally, you will learn some handy techniques for gathering ideas to use in your essay.

Myths About Writing

> "Anyone who's not dead has something to write about."

If you can talk English, you can learn to write it. Indeed, you already know more about writing than you think. However, if you are like most students, you probably believe some common and harmful myths about writing—our own students often do. Most likely, you use these myths to belittle your natural writing skills.

If a myth leads you to think that you write badly, for example, you'll try to avoid writing. Since practice makes perfect in writing as in nearly everything else, if you avoid writing, you won't get any better at it. To think you are naturally bad at writing is to plant a nagging critic inside your head who will scold every sentence you write. No one works well with constant scolding; everyone works better if encouraged. Human nature swims on "You can!" and drowns on "You can't!"

Let us begin then with a discussion of some myths about writing and how believing them can stunt your growth as a writer.

Myths About Writing

A *myth* is a popular but false belief. Among the many myths that students believe about writing are the following:

- I have nothing to write about.

- I can't write the way you're supposed to—with big words and long sentences.

- Writing is so difficult for me.

- English teachers are too picky.

- I hate to write because I make too many mistakes.

We will take up these myths one by one.

I have nothing to write about.

Anyone who's not dead has something to write about. All of us have opinions that can be used as writing topics. The problem is that students often think that only stuffy, academic topics are suitable for college essays.

You can, however, write about many topics that are neither academic nor stuffy. You can write about an everyday event in your life, such as dating, or an idea that interests you. You can write about a friend, a hobby, your job. You can tell about an exciting experience, a favorite teacher, a kindly uncle, or a cruel aunt. One student we know wrote a funny essay about a goldfish. Another wrote a moving essay about burying a hamster. Everyone alive is interested in something; that *something* is what you can write about.

To see that you do have ideas worth writing about, do the following activity, which we call "Practicing." Chances are that everyone in your group will be able to come up with an idea suitable for a paragraph.

PRACTICING 1

Form a group of three or four students. Choose one topic from the list below. Everyone in the group should take turns talking about the same topic.

1. A teacher I really like (or dislike)
2. A movie that should have won an Oscar but didn't
3. My mother's (or father's, sister's, brother's) best trait
4. My least favorite relative
5. How I choose my close friends

I can't write the way you're supposed to—with big words and long sentences.

The first aim of any writer is to communicate. If using big words and long sentences will get a message across, a writer will use them. Ask yourself, though, how often do big words and long sentences help anyone communicate? The answer is, almost never. Writers therefore use big words and long sentences only when small words and short sentences will not do the job. Small words and short sentences often make the point as well, if not better, than big words and long sentences.

Furthermore, few people like reading big words clumped together in jaw-breaking sentences. Understanding such writing simply takes too much effort. Look at the following passages, for example. Which one do you think is better written and easier to understand?

> The audience was lachrymose at the termination of the drama, especially expressing a predilection for the heroine's experienced reunification with her long-lost progeny.

> The audience was tearful at the end of the play. They especially liked when the heroine was reunited with her long-lost children.

The first passage consists of big words in one python-long sentence; the second uses simple words and two straightforward sentences. The second passage, by being direct and clear, is better than the first because it is easier to read and understand.

Directness and clarity: These are desirable qualities of good writing, not big words and long sentences. This book will teach you to write clearly, directly, and always understandably.

PRACTICING 2

Get together in a small group. Each student should choose one topic from the list below and "talk a paragraph" about it. Be as clear and direct as you can. You might want to scribble down a few ideas in advance.

1. Your most valued personal possession
2. How to get to the nearest fast-food restaurant
3. Where you live
4. A piece of good advice
5. A piece of bad advice

Writing is so difficult for me.

"I hate to write, but I love having written." So said Eudora Welty, a famous American writer whose works are widely read. The fact is that writing is hard for almost everyone. There are some rare exceptions, but for most of us, writing is one of the most difficult tasks we do. It is easy to scribble a note to leave on the refrigerator: "Roy, did you pay the rent? The landlord called." It is equally easy to send a friend a quick e-mail message: "Kelly, see you at the ball game." But writing that requires us to frame a complex thought, explain it in detail, and back it up with facts and opinions gives everyone trouble.

That writing is hard for everyone is a pesky fact but one that does not have to get in a writer's way. Trouble, however, crops up if you begin to believe that you're the only one who finds writing hard. The raw truth is simply this: Writing is hard work for the great, the near great, the professional, the amateur, for your Aunt Susie, your Uncle Albert, for me, and for you. If you accept that writing is difficult, you will at least begin with a realistic outlook. Say to yourself, "Writing is hard." Now, having admitted that, you can simply roll up your sleeves and get to work.

PRACTICING 3

Try your hand at some "easy writing." Write a refrigerator note on each of the following topics. Address it to someone specific, your apartment-mate or someone in your family. Keep the message short and to the point.

1. You're going to be late. Say why.
2. Describe a phone message you took for someone.
3. Ask a roommate or family member to leave you money on the kitchen table.
4. You're doing something with a friend and won't be home for dinner. Tell who and what.
5. Apologize for something (being a grouch this morning, etc.).

English teachers are too picky.

Everyone who has had an English class, even English teachers themselves, have felt this way at one time or another. But it is the role of the English teacher to be your editor, and any editor who is not picky is useless. By picky, students usually mean that their teacher finds many "small" mistakes. But what may seem a small mistake to you may lead your reader to misunderstand you. Here is an example. A former student of ours has recently begun writing for a free neighborhood newspaper. One of her articles contained the following sentences:

> When it comes to gambling; the professional is no better than the amateur. It might even be said that the amateur has a better chance; by not knowing the real risk involved.

Did you spot the mistake in these sentences? It is in the use of semicolons. Obviously, we should have picked at her more vigorously about punctuation than we did. This mistake may seem trivial to you, but it is no small mistake. Writers who repeatedly make it will find themselves ridiculed by fellow-reporters or misunderstood and may even find the way to promotion blocked. This is not to say that using a semicolon properly is an earthshaking skill; it isn't. But even such a small misuse can embarrass you and harm an otherwise promising career since most professions require some amount of writing. As an old Chinese proverb says, "People do not fall over mountains; they trip over pebbles."

PRACTICING 4

Here is a chance to exercise your skill at being picky. Each of the sentences below contains an error that our students have called "picky." Find and correct the error. If you need help, ask your teacher!

1. We're having pecan pie for desert.

2. Between you and I, the band was awful.

3. She is the most hardest worker.

4. For a man of his size; he is very quick.

5. I'm majoring in biology, I want to be a veterinarian.

6. She moved to Florida. Which really surprised me.

7. For a person to get ahead, you must work hard.

8. A doctor know best.

9. A lawyer should respect his client's confidentiality.

10. That car is her's.

I hate to write because I make too many mistakes.

Everyone who writes or talks makes mistakes occasionally. We came across this sentence, for example, in a scholarly book about the Civil War Union General William Tecumseh Sherman:

> When victory was achieved, however, [the army should] stop the bloodshed and destruction immediately and help those in need irregardless of any oaths of allegiance.

Irregardless is not a standard word. If you check your dictionary, you'll see that the author should have written *regardless*.

In speech every one of us has, at one time or another, mispronounced a word, addressed someone by a wrong name, or misspoken a common phrase. Mistakes in speech are so common that many even have names. Here, for example, is a **spoonerism**, a mistake where a speaker mixes up the beginnings of words:

> Will someone please hick up my pat?

Of course, what the speaker meant was, *Will someone please pick up my hat?*

Yet even if you do make the occasional mistake, you also know a great deal more about language than you think. This knowledge—sometimes called an *ear* for the language—comes naturally from the thousands of hours you have spent listening to and speaking English. Using your ear for language can help you with your writing.

Of course, you do not know everything about the language. Like the rest of us, you have your weaknesses. However, you also have your strengths, and they are considerable. This book can help you use what you do already know by ear about language. What you don't know, this book can teach you.

Let us begin with what you know. Take the following quiz. We think you will be pleasantly surprised to find out how much you already know about English.

PRACTICING 5

Using your ear for the language, make an *X* in the space beside any sentence you think is incorrect. If you think the sentence is correct, leave the space blank.

1. _____ I love to sailing.

2. _____ Jamaica is a beautiful island.

3. _____ Uncle never went Vietnam.

4. _____ Between you and me, I'm very tired.

5. _____ He have a twitch because he is nervously.

6. _____ She a good poem writes.

7. _____ What should we have for dinner?

8. _____ I gived the man a dollar.

9. _____ Stay sitted in your chair, please.

10. _____ Jim is a faster talker than me is.

Here are the correct sentences:

1. I love to sail. *Or* I love sailing. (Omit the *to* or change to *to sail.*)
2. Jamaica is a beautiful island. (Correct as written.)
3. Uncle never went to Vietnam. (Should be *went to,* not *went.*)
4. Between you and me, I'm very tired. (Correct as written.)
5. He has a twitch because he is nervous. (Should be *has;* no *-ly* needed after *nervous.*)
6. She writes a good poem. (Original misplaced the verb *writes.*)
7. What should we have for dinner? (Correct as written.)
8. I gave the man a dollar. (*Gived* is not a word.)
9. Stay seated in your chair, please. (*Sitted* is not a word.)
10. Jim is a faster talker than I am. (Not *me is.*)

To sum up, don't approach writing as if it were a kind of communication utterly different from the talking you normally do. See it first as a kind of talking—but on paper. Remember that if you can speak English, you can use your ear to become a better writer.

In a Nutshell

There are five common myths about writing:

- I have nothing to write about.

- I can't write the way you're supposed to—with big words and long sentences.

- Writing is so difficult for me.

- English teachers are too picky.

- I hate to write because I make too many mistakes.

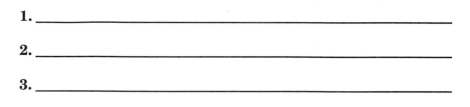

State what you believe to be the three most serious difficulties you have with writing. State each in a separate sentence.

1. _____

2. _____

3. _____

PRACTICING 7

Form a small group of three or four classmates and discuss the difficulties you have with writing and what you might do about them.

Standard English

If you can speak English well, why do you sometimes have trouble writing it? The answer is simple. Writing is, for the most part, done in Standard English, which is not the English we commonly speak.

Standard English is English that is universally accepted by dictionaries and respected authorities. It is the universal English that all people who speak and understand English can use to communicate. Just as plumbing pipes have standardized sizes and fittings, Standard English has a standard vocabulary—no slang or street-talk—and a standard grammar. Without standards, English would become so regional that a New Yorker might have a hard time communicating with a Californian. With Standard English, however, all who speak the language can make themselves understood, at least on one level.

Consider, for example, these pairs of sentences:

Standard: You understand?
Nonstandard: You dig?

Standard: The game was exciting.
Nonstandard: The game rocked.

Standard: You're joking.
Nonstandard: You jiving.

Realistically, which sentence in each pair do you think, say, a native Russian who also speaks English would more likely understand? The nonstandard sentences would be understandable only to those who have an ear for nonstandard English.

Even if you speak mainly nonstandard English, you also have an ear for Standard English. Every day you hear it in television newscasts and read it in magazines and newspapers. Most publications, including the supermarket tabloids with their alien three-headed babies and prowling bigfoots, are written in Standard English. In fact, you are more likely to read this Standard English headline in a tabloid,

> Alien Spacecraft Sighted!

than this nonstandard one,

> Alien Spacecraft in the Hood!

Your ear cannot help you, however, with some finer points of Standard English. For instance,

> "Let's keep this news between you and I."

This commonly used construction, which probably sounds right to your ear, is actually wrong. The *I* is technically wrong. The correct sentence should read,

> "Let's keep this between you and me."

Yet practically every day we hear people say *between you and I*. In Standard English, that is wrong.

When we think we see a situation where your ear for spoken language might trick you, we will warn you with an "Ear Alert" such as this one.

To sum up, use your ear for the language to help you with your writing although bear in mind that sometimes your ear can mislead. To become the best writer you can be, you must also learn certain ground rules for written work. You must learn the rules of capitalization and punctuation. You must learn how to use prepositions correctly (*between you and me* not *between you and I*), adverbs (*I speak quickly* not *I speak quick*), and verbs (*seated* not *sitted*). You must learn how to organize your thoughts into paragraphs and how to assemble your paragraphs into a clear essay.

In short, you must learn some grammar as well as some techniques for writing paragraphs and short essays. This book will not only teach you grammar, it will also teach you how to use the paragraph to make a point and how to knit paragraphs together into an essay.

The good news is this: As a speaker of English you are already ahead in the race to learn these skills. Indeed, many of the skills you need to be a good writer you already practice in your everyday talking. You know much more than you think!

In a Nutshell

- Standard English is English that is universally accepted by dictionaries and respected authorities.

- Even if you speak nonstandard English, you still have an ear for Standard English.

• Your ear for English can usually help you with your writing. When it can't, this book will warn you.

PRACTICING 8

For each of the following pairs of sentences, check the one written in Standard English.

1. **a.** _____ It ain't necessarily so.

   b. _____ It isn't necessarily so.

2. **a.** _____ You can't hang that one on me.

   b. _____ You can't blame that on me.

3. **a.** _____ Stop hound-dogging me about money.

   b. _____ Stop pestering me about money.

4. **a.** _____ He doesn't care about it.

   b. _____ He don't give a rap about it.

5. **a.** _____ I bought the coolest earrings.

   b. _____ I bought some very pretty earrings.

6. **a.** _____ She's preparing to go to the beach.

   b. _____ She's fixing to go to the beach.

7. **a.** _____ There's too much chin music at those meetings.

   b. _____ There's too much talking at those meetings.

8. **a.** _____ They spared no expense for the party.

   b. _____ They went whole hog for the party.

9. **a.** _____ I went to the seashore to relax.

   b. _____ I went to the seashore to chill out.

10. **a.** _____ I was, like, feeling real mellow.

    b. _____ I was feeling very calm.

PRACTICING 9

Below is an e-mail message written in everyday informal language by one student to another. Rewrite the paragraph in Standard English.

Hey, Marcy What a blast to hear from you! I just been down here kicking around in the new hood, chilling out every day, and having a ball. My Mom's been cool about everything She hasn't been on my back even once about school work. It just goes to show you that the old lady is not as over the hill as I had thought. As for friends, so far I've got zip, zero, zilch. My love life is equally exciting. I met a couple dudes in the cafeteria, but, I mean, like, guys always think they're so hot. It makes me want to puke. . This one guy I met, like, every second word out of his mouth was "I, I, I, I." I felt like saying, "gimme a break, will ya?" Well, whatever. So what's new by you?

_____

_____

_____

_____

_____

_____

_____

_____

_____

_____

PRACTICING 10

On a separate sheet of paper write two paragraphs on one of the topics below. In the first paragraph feel free to use nonstandard English. In the second use only Standard English.

1. A personal desire
2. Portrait of someone I really admire
3. A time when I was lucky
4. A time when I was unlucky
5. Something that makes me laugh just thinking about it

TALK WRITE

In this Talk Write exercise and the ones to follow, you are asked to convert a spoken paragraph into a more structured written one. The exercise is designed to apply your speech skills to your writing. To do the exercise, turn the spoken sentences under *Talk* into Standard written English.

This particular assignment presents one student's comments during a class discussion about personality. Here is what the student actually said in response to the question, "What is the most interesting part of your personality?" Rewrite the casual spoken speech into Standard English in the lines provided.

Spoken Paragraph

Actually, I'm sort of a funny guy, I guess. Mom always called me the clown of the family. Come to think of it, kids in grade school used to—I just think they did—look to me for monkey tricks—like giving smart alecky answers to questions asked by teachers. Some times I'd cross my eyes, bare my teeth, and stick out my tongue—just to look geeky, you know. The kids always laughed. I mean, I still play that role. Trouble is, I don't always feel like being funny. Some times I just want to tell everyone to bug off and leave me alone, but when you've gotten the reputation of goofy Joe, you kinda feel obligated, you know. It's like, you know, they're expecting you to make 'em laugh. Even you guys in this class put pressure on me, you know. The other day our psych teacher asked us to define *pessimist.* She probably expected some high-falutin answer from our textbook assignment, but I couldn't resist being the class joker by waving my hand high above my head as if I had the perfect answer. "Yes, Fred?" The teacher asked—and, of course, all heads jerked around as if to say, "O.K., goofball, say something funny . . ." With triumph I belted out my dad's saying, "A pessimist is a guy who looks both ways when crossing a one-way street." Naturally, the class giggled, and some looked at the ceiling as if to say, "There goes that nut case." What can I tell you? I'm a total joker.

Written Paragraph

_____

_____

_____

_____

_____

_____

_____

UNIT TALKING ASSIGNMENT

Get together with a classmate and describe to him or her a time when you lacked self-confidence. Have the classmate ask you questions about the circumstances involved and how you felt. Then use your discussion to write a paragraph written in Standard English.

UNIT WRITING ASSIGNMENT

Write a paragraph about a time when you got something you wanted and found it wasn't as desirable as you thought. Use Standard English.
    Here is how one student accomplished the assignment:

I always thought it would be wonderful to be in charge of our household. But when this opportunity actually came my way, the task proved extremely hard. For eight months while I was in high school, while my mother toured Iran, I was completely in charge of my dad's household. I was the woman of the house. I became a master of finding the right kinds of detergents and bathroom cleaners. I clipped supermarket coupons to get special discounts. I found a little Armenian market where I could buy fresh vegetables at modest prices. I even discovered that with the right amount of club soda I could get out any stain from our carpet. At three o'clock in the afternoon, when I came home from school, I would put away my books and put on my apron. Cookbooks no longer scared me because I learned to follow their instructions and make scalloped potatoes, stuffed grape leaves, and lamb kabobs. My dream had come true: I was in charge of my house. But I was not happy. First of all, I had no time for studying. Then too, as soon as my mother had left, my father began to brood and to keep himself away from me and my sister. He would leave at eight in the morning and come back at eight at night. I did my best to cook his favorite foods, hoping that it would cheer him up, but he continued to be sad. Then, one early September morning I received a surprising phone call from my mother. She said she would be home a month earlier. "Hooray!" I thought. At last I can lead a normal teenage life again—with Mother in charge of the household.

PHOTO WRITING ASSIGNMENT

The following photo depicts a place where young people "hang out."
First, in a small group of classmates, discuss favorite gathering places.
Then write a description of a place where you or your friends hang out
regularly. State why the place is popular. Use only Standard English.

Purpose and Audience

> "Purpose is why you are writing. The audience for your writing is the person for whom you write it."

We write for different reasons, in different ways, and with different tools. Some of us sit at a desk and write with a computer. Others curl up in a chair with a legal pad and scribble away with a pencil. Some of us outline what we want to say before we begin, while others discover their ideas as they write. Our reasons for writing likewise vary. They can range from a letter applying for a job, to a report on U.S. history, to a personal note jotted in a birthday card.

Yet all writing has at least two things in common: *purpose* and *audience*.

Purpose

Purpose is *why* you are writing. Knowing the purpose of an assignment can actually help you with its writing. However, you'll get no help from thinking that your purpose for writing an essay is to get a grade. A newspaper reporter writes for money—but imagining a paycheck as the purpose for a story about a local bus strike will not tell the reporter how to write it.

On the other hand, the reporter who understands that the purpose of a story is to *inform* the public about the local bus strike knows exactly what to do: *inform*. State the facts. Give background information. Stick to the point; don't make jokes, just tell the story behind the strike. *Why* you write, in short, will always affect *how* you write. To know your purpose is to understand not only *what you must do* but, equally important, *what you must not do*.

Basically, all writing serves one of three purposes:

1. To entertain
2. To inform
3. To persuade

Writing to entertain

Writing to entertain is fun to do because it is writing at its most informal and lighthearted. Your main purpose is to amuse your reader. You do not have to be faithful to logic or facts. You do not have to do any research. You can exaggerate, twist situations, and use colorful language.

Students are often hesitant to use *I* in their college writing, and this hesitation is well-founded. In a research paper, for example, many teachers prefer that students not use *I*. In writing to entertain, however, the *I* is not only welcome, it is unavoidable. How could you tell the story of your funny summer vacation, for example, without calling yourself *I*? After all it happened to you, not to *one* or to nobody. Writing meant to entertain, therefore, is often told by an *I*, as it should be.

Here is an example from a very funny writer, Mark Twain. His purpose is to entertain an audience of young people by giving them tips on how to live a moral life.

> Always obey your parents, when they are present. This is the best policy in the long run, because if you don't they will make you. Most parents think they know better than you do, and you can generally make more by humoring that superstition than you can by acting on your own better judgment.
>
> *Mark Twain, "Advice to Youth."*

Here is another example, from a student paper, about visiting the dentist:

> Most dentists have been taught in school to put their trembling patients at ease by talking to them. My dentist is a pro at this. He waits until my mouth is packed to the brim with cotton and dry from the saliva suction tube. When I am helplessly pinned to the chair, he will ask a heavy question such as, "So, you're taking philosophy in school? What's your take on Plato's 'Myth of the Cave?'" As I try to answer, he'll say, "Open wider and turn toward me," with the result that I can't get a word out. If I do manage to blubber an opinion and he disagrees with me, he immediately starts drilling below the gum line until I take it all back.

PRACTICING 1

For each of the following pairs of topics, check the one whose primary purpose is more likely to entertain.

1. **a.** _____ Being completely broke is a great way to keep your roommate from borrowing your money.

   b. _____ Bird-watching is an educational hobby.

2. **a.** _____ The homeless problem in the United States is getting worse.

   b. _____ I love to help out hypocrites—just to listen to their extravagant praise.

3. a. _____ Medical research is offering new hope for AIDS patients.

    b. _____ The most effective labor-saving device on the market is a spouse with lots of money.

4. a. _____ Usually, progress means exchanging one nuisance for the other. Consider garbage disposals.

    b. _____ I believe strongly that NASA should send more humans into space.

5. a. _____ Marriage is a great institution, but I'm not ready for an institution yet.

    b. _____ Banking is a sensible career choice.

PRACTICING 2

Write a letter to your best friend relating something that happened to you. Your purpose is to entertain.

Writing to inform

"Just the facts, ma'am." Years ago a beloved television cop made that statement popular. It neatly sums up what should be your aim when you write to inform: to give the facts.

When you write to inform, your aim is usually to explain something to your reader. You might define the meaning of a little-known term. You might describe what bacteria look like under a microscope. You might compare running to power walking. You might explain the stages of a process: First you do this, then you do that. In all cases, though, you remain mainly serious while trying to be as clear and understandable as possible. Here is an example of informative writing.

> In the United States, we seem to awaken to social problems in stages: In the case of family violence, awareness of child abuse increased during the 1960s, spousal abuse was the issue of the 1970s, and abuse of the elderly was publicly acknowledged in the 1980s. Abuse of older people takes many forms, from passive neglect to active torment, and includes verbal, emotional, financial and physical harm. Most elderly people suffer from none of these things; but research suggests that some 1 million elderly people (3 percent of the total) suffer serious maltreatment each year, and three times as many sustain abuse at some point.
>
> *John J. Macionis,* Sociology, *Prentice Hall, 1999.*

The writer focuses on an emerging social problem—abuse of the elderly.

Here is another example, this one from a student paper about *ki*, a martial arts concept:

How can a man in a threatening situation jump higher or run faster than he thought possible? How can another lie on broken glass with a 150 lb. concrete slab on his chest while enduring the blows of a sledgehammer and not be harmed? The answer, known to those advanced in the martial arts, is a phenomenon called *ki*— an invisible force present in all living things that can be developed by anyone. Ki consists of four powers that are classified as *lightness (kyung ki), heaviness (hung ki), hardness (chul ki),* and *numbness (ma ki).* With proper training and discipline, anyone can attain these powers and use them to perform extraordinary feats of strength and athleticism.

This writer is informing us about a martial arts concept by defining it. Later in this book you will learn to use definition in your writing.

PRACTICING 3

Both paragraphs that follow try to inform, but one does a better job than the other. Read both paragraphs and decide which one is better. Then, in the space provided, state the reasons for your choice.

A.

Cable TV offerings have become really ridiculous. There are too many choices. A viewer can have many, many choices. There's something for everyone. There's something for the sports fan and something for the cook. The gardener has a special program, and children have many choices. If you are history buff, there's a program for you, and if you love music, there are music programs, too. For the weather enthusiast, there are live radar displays of local weather. Yet in spite of all these choices, you still hear people say, "There's nothing on TV."

B.

Cable TV offerings have become ridiculous. One local cable company in my area offers 160 channels in its regular subscription. There are programs for gardeners, history buffs, sports fans, cooks, and just about anyone else with a special interest. Premium subscribers can choose another dozen or so channels offering nonstop movies, and even these are specialized. There are channels called Classic Movies, Romance Classics, Independent Film Classics, True Stories, and Science Fiction. The Cartoon Network shows nonstop children's cartoons. One station, called *Animal Planet,* screens nothing but wildlife shows. In addition, there are 30 stations devoted to playing music of all types, from classical to rap. Yet with all these choices, people still complain, "There's nothing on TV."

_____

_____

_____

_____

_____

_____

_____

_____

_____

_____

PRACTICING 4

Check the topics listed below that would make good informative paragraphs.

1. _____ Guide-dog training is a complicated process.

2. _____ Grafting plants is not as simple as it might look.

3. _____ My Aunt Trudi reminds me of a horse.

4. _____ The popularity of golf in the United States is soaring.

5. _____ Finches are the largest family of birds and include several distinctive types.

6. _____ There are several ways to improve your neighborhood watch program.

7. _____ Three kinds of students annoy me: Vapid Vivian, Stupid Steve, and Holy Herbie.

8. _____ My brother is a rat.

9. _____ Let me tell you about my operation.

10. _____ Jefferson Davis accomplished four major goals while he was president of the Southern Confederacy.

Writing to persuade

Your primary aim in writing to persuade is to win over your reader to your point of view. You wish either to change your readers' minds or to prod them into taking some action. You do so by stating the facts, making logical arguments, and quoting the supporting views of experts. Often, you present the opposing viewpoint to spell out its inconsistencies or weaknesses. You always aim for a logical presentation of your case.

Here is an example of a paragraph written to persuade:

> Extremists within the animal-rights movement take the position that animals have rights equal to or greater than those of humans. It follows from this that even if humans might benefit from animal research, the cost to animals is too high. It is ironic that despite this moral position, the same organizations condone—and indeed sponsor—activities that appear to violate the basic rights of animals to live and reproduce. Each year 10,000,000 dogs are destroyed by public pounds, animal shelters, and humane societies. Many of these programs are supported and even operated by animal-protectionist groups. Surely there is a strong contradiction when those who profess to believe in animal rights deny animals their right to life. A similar situation exists with regards to programs for pet sterilization, programs that deny animals the right to breed and bear offspring and are sponsored in many cases by antivivisectionists and animal-rights groups. Evidently, animal-rights advocates sometimes recognize and subscribe to the position that animals do not have the same rights as humans. However, their public posture leaves little room for examining these subtleties or applying similar standards to animal research.
>
> *Frederick A. King, "Animals in Research:*
> *The Case for Experimentation."*

This writer is trying to persuade us that animals should be used in medical research. His argument attacks those who disagree and points out inconsistencies in their views.

Here is an example of a student paragraph written to persuade:

> If you're like many people, you've probably passed by runners, seen the look of agony and pain on their faces, and said to yourself, "I'd rather die." Runners do not look happy, but walkers do, and walking is every bit as good for you as running. Walking reduces the risk factors for heart disease and stroke as much as running. Walking also produces the same healthy cellular changes as running does, with the same beneficial effects upon the heart and the lungs. Moreover, walking helps prevent diabetes, strengthens bones, and improves the immune system. Best of all, you do not have to walk until you're ready to drop like runners often do. In fact, walking for 20 to 30 minutes a day has been shown to have

a highly beneficial effect on a person's overall health. This was recently proved again in a study conducted by the National Institutes of Health. Next time you come home worn out at the end of the day, don't just slump in a chair and watch TV. Get out and walk. Not only will it be good for you, it'll make you feel better.

This student presents the advantages of walking with straightforward logic. She is serious, but not stuffy as she tries to persuade others to her point of view.

In a Nutshell

• The three broad purposes for writing are to *entertain*, to *inform*, and to *persuade*.

• Knowing the purpose of your essay tells you *what to do* as well as *what not to do*.

PRACTICING 5

Some students live in dorms while attending college. Others choose off-campus apartments, while still others live at home. Which do you prefer? List three reasons you would use to persuade someone to your opinion.

1. _____

_____

_____

2. _____

_____

_____

3. _____

_____

_____

PRACTICING 6

Compose an argument against the use of animals in laboratory or medical testing.

Audience

The **audience** for your writing is the reader, *the person for whom you are writing*. Most writing is aimed at a specific audience—an individual or a specific group of readers.

From your daily talking you already know more about audience than you think. For example, you know that you can talk to your roommate using language you would not say to your grandmother. Indeed, so sophisticated is your sense of language and audience that you can tell about a social situation just from a line of casual talk. Take the following quiz to test your intuitive sense of how language is used for a specific audience. We will use as an example the everyday greeting, "Hey girl, what's going on?"

Quiz: *Hey girl, what's going on?*

1. Who do you think the greeter is?
   a. An elderly relative.
   b. A teacher.
   c. A boss.
   d. A close friend.
2. How old do you think the greeter is?
   a. Over 50.
   b. A teenager or other young person.
   c. Over 60.
   d. At least 80.
3. What is the sex of the person being greeted?
   a. Male.
   b. Female.
   c. Could be either male or female.

The answers we had in mind are (d), (b), and (b).

You know that you'd greet only a close friend so informally, not a professor, boss, or elderly relative. You also know that a young person would most likely use this particular greeting, and that "girl" is a popular term among young female friends today. All of us, from our use of daily speech, already have a grasp of the language that is suitable for different audiences.

In talking we choose appropriate language on the spot with surprising sophistication. When we make mistakes, people tend to overlook them during the give-and-take of conversation. Writing is not so forgiving of mistakes. You can still use your intuitive understanding of audience when you write, but you must use this sense more carefully, taking the time to edit your work until it fits its audience.

The instructor as audience

Whenever you write anything, you always should ask yourself, "Who will read this?" Naturally, in your present circumstance, the expected answer is, your instructor. Yet your instructor is only your symbolic audience. That is, your instructor stands for someone else.

In the classroom your instructor is, first, an editor who will suggest ways to improve your writing. Your instructor also has a second role—to stand for the educated reader. This is the reader for whom most of us write in the everyday world of work and business—someone who is educated but not an expert on our topic.

Asking questions about your audience

After you ask the question, "Who will read this?" you must ask yourself two more questions: "What does my audience know about this topic?" "What does my audience need to know for me to achieve my purpose?" The answers to these two questions will tell you what information you must provide and what you can safely leave out.

For example, if you are a sailor writing to another sailor, you can use common sailing terms and know you will be understood. Here, for example, is one sailor writing to another about upwind sailing:

> To head upwind, ease the tiller in the direction of the heel until the mainsail gives signs of luffing. Do not head up any higher or you'll find yourself in the irons. Once you've reached the luff line, fall off five points to weather until the sail is drawing fully without further signs of luffing. That is your tack.

This description would puzzle anyone but a seasoned sailor. For the average educated reader, therefore, your explanation might be given this way:

> A sailboat can sail with the wind behind it, with the wind coming from the side, or with the wind blowing off the bow (the front). This last course is known as "upwind sailing." To sail upwind, ease the tiller (the steering stick) in the direction of the heel (the tilt of the boat) until the mainsail begins to sag and flap where it is joined to the mast. This is known as luffing. Do not head up any higher or you'll find your sails flapping wildly and your boat at a standstill in the water. This condition is known as being "in the irons" and can pose a danger to the boat on a blustery day. Once the sails have begun to luff, slowly pull the tiller away from the direction of the heel until the sail is drawing fully and showing no signs of luffing. The boat should be heeling and driving ahead. You are now sailing upwind.

The writer now defines all the terms. Although a fellow sailor will know the meaning of *bow, tiller, luffing, in the irons,* and *heeling,* these terms would stump the average educated reader who's never been on a sailboat. Yet someone with a general knowledge can be expected to know the meaning of *mast* and *mainsail* so the writer doesn't define these terms. This is what writers do—they adapt their work to their audience.

Similarly, if you are writing an essay about how to tune a car for a reader who can't tell a fender from a bumper, you know right away that not only must you explain the process, you must also name and explain basic parts. You must say, these are the sparkplugs. You can find them here. This is what they look like. This is what they do. Here is why they must be changed when you tune the car.

If your reader knows the difference between a fender and a sparkplug, you can start your explanation at a higher level and skip the basics. In either case you know which information to include and which to omit by asking the two basic audience questions: "What does my audience know about this topic?" "What do they need to know for me to achieve my purpose?"

In a Nutshell

- Your audience is the person or group for whom you are writing.

- The two questions you should ask about audience are, "What does my audience know about this topic?" "What does my audience need to know for me to achieve my purpose?"

PRACTICING 7

The following writing assignment is aimed at three different audiences. What details about your family life would you focus on for each audience?

1. Describe your family life for a cousin who is planning to spend the summer with you.

_____

_____

_____

2. Describe your family life to a college admissions officer.

_____

_____

_____

3. Describe your family life for a student living in China.

_____

_____

_____

PRACTICING 8

Fill in the spaces as indicated.

1. Write an appropriate greeting for a distinguished professor you meet in the cafeteria.

_____

2. In the same cafeteria you leave the professor and sit down with a friend. Write an appropriate greeting for him or her.

_____

3. A student you've seen around and would like to know better sits at your table and makes eye contact. Write down how you greet him or her.

_____

TALK WRITE

We spend much of our talking time trying to persuade, and we use different techniques, depending on our audience. Sometimes we make an emotional argument, sometimes a logical one. What we say is often not what we would write in a more formal written argument.

The *Talk* section below presents a spoken paragraph that is persuasive. A student is talking to her apartment-mate about a city council proposal to tag all cats, just as dogs have to be tagged. Cindy, the speaker, is heatedly against the proposal and decides to write her council representative. Your assignment is to rewrite Cindy's spoken paragraph into Standard English. Consider the different audience and the reasons she presents. Add whatever you think is necessary to improve her argument.

Spoken Paragraph

Obviously our City Council has no clue about cats. What a bunch of boobs. Really. I can't believe real people would come up with a moronic idea like that. Cats aren't like dogs. I mean, can you imagine a cat wearing a license tag around the neck? My Siamese cat,

Rama, would have a conniption fit if you tried to tie anything around her neck. I'm not kidding. She would claw and spit and scratch like a crazy witch before being dissed by a tag. "Just like a stupid dog," she would sniff to herself. Can't be on a leash, either. Doesn't everybody know that cats are boss when it comes to being completely independent? You can't wow them; you can't push them around; you can't threaten them; and you can't tag them. No way, Jose! They live in their own world where they reign like kings and queens. Forget this tag stuff. I'll bet you any amount of money that the dummy politicians who came up with this stinker don't own a cat or they'd know better. Cats have to be allowed to stalk, hunt, chase, and track—day or night—whenever they feel like it and without some crummy necklace bothering their necks. I'm telling you, keep tags away from cats.

Written Paragraph

_____

_____

_____

_____

_____

_____

_____

_____

_____

_____

UNIT TALKING ASSIGNMENT

Choose one of the topics below and decide what kind of paragraph you would like to write—a paragraph to entertain, inform, or persuade.

1. A favorite outdoor activity
2. The benefits of fairy tales
3. A popular television sitcom
4. A sport I enjoy
5. What I would like to do with my life

Pair up with a partner and talk about the details you might use and how you would go about developing the paragraph for an average educated reader. Now switch places with your partner, who should do the same.

UNIT WRITING ASSIGNMENT

On a separate sheet of paper develop the topic you discussed above into a paragraph. Before you begin, write down your purpose and audience. Then stick to your purpose and write with your audience in mind.

PHOTO WRITING ASSIGNMENT

The following picture shows concert-goers enjoying a live performance at a rock concert. Choose a specific person—an elderly relative, a roommate, a teacher—and write to persuade him or her that rock concerts are fun, boring, or whatever else you think about them.

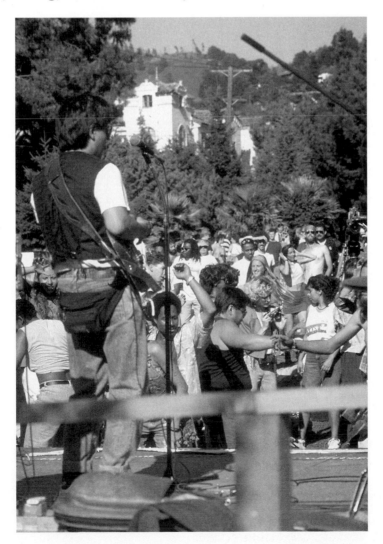

Gathering Ideas

*"The skill of writing is like a muscle:
The more you use it, the stronger it gets."*

Writing is always hardest at the beginning when the page is blank. We start to write, find the going slow, and imagine our secret fears about our inability to write confirmed.

The truth is that for nearly everyone, writing is hard and slow work; the only solution to the slow start is to get started quickly. Once the words are flowing, self-doubt will give way to the practical business of writing.

In their working habits writers tend to resemble baseball pitchers. For both *warming up* is essential. Pitchers throw practice balls to flex their arms; writers warm up their writing skills by scribbling words on the page. Indeed, the longer you sit and write, the better you will gradually find yourself getting at it.

There are several things you can do to start yourself writing:

- Talking writing

- Freewriting

- Brainstorming

- Clustering

All these activities will help you warm up, get ideas, and arrive at a suitable writing topic.

Talking Writing

One of the simplest ways of getting ideas is to talk aloud about your topic to a friend, yourself, your cat, or even a chair (better not to do this in public, however!). The idea is to use talking to inspire thinking. Most of us feel better after we talk over our troubles with a friend. Similarly, discussing your topic with a friend will give you a clearer picture of what you want to write.

The talking we have in mind is not hit-or-miss gabbing, but talking aimed specifically at your topic. Begin by opening a notebook so you can jot down any ideas or suggestions that you get during the talking. If you have a friend with whom to share your thoughts, start by simply stating your topic. No one can predict what will happen next, but an idea of what might possibly follow is shown on page 32.

You: I've got a paragraph to write.

Friend: What about?

You: Someone I admire.

Friend: So who are you going to write on?

You: I don't know. Maybe Sandy, a girl I work with. She is someone special.

Friend: What's so special about her?

You: She's so down-to-earth. When she walks into a room, she always says hello to everyone. She always tries to say something cheerful or positive.

Friend: Oh, yeah? What's she look like?

You: She always looks great. The other day she walked in with a black sweater. She was a knockout.

Friend: I hate her already.

You: No, you'd like her. She's always nicely dressed. It isn't often that I see her wearing the same outfit twice. She has black hair, and never a strand out of place.

Friend: Where's she from?

You: California. But she lived for years in London. She has this British accent that makes her sound so cool on the phone. But she's not snobby. Just nice and straightforward.

Friend: That's good.

You: And when you're talking to her, she always looks right at you and really listens. It doesn't matter if you are the janitor or the President of the United States. I definitely admire her.

Talking can help you come up with the kinds of details your reader will be interested in. Notice, for example, that in this exchange the friend asks where Sandy is from, which leads to interesting information that might be included in the paragraph. Talking can also help you decide what your purpose is and how you need to approach the topic for your particular audience. It is even possible to talk out a topic sentence that you can refine later. The point is to use talking to start yourself thinking about the topic and to get ideas about it.

In a Nutshell

Talking to yourself or a friend about your writing topic can help you find things to say about it.

> ### PRACTICING 1

Your teacher has asked you to write a paragraph about one change that you would like to see at your college and why. Choose a friend and talk out the assignment. Jot down notes.

> ### PRACTICING 2

Write the paragraph you talked about in Practicing 1.

Freewriting

A good warm-up exercise for the writer is freewriting. To **freewrite**, you write about a topic for a timed period of about ten minutes. Forget about grammar, spelling, and punctuation. Just sit and write freely. If you have nothing to say, write, "I have nothing to say," until you do say something. The result of such freewriting will be sense mixed with nonsense, but gradually you'll find yourself warming up to the topic.

Here is an example of student freewriting:

> How I spend my free-time? Most of the time, I don't have none. Between school and work, I hardly have time for anything else. I don't know what else to say. What can I say? When I have a day off, I like to fix cars, I like taking them a part. If I thought I could get a good job in a garage without going to school, I would. But today, even the garages want someone with at least a junior college degree. I don't know what else to say. If I had any free time, I wouldn't spend it, I would save it. But I never have any. I get up around six. Then I feed the dog and the cat, make myself coffee, and read the paper. At least, I read the funnies. Sometimes the sports page. Then I go to work for most of the morning. In the after-noon I go to school, and try to make heads and tails of English. Usually I have to write essays such as this one about topics that have nothing to do with cars. Then I go home and play with the dog and the cat and watch TV and do my homework and try to write essays like this one, which is supposed to be about how I spend my free time, which I never have any of.

Notice that the paragraph contains several grammatical errors, which is fine in freewriting. For example, the writer says, " most of the time, I don't have none," which is a double negative. He says about cars, "I like taking them a part" when what he really means is, "I like taking them apart." What other errors do you find? Errors are normal and expected in freewriting. The idea is not to write perfectly, but simply to think out loud on paper. As a result of this freewriting session, the student decided to write his essay on the topic, "Not having any free time." The freewriting session did its job: It generated an idea for an essay.

Your own attempts at freewriting should be similarly loose. Don't try to correct your mistakes, control your writing, or muzzle your thoughts. Freewriting should be as free and uncontrolled as a pitcher's warm-up tosses. The goal in both cases is the same: to warm up.

In a Nutshell

You can warm up to a topic by freewiting about it.

PRACTICING 3

Freewrite for five or ten minutes on one of the topics below.

1. A job I once had
2. What I like to cook
3. A favorite singer
4. Dreams
5. A movie I think is overrated (or underrated)

PRACTICING 4

Write a paragraph based on your freewriting session (Practicing 3).

Brainstorming

The aim of freewriting is just to get you writing. Once you're warmed up and are ready to write, however, you need to focus on finding ideas to put down on paper. One especially good technique for finding ideas is brainstorming.

Brainstorming is an exercise in thinking. You simply list every thought that pops into your head about a particular topic. Don't try to write in sentences. Don't worry about logic or whether your ideas are good or bad. Just jot down your thoughts. You can always sort them out later.

Brainstorming produces a random list of ideas, as you can see from this student's list on the topic "things I like:"

apple pie

riding my mountain bike

dressing up

fancy restaurants

watching my little sister eat

teasing my brother

popsicles

caramel apples

popcorn

walking

birdwatching

Uncle Fred

quiet

alone

peaceful

saw a blue heron once

fabulous

lifted off like some spirit

huge wing span

slow, beating wings

breathtaking

bird watching is actually fun

When you are finished brainstorming, you look over the ideas scribbled on the page to find out what you really think about the topic. Odd as it may seem, many writers learn what they really think about a topic only when they try writing about it.

For example, this student remembered the excitement he felt when he saw a rare blue heron in the park last summer. He decided to write a paragraph on that one thrilling moment in his hobby of birdwatching, which he'd learned from his uncle. That experience became the focus of his paragraph. Brainstorming will often give you this kind of new slant on your topic.

In a Nutshell

Brainstorming is a warm-up technique of freely jotting down ideas about a topic.

PRACTICING 5

Brainstorm by yourself on one of the following topics.

1. Why your room is important to you
2. Showing love
3. A hobby or special interest
4. Planning a surprise party
5. Your favorite sport

> **PRACTICING 6**

Brainstorm in a group session on one of the following topics.

1. How to become more organized
2. What makes a good boss
3. What makes a good employee
4. What makes a good parent
5. How to eat well on a tight budget

> **PRACTICING 7**

Write a paragraph on one of the topics that you brainstormed on in either Practicing 5 or Practicing 6.

Clustering

Clustering is thinking with the help of a diagram. As with brainstorming, you don't worry about grammar or wording. You simply think about your subject, jotting down your ideas in circles.

One aim of clustering is to narrow a broad subject to a manageable topic. For example, clustering can help you narrow the broad subject of the Internet to a manageable topic, such as how being online helps you do your homework. It is always harder to find things to say about a big topic than about a smaller one. Indeed, what can you say about the Internet? That it is a new frontier? Everyone already knows that. On the other hand, try writing about how the Internet helped you complete a difficult homework assignment, and the examples and details will probably gush out in a flood of words.

Here is how clustering works. You begin by writing down the main word of your subject and circling it. From this core word you draw spokes. Then you write down any other idea that comes to mind. Page 37 shows a cluster diagram on the Internet.

Clustering goes a step beyond brainstorming because it groups—clusters—related ideas. You take the big subject in the middle and reduce it to smaller ideas that you put at the ends of spokes. From each smaller idea, you can branch off other ideas that are even smaller. Eventually, you will not only find an idea small enough to be a manageable topic, you will also find you have much to say about it. For example, in the diagram on page 37, *Homework Help* is a manageable topic. The smaller circles suggest details that you can use in a paragraph or essay on it. You can begin by talking about how the Internet helps you with your homework in general and then get down to a specific case, giving appropriate examples. You can cite the help you got from using Yahoo!, from consulting online encyclopedia, or from reading online magazines.

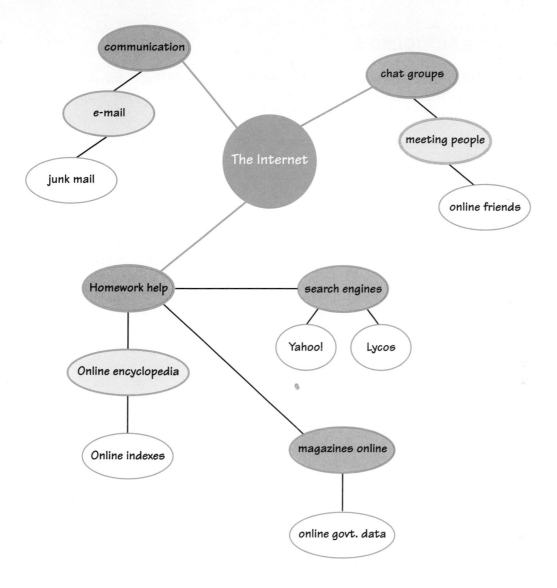

In a Nutshell

Clustering is using a diagram to think about your topic.

PRACTICING 8

Do a cluster on one of the topics below.

1. Neighbors
2. Exercise
3. Music
4. College sports
5. High school teachers

PRACTICING 9

Examine your cluster diagram from Practicing 8 for a manage-able topic about which you have lots to say and write a paragraph about it.

Journal Writing

The skill of writing is like a muscle: The more you use it, the stronger it gets. If you never write, your writing muscle will shrivel up. One way to keep the writing muscle exercised is to keep a daily journal.

The **journal** is a notebook in which you pour out your heart about everything and nothing. Because a journal is private, you can write anything you like in it. Getting in the daily practice of expressing your deepest self on paper can help you to get used to writing.

You can use your journal as a source of ideas for writing topics. You can add to it anything that interests you: cartoons, magazine clippings, newspaper articles, quotations, notes from friends, and so on. Here are some sample entries from a student's journal:

1/5/99—Sometimes the news is so depressing. Now we're worried about other countries getting the nuclear bomb. You'd think that whole thing would be over by now, what with the collapse of Russia. But it turns out that instead of getting better, things are getting worse. Now more countries have the bomb, like India and Pakistan. Then there's Sadam Hussein and biological warfare. It looks like we've gone from the frying pan to the fire.

1/17/99—Today was a stinky day. My alarm clock didn't go off, and I was late for my 8:00 psych class. The professor gave me a dirty look, and when I tried to explain to him after class that my alarm clock wasn't working, he said he didn't care. Well, if he doesn't care, I don't care either. Then John, who I usually eat lunch with, was in a stinky mood over some stupid girl. I told him not to take it out on me, that my day was hard enough already. Later, I found out at my job that the new fry cook quit, which meant I had to work a double shift and close up. When I got home it was late, and I found that my cat had eaten a bird and left the feathers and bones all over the living room floor. Maybe a bird will eat her one day. I'm in a bad mood. Then there's this whole business about the nuclear bomb hanging over my head, too. As if I didn't have enough to worry about.

1/18/99—I heard a poem today on the radio that I really like. It's short:

Whether the weather be cool

or the weather be hot,

we'll weather the weather

whether we like it or not.

I wonder who wrote it?

1/20/99—Today I got a raise at work. It's only 50 cents an hour, but I can sure use it. My boss said I've been doing a good job and deserve it. She said she wished she could give me more, which I thought was very sweet. Maybe one day I'll be able to get a better car.

Here are a few suggestions for keeping a journal:

1. *Write regularly.* Keep your journal regularly, even if you have nothing special to say. If you get in the habit of writing regularly, you'll find something to say about even a boring day.

2. *Don't worry about grammar or spelling.* Write from your heart. Don't edit your entries, and don't think you have to be in a cheery mood. If you're upset or angry about something, use the journal to get it off your chest. Just write about anything that's on your mind.

3. *Keep your journal handy at all times.* Keep your journal with you so you can pick it up whenever you get the urge to write. Some people like a small spiral notebook, while others prefer a regular class notebook. The choice is yours. Use whatever notebook you prefer—small, big, spiral, or bound. Some students have even used exam *blue books* as journals.

4. *Date your entries.* Dating your journal entries will help you remember when you made them. You'll have fun looking back at specific events that happened during the year. You'll also be able to watch your writing skills grow over the passing months and years.

In a Nutshell

Keeping a daily journal can help exercise your writing muscle.

PRACTICING 10

To get a feel of what it's like to keep a journal, write a brief journal entry on what you did this morning.

_____

_____

_____

_____

_____

_____

_____

PRACTICING 11

From the journal entry that follows, written during the Civil War by a 16-year-old Southern girl just out of school, extract an idea that could be used for writing a paragraph. Use the space below to write.

Charleston, June 20, 1863. It is too delightful to be at home! In spite of the war everyone is so bright and cheerful, and the men are so charming and look so nice in their uniforms. We see a great many of them, and I have been to a most delightful dance in Fort Sumter. The night was lovely and we went out in rowing boats. It was a strange scene, cannon balls piled in every direction, sentinels pacing the ramparts, and within the casements pretty, well-dressed women, and handsome well-bred men dancing, as though unconscious that we were actually under the guns of a blockading fleet. It was my first party, and the strange charm of the situation wove a spell around me; every man seemed a hero— not only a possible but an actual hero! One looks at a man oh so differently when you think he may be killed tomorrow! Men whom up to this time I have thought dull and commonplace that night seemed charming. . . .

From the diary of Esther Alden

UNIT TALK WRITE ASSIGNMENT

A good way to get ideas on a subject is to talk with friends and class-mates. Below is the transcript of a conversation among four students who were assigned to write a paragraph about television sitcoms.

Use the space provided below to turn this four-way conversation into a paragraph that either supports or opposes the view that sitcoms benefit society. You may use the ideas reflected in the four-way conversation as if they were your own. You may also want to add your own ideas.

Conversation

Dexter: I think sitcoms are a stupid waste of time. I'd much rather watch the history channel.

Sonik: I disagree completely. A good sitcom is like an extended family.

Armineh: Sonik is right. My friends and I discussed every *Seinfeld* episode. My best friend swooned over Jerry, and I think George is adorable. And Kramer! He's hysterical! All of my friends loved rehashing the episodes. It kept us close—we knew something special—we were insiders—like belonging to a private club.

Sonik: I agree. I always felt as if I knew everyone personally, like they were part of my life. I really felt bad when something happened to Jerry or Elaine.

Dexter: You've got to be kidding. How could you take a tv show seriously? The show was hot air, about nothing. The characters stood for nothing. Nothing important ever happened—nothing—just silly stuff. It was worse than a soap opera.

Bryan: Now *Mash*—I've seen re-reruns of that show—*that* was a sitcom worth tuning in on. You could learn about the Korean war, about petty human jealousies, about true friendship, about how military big shots can make your life miserable.

Bryan: Have you guys ever seen re-runs of *All in the Family?* My dad loved that show.

Sonik: What was it about?

Bryan: About a middle-aged guy who was really politically conservative, and everything his liberal son-in-law said or did drove him crazy. He called him "Meathead." The old guy was really stupid, but you got sucked into watching him and even liking him.

Armineh: What do you mean?

Brian: Well, he said stupid stuff, but then he'd always try to do the decent thing.

Dexter: If I want opinions about politics, I'll watch the news.

Armineh: Wasn't the main character Archie Bunker? And didn't he become a household word for stupid conservatism?

Bryan: Yeah.

Dexter: You're all talking about how popular these shows are. But people get addicted, and that's bad. My sister lives for Monday night and *Ally McBeal.* When I was in the hospital, she left early so she could get home in time to see it.

Sonik: Oh, come on. It's comforting to know that anything can pull together a whole country, even a TV show.

Dexter: Well, I don't think sitcoms contribute anything worthwhile to our society.

Bryan: I think anything that gives people a common experience is good.

Written Paragraph

_____

_____

_____

_____

_____

_____

_____

_____

_____

_____

_____

_____

UNIT TALKING ASSIGNMENT

Pair up with another student. Choose one of the topics below and talk out a paragraph. Take notes on your ideas.

1. A serious problem that exists in your community
2. Raising responsible children
3. An obsession of yours or of a friend
4. How country music has changed
5. The problem with being too in love

UNIT WRITING ASSIGNMENT

From the notes you took in the Unit Talking Assignment above, write a paragraph.

PHOTO WRITING ASSIGNMENT

Study the following photo. Use talking, freewriting, brainstorming, clustering, or journal keeping to develop ideas for writing a paragraph. Then write the paragraph.

Writing Good Paragraphs

This part of *Writing Talk* leads off with the topic sentence and its importance to an essay. You will learn how to compose good, workable topic sentences that will make writing an essay easier. You will learn the kinds of details you need to include to make your writing convincing. Finally, we will introduce you to some techniques for linking your sentences into coherent and unified paragraphs.

The Topic Sentence of a Paragraph

> "One of the best features of my apartment is its convenient location."

Before the invention of the printing press, writing was done on long rolls of paper called *scrolls*. The writing itself appeared as a solid, unbroken block of print. To help readers follow the writing, *scribes*, those workers who hand-copied the scrolls, would make a small mark in the margin of the manuscript wherever a new idea appeared. This mark was known as a *paragraphus*. From that word comes the word *paragraph*.

Today, instead of making a mark in the margin, we indent five spaces to signal the beginning of a new paragraph. In other words the idea behind the paragraph has remained unchanged through the centuries. A paragraph is still a group of sentences discussing a single idea. What makes a paragraph is not the indentation or blocklike shape but the focus of all its sentences on a single idea.

Here are two examples. Which of these is the better paragraph?

A.

Alzheimer's disease is a dreadful disease that hits many of the elderly at an alarming rate, including my grandmother. Grandmother soon forgot her identity, her relatives, and her past. For five years she lived with us at home. Sometimes, Grandmother would insist that the house next door was her house and that she wanted to go there. One afternoon, she asked me who "the lovely lady" was visiting her. I had to tell her that it was her own sister. "Oh, how nice," she exclaimed, without a glimmer of recognition. Her condition worsened as the months passed until she lost complete control of most bodily functions. After much inner turmoil my parents decided that it would be in everyone's best interest if Grandmother went to an extended care facility. Today my grandmother just lies in bed, staring at the ceiling. We visit her and hold her hand and wonder why her "golden years" have to be so horrible.

B.

"The cows don't care how smart you are, and General Motors doesn't require a degree." That's what a counselor told me at Juniper High in Michigan. Being book-smart, artistic, and cultured were not admirable qualities in this community, where most people went into farming or into factory work. One of my best friends became a farmer. In fact, he's been very successful. He has a big dairy, and he sells most of his milk to the Miller Cheese Factory. In the fall of 1995 I entered Southwest Institute, where I enjoyed the courses in art and literature. When I studied van Gogh's paintings, I wished I could paint like him. My teacher became a sort of guru for our whole class. He was a model teacher—always prepared, very fair, and very interesting. He really helped us gain insight into our own inner selves.

The first paragraph focuses its every sentence on one single point, namely that Alzheimer's is a dreadful disease. The second paragraph has no unifying topic to hold together its sentences. Separately, they are good sentences, but jointly they go nowhere. Paragraph A is a paragraph, whereas Paragraph B is a block of sentences.

The lesson the examples teach is this: Just because a block of print is indented, it is not a paragraph unless it functions like one. To be a paragraph, all the sentences must focus on and add to the same single point.

In a Nutshell

A block of print is a paragraph only if all the sentences are focused on the same topic.

PRACTICING 1

The block of writing below contains some good ideas, but it is not a paragraph. The topic sentence is underlined. Delete all details that are off the topic.

<u>My dog Fazzi is a kick.</u> I found him one late afternoon about two years ago, hovering behind a fence, sick and scared. He has taught me what it means to love unconditionally. I can truthfully say that no one has given me more pure joy in life than this little mutt. He rarely makes demands. All he seems to want to do is give affection and receive it. His loyalty is so fierce that he would attack Godzilla to defend me. I wish human beings would learn certain character traits from dogs. Society might be improved if it could be more like dogs. Too many people today just live the "gimme, gimme" life of greed

and ambition. In fact, most politicians, businesspeople, and profes-sionals just want to climb the social ladder and make money. Little Fazzi couldn't care less about ambition and power. He's happy just walking with me or riding in my car when I have to run an errand. People who don't have dogs miss a great opportunity for genuine friendship.

Talking and the Paragraph

Although the paragraph is an invention of writing, for the most part we also talk paragraphs. For example, here is a "spoken" paragraph:

> My new apartment is very convenient. It's close to everything. The bus passes right in front of the building. Right across the street is a mini-grocery store that is always open. Next to that is a shop-ping plaza that has a laundromat, supermarket, drugstore, and Radio Shack. The campus is only a mile away. I can easily walk to my classes. Also, my best friends live only a half-mile away.

How is this description a "spoken paragraph"? First, it discusses a single point—that the speaker's new apartment is convenient. Second, every sentence adds another detail about that single point.

Of course, we do not always talk in paragraphs. Sometimes, we exchange rat-a-tat single sentences. Other times, we talk in scatter-shot fashion, hopping from one topic to another like a bumble bee in a garden. If you listen carefully, you'll find many instances of talk all around you that sound remarkably like paragraphs.

PRACTICING 2

Get together with a classmate and take turns talking paragraphs on one of the following statements. Remember to stick to the point. Tell your partner if he or she strays from the subject.

1. I really get stressed out during final exams.
2. I can't stand (or I love) vegetables.
3. My parents treat me like a little kid.
4. I wish my girlfriend (or boyfriend) weren't so demanding.
5. I like (or I hate) cooking.

The Topic Sentence

The **topic sentence** of a paragraph is a single sentence that sums up what the paragraph is about. The topic sentence is like a road sign telling your reader where your paragraph is heading. If your topic sen-tence is *Baseball is a boring sport*, your reader knows what's ahead: a discussion of why baseball is boring. Obviously, it makes sense to put this road sign before, rather than after, the discussion. Typically, then, the topic sentence comes first in a paragraph.

Not every sentence, however, can be a topic sentence. Indeed, some sentences simply won't work as topic sentences. The ideal topic sentence should do the following:

- Make a single point

- Make a discussible point

- Not be too narrow

- Not be too broad

The topic sentence should make a single point.

How many times has someone come up to you and said, "I want to tell you about my girlfriend and my new car"? Hardly ever. We usually don't mix two topics in a single breath. It is far more likely that you will hear first about the girlfriend and then about the new car.

Yet students will often write topic sentences that propose to take up two topics in one paragraph. Here are some examples:

Two topics: My neighborhood is beautiful, and it has the best bakery in town.

One topic: My neighborhood is beautiful.

or

My neighborhood has the best bakery in town.

Two topics: The best time to form good habits is when you're young, and bad habits have a way of staying with you as you get older.

One topic: The best time to form good habits is when you're young.

or

You should get rid of bad habits while you're young.

Two topics: My best friend helped me get over my fear of computers, which really helped me write essays for English composition.

One topic: My best friend helped me get over my fear of computers in one easy lesson.

or

A computer is a wonderful tool for writing English class essays.

The paragraph that tries to take up two topics at once is doomed to be confused. It is hard to keep two topics straight in a spoken paragraph; it is even harder to do in the written one. Read your topic sentence aloud to be sure that it commits you to discuss a single topic. If it does not, rewrite it.

PRACTICING 3

Place an *S* in the blanks provided for each sentence that makes a single point. Leave the others blank.

1. _____ Your vocabulary can be improved if you force yourself to use new words, but a good vocabulary alone will not guarantee good writing.

2. _____ If you want to get along with people, learn which battles to fight and which ones to ignore.

3. _____ It's important to buy the right shoes for mountain hiking, and you should maintain good health so that you can make it up steep inclines.

4. _____ My brother lacks consideration for the other members of our family.

5. _____ His optimistic attitude makes my 80-year-old grandfather one of the most popular people in our neighborhood.

The topic sentence should make a discussible point.

To be discussible, your topic sentence should give you something to say. It should state your opinion, point of view, or feelings on the topic. Consider this sentence:

Yesterday I went to a baseball game.

If this were a line of talk, your listener would probably reply, "Oh? What game did you see?" The conversation would pick up from there and could lead to a friendly chat about sports.

Writing, however, is not a dialogue. There's no one to ask, "Oh? What game did you see?" Your topic sentence must therefore do the work of asking for you. Indeed, the ideal topic sentence not only says, "Oh?" it also says, "Prove it!" Here is an example:

Baseball is a boring sport.

"Oh? Prove it!" which you then do:

Baseball is a boring sport. For example, yesterday I went to a baseball game. It lasted nearly three hours. During that time there was one home run and three singles hit over nine innings. The rest of the time the game consisted of "strike one, strike two, strike three," or, "ground ball to the shortstop, a throw to first, and he's out." For some innings—six to be exact—almost nothing happened. The sun was hot, the seats were hard, and the hot dogs were gummy. I spent $15 to get sunburned, eat bad food, and see a dull game with no athletic feats whatsoever.

One way to check whether or not you have a suitable topic sentence is to apply the "Oh? Prove it!" test. The topic sentence that passes this basic test will at least give you a discussible topic.

PRACTICING 4

Turn the following dead-end topic sentences into discussible ones.

Example: Harriet wore a brown suit to the bridal shower.

Harriet always wears understated clothes

1. The other day Laurie used a cussword.

_____

_____

2. Banana cream pie is high in calories.

_____

_____

3. Mr. Wang makes jokes in our algebra class.

_____

_____

4. I like my new computer.

_____

_____

5. Sometimes we get carry-out for dinner.

_____

_____

The topic sentence should not be too narrow.

If your topic sentence is too narrow, you will have a hard time finding anything interesting to add to it. Here are some examples:

Too narrow: Dallas parking meters have a parking limit of 30 minutes.

Discussible: The parking in our city should be improved in order to increase business.

Too narrow: There are always a lot of dishes after a party.

Discussible: Doing the dishes with my roommate after a party can be as much fun as the party itself.

Too narrow: The international student center contains 20 foreign flags.

Discussible: The international student center serves our F-1 Visa students well.

An overly narrow topic sentence is seldom discussible without strenuous effort. It will often flunk the "Oh? Prove it!" test. Even if it can pass that test, its narrowness is still likely to make it boring to the general reader. The best course for the beginning writer is the middle ground: the topic sentence that is discussible and not overly narrow.

PRACTICING 5

Rewrite the following narrow topic sentences into discussible ones.

Too narrow: My basketball team wears old-fashioned yellow shorts.

Discussible: Basketball uniforms should be modernized to keep up with new styles.

1. My car needs a tune-up.

   _____

   _____

2. My sister works at McDonald's.

   _____

   _____

3. Every morning I read my horoscope in the newspaper.

   _____

   _____

4. We have 300 Vietnamese students and 250 Korean students on our campus.

   _____

   _____

5. A television soap opera writer earns as much as $250,000 a year.

   _____

   _____

The topic sentence should not be too broad.

The opposite of a too-narrow topic sentence is the topic sentence that is too broad. The broad topic sentence proposes too big a topic for a paragraph. It is so general that the writer will struggle to find anything specific to say about it. Here are some examples:

Too broad: The Olympics has a long history.

Discussible: Michael Johnson is my favorite sprinter.

Too broad: The U.S. family has changed over the last 100 years.

Discussible: My mother did a great job as a single parent.

Too broad: A good education is the basis of a good life.

Discussible: You have to know Standard English to get a good job.

Each of the too-broad topics could fill a book, but they cannot be covered in a paragraph unless the writer is very skilled. Use your common sense. Ask yourself whether you could talk an intelligent paragraph—not an essay, but a single paragraph—on the topic. If you can't, you can't write one about it, either.

In a Nutshell

The topic sentence of a paragraph should make a single discussible point. A good topic sentence is neither too narrow nor too broad.

PRACTICING 6

Rewrite each of the following broad topic sentences so it presents a single discussible point.

Too broad: The history of skyscraper architecture is a colorful one.

Discussible: Skyscrapers were built in New York in the mid-nineteenth century.

1. Sports build character.

_____

_____

2. People in the United States love to go on diets.

_____

_____

3. Music is an important part of life.

_____

_____

4. If you don't have your health, you don't have anything.

_____

_____

5. Computers run our lives today.

_____

_____

UNIT TALK WRITE ASSIGNMENT

The following conversation in the student lounge took place between two students. The topic was drinking water—a subject covered in a television special report one student had seen the night before. From the discussion, extract a discussible topic sentence and develop it into a paragraph written in Standard English and supported by appropriate ideas and details. You may use any sentences and ideas found in the discussion as well as add your own. Write your paragraph in the lines provided.

Conversation

Francine: Cool. You like Evian water, too.

Chuck: This is my last bottle. I'm going on the wagon.

Francine: Gee, you sound like you're addicted.

Chuck: Yeah, I know, but didn't you watch Channel 4 last night when they reported on bottled water?

Francine: Nah, I was too busy doing homework. What'd they say?

Chuck: They reported on some lab tests done on bottled water— you know, Evian, Naya, Sahara, Arrowhead, Alpwater, Crystal Geyser, and others I can't remember.

Francine: So?

Chuck: Well, it was awesome. They found that these so-called designer waters had just about the same level of purity as tap water. Can you believe that?

Francine: You're kidding? How can that be?

Chuck: I don't know, but that's what the lab tests showed. Maybe microbes accumulate while the water sits on shelves, or maybe tap water just isn't that dirty.

Francine: Well, I don't care. I'll pay a few pennies more; the taste is worth it.

Chuck: It's more like bucks more.

Written Paragraph

UNIT TALKING ASSIGNMENT

A. All of the following sentences could be written in a paragraph, but they are missing a topic sentence. Read them aloud to a partner, who should then supply a topic sentence for you to write below. Working together, make the topic sentence clear and discussible.

1. Benjamin Franklin invented the lightning rod, bifocals, and other practical items.
2. He was apprenticed to a printer and became a successful editor.
3. He became the U.S. ambassador to France.
4. He started the first lending library.
5. He helped draft the Declaration of Independence.
6. He was a member of the 1787 Convention that produced the U.S. Constitution.

Topic sentence: _____

_____

B. Now have your partner read you the following sentences, and then you try to supply an appropriate topic sentence.

1. The curtains are grimy and torn.
2. The posters on the wall are old and falling off the wall.
3. Mark's bed is unmade.
4. Dirty dishes and coffee mugs litter Mark's desk.

5. Clothes are flung over chairs and even on the floor.

6. Candy wrappers lie all over the stained carpet.

Topic sentence:_____

_____

UNIT WRITING ASSIGNMENT

Choose one of the numbered topics listed below and write a paragraph about it. Be sure to do the following:

- Decide on a purpose—to entertain, inform, or persuade.

- Take your audience into account.

- Gather ideas by talking, freewriting, brainstorming, clustering, or journal writing.

- Write a topic sentence that makes a single discussible point.

- Check that all the sentences in your paragraph are about that single point.

1. High salaries paid to sports stars
2. A valuable lesson you learned in high school
3. Your opinion of sex and violence in movies
4. Your favorite restaurant
5. Why college students drink

PHOTO WRITING ASSIGNMENT

The following picture shows a scene from a garage sale. Write your opinion about why these kinds of neighborhood events are so popular today. Begin with a discussible, single-point topic sentence.

Adding Details

> "What kinds of supporting details do paragraph writers most often use? That depends on the topic sentence."

A typical paragraph consists of two main parts: a topic sentence and supporting details. The topic sentence is the sentence—usually the opening one—that states the main point of the paragraph. Supporting details are sentences that back up this main point with specifics. Here is a typical paragraph with the topic sentence underlined:

> <u>For all its popularity, satellite dish television is still riddled with drawbacks.</u> The first drawback is the most serious. Most satellite dish television systems do not pick up local channels. If you want to watch the local news or local programming, you have to have a separate antenna. The second drawback is the expense. Satellite dish television can be quite expensive. In addition to installation charges, you also have to pay monthly subscription rates to a service provider. These charges can easily add up to a substantial monthly fee. The third drawback may seem odd, but it is nevertheless real. Satellite dish television systems offer too many program choices. Depending on the system you have and the server you subscribe to, a satellite dish system can offer in excess of 200 programs. Just navigating the maze of programming choices is a challenge and a headache. Finally, a satellite dish is not suitable for every home site. In fact, a lot of homes cannot use satellite dishes because of surrounding hills.

Supporting Details

What kinds of supporting details should writers use in a paragraph? That depends on the topic sentence. A good topic sentence suggests the kinds of details needed for its support. Basically, there are five kinds of supporting details:

- Examples
- Facts
- Testimony
- Reason and logic
- Personal observation

We'll cover each type of supporting detail separately.

Examples

An **example** is a part used to represent the whole. You say that working at Joe's Diner is hard. Someone asks, "What do you mean by hard?" For example, you say, employees must work 12-hour shifts without a break. Working long hours without a break is one small part of why working at Joe's Diner is hard.

The example is an effective supporting detail that is used as often by writers as by speakers. Here is an example from a student essay on the usefulness of the Internet:

> <u>There's a lot of useful information available on the Internet.</u> For example, I needed to find the words of the national anthem of Trinidad. I went to Yahoo!, entered "national anthem" in the search box, and was directed to a site called the World National Anthem Database. There I found the entire text of the national anthem for Trinidad. Another time, my mother wanted to find the exchange rate for Singapore dollars to send some money to a relative. Again, this information was readily found on the Internet, merely by going to a search engine and typing "foreign currency rates." It took all of two minutes to find what I was looking for. Indeed, almost anything you need to know can be found on the Internet. Here's another example: Not too long ago, I was doing a paper on old television shows and needed information on the sitcom "The Farmer's Daughter." I found an entire Web page devoted to the star, Inger Stevens. It contained all that I was looking for. Before the Internet, I would have had to go to the library and manually dig through reference books. What would have taken me a half a day to find, I found on the Internet in a matter of minutes.

To use examples, all you have to do is introduce them with a suitable phrase such as *for example*, *for instance*, or *take the case of*, and then spell out the example you have in mind. Naturally, any example you use should support your point. For instance, Joe's Diner may have a wonderful employee training program but mentioning that won't support your point that *working at Joe's Diner is hard*.

PRACTICING 1

Write two appropriate examples that support the following topic sentences.

1.   **Topic sentence:** The sound in movie theaters today is deafening.

First example: _____

_____

Second example: _____

_____

2. **Topic sentence:** There are some advantages to owning an ordinary wristwatch with a minute hand.

First example: _____

_____

Second example: _____

_____

3. **Topic sentence:** Telling lies can ruin a friendship.

First example: _____

_____

Second example: _____

_____

Facts

A **fact** is a statement that is accepted or can be verified. Anyone who is curious can look up the statement in a proper source and verify its truth. For instance, the fact that George Washington was born on February 22, 1732, can be confirmed by checking the encyclopedia or any biography of our first president. Some facts are simply accepted by everyone because they have never been proven untrue. That sooner or later all humans die is one such fact.

The opposite of a fact is an opinion. Unlike a fact, an **opinion** is a personal belief that cannot be proved either true or false. Here are some examples of facts and opinions:

Accepted fact: The sun rises in the east.

Verifiable fact: Toni Morrison wrote *The Bluest Eye.*

Opinion: Toni Morrison's best book is *The Bluest Eye.*

That the sun rises in the east is a universally accepted fact, and every morning nature again confirms its truth. Anyone can look up who wrote *The Bluest Eye,* and every book consulted will give the same answer: Toni Morrison wrote it. However, it is not universally accepted that *The Bluest Eye* is Morrison's best book. Some readers will argue that *Song of Solomon* is her best, whereas others will make that claim just as strongly for *Sula.* The third statement is therefore an opinion because it is not universally accepted like the first nor verifiable like the second.

Here is a paragraph that supports its topic sentence with facts:

The prices of computers have come down dramatically. Just a little over a year ago I bought up a 233 MHz computer with 32 megabytes of RAM, a CD-ROM drive, and a 14 inch monitor. I paid a little over $1800 for it. Today in the newspaper that same system with the same amount of memory and same size monitor, was advertised for $799. To make matters worse, my system was a clone—meaning an off-brand that was assembled locally. The $799 system was a Hewlett-Packard Pavilion, which is a known national brand backed up by a good warranty. But when it comes to buying a computer, it's no use waiting. Prices are always coming down.

Properly cited, facts add believability to a paragraph. Of course, you must always be sure that your facts are indeed facts and not opinions. Ask yourself, can a reader look up this statement and confirm its truth? If not, the statement is an opinion, not a fact.

Unfortunately, facts do not grow on trees. Seldom do writers have at their fingertips all the facts they need to write about a particular topic. Most of the time, they have to dig them up before they can do the writing. Digging up facts may involve interviewing particular people or even conducting a mini-survey. Some assignments may require you to interview certain professors or even your fellow students.

Generally, the best place for finding facts is the library. Encyclopedias there are literally brimming with helpful facts on nearly every topic. Moreover, many libraries are staffed by friendly librarians who can help you find facts on almost anything. All you have to do is ask. In addition to the books and magazines available in your local library, another vast storehouse of facts on virtually any topic is the Internet. To search the Internet, you merely go to a search engine such as *yahoo.com* and type in your topic. Many libraries provide Internet hookups through their local computer systems. Ask your library what's available in your own local library.

PRACTICING 2

Support the following topic sentences with at least three facts. You may need to interview or survey classmates or visit your library or log on to the Internet.

1.   Topic sentence: Foreign students are a large and important part of my college campus. *Or,* There are few foreign students in my school.

First fact: _____

_____

Second fact: _____

_____

Third fact: _____

_____

2. Topic sentence: The school cafeteria serves a nutritious menu at reasonable prices. *Or,* The school cafeteria serves bad food at high prices.

First fact: _____

_____

Second fact: _____

_____

Third fact: _____

_____

3. Topic sentence: Riding a motorcycle can be dangerous and expensive.

First fact: _____

_____

Second fact: _____

_____

Third fact: _____

_____

Testimony

Testimony is expert opinion that backs up your topic sentence. The expert may be someone who is recognized in the field or who has had personal experience with your topic. Of course, getting the testimony you need may require you to do research or interview the right people. Here is a paragraph that has both kinds of testimony—the personal experience and expert opinion. The topic sentence is underlined.

<u>When it comes to swimming in an unfamiliar place, it is always wise to look before you leap.</u> I found out that truth one day when I dove into an unfamiliar river and hit the bottom. Fortunately, I was only dazed, not seriously hurt. My friend, Brenda, who is a park ranger, says that almost every week she is called to the scene of a diving accident. She says the accidents are usually caused by reckless diving into unfamiliar water. Only last year she pulled a young boy out of the Chattahoochee River, who had dove and hit his head against a rock. He'd never swum in that stretch of the river before and was showing off to his friends. Although he broke his neck, he was lucky because he regained the use of his legs after physical therapy. "Two summers ago, another boy did the same thing in the same stretch of river, and is now confined to a wheel-chair for the rest of his life," Brenda said. "When it comes to a

strange stretch of water, never dive without knowing the depth and first checking for submerged rocks and trees," Brenda advises.

As testimony, the writer first cites his own experience, and then quotes the expert opinion of his friend, Brenda.

PRACTICING 3

Cite at least two opinions as testimony supporting the following topic sentences.

1. Topic sentence: Students who study invariably get better grades than students who don't.

First opinion: _____

_____

Second opinion: _____

_____

2. Topic sentence: Speed reading techniques do not help in understanding poetry.

First opinion: _____

_____

Second opinion: _____

_____

3. Topic sentence: Living in a college dorm can be stressful.

First opinion: _____

_____

Second opinion: _____

_____

Reasons

Some topic sentences are best supported by **reasons**—explanations based on common sense, good judgment, clear thinking, and logic. This kind of support is most commonly used when a writer is trying to persuade the reader to change an opinion.

In the following paragraph reason is used to support the writer's argument that a constitutional amendment against flag burning should not be passed:

<u>A constitutional amendment outlawing flag burning is a bad idea and should not be passed.</u> To most Americans, flag burning is a repugnant gesture. I myself do not believe in flag burning and would

never burn the American flag. Yet common sense tells us, and a 1989 Supreme Court decision agrees, that burning the flag is a form of political speech protected by the First Amendment. As a matter of fact, according to flag etiquette, the proper way to dispose of an old flag is to burn it. What we should respect and honor, above all else, are the principles of freedom enshrined in the Bill of Rights. That, in part, is what the American flag stands for—the right to protest, even if the protest is unpopular, as protest frequently is. It makes no sense to desecrate what the flag stands for—freedom—in a misguided attempt to protect it.

Of course, not every topic sentence can be supported by reason. However, for those topic sentences that can be—and your common sense should be the judge—reason and logic can be highly effective support.

PRACTICING 4

Use reasoning or logic to support one of the following topic sentences.

1. **Topic sentence:** Imprisonment without the possibility of parole is cruel and unusual.

   _____

   _____

   _____

   _____

   _____

2. **Topic sentence:** For certain inhuman crimes, imprisonment without the possibility of parole is just punishment.

   _____

   _____

   _____

   _____

   _____

Personal observation

Some topics are strictly personal and must be supported mainly by your own personal observation. That old standby topic, "How you spent your summer vacation," is a classic example of a personal topic. Unless he or she vacationed with you, no librarian can help you find support for it. You must draw entirely on your own personal observations for support.

Personal observation includes descriptive details and examples. Here is an example of the use of both descriptive details and examples in a paragraph:

<u>About a year ago I tried water skiing and hated it.</u> Getting up on the skis was a battle to begin with, and once I got up, I found the ride frightening. I found myself stung by spray from passing boats, bumped by waves, and occasionally flattened by the wake of a passing boat. Falling was no joke. It hurts. Being slammed against the water when you're traveling over twenty miles an hour might look good in a television commercial, but in real-life it's painful. I fell three times. Once I thought I'd dislocated my shoulder. The second time I got water in my ear, and it took more than a week for it to come out. The third time I was almost knocked unconscious. That's when I decided water skiing was not for me.

The details this writer uses are not available in any library, but come solely from memory. Similarly, paragraphs written on such topics as a favorite place, a special friend, or the first day on a new job must be supported by such personal observations.

In a Nutshell

The supporting details of a paragraph typically consist of examples, facts, testimony, reasons, and personal observations.

PRACTICING 5

Develop a topic sentence on one of the following subjects and write a paragraph about it, supporting the topic sentence with personal observations.

1. The best summer vacation I ever had
2. A family celebration
3. An encounter with prejudice
4. The first time I fell in love
5. A spectacular act of nature I once witnessed

UNIT TALK WRITE ASSIGNMENT

In both talking and writing, we often use examples, facts, testimony, reason and logic, and personal observation to support our ideas. You can see this in the following example. Students in an English class were asked to talk to a classmate about the topic "useful inventions of the past twenty years" using at least two kinds of these supporting details. Here is what one student did. Using this paragraph as your source, write a paragraph in Standard English on the lines that follow. Begin with a topic sentence, and use at least two kinds of supporting details.

Spoken Paragraph

I'm getting mixed up here because I can't member when the computer was invented. It would have my vote. Let's see . . . hmm . . . I think it was invented earlier than twenty years ago, so I guess that won't count. What was invented in the last twenty years—a useful invention? . . . hmm. I know there're lots of things, but it's hard to come up with something right off the bat . . . Oh, I got it! I love my strawberry toothbrush! My toothbrush tastes and smells like strawberries. It's a product that was invented by a woman who lives in Southern California right next-door to my family. Her company is called Plak-smacker, Inc. She also invented dentists' rubber gloves that smell like different fruit, but my dentist doesn't use these gloves, so I haven't smelled them. Anyway, they're probably more for little kids. But I think they are so cool. The newspaper said she started her company 11 years ago and now it's worth ten million dollars. Wow! I mean, why can't I think up something like a neat-smelling toothbrush? It's such a simple idea . . . man, it's almost stupid it's so simple. But, I suppose just having the idea ain't enough. You have to figure out how to make it, how to advertise it, and how to distribute it. But, man, you'd be independent with that kind of business. You'd be your own boss. I'd sure like that. So, anybody here want to start a business with me?

Written Paragraph

_____

_____

_____

_____

_____

_____

_____

_____

_____

_____

_____

_____

_____

UNIT TALKING ASSIGNMENT

Get together with two or three students in the class and talk out a paragraph on each of the following topic sentences. Discuss what types of supporting details the topic sentence requires and suggest some specific details that could be used.

1. Bicycle riding is good exercise.
2. It is hard to write without using "I."
3. Alcoholism is a disease, not a choice.
4. Doctors often keep their patients waiting too long.
5. Car phones are dangerous.
6. Television shows often give an unrealistic view of life.
7. The movement to rid the language of sexism has gone too far.
8. The movement to rid the language of sexism needs to go further.
9. Exercise is the best thing you can do for your health.
10. Polygamous marriages should be permitted for people over 75.

UNIT WRITING ASSIGNMENT

Devise a discussible topic sentence on one of the topics listed below. Then develop a paragraph by supporting it with appropriate examples, facts, testimony, reason and logic, or personal details.

1. A boring event
2. Career moves
3. Tests are overrated as a predictor of success
4. Living with an older relative
5. The computer as an aid to education
6. What I would do if I won the lottery
7. Dealing with a phobia
8. The best way to meet people
9. Morality in politics
10. Going to the theater

Follow these steps:

▪ Choose the topic.

▪ Warm up by freewriting.

■ Gather ideas by brainstorming.

■ Narrow the subject to a manageable topic by clustering.

If you aren't happy with your topic at this point, put away what you've done, choose another topic, and repeat the listed steps.

Check your topic sentence by asking the questions that follow.

■ Is it discussible, or is it too dry and narrow?

■ What kinds of supporting details does it need?

Now complete your paragraph.

PHOTO WRITING ASSIGNMENT

The following photo shows a politician campaigning for office. Write about why candidates often do things during a political campaign that make them look silly. Begin with a discussible topic sentence, then prove it with appropriate details.

Sticking to the Point and Linking Sentences

> "The sentences of a true paragraph always function to make a common point. They are like horses pulling a cart in the same direction."

A paragraph has structure: It consists of lines of print, it is usually rectangular, and its first line is indented five spaces. A paragraph also has function: All the sentences are about a single point. If its sentences do not function this way, then the block of print cannot be called a paragraph.

Basically, here is what a paragraph does. First, it makes a point in the topic sentence. Second, it sticks to that point. Third, it tries to prove the point with details. Finally, all its sentences are linked together so that it is easy to follow the train of thought.

To write a solid paragraph, you should therefore do the following:

- Begin with a discussible point.

- Stick to the point.

- Prove the point; don't merely repeat it.

- Link your sentences to make your ideas easy to follow.

Unit 4 talked about the importance of making the point of a paragraph discussible; Unit 5 discussed how to prove your point by adding details. In this unit we will focus on how to stick to the point and how to link the sentences of your paragraphs.

Stick to the Point

A block of print on the page is not necessarily a paragraph just because it looks like one. Consider this example:

> Coach Burns is the opposite of what a coach should be. The clock in the kitchen is broken. The *Type A personality* is always nervous about something. Sailing is my favorite hobby. My mother saves everything—money, string, even rubber bands. This winter was unusually cold.

Although this block of print looks like a paragraph because its first sentence is indented, it isn't really one. Its sentences do not *function* like the sentences of a paragraph: Namely, they do not make a common point. Rather, each sentence is like a horse galloping in a direction different from the others. The sentences of a true paragraph, on the other hand, always function to make a common point. They are like horses pulling a cart in the same direction.

If you begin to write a paragraph about fairy tales, discuss only fairy tales—nothing else. Save all your other thoughts for another paragraph. Here is an example of a paragraph that drifts from the point:

> A fairy tale is a story about a someone who faces difficulties but overcomes them. The lovely Cinderella is forced to stay home and clean the fireplace while her mean stepsisters go the royal ball. Sleeping Beauty is poisoned by her envious stepmother and falls into a deathlike sleep. As far as I'm concerned, fairy tales are silly. The kinds of stories I like are murder mysteries. I love Sherlock Holmes. He is the best fictional detective ever created. On a dull, rainy day, I love to sit home and read murder mysteries. In a sense, fairy tales reflect life as a challenge to succeed despite overwhelming odds. But fairy tales always have happy endings: Goodness is rewarded whereas evil is punished. In the end, Cinderella marries the handsome prince, and Sleeping Beauty is awakened by her lover's kiss. Of course, real life doesn't always have happy endings. Fairy tales are the ideal and represent life with hope.

It is easy to spot the annoying drift in the above paragraph. Here is the paragraph without it:

> A fairy tale is a story about a someone who faces difficulties but overcomes them. The lovely Cinderella is forced to stay home and clean the fireplace while her mean stepsisters go the royal ball. Sleeping Beauty is poisoned by her envious stepmother and falls into a deathlike sleep. As far as I'm concerned, fairy tales are silly. Yet in a sense, fairy tales reflect life as a challenge to succeed despite overwhelming odds. But fairy tales always have happy endings that teach moral lessons: Goodness is rewarded whereas evil is punished. Cinderella marries the handsome prince, and Sleeping Beauty is awakened by her lover's kiss. Of course, real life doesn't always have happy endings. Fairy tales are the ideal and represent life with hope.

When the writer sticks to the point, the resulting paragraph is always sharper, crisper, and easier to read.

PRACTICING 1

Cross out the sentences that stray from the point in the paragraph below. The topic sentence is underlined.

<u>If you're nervous about flying, here are a few tips to help you overcome your anxiety.</u> First, before your trip, avoid coffee and candy

or sweets. Caffeine and sugar raise your blood sugar level and will just make you more nervous. Second, take along something to do: A good book or some magazines or music tapes can take your mind a million miles away. On my last plane trip, I read the best book. I can't remember the title, but it was about a girl growing up and how she just eats and eats to smother the pain in her life. Some parts were very funny, but other parts were so sad. Sometimes it made me laugh; sometimes it made me cry. Another good way to avoid anxiety when you're flying is to practice deep-breathing. Put your head back, close your eyes, and breathe deeply. Inhale through your mouth; exhale through your nose. Fourth, try systematic muscle relaxation. Again, close your eyes and loosely fold your hands in your lap. Tense your toes, count to five, and relax them. Then do the same with your calves. Go all the way up your body to your jaw— tensing, counting, and relaxing. Don't expect to get over a fear of flying in one trip, but if you regularly practice these techniques, you'll soon be taking off and landing like a bird.

Prove the Point; Don't Merely Repeat It

Proving a point is not the same as repeating it. When you prove a point, you add something new to it—an example, a fact, a reason, an expert's opinion. Look at this paragraph, for example:

> A sensible diet is an important part of keeping healthy. But many people just don't eat well. They are content to gobble on the run, paying no attention to what they eat. Gobbling down food without regard to what you're eating is unhealthy. You should always ensure that the diet you eat is good for you. How can you expect to avoid illnesses if you pay no attention to your eating habits? Truly, poor diets lead to poor health.

The paragraph adds nothing to the underlined topic sentence, but merely repeats the idea in different words. Here, on the other hand, is a paragraph that adds supporting details to the same topic sentence:

> A sensible diet is an important part of keeping healthy. By "sensible diet," I mean eating the following foods on a daily basis: whole grains, fresh vegetables and fruit; low-fat or nonfat dairy products; small portions of chicken, fish and occasionally red meat; and 4 to 5 servings of nuts and seeds per week. Whole grain breads and

pastas supply necessary fiber. Vegetables and fruits are also good sources of fiber as well as vitamins and minerals. Some vegetables, such as broccoli and cabbage, even have cancer-fighting agents. Nonfat dairy products add calcium to the diet. Fish, chicken, and beef are important for protein. Nuts and seeds are good sources of fiber and unsaturated or "good" fat. Following such a diet seems a sensible and easy way to feel energetic and safeguard your health.

The writer moves quickly from the assertion that a sensible diet is healthy to explaining exactly which foods are healthy and why.

In a Nutshell

To write a solid paragraph, you should do the following:

- Begin with a discussible point.

- Stick to the point.

- Prove the point; don't merely repeat it.

PRACTICING 2

The following topic sentence is followed by a number of details. Mark a plus (+) beside the statements you think add something specific to the topic sentence and a minus (–) beside those that merely repeat it.

Topic sentence: The prices of new cars are coming down for several reasons.

1. _____ Rather than going up, new car prices have been coming down.

2. _____ The U.S. dollar has been strengthening against the Japanese yen, allowing Japanese car manufacturers to lower their prices without sacrificing profit.

3. _____ My dad, who sells new cars, says now is the time to buy—when prices are low.

4. _____ Many analysts project that U.S. sales of cars and light trucks will fall in 1998 by nearly one million units. Less demand means lower prices.

5. _____ The return of leased cars to the market contributes greatly to lower demand for new cars.

6. _____ Some sticker prices have fallen as much as eight percent.

7. _____ Sports utility vehicles, compact cars, luxury cars— they all cost less today.

8. _____ To increase sales, many manufactures have not only lowered sticker prices, they've also increased their rebates.

9. _____ If you've been trying to decide between a new and a used car, bear in mind that new car prices are down.

10. _____ Because of lower demand, many new car dealers are willing to sell their vehicles for only 3 to 4 percent over dealer costs.

Link the Sentences

A paragraph is a block of print with all its sentences on the same topic. Consider this example:

> Coaching a youth soccer team may look like fun, but it's actually hard work. You have to teach the children which goal to score on and which one to defend. I line them up with their backs toward the goal they are to defend. I point to the goal they are facing and tell them that that is their target. You have to teach them how to dribble. You have to teach them the stutter steps that soccer players use when they run with the ball. They trip and stumble. They get the hang of it. You have to teach them how to shoot a goal. They must kick the ball with their toes, not their insteps. They do drills. They learn how to make the basic soccer shot. You have to teach them how to make a soccer tackle. It takes a while. They get the idea that they should go for the ball, not for the opponent's foot. They thoroughly enjoy the game, especially the running up and down the field, which exhausts them but leaves them feeling good.

By our definition, the above is definitely a paragraph, but it is not a good one. The writing is choppy, and the writer's train of thought is hard to follow. Helpful links between its sentences are missing. Here is the same paragraph rewritten to add sentence links:

> Coaching a youth soccer team may look like fun, but it's actually hard work. The first thing you have to teach the children is which goal to score on and which one to defend. I do that with a simple exercise. I line them up with their backs toward the goal they are to defend. Then I point to the goal they are facing and tell them that that is their target. The second thing you have to teach them is how to dribble. You have to teach them the stutter steps that soccer players use when they run with the ball. Usually, at first they trip and stumble, but then they get the hang of it. The third thing you

have to teach them is how to shoot. At first, they kick the ball with their toes, not their insteps. But usually after a few drills and a few practice shots, they learn how to make the basic soccer shot. <u>Finally,</u> you have to teach them how to make a soccer tackle. It takes a while, but again, after a few drills, they get the idea that they should go for the ball, not for the opponent's foot. <u>When they finally get it together,</u> they thoroughly enjoy the game, especially the running up and down the field, which exhausts them and leaves them feeling good.

Now we can easily follow the writer's thinking. The words *first thing, second thing, third thing,* and *finally* specify what the writer has to teach young children who play soccer and in what order. The transition sentence, "I do that with a simple exercise," and the transition phrase, "when they finally get it together," also help make the writing smooth, not choppy.

To link the sentences of a paragraph, writers use the following techniques:

- Transition words and phrases

- Repeated key words and pronouns

- Similar sentence patterns

Transition words and phrases

A **transition** is a word or phrase that links the sentences of a paragraph together. In the following paragraph, the transitions are underlined:

A simple but nutritious meal you can prepare is Jamaican stew peas. Moreover, it can be prepared in advance. Begin by soaking the peas overnight—actually, kidney beans but Jamaicans call them "peas"—until they soften somewhat and swell. <u>The next morning,</u> put the peas in a big pot with a ham bone that has just enough meat left on it to add flavor to the dish. Cover the peas and ham bone with water. Then add half a green pepper. Usually the best pepper to use is a Scotch Bonnet, which is found in the produce section of most big supermarkets. <u>However,</u> be sure to take the seeds out before you put the pepper in the pot. <u>Remember, also,</u> to leave out the salt; the ham bone adds enough salt. <u>Next,</u> add a sprig of fresh thyme. <u>Now,</u> partly cover the pot and allow the dish to stew down. Gradually, the mixture will turn brown and thicken. This can take anywhere from 5 to 7 hours. <u>All you have to do then</u> is serve the stew peas hot over rice for a delicious and unusual main dish that will stick to the ribs.

The writer makes it easy to follow the directions by linking the sentences with transitional words—*you begin, the next morning, however, remember also, after that,* and *all you have to do next.* Here are some other common words and phrases used to link sentences:

Common transitional words or phrases

after all	but	however	in spite of	plus
also	finally	in addition	moreover	therefore
and	for example	in contrast	nevertheless	what's more
as a consequence	for instance	in fact	next	

PRACTICING 3

Link the following sentences to make it easy for the reader to follow the train of thought.

Example: He knew that no one could blame him for being late.
It was not his fault that his car broke down.

Answer: He knew that no one could blame him for being late.
After all, it was not his fault that his car broke down.

1. It rained and stormed the whole night long. We enjoyed ourselves.

_____

_____

_____

2. I love my English class. I like grammar.

_____

_____

_____

3. First I stopped at an ATM. I went to the bookstore.

_____

_____

_____

4. Chang skipped breakfast that morning. She skipped lunch.

_____

_____

_____

5. We stood in line for hours. The box office opened.

_____

_____

_____

6. I have three goals. I want to get my diploma. I want to find a job in Seattle. I want to go to Australia.

_____

_____

_____

7. He's very organized. He's the most organized person I know.

_____

_____

_____

8. I had a lot to do this morning. I still found time to study.

_____

_____

_____

9. My mother paid me a surprise visit. I couldn't go out on a date.

_____

_____

10. My sister Jane is tall and skinny. My sister Elizabeth is short and muscular.

_____

_____

_____

Repeating key words and pronouns

Another way to link the sentences of a paragraph is to repeat key words and pronouns. **Pronouns** are words that take the place of nouns, such as _he_ for _Uncle Bertie_ or _it_ for _the book_. Here is an example (the topic sentence is also underlined):

> My uncle Bertie is an avid fisherman. He has caught more fish than anyone I know. When he sets out on a fishing trip, it's like he is going on an expedition. He generally packs at least two tackle boxes full of fishing equipment. One time I went trout fishing with him in the mountains of Reno, and we spent the night camping at the trout stream. He showed me how to tie a fly and how to cast in the whirlpools where trout like to hide. He taught me so well that I caught five trout. Uncle Bertie is not only a great fisherman, he's a great teacher, too. His love for fishing is catching.

The sentences of this paragraph are tightly linked by the repetition of the key words *Uncle Bertie* and *fisherman* and the pronouns *he* and *him*.

PRACTICING 4

Read the following paragraph to understand what is happening. Then write the appropriate key word or its pronoun in each blank.

Mary decided her dog needed a bath _____ grabbed the doggy shampoo, and then _____ grabbed _____ as _____ was trotting past. Before _____ knew what was happening, _____ dunked _____ in a basin filled with water. _____ , whose name is Francois, put up a fight, but _____ was no match for _____ . First _____ wriggled furiously, but _____ held _____ firmly and refused to let go. Then, _____ began an unearthly howling, but it had no effect whatsoever on _____ . In fact, _____ began howling too as if _____ were playing a game. Suddenly, _____ gave a huge leap and nearly bounded out of the basin. But _____ was ready for this tactic, which _____ had tried during previous baths. No matter how _____ struggled, _____ could not escape _____ grip. Eventually, the poor dog surrendered, and _____ scrubbed _____ until _____ was the cleanest _____ on the block.

Similar sentence patterns

This linking technique simply means that similar ideas are expressed in similar words. For example, you could use the same sentence patterns to compare people, places, things, or ideas, as the writer does below (the topic sentence is also underlined):

My Aunt Rosa and my Uncle Harry are so much alike that it's almost scary. Aunt Rosa worries constantly and about everything. Uncle Harry also worries about everything. When Aunt Ross goes on an airplane trip, she always buys millions of dollars worth of flight insurance. When Uncle Harry goes on an airplane trip, even a short one, he always makes sure that his will is up-to-date. If Aunt Rosa is driving to the neighborhood grocery store, she always gets dressed in her best clothes so she will look good if she's killed in an accident. If Uncle Harry is driving to the convenience store, he likewise always dresses up in his best clothes for the same reason. <u>Should a black cat cross</u> Aunt Rosa's path, she'll turn around and come right back home. <u>Should a black cat cross</u> Uncle Harry's path, he'll go to bed for the rest of the day. Both, however, have a sense of humor about the way they are. <u>Aunt Rosa laughs</u> at Uncle Harry and tells him he's foolish. <u>Uncle Harry, in turn, laughs</u> at Aunt Rosa. Yet both of them are unable to see how much alike they are.

Notice the definite pattern used in this paragraph to compare Aunt Rosa to Uncle Harry. For each point the writer first talks about Aunt Rosa and then Uncle Harry, using the same sentence pattern. This technique makes the ideas in a paragraph easy to follow.

In a Nutshell

Help your reader follow your train of thought by:

- Using transitions.

- Repeating key words and pronouns.

- Using similar sentence patterns.

PRACTICING 5

In the following passages underline the repeated sentence patterns.

Example: Emotion <u>has taught people</u> to reason; reason <u>has taught people</u> the importance of emotion.

1. Exercising is a habit; not exercising is also a habit.

2. I hate opera almost as much as I hate ballet.

3. In the 1960s, it was rock and roll; in the 1970s, it was disco; and in the 1980s, it was hard rock.

4. Are we here to talk or are we here to work?

5. Love is ennobling; hate is demeaning.

6. I have many a dream. I also have many a nightmare.

7. To feed a man for a day, give him a fish. To feed a man for a lifetime, teach him to fish.

8. I clean the basement every spring, and I clean the garage every fall.

9. The food we like to eat as adults is the food we liked to eat as children.

10. Soon we fell in love. Even sooner we fell out of love.

UNIT TALK WRITE ASSIGNMENT

When we talk, we do not always take the time to **make a point, stick to the point, prove the point, and link sentences so that they make sense**—the main lessons of this chapter. However, in the passion of an argument, we generally make a point, stick to it, and try to prove it. Here is an example, a paragraph spoken by a student who thinks dog owners ought to train their pets properly. Her grammar is not always correct nor are her sentences perfectly linked, but she does stick to her point and try to prove it. Your job is to turn this spoken paragraph into one that obeys all the rules in this chapter (boldfaced above) and is written in Standard English. Feel free to add more or better supporting details that prove the point. Use the space provided below.

Spoken Paragraph

I get so ticked at people who just let their dogs run wild. It's so disgusting how many dog owners don't train their dogs to behave right. Really, it is. They must think that dogs will just outgrow their bad habits—puff! Magic!. Now that's just doggone stupid—oops, excuse the pun. Dogs don't know nothing about manners if you don't teach them. They're like children. They'll chew furniture, jump on strangers, bark when you leave the house, poop all over the place, and generally cause gross problems. Getting a dog is like having a child. You've got to be responsible. You can't just let a dog run wild cause once its growed up, you won't be able to control it. If you're too lazy to teach your dog, then take him to obedience school, where dog trainers will do the job for you. What I'm trying to say is that owning a dog means more than just providing food, water, and shelter, for Pete's sake. A good dog has to show respect for people. Our neighbor's dog terrifies me. Every time he sees me or anyone he growls and puts out his front paws in a weird way; then he tries to attack me even when he is on a leash. Our neighbor keeps his yard nice and his lawn mowed, and that's O.K., but he sure hasn't trained his mutt.

Written Paragraph

_____

_____

_____

_____

_____

_____

_____

_____

_____

_____

_____

_____

UNIT TALKING ASSIGNMENT

Pair up with a classmate. One person should read the following paragraph aloud. Discuss how the paragraph can be improved according to what you have learned in this unit. Check the following:

- Does it have a discussible topic sentence?

- Does it stick to the point?

- Does it prove the point, or merely repeat it?

- Are all the sentences linked so the reader can easily follow the train of thought?

Then, you and your partner should work together to correct the paragraph. The topic sentence is underlined. Do all the sentences stick to the point? Are there enough details to prove the point? Are the sentences smoothly linked?

<u>My grades would improve if I just learned to manage my time better.</u> I could do some of my homework immediately after class. I have at least one free period after every class. I usually just goof around. I love hanging out with my friends. We go to the student union. We watch television together. We get something to eat. We look for girls to talk to. In the afternoons that I don't have to work, I could do homework. I don't. I read the sports pages. During the baseball season. I like to read the box scores for each game. Since I used to be a pitcher in high school, I especially like to read the stats on the pitchers. Greg Maddux is my favorite pitcher. He has the best ERA of any working baseball pitcher today. He's sure to get into the baseball Hall of Fame even if he never pitches another game. I don't know why I don't spend more time on my homework. My grades would improve. The only thing I can think of is that I should learn to manage my time better.

UNIT WRITING ASSIGNMENT

Choose one of the numbered writing topics listed below. On a separate sheet develop a strong paragraph, observing the following guidelines:

■ Begin with a discussible topic sentence.

■ Support the topic sentence with appropriate examples, reasons, or personal observations.

■ Stick to your point.

■ Link your sentences smoothly.

You may want to first gather ideas by talking, freewriting, brainstorming, clustering, or journal writing.

1. Why you chose the college you did
2. A time when you felt loved and appreciated
3. A funny experience on the job
4. What you like to do for exercise
5. Expensive shoes

PHOTO WRITING ASSIGNMENT

The person in this picture is trying to make a fashion statement. Write your reaction to the person's taste. Make sure that your writing has a discussible topic sentence, is supported by appropriate evidence, sticks to the point, and contains smoothly linked sentences.

Paragraph Strategies

The paragraph strategies taught in this section of *Writing Talk* are patterns for organizing your ideas. Once mastered, they will allow you to write solid paragraphs on any topic. Each unit focuses on one particular strategy, opening with a real-world example of how it might be used. Then the unit gives advice on how to use the strategies under the following headings: *What Am I Trying to Do? How Can I Do It?* and *What Do I Need to Look Out For?*

Narrating

"The most frightening day of my life was when I blew out to sea in a small rowboat."

You are a careful driver, but one day as you sit at a stoplight minding your own business, someone rear-ends you and drives away. Fortunately, an alert pedestrian gets the hit-and-run driver's license plate, which you turn over to the police. You call your insurance agent, who asks you to write a paragraph telling how the accident happened. She says doing so might prevent an increase in your premium. This is what you write:

> The rear-end accident I was involved in last Tuesday, August 5, 1999, was not my fault. I was stopped at a red light at the corner of Chamblee Road and Harts Mill, waiting for the light to change. I glanced in my rearview mirror and noticed a pickup approaching very fast from behind. Before I could react, the pickup was on top of me. At the last second, the driver swerved to avoid me, but still clipped my right rear fender. Then he ran the red light and sped away. Fortunately, a woman who lives in the neighborhood, Ms. Smith, was out walking her dog and got the pickup's license plate number, which I turned over to the police. I am a careful driver who pays all premiums promptly. I hope this accident, which was not my fault, doesn't increase my premium.

Without even knowing it, you have written a narration.

What Am I Trying to Do?

Tell a story: That is your assignment. It may be a make-believe story—fiction—or something that actually happened to you—a personal recollection. Telling a story of any kind requires you to use the strategy called **narration.**

Here is an example of a paragraph developed by narration:

> <u>The most frightening day of my life was when I blew out to sea in a small rowboat.</u> My father had warned me not to row out, saying that it was too windy, and I would have trouble controlling the boat. But I was 13 and knew it all. So I set out in the sound off Hilton Head Island and soon I was out in deep sea. Two dolphins swam up to the boat and began playing. I became so fascinated with them that I lost track of where I was and how hard the wind was blowing. By the time I looked around, I had drifted to the mouth of the sound. I ran out the oars and began pulling, but it was no use in that wind. The boat was being blown out to the Atlantic. I screamed.

I waved at passing boats. But no one heard or saw me. Soon I was in dark blue water and bouncing in a strong sea. Suddenly, I saw a motorboat slicing through the whitecaps, heading for me. It was Dad. He threw me a rope and towed me to shore. He never said a word. He didn't have to. I had learned my lesson.

This is a typical narration. It has a beginning, middle, and end. It occurs in time and makes a point.

Any assignment that asks you to recollect an incident, relate a memory, or tell a story is asking for a narration. Of all the strategies for writing, narration is probably the one you use most in daily talk. We all tell stories during the course of our waking hours, whether brief little incidents that happened to us or longer, more involved episodes. We may tell those stories off-the-cuff and without any conscious eye to technique, but a story is a story, whether it is written or told orally. In sum, you know how to do a narration because you have a lot of experience with talking the form.

The aim of most narratives is to entertain. Long before radio or television, people got together and told stories. Some narratives, however, aim to inform or even persuade. The rowboat story, for example, preaches a valuable lesson: We should heed the advice of those who are more experienced. If we don't, we put ourselves at risk and may pay a high price.

In a Nutshell

- Narration is the strategy of storytelling.

- Most narratives are written to entertain, but they may also inform or persuade.

PRACTICING 1

In the blanks provided check the sentences that would best be developed by narration.

1. _____ Something dreadful happened to me on the afternoon of my graduation from Freemont High School.

2. _____ Thousands of criminal shootings each year prove that no one except police officers or military personnel should be allowed to carry guns.

3. _____ Martha's career has taken some interesting twists and turns.

4. _____ Let me tell you about how I risked my life when I flew in a private plane.

5. _____ I thought my first fishing trip would be my last.

6. _____ Donations of body organs are increasing annually.

7. _____ It is easy to learn to play the piano if you follow these four tips.

8. _____ The day of my parents' divorce was one of the most difficult of my life.

9. _____ Rats live in many neighborhoods where ivy grows abundantly.

10. _____ It was time to say goodbye to my family.

How Can I Do It?

Even though you've told hundreds of stories in your everyday chats, you probably have done so without consciously thinking of any technique. On the other hand, in *writing* a story it is best to start off with a definite idea of what to do. These are the steps you should take:

1. Compose your topic sentence.
2. Use enough details.
3. Connect the details.

Compose your topic sentence.

An old Chinese proverb says that a journey of one mile or 5000 miles begins the same way: with a single step. To write a narration, this first step should be to compose a topic sentence.

The topic sentence is the point of a narrative. It is a single sentence that tells what your story is about. A story without a topic sentence is pointless. Here is an example:

> We would pretend to be making mud pies. Sometimes, we would splatter each other in a game of war. One day we imagined that we were pigs and flopped down on our backs in a mud puddle. Then we had a contest to see who could make the most convincing oink. My mother came home, caught us wallowing, and threw a fit. She said that we had gotten our clothes filthy and would have to wash them ourselves. And then she made us do it, too!

What is this all about, we wonder? We can't tell because, without a topic sentence, the story has no main point. Notice how much the paragraph is improved when we add a topic sentence:

> <u>When I was 11, my cousin and I discovered how much fun it was to play in mud.</u> We would pretend to be making mud pies. Sometimes we would splatter each other in a game of war. One

day we imagined that we were pigs and flopped down on our backs in a mud puddle. Then we had a contest to see who could make the most convincing oink. My mother came home, caught us wallowing, and threw a fit. She said that we had gotten our clothes filthy and would have to wash them ourselves. And then she made us do it, too!

A pointless story is not interesting or funny. Yet it is easy to fix. Simply express the point—whatever it is—in a topic sentence. Note, however, that some topic sentences are more interesting than others. You should word your topic sentence in a way that arouses your reader's interest. A dull topic sentence does not make someone want to read on. An interesting topic sentence has the opposite effect. It pulls the reader in. Here are some examples:

Dull: Once I almost got lost at sea.

Interesting: The most frightening day of my life was when I blew out to sea in a small rowboat.

Dull: My first kiss happened when I was 13.

Interesting: I'll never forget that thrilling moment when I was 13 and experienced my first kiss.

Read aloud your topic sentence, asking yourself whether it would make you want to read on or run out and see a movie.

PRACTICING 2

Rewrite the topic sentences below to make them more interesting.

1. We almost missed our plane.

_____

_____

2. An interesting thing happened last Saturday.

_____

_____

3. My latest run-in with a family member bothered me.

_____

_____

4. Some things take courage.

_____

_____

5. From personal observation I know that drugs can ruin
lives.

_____

_____

Find enough details.

The details of your story will most likely come from your personal observations. Vivid details add to any story. To give you an idea of how important details are, here is the rowboat story with its details omitted:

> Once I almost got lost at sea. I was in a rowboat, which my
> father told me not to take out, but I did. Before I realized what was
> happening, I had drifted far from shore. But then my father came
> in a motorboat and got me.

Without details the story is dull and bare. All kinds of questions are
left unanswered. When did this happen? Where? Why didn't you notice
that you were drifting out to sea? How did your father find you?

Details flesh out the drama of your story and give your reader a
sense of "being there." They add believability and realism. Your reader
will be swept along with your narrative if its details are convincing.

PRACTICING 3

The following paragraphs are vague and empty because they lack
details. Rewrite them, using details that make the narrative livelier.

1.

My uncle told me about something that happened to him. While
on a business trip, he decided to buy gifts for his wife and daughter. He strolled around, looking into shop windows for ideas. He
was getting tired so he decided to have a cup of coffee and rest.
The man sitting next to him looked somehow familiar. Gradually my
uncle recognized that the man was his college roommate, whom he
had not seen for 20 years.

2.

My first day in Math 101 was bad. The teacher's name was Mr.
Goodman. At the stroke of 10:00 A.M., he called the roll, handed
us a syllabus, and announced that usually 40 percent of the class
dropped out because it was too difficult. I was concerned because
I needed this class to graduate. I looked around and noticed that
all the students looked worried. But I studied hard, and I got an A.

3.

Today my bird died. I had gone to work as usual. When I returned
home, I opened the bird cage to let her out. I could tell something
was wrong. I put her back in the cage, placed a warm towel under her,
and tried to get her to drink some water. She wouldn't move. I went
to the kitchen, and by the time I returned, she had died.

Connect the details.

Most stories are told in a simple chronological, or time, order. First this happened, then that, with one episode following another. Here is an example:

> My most memorable experience from elementary school happened in Ms. Higgins' geography class. She gave us a pop quiz that I hadn't studied for. When I saw the ten questions, I knew I was dead. I didn't know a single answer. I decided to guess. So I sat there at my desk, pencil in hand, and took a stab at giving my answers: A, or B, or C, or D. The next day Ms. Higgins returned our papers with a big orange smiley face drawn on mine. That meant only one thing— I'd gotten the highest mark in the class. And I had. I'd guessed nine of the ten correctly. Later, Ms. Higgins said to me that this just went to prove what I could do if I would only study!

This narrative takes place in time, as do all narratives, and the writer uses transitions to move the story along—*when*, *so*, *the next day*, and *later*. Without these transitions, the story loses its sense of episodes occurring in time. Here it is with the transitions omitted:

> My most memorable experience from elementary school happened in Ms. Higgins' geography class. She gave us a pop quiz that I hadn't studied for. I saw the ten questions. I knew I was dead. I didn't know a single answer. I decided to guess. I sat there at my desk, pencil in hand, and took a stab at giving my answers: A, or B, or C, or D. Ms. Higgins returned our papers with a big orange smiley face drawn on mine. That meant only one thing—I'd gotten the highest mark in the class. And I had. I'd guessed nine of the ten correctly. Ms. Higgins said to me that this just went to prove what I could do if I would only study!

Some common time transitions are listed below:

afterward	later	when	immediately
shortly afterward	soon	while	suddenly
the next day (or night)	before	then	now

When you write your own stories, use suitable transitions to link the episodes together.

In a Nutshell

To write a narrative, do the following:

- Compose your topic sentence.

- Use enough details.

- Connect the details.

PRACTICING 4

Choose one of the topics listed below and write four episodes that make up the narrative. Use a transition to link each episode.

1. Recalling of a severe or unjust punishment
2. Meeting an unusual person
3. Making peace after an argument
4. A funny adventure
5. How I survived (an earthquake, a flood, a fire, a car crash, or some other disaster)

Episode #1: _____

_____

Transition: _____

_____

Episode #2: _____

_____

Transition: _____

_____

Episode #3: _____

_____

Transition: _____

_____

Episode #4: _____

_____

Transition: _____

_____

PRACTICING 5

Supply the missing transitions in the following sentences. Try to vary the transitions you use.

1. For six days, he worked steadily, but made little progress.

   _____ he gave up and went home.

2. The whole room broke into loud noise. Some people were singing; others were praying; and yet others were shouting. _____ it was dead still.

3. That morning, we parted in great anger. _____ he called me on the telephone and apologized for being so immature.

4. Life in Samoa begins at dawn when the cock crows. _____ mothers wake up to feed their babies, children drowsily roll out of their beds, and men get ready for early fishing.

5. I arrive at the airport and begin the aircraft check while my instructor waits. The check takes about 15 minutes, and I wish it were over. _____ my instructor and I climb into the cockpit.

What Do I Need to Look Out For?

Narratives are usually easy and fun to write. Nevertheless, here are three tips to help anyone write better narratives:

- Pace the story.
- Stay in character.
- Stick to one time frame.

Pace the story.

Pacing the story means including the most important episodes and details. Although providing some of the details makes a story more interesting, good storytelling does not include every picky little detail that happened. Narrating is not the same as keeping a diary in which you note every event in a day. Instead, a good narration is paced to include only the events and details that are important to the point of the story.

Let us assume, for instance, that you have been asked to narrate an experience with crowds. Here's one student's first draft:

The only experience I've ever had with a crowd occurred at a rock concert where I was nearly crushed. As I waited for the concert to start, I was worried about how I would get home. My friend and I were wondering if we should take the bus or the train. My friend, whose name is Hazel, was saying that the bus might be slower but since everyone would probably want to take the train, we might be better off on the bus. We were deep into this discussion when a loud G-flat rang throughout the arena, and the concert got underway. About six songs into the concert, the mass hysteria began. The crowd began surging toward the stage, carrying me along like a riptide, and shoving me against the apron of the stage. The sweaty, pressing bodies of the audience crushed against me. I couldn't breathe. Somehow, I managed to escape, and the next thing I knew I was being swept to the side of the theater. There I saw Hazel, terror in her eyes. We wriggled along the wall until we reached an exit door. Frightened and bruised, we decided to leave, even though we could hear the concert in full, blaring swing. We didn't take the bus as we had decided we would. Instead, we took the train because it wasn't at all crowded.

This narrative is not well-paced because it bogs down in unnecessary details about whether the narrator and her friend would take the bus or the train home. When the student was asked why she included the details about whether to take the train or bus, her answer was, "Because that's what happened."

But putting in everything that actually happened, especially if it has nothing to do with the point of your story, is a mistake. Notice how much the story is improved once its pacing is tightened:

<u>The only experience I've ever had with a crowd occurred at a rock concert where I was nearly crushed.</u> With the playing of a loud G-flat, the concert got underway. About six songs into the concert, the mass hysteria began. The crowd began surging toward the stage, carrying me along like a riptide, and shoving me against the apron of the stage. The sweaty, pressing bodies of the audience crushed against me. I couldn't breathe. Somehow, I managed to escape, and the next thing I knew, I was being swept to the side of the theater. There I saw Hazel, terror in her eyes. We wriggled along the wall until we reached an exit door. Frightened and bruised, we decided to leave, even though we could hear the concert in full, blaring swing.

Remember, pace your story. Skip over boring details that are beside the point. Focus only on what matters to the point you are making.

PRACTICING 6

Imagine that your assignment is to write a narrative paragraph with the following topic sentence: *My roommate, Buto, from West Nigeria, taught me a lesson about the dangers of stereotyping.* Read through the 12 sentences; then, go back and, in the blanks provided check the details that would slow down the pace of the narrative and make it boring.

1. _____ My first meeting with Buto.

2. _____ My feelings about dorm life.

3. _____ How I stereotyped Buto as unsophisticated because he was from Africa.

4. _____ My reaction to other foreign students in our dorm.

5. _____ What happened when I was asked to join a fraternity.

6. _____ One day I saw Buto working on a laptop computer.

7. _____ How I overcame my own computer phobia.

8. _____ Buto was setting up a database for a large travel agency.

9. _____ He seemed to click on varied icons with enormous speed.

10. _____ A description of every computer command Buto gave.

11. _____ Later, I found out that because of his brilliance, Buto had received a $10,000 grant to study computer science at my university.

12. _____ My decision never again to prejudge an individual.

Stay in character.

Many narratives are told from the first-person viewpoint, that is, *I*. Often, using this viewpoint requires us to assume a certain voice. Whatever voice you begin with is the one you must use throughout the story, or its believability will suffer. Here is a narrative in the first person *I* that uses the voice of a young child:

> When I was six years old, one of my Texas relatives tweaked my nose and told me that I had a "cute potato nose." I remember looking up at this towering woman and telling her, "No, I don't, and you have a fat bottom." My mother, who was standing close by, looked at me in shocked horror, exclaiming, "Now, Marcie, that's no way to speak to Aunt Dorothy." I wondered, <u>"Why not? This woman has humiliated me by castigating my nose. She has hurt my ego, and she deserves to have me retaliate; it's only just."</u>

The underlined passage is a lapse in point of view because a six-year-old child would not use words like *humiliated*, *castigating*, *retaliate*, or even know the meaning of *ego*. A rewrite follows.

When I was six years old, one of my Texas relatives tweaked my nose and told me that I had a "cute potato nose." I remember looking up at this towering woman and telling her, "No, I don't, and you have a fat bottom." My mother, who was standing close by, looked at me in shocked horror, exclaiming, "Now, Marcie, that's no way to speak to Aunt Dorothy." I wondered, <u>"Why not? She hates my nose. I hate her fat bottom."</u>

The decision about which voice to use is largely a matter of common sense. Whichever voice you do use, you must stick with that voice (and character) throughout.

PRACTICING 7

The following narration has an inconsistent voice. It is supposed to be written from the point of view of a dignified elderly woman. Cross out and rewrite the paragraph as necessary to keep the voice consistent.

Last Friday, I dented the passenger side door of my 1980 Buick. Gee whiz, what a bummer! I was sure ticked when I realized what had happened. I had reason to be seriously concerned because I am 78 years old and wondered if the state would renew my license. Unfortunately, three months earlier I had slammed into a car as I was backing out of a parking space in front of Target's. Wow! When it rains it pours! It made me nuts. Alas, we "senior citizens," as society labels us, are treated as if we were a terrible hazard to car traffic, no matter how carefully we drive. I expected some big dude driver to jump out of the other car and yell at me. Thank goodness, the person who had run into me was a pleasant young girl. She admitted that she didn't see me and couldn't stop fast enough to avoid my door. We exchanged insurance information and telephone numbers; then I drove home, upset and shaken, but nonetheless relieved.

Stick to one time frame.

Whenever you tell a story, you must choose one time frame and stick with it. If you are recalling an incident that happened in the past, you must begin in the past and end in the past. If you are telling the story in the present tense, you must stay in the present. You should not, say, switch midway, as in this sentence:

Shifting: I ran into the house and says to Jim, "Where have you been?"

Here is the sentence rewritten entirely in the past, and then entirely in the present. Either one is fine, as long as you are consistent.

Consistent: I ran into the house and said to Jim, "Where have you been?"

Consistent: I run into the house and say to Jim, "Where have you been?"

Hopscotching from past to present while telling a story is a common error. Here is an example:

> <u>My cousin Lisa has proved once again that she is a perfect slob.</u> Yesterday, at the First Presbyterian Church service where everyone dresses up, Lisa appears in an oversized sweatshirt, worn over bright red tights with a large hole in the left knee. Young and old members alike look away—anywhere but at Lisa—so they would not reveal their shock. But Lisa sits in her pew, quietly chewing gum as if she were a saint.

The story is easier to follow when the writer stays in one time frame, as in the corrected version below:

> <u>My cousin Lisa has proved once again that she is a perfect slob.</u> Yesterday, at the First Presbyterian Church service where everyone dresses up, Lisa <u>appeared</u> in an oversized sweatshirt, worn over bright red tights with a large hole in the left knee. Young and old members alike <u>looked</u> away—anywhere but at Lisa—so they would not reveal their shock. But Lisa <u>sat</u> in her pew, quietly chewing gum as if she were a saint.

In a Nutshell

When you write a narrative, be sure to pace the story, stay in character, and stick to one time frame.

PRACTICING 8

Correct the following paragraph so that it remains in one time frame—the past.

Last Wednesday I cleaned out my mother's garage, which made me feel proud of myself. It is spring vacation and I am home for the week. Each time I drive into the garage, I think to myself, "I really should help clean out this mess," but I let the first two days go by without acting on these better instincts. Mom did not say a word; in fact, she just washes all of my clothes, bakes me my favorite peanut butter cookies, and lets me use her car to go visit my friends. When I arrived home past midnight, she did not scold me or complain. She probably thinks that because I am a college student I am mature enough to keep whatever hours I choose. But midweek, my conscience just won't let me continue to take and not give. I announced, "Mom, today I am going to clean out the garage because it's too hard a job for you." Well, my mother was so grateful, she almost had tears in her eyes. To tell you the truth, once I was finished, I couldn't remember any job that had given me more satisfaction.

UNIT TALK WRITE ASSIGNMENT

If you think that nothing worth writing about ever happens to you, you're wrong. If you have a topic sentence, pace your story, and include vivid details, the most ordinary experience can be made interesting, funny, or even suspenseful. Here is one student's spoken story of a frightening experience. Read the account carefully, and then turn it into a well-developed narrative, paced properly, supported by vivid details, and with a clear sense of an adult looking back on a childhood experience. Use the blanks provided.

Spoken Paragraph

When I was eight years old, I thought I was going to drown. Water is such a scary thing anyway. Even as I stand here remembering the experience, I feel a shiver go through my body. Man, it was such a . . . I mean, I'll never forget it. Moments like that stay glued to your brain for sure. Let's see, how did it all start? Oh yeah, my home town had a municipal swimming pool that created waves for five minutes every hour on the hour. I can't remember exactly how they did it, but it involved a machine that forced air out through an iron grid with bars about 1 inch apart. We loved going to this pool and would beg our parents for the $1.00 entrance fee. My brother, my little sister, and me would go every Saturday. We'd have so much fun. "Come on, let's dive the waves!" we'd scream as soon as it was wave time. Then we'd jump in the water, shoving each other, laughing, and spitting water in the air like fountains. We would dive under the surface and make faces at each other under water. Man, we had fun. One afternoon, I decided to swim under water to the end of the pool to see how the air was pushed through the grid. Whoa, what a bum idea! I was practically out of breath when I reached the grid. But in order to hang on and look inside, I grabbed the iron bars with my hands as well as one foot. Remember that all the time I'm under water. For some weird reason, my big right toe got stuck between two bars. I couldn't pull it out. I yanked, I tried to turn my toe sideways where it was thinner, but I couldn't move it. I started panicking and swallowing water. I figured I had had it. Finito! One thing I know, my whole life didn't pass before me as people say it does. I just felt scared, big time. In total desperation I yanked at my toe one more time, practically breaking the bone and scraping off the skin. Miracle! I was loose. I floated to the top. Then—get this—my brother yells, "Hey, Marty, let's play Blind Man's Bluff." "Yeah, Marty, come on," says my sister. These clowns never even noticed I was gone—and here I'd almost drowned!

Written Paragraph

UNIT TALKING ASSIGNMENT

Choose a partner and take turns narrating to each other a humorous or embarrassing incident. Try to keep your partner interested in your story by practicing the lessons in this unit—pace your story, use enough details, keep a consistent voice, and stay in one time frame. The purpose of this exercise is to prepare you to write a good narration.

UNIT WRITING ASSIGNMENT

Select one of the two following assignments:

1. Narrate an event that helped you mature. Start with a topic sentence that gets your reader's attention. Pace your story to emphasize important actions and gloss over less important ones. If your event occurred during childhood, maintain a child's point of view throughout. Also, stay in the same time frame—the past. When you have completed your narration, read it aloud to someone whose opinion you value but do not fear. See what effect the narration has. If you are not satisfied, pace yourself better or add more vivid details.

2. Write a paragraph describing the last time you quarreled with someone important to you. Arrange the main episodes in the most effective order and use transitions. Practice the other tips given in this unit.

PHOTO WRITING ASSIGNMENT

Study the following photo. Then use your imagination to tell a story about the picture. Keep in mind these rules: (1) watch your pacing and do not get bogged down in details that are off the point of the story; (2) use a consistent voice; and (3) use a consistent time frame.

Describing

"What I saw was life on the edge of decay."

Picture this: You work in maintenance for an apartment complex. A renter has filed a complaint about a neighbor's messy patio. Your boss sends you to inspect the patio and write a report of what you see. You pay a visit to the apartment, look around, and write the following paragraph:

> The patio of apartment 14B is dirty and unsanitary. From the street you can see old tires and the rusty frame of a bicycle. When you get closer, you can see debris of various kinds—cans, empty soda bottles, and clothes. Stacks of old newspapers create a fire hazard. A rotten odor wafts up from the rubbish and over the entire backyard. The patio is clearly a filthy mess.

You have just written a description.

What Am I Trying to Do?

A **description** is a word picture. When you write a description, you try to portray a scene as you see, hear, taste, smell, and feel it, using nothing but words. Writing a good description requires close and careful observation with all your senses—sight, sound, taste, smell, and touch. Here is an example of one student's description:

> Rainbows add to the fairy-tale atmosphere of Hawaii. Warm showers are part of each day's weather. Lasting from five to ten minutes, these pleasant showers are followed by beautiful rainbows. The rainbows on the island of Maui are particularly beautiful because Maui is mostly mountainous and filled with lush, green vegetation and brilliantly colored flowers. Driving through the mountains of Maui, you can suddenly spy a fully arched rainbow in the mist of a waterfall, with its orange, violet, and green bands bleeding into each other. Framing the picture is a shiny jungle of blooming vines and trees. The sight could be entitled "Rainbow Magic." It is absolutely breathtaking.

We use descriptions all the time in the business and academic worlds, in both writing and talk. Indeed, next to narration, description is probably the strategy we most use in our everyday chatting. You may have to describe for an insurance adjuster the damage a storm did to your property. Lab reports describe how cells look under a microscope. Eyewitnesses describe fleeing felony suspects. We write descriptions of missing pets and post the notices on lightposts. Indeed, description is quite possibly the most commonly used way to develop paragraphs.

In a Nutshell

Description is a word picture.

PRACTICING 1

In the spaces provided check the topics that require a description.

1. _____ The techniques of safe driving

2. _____ A portrait of your mother

3. _____ What your room at home looks like

4. _____ The long-term effects of eating poorly

5. _____ Why good manners are important

6. _____ Typical student excuses for not doing homework

7. _____ Your new sofa

8. _____ How to deal with a grumpy boss

9. _____ What a typical gang member wears

10. _____ Your favorite scenic view

How Can I Do It?

To write a description, follow these three steps:

1. Decide on a dominant impression.
2. Use vivid supporting details.
3. Organize the details.

Decide on a dominant impression.

To write a vivid description, zoom in on a dominant impression. The **dominant impression** is the one feature that most stands out about what you are describing. It will become the topic sentence of your descriptive paragraph and guide you in selecting supporting details.

For example, let's say that you are describing a really nasty slum. You begin by asking yourself, "What feature of the slum most stands out?" Then you make that feature your topic sentence. Here is an example:

> Cabbagetown is a hellish part of town where life is in a process of decay. Its streets and dingy alleys are blanketed with a smelly humidity. Glancing at the wall to my left, I notice an ancient advertisement, rotting under years of dirt and dust. It reads, "Taylor's Drugstore—Coca-Cola 5 cents." An ugly, huge iron door dangles off its hinges under the Coca-Cola sign. Streams of water leak down the wall from the rusted roof gutters, like long fingers trying to claw the cement floor. Not far from where I stand is a soggy pile of wrappers, milk cartons, toilet paper, and rotting food. Next to my foot lies a faded, yellowish wrapper from a Mallow Cup. I jump instinctively when I hear a strange rustling noise, and see a grinning rat carrying a rotten apple core across the cracked concrete. A sudden mental slap reminds me of where I am. I turn and hurry away from this black hole of decay.

In deciding on a dominant impression, use your common sense: Pick the feature that most stands out about what you are describing. For example, a hummingbird generally appears to the naked eye as a whirring, fidgety blur. If you use "whirring, fidgety blur" as your dominant impression, writing the description will be fairly straightforward. You have lots of details to draw on. On the other hand, if you select as a dominant impression the brief glimpse you had of a hummingbird at rest, writing that description will be hard to do. Because hummingbirds are always moving and seldom still, it is far easier to find details to describe one that is whirring and fidgety than one that is at rest.

In other words if you choose as your dominant impression a rare rather than a dominant feature, you make your job harder. An elephant can be described in terms of its delicateness rather than its massive bulk, but it is not easy to do. The feature that most stands out about a scene, person, animal, or object is always easier to support with details than the one that is rare and seldom seen.

In a Nutshell

Use as a topic sentence the most dominant feature of what you are describing.

PRACTICING 2

Supply a dominant impression that might work for each of the following.

1. A baby lying in a crib

2. Your local supermarket

_____

3. An elderly neighbor or relative

_____

4. The front of the main building of your college

_____

5. Some musical instrument

_____

Use vivid supporting details.

The details of a good description come from your personal observations. They consist of what you see, smell, hear, taste, and feel. The trick in writing descriptive details is to be concrete, so your reader can see the picture you're creating. Here are some examples:

Vague: He was a big man.
Concrete: He was six feet five inches tall, weighed 250 pounds, and was bursting with muscles.

Vague: I bought a blue rug.
Concrete: I bought a deep blue rug with flecks of beige and a wide maroon border.

Vague: The restaurant was noisy.
Concrete: The restaurant was so noisy that we could barely talk above the blaring jukebox and clattering dishes.

Rich sensory details give your description believability and realism. To write with rich details means to use specifics. You name the colors and describe the sounds and odors, using language that is as exact as possible. Don't be satisfied with the dim picture. Brighten it by being as specific and detailed as you can.

Here is a description of a person that lacks specific sensory details:

My political science teacher takes looking natural to an extreme. She doesn't wear makeup and dresses very casually. Professor Lola Bloodgood is what I call a granola woman.

Here is the same paragraph with specifics and sensory details added:

My political science teacher takes looking natural to an extreme. She wears her stringy blond hair straight down to her shoulders, without even bothering to tie it back. Although her skin is pale, she wouldn't dream of using a light shade of blush on her cheekbones or a soft pink lipstick. She prefers khaki pants and gray sweatshirts to more attractive outfits. Whether it's cold or hot, she wears leather sandals, so she always looks as if she's going camping rather than about to lecture in a college classroom. What can I tell you? Professor Lola Bloodgood is what I call a granola woman.

Comparisons can add sparkle to descriptions. Two such types of comparisons are the simile and the metaphor. The **simile** is a comparison that uses *like* or *as*. A **metaphor** is a comparison drawn without the use of *like* or *as*. Here are some examples:

Simile: He was <u>like a raging bull</u> when he saw the smashed fender.

He was <u>as angry as a raging bull</u> when he saw the smashed fender.

Metaphor: He <u>was a raging bull</u> when he saw the smashed fender.

Simile: He <u>cooed like a dove</u> when he first saw his newborn daughter.

Metaphor: He <u>was a cooing dove</u> when he first saw his newborn daughter.

Similes and metaphors add color to descriptions by creating images—pictures that spring to mind. We can well imagine the anger of a bull thundering with rage. Here are some other examples:

Simile: The ballerina leaped into the air and landed as delicately <u>as a butterfly</u>.

Metaphor: The ballerina <u>was a delicate butterfly</u>.

Simile: He ran the race <u>like a gazelle</u>.

Metaphor: He <u>was a gazelle</u> running the race.

Although similes and metaphors add color to a description, they should be used sparingly. They are like pepper in a stew: The trick is to add enough for flavor, but not too much to burn the tongue.

In a Nutshell

• The supporting details of your description should back up your dominant impression.

• Use similes and metaphors in your descriptions.

PRACTICING 3

In the blanks provided indicate whether the comparison in each of the following sentences is a simile or a metaphor. Use *S* for simile and *M* for metaphor.

1. _____ I was as tired as the 1000-year-old man.

2. _____ Her eyes were two burning black coals.

3. _____ His heart beat like a drum.

4. _____ He was as stingy as old Scrooge himself.

5. _____ What an angel she turned out to be!

6. _____ He looked like a great big shaggy dog.

7. _____ My dorm monitor is all heart.

8. _____ She stood as still as a statue.

9. _____ The coffee was like hot lava flowing down my throat.

10. _____ She is my alarm clock.

PRACTICING 4

Try your hand at making an interesting comparison about each of the following subjects. Write in complete sentences, and tell whether you have written a simile or a metaphor.

Example: People crowding onto a bus

People crowded onto the bus like pigs trying to get to a mud hole on a hot day.

Simile or metaphor? Simile

1. A pizza with everything on it

_____

_____

Simile or metaphor? _____

2. Someone dressed up for a fancy party

_____

_____

Simile or metaphor? _____

3. The taste of chocolate fudge pie (or some other favorite food)

_____

_____

Simile or metaphor? _____

4. Standing in a line for a long time

_____

_____

Simile or metaphor? _____

5. A soft breeze blowing across your face

_____

_____

Simile or metaphor? _____

Organize the details.

Most descriptions lend themselves naturally to spatial organization—that is, moving from top to bottom or from bottom to top, from left to right or from right to left. However you organize your description, you should make this spatial movement consistent. For example, if you are describing a person from head to toe, don't go from the head to the midriff, and then shoot back up to the head. Instead, choose one direction for the movement of your description and stick to it. Here is a description that moves from top to bottom:

> My favorite possession is a handcarved wooden fox, given to me by one of my closest friends. The fox is painted a dark burgundy, and he stands on his hind legs. His ears stand straight up as if he is alert for guests. He holds his head high, proud of his position in life. In his two front paws, he carries a little round crystal candleholder containing a burgundy candle. When I look at this adorable little carving, I feel my fox is offering to light my way through darkness. His tail trails along the ground, and he looks as if, any minute, he could set down the candle and start dancing a waltz. He's an elegant fox, and I never get tired of studying him.

There is a built-in logic to using spatial organization for a description: After all, you are physically present in one place and your eye travels along a path like a camera. It doesn't hop erratically from here to there. Moreover, moving slowly and in a predictable path in your description makes it easier for your reader to follow. You might describe a cave from its entrance to its back wall. A boat may be described from bow (front) to stern (back). A tree may be described from its roots to its crown or its crown to its roots. If you look again at the descriptions that begin this unit, you will notice that they use the same kind of deliberate movement.

Spatial order works for most descriptions, but not all. If, for example, you want to describe how you feel when you see your latest love, you'd probably just use a lot of comparisons—similes and metaphors—rather than a spatial organization. For most descriptions, though, spatial organization works fine.

In a Nutshell

Use a spatial organization for most of your descriptions.

PRACTICING 5

In the spaces provided tell how you would move through a description for each of the following topics.

1. An unusual-looking person with whom you are acquainted

   _____

2. A remarkable tree you see often

   _____

3. The inside of an interesting room

   _____

4. A view seen from some height

   _____

5. Your car, or a car you'd like to own

   _____

PRACTICING 6

Write a one-paragraph description of someone you personally know and admire. Begin with a dominant impression expressed in your topic sentence. Use sensory details and perhaps a simile or metaphor. Organize the details to make it easy for your reader to follow your description.

PRACTICING 7

Write a paragraph developing one of the following dominant impressions.

1. It was a dreary late afternoon by the lake.
2. The living room was a shambles after the party.
3. It was the most beautiful wedding dress I'd ever seen.
4. The motorcycle stood at the curb, gleaming in the sun.
5. The closet couldn't hold one more thing.

What Do I Need to Look Out For?

Many descriptions rely too heavily on only the visual sense; however, we have five senses. We also hear, taste, smell, and touch. So if, for example, you want to describe your beloved Persian cat, don't mention only her dazzling white fur and proud stride. Talk also about how soft her fur is (touch), her motorboat purr when she's content (sound), or even her fish breath after eating (smell). At the same time be sure you select only those details that support your dominant impression. Here is a student example:

> Uncle Jack, who is normally a handsome, athletic man, looks pitiful. About three weeks ago, as he was driving along the freeway on his Harley Davidson, he was sideswiped by a truck. Down he went on the pavement, shattering his right foot into 16 pieces. Now he uses a walker, and you hear him before you even see him. Click, click, click goes his walker, accompanying his winded "huh . . . huh . . . huh." Every move he makes is painful. His hair is uncombed, and his face is pale. His eyes have no gleam in them. His jogging suit hangs on his thin frame—a frame that used to be hefty and muscular. In the past Uncle Jack always smelled like Allspice, his favorite aftershave lotion, but now he smells like someone who hasn't taken a shower for a week. It is hard to reconcile this frail, rumpled little man with the dapper uncle I had admired all of my life. He seems so much smaller.

In a Nutshell

Use all your senses—not just vision—in your descriptions.

PRACTICING 8

Write a one-sentence dominant impression of each of the following places. Then choose one of the topics and write a descriptive paragraph about what you **hear**, **smell**, **taste**, **touch**, as well as what you **see**.

1. Your favorite restaurant _____

_____

2. Your local supermarket _____

_____

3. The inside of a church _____

_____

4. An auto body shop_____

_____

5. A dentist's office _____

_____

UNIT TALK WRITE ASSIGNMENT

The writing assignment was to describe a familiar person, animal, place, or thing from memory. In preparation, students paired up to talk about their descriptions and work out a dominant impression and supporting details. One student, Maggie, decided that it would be easier to describe something offbeat, different, or even ugly than something perfectly normal and routine. So she did a description of "Sir George," a stuffed animal in the living room of her home. Her description is a good start but needs polishing. After you have read it, use the blanks provided to write an improved version—beginning with a dominant impression that is supported by vivid details.

Spoken Paragraph

One of my favorite things is "Sir George," a stuffed, life-size Chinese pug who stands near the fireplace in our living room. I guess my mom fell in love with him at a flea market in Arizona. He is made of dark greenish-gray velvet. His ears stick up like two little triangles. He has goldish eyes—I mean the color of that stuff people wear as jewelry—oh yeah, amber. And the pupils are black and huge. His eyes are surrounded by bulging wrinkles. His nose looks like a black prune, wrinkled and stuck right above his shut mouth. Around his fat neck the person who made this dog placed a leather band studded with big brass tacks. Now, to give Sir George the aristocratic bearing he deserves, a small silk Persian carpet covers his back. The design is typically Persian—sort of mythology, I think. It has gold and royal purple fringes. "What a dude!" as my dad has said. The blanket has a hole for his stubby little tail to stick through. Officially, Sir George is a footstool, but no one ever has the nerve to use him that way. He just stands by our fire place, staring into space—a miniature monster—no, not really, just a fierce aristocrat.

Written Paragraph

_____

_____

_____

_____

_____

_____

_____

_____

_____

_____

_____

_____

_____

_____

_____

UNIT TALKING ASSIGNMENT

Get together in small groups of three or four and brainstorm a list of people who have been in the news lately. Then talk about dominant impressions that could be used to sum up each one in a descriptive topic sentence.

UNIT WRITING ASSIGNMENT

Write a description of one of the people discussed by your group in the Unit Talking Assignment above. Use what you have learned in this chapter about writing good descriptions.

PHOTO WRITING ASSIGNMENT

Study the face of the child in the following picture. Use a dominant impression in a topic sentence. Choose vivid details that support your dominant impression. Organize your description with a suitable spatial order.

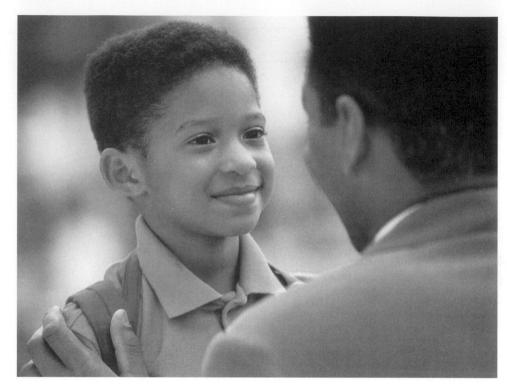

Illustrating

> "My cat, Tabby, is a snobby eater.
> For example, she refuses to eat anything
> but roast duck and fresh trout."

You have a job selling a new miracle furniture polish at flea markets, but lately you've been getting some bad feedback about the product. It doesn't work. Worse yet, it actually ruins the finish on wood. You are bombarded by complaints, and many angry customers prove its worthlessness by bringing Polaroid pictures of their damaged furniture. You tell your boss, but she's disbelieving. She finally asks you to write a brief report about the customer complaints. Here is what you write:

> Brand X, our new furniture polish, not only does not work, it leaves furniture looking streaked and dull. In some cases, Brand X has even taken off the finish. We have many complaints from our customers. For example, Ms. Phillips of Lithonia applied our polish to a table inherited from her grandmother. She said it left the table looking as streaked as if it had been left out in the rain. Three customers from Richfield came to complain, and one from Morton Grove even brought Polaroid pictures showing how her furniture was left streaked and dull from Brand X. Finally, Mr. Prentiss of Stone Mountain may need to have a chair refinished because of the damage Brand X did to its veneer. These are just a few of the complaints I've received in the past weeks.

What you've done in your report is develop a paragraph by examples.

What Am I Trying to Do?

To support a topic sentence with **examples** means to give some instances or cases that illustrate your point. For example, you say that Janet is a good friend. Then you add that once when you badly needed help with a paper you were writing, Janet came over and worked with you through the night. Giving such help is an example of why you think that Janet is a good friend.

Illustrating with examples is as natural as breathing. Every day in our ordinary conversations we use such expressions as *for instance*, *for example*, and *just to show you*. We constantly give examples to back up what we're saying. Often, in everyday talk we even give examples without introducing them. Here is an example we overheard:

> I hate shopping at the mall because it's so big it takes too long to find what you want. [For example] Yesterday it took me almost

two hours to find a store that carries the kind of sunglasses I was looking for.

Although the speaker didn't say *for example*, she clearly meant the incident about hunting for sunglasses to serve as an example. Examples are important because they keep us from making wild generalizations.

Examples also serve as supporting details. Without examples, a statement will often seem thin and unconvincing. Here, for example, is a topic sentence that desperately needs the support of examples:

> Everything bores my friend Merrilee. Nothing seems to interest or excite her. She begins the day convinced that it will be dull and that nothing interesting will happen. This attitude, of course, requires no energy from her. She can just give in to it and let it overcome her. Sometimes, I wonder what would happen if an earthquake hit. Would that raise Merrilee's blood pressure?

Something is obviously missing, for the writer repeats herself without proving her point. Each sentence merely parrots the one before.

Here is the same paragraph with its main point supported by examples:

> Everything bores my friend Merrilee. Nothing seems to interest or excite her. For instance, last week a group of us decided to rent a conversion van and go camping in Yosemite over spring break. The more we planned our adventure, the more thrilled we got. But when we asked Merrilee to join us, she just shrugged her shoulders and said, "That sounds pretty pointless to me." On another occasion, I wanted Merilee to teach me how to make a decorative wreath out of twigs and dried flowers because she is very talented in arts and crafts. At first she agreed, but before I could even collect the materials, she decided that making wreaths sounded like a lot of work for nothing. On still another occasion, when I was completely heartbroken after watching one of my favorite soap operas, Merrilee looked at me with scorn and commented, "That was so dull; I fell asleep watching it." Sometimes, I wonder what would happen if an earthquake hit. Would that raise Merrilee's blood pressure or would she just yawn and say, "So what?"

What makes the second paragraph better than the first is its use of examples. They convince us of the writer's topic sentence, *Everything bores my friend Merrilee.*

In a Nutshell

An example serves to illustrate a general statement.

PRACTICING 1

List three examples that would appropriately illustrate each of the following topic sentences.

1. I am definitely an indoor (or outdoor) person.

   a. _____

   b. _____

   c. _____

2. My roommate is annoying (or pleasant) to live with.

   a. _____

   b. _____

   c. _____

3. Personal service is being replaced by technology.

   a. _____

   b. _____

   c. _____

4. Old age has its privileges.

   a. _____

   b. _____

   c. _____

5. People treat the homeless in a variety of ways.

   a. _____

   b. _____

   c. _____

How Can I Do It?

You can use examples effectively in your writing if you follow these tips:

- Introduce the examples.

- Use strong examples that fit.

- Give enough examples.

Introduce the examples.

It is always a good idea to introduce an example with a simple *for example*, *for instance*, or similar phrase. This lead-in mentally prepares the reader for what is to come. If you are giving several examples in a row, introducing each one will also help your reader keep them straight and follow your train of thought. Here is a paragraph with lead-ins missing:

> <u>This year, I am trying hard to practice good study skills.</u> After every lecture, I go over my notes and make a list of questions about anything I didn't understand. When I do reading assignments, I highlight key ideas and answer the review questions. I start studying for tests early, instead of cramming at the last minute. My efforts seem to be paying off. I got all As and Bs on my midterms.

Notice how much clearer the paragraph is when appropriate lead-ins are used:

> <u>This year, I am trying hard to practice good study skills.</u> <u>For example</u>, after every lecture, I go over my notes and make a list of questions about anything I didn't understand. <u>Also</u>, when I do reading assignments, I highlight key ideas and answer the review questions. <u>Perhaps most important of all</u>, I start studying for tests early, instead of cramming at the last minute. My efforts seem to be paying off. I got all As and Bs on my midterms.

Here are common phrases used to introduce examples:

for example	for instance	another example
another instance	on another occasion	once
another time	that is	namely
in particular	specifically	first, second, etc.
finally		

PRACTICING 2

For each of the following topic sentences supply at least three examples. Underline the introductory phrase used for each.

Example: This was the most relaxing vacation I've ever had.

Answers: **a.** <u>For one thing</u>, I didn't set my alarm clock, so I just woke up whenever I felt like it.

b. <u>Also</u>, I didn't do anything but sit on the bench and read.

c. <u>Finally</u>, I didn't tell my boss where I was going, so I couldn't get any phone calls about work.

1. It takes planning if you want to avoid junk food and eat right.

    a. _____

    b. _____

    c. _____

2. _____ is one of the funniest people I know.

    a. _____

    b. _____

    c. _____

3. I am amazed at how badly some children are allowed to behave in public.

    a. _____

    b. _____

    c. _____

4. A good restaurant server should be available but not pushy.

    a. _____

    b. _____

    c. _____

5. Some slang is colorful and enhances the English language.

    a. _____

    b. _____

    c. _____

Choose strong examples that fit.

Your examples should both fit your point and clearly prove it. To do both, examples have to be strong. If your point is that your friend is stingy, you must give strong examples of that stinginess. For example, this would be a weak example of your friend's stinginess:

> My friend Bob is very stingy. For example, I asked him to lend me $1000 and he said no, even though he could easily afford it.

Refusing to lend someone $1000 is hardly an example of stinginess. Here is a stronger example:

> My friend Bob is very stingy. For example, he refuses to go to any birthday parties because he might have to buy presents.

Here is another weak example, this time of your hometown's friendliness:

> My home town is a very friendly place. For example, many people say good morning back if you greet them first.

A stronger example would be people going out of their way to say good morning instead of just responding. Here is a still stronger example:

> My home town is a very friendly place. For example, one day my mother got a flat tire on Main Street, and five people stopped and offered to help her change it.

Here are some more weak and strong examples:

Topic sentence: My Uncle Bob is a great cook.

Weak example: For example, he makes good chili.

Strong example: For example, his chili is so good that people have offered him money for the recipe.

Weak example: For example, he often cooks the Thanksgiving dinner for the family.

Strong example: For example, his Thanksgiving feast last year was so delicious that for months afterward it was the talk of the family.

PRACTICING 3

List three strong examples for each topic sentence.

1. **Topic sentence:** Some movies are a waste of time.

   a. _____

   b. _____

   c. _____

2. **Topic sentence:** I have some bad habits I would like to overcome.

   a. _____

   b. _____

   c. _____

3. **Topic sentence:** People are becoming more polite.

   a. _____

   b. _____

   c. _____

   4. Topic sentence: Little things matter, sometimes the most.

   a. _____

   b. _____

   c. _____

   5. Topic sentence: _____ is a very _____

   person.

   a. _____

   b. _____

   c. _____

Give enough examples.

Always give enough examples to support your point. How many are enough is largely a matter of common sense. If you are making a small point, one or two examples may be enough. Here is an example:

> My boyfriend sometimes spends money foolishly. For example, last week he sent me a huge bouquet of flowers that cost him $50. It was his way of apologizing. Another time he bought front-row tickets to a show that was in town. That set him back $75, which was half of what he earned that week in his part-time job.

To support a small point about her boyfriend's foolish spending, the writer cited two cases—which were enough.

Here is a bigger point that requires more support:

> My school, a community college of 13,000 students, is always being sued. For example, this year alone, three students filed formal grievances against teachers for what I consider silly reasons. The first was a returning student who had been caught red-handed cheating on an exam. He screamed and yelled that he was innocent and filed a formal grievance accusing the teacher of abusive treatment. Another student decided that her accounting teacher should be fired because she thought he lacked patience. That particular teacher had consistently received outstanding student reviews, yet this angry student blamed him for her own poor performance. A third student decided that his dance teacher was deliberately humiliating him in front of the class because he could not get the movements as quickly as the other students and was holding up the class. All three cases were either dismissed by the Judiciary Board or settled between student and teacher.

Sometimes, however, one extended example may be enough to support a topic sentence. An **extended example** is an example developed in some detail. Here is an example:

> Sometimes no matter how carefully you drive, you can still have an accident through no fault of your own. For example, last month I

had just moved off at a red light and was going no more than ten miles an hour, when a car traveling in the opposite direction suddenly crossed the center line and headed straight for me. I honked and tried to get out of the way, but the car bore down on me like a heat-seeking missile. It raked the side of my car, jumped the curb, and crashed into a wall. Angry and scared, I jumped out and ran over to the driver. When I got there, I found a young man behind the steering wheel in convulsions. It turned out that three months before, he'd had a brain tumor removed and had suffered occasional black-outs since then. When he came to, he was very apologetic and admitted that he shouldn't have been driving. I was no longer angry, however. I figured it was just one of those days.

In a Nutshell

When using examples, do the following:

- Introduce the example.

- Use examples that fit.

- Use strong examples.

- Use enough examples.

PRACTICING 4

Reread the paragraph on the bad furniture polish on page 115. How many examples does it give? Could any of these examples have been omitted? If so, which ones and why? What is the purpose of the last line, "These are just a few of the complaints I've received in the past weeks"?

PRACTICING 5

Pick one of the topic sentences below and develop it into a paragraph with one extended example.

1. If you believe in yourself, you can do anything.
2. Rules are often annoying, but sometimes they can protect you.
3. Once in my life, I had a serious case of hero worship.
4. It's better to act than just complain.
5. Sometimes when you least expect it, something wonderful will happen.

What Do I Need to Look Out For?

Writers often make the mistake of saying *for example* and then merely repeating the topic sentence in different words. This is a false example. A true example does not simply repeat the topic sentence, but supports it with a specific instance. An example of a false example follows.

> My Uncle John is a generous man. For example, he is always being helpful and kind.

In spite of the lead-in, this is not an example. *Generous*, *helpful*, and *kind* all mean the same thing. The writer has not given a specific instance of Uncle John's generosity. Here is a true example:

> My Uncle John is a generous man. For example, when he learned that the house of an elderly couple in our neighborhood had been spray-painted by vandals, Uncle John organized some neighborhood volunteers to repaint it.

Here are two more examples:

False example: My Uncle John is a generous man. For example, he has a soft heart.

True example: My Uncle John is a generous man. For example, every year he spends one week of his vacation working with a group that builds houses for the homeless.

False example: My Uncle John is a generous man. For example, he feels sorry for the sick.

True example: My Uncle John is a generous man. For example, he takes part in nearly every charity walk there is, such as the Cancer Walk, the AIDS Walk, and the Annual Walk for Diabetes.

Always be sure your example is more specific than the point it is meant to support.

In a Nutshell

The example must always be more specific than the point it supports.

PRACTICING 6

Check the true example in each case, the one that is clearly more specific than the point it supports.

1. Appearances can be deceiving. For instance,

_____ **a.** Mrs. Parker lives in a big house on the lake, but she can't pay her telephone bill.

_____ **b.** you can't know a person's real circumstances just by looking at them.

2. Learning something new can be really exciting. For instance,

_____ **a.** classes make you feel good because they are full of interesting information.

_____ **b.** there is great satisfaction in understanding a new poem or discovering how sociology applies to everyday life.

3. Not following directions in a welding class can be disastrous. For instance,

_____ **a.** most activities connected with welding are dangerous.

_____ **b.** if you do not light your torch correctly, you can set yourself on fire.

4. Children have such lively imaginations. For example,

_____ **a.** they make up imaginary friends and talk to them.

_____ **b.** they fantasize a great deal and make up things.

5. You can save a lot of money at the grocery store by using coupons. For example,

_____ **a.** clipping newspaper coupons can result in big savings.

_____ **b.** tuna fish was on sale and with a coupon, I got another 25 cents off.

UNIT TALK WRITE ASSIGNMENT

What follows below is a three-way conversation among students discussing people who lie because of a poor self-image. After studying the passage, assemble the examples into a paragraph, written in Standard English. Come up with a topic sentence that the examples support. Introduce each example, and leave out any that is irrelevant.

Conversation

Ben: I'll tell you an example that happened in my own family. When my sister was in the sixth grade, we had just moved from Iran to the United States. She felt so strange and unwanted in her class that she announced one day that she was the great granddaughter of the Shah of Iran. She came up with a bunch of baloney about how she was brought up in a palace, had her own personal maid, and took ballet lessons from a famous Russian teacher. She even described her bed, covered with pink satin and beautiful dolls. At first her story worked, and the other kids in the class stuck around her like she was a princess. But the teachers didn't buy her story and called my parents. Poor kid. If she had felt good about herself, I don't think she would've done that.

Rita: I'm telling you, people who make up stories about their backgrounds are everywhere. I read where some guy who owned the *Phoenix Gazette*—can't remember his name—something like Bully or Mully—no, I think it was Tully. Anyway, this guy grew up a nerd—you know, reading all the while his older brother was one of these super athlete types. The brother eventually became a Marine lieutenant and was killed in an air collision. Now get this—this nerd made up an entire war record for himself. Pretended he had been in combat flights, had earned every kind of medal. All of this totally made up—not a bit of truth in it. He lived these lies for 30 years until one day, the military found him out. Then, his whole lie fell in on him. He was ruined.

Jean: Well, I have to admit that I like to fantasize. I admit it. But I'll bet lots of you do the same thing. I'll sit on a bench at the mall, watching handsome guys pass by, and I'll pretend the most handsome one wishes he could meet me. At other times, I'll daydream that I'm dating someone like Taye Diggs or Will Smith. Don't laugh. I'm convinced we all fantasize that way. It makes life more exciting.

Ben: Wait a minute; day dreaming is different from lying. I'll tell you about lying. My cousin tells everyone he graduated from college with a degree in journalism. But he didn't. He flunked out his senior year. I guess he felt so bad about flunking out that he thought he could build up an image by lying. I don't know why he doesn't just go back to school and finish.

Written Paragraph

UNIT TALKING ASSIGNMENT

Get together with a partner and discuss good teachers you've had in other classes. You and your partner should then each decide on your favorite teacher. Next, each of you should talk out a topic sentence that sums up what made your teacher so good. Then you should both give examples to support your topic sentences.

UNIT WRITING ASSIGNMENT

Develop a paragraph on the topic of good teachers, using as material the ideas in the above Unit Talking Assignment. Be sure to introduce your examples, make them strong, and cite enough of them to support your point adequately. Also be sure you are not merely repeating the topic sentence but are instead using true examples.

PHOTO WRITING ASSIGNMENT

The following photo shows someone in a ridiculous situation. Use the photo as a basis for writing about how a sense of humor can help you through difficult times. You may give a single extended example or several examples.

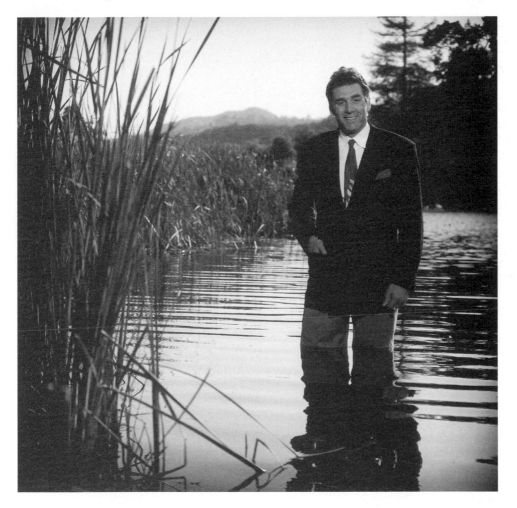

Explaining a Process

"Four simple exercises can help you warm up before exercising vigorously."

You work as a fry cook in a restaurant. It is your job to stand at the grill and cook hundreds of eggs in specially maintained egg frying pans. Because of the high turnover among grill cooks, the egg pans are often improperly maintained and become sticky. The chef asks you, the most experienced cook, to write and post directions detailing how the egg pans should be maintained. This is what you write:

> To keep the egg pans in good condition, all cooks should follow these steps: First, never allow metal utensils to come in contact with the cooking surface. Always use plastic, rubber, or wooden spoons or spatulas on the pans, since even the slightest contact with metal can pit the cooking surface and cause the pans to stick. Second, never stack egg pans on top of each other, for the same reason given above. Third, never wash the pans in water. Instead, wipe them with a clean towel. The high temperatures at which the pans are used make them sterile. Fourth, always begin and end a shift by wiping the pans with a thin coating of cooking oil. This creates a protective barrier that keeps the pans slick so they never become sticky. Finally, if you notice a pan sticking, throw it away immediately and bring in a new one. Once a pan begins to stick, it will never be completely slick again. It will cause problems for other cooks during the rush hour. Let's follow these simple directions and make life easier for all of us.

What you have just written is a *process* paragraph.

What Am I Trying to Do?

A **process** is any task that is done step by step. Learning how to write is a process; so is making beef stew. Getting ready for work or school is as much a process as shaving, tying shoelaces, or warming up the car. Indeed, nearly every waking hour of our lives finds us involved in one process or another.

Process paragraphs are usually one of these three types:

1. How to do something (giving directions)
2. How something works (giving information)
3. How something happened (giving the history)

Here is an example of the first and most common kind of process writing—giving directions on how to do something:

Opening up a swimming pool after a long winter requires five separate steps. First, stick the hose under the winter cover and fill the pool. Raising the water level this way makes it easier to take off the cover. Second, pump any accumulated rainwater off the cover and remove any debris, such as pine needles or dried leaves. Third, remove the cover, drag it over to the lawn, hose it down, and swab it with a yard broom. Fourth, with the pool now full, run the pump for at least 24 hours to circulate the water thoroughly. If you test for chemicals before taking this fourth step, you are likely to get a false reading of the city's tap water rather than of the water in your pool. Fifth, check the chemical balance, paying particular attention to the calcium hardness, total alkalinity, and chlorine content. Opening up a pool is not a difficult process and can usually be done in a day or two. You are now ready for a summer of poolside fun.

Here is an example of the second kind of process paragraph—one that explains how something works:

My computer printer is very easy to use. In fact, if anything is wrong, it tells you exactly how to fix the problem. All you need to do is look at the status panel at the top. It has three amber lights that indicate problems. First, there is the "error" light. When lit, it indicates a problem such as a paper jam, empty toner cartridge, or open printer cover. Second, there is the "tray 1" light. When it is lit, the main paper tray is empty and must have paper added before the printer can function. Third, there is the "tray 2" light. When it is lit, paper must be added to the number 2 tray. If none of these lights is on and the printer still isn't working, I check my printer manual. I also check to be sure that the printer is plugged in!

The third kind of process paragraph—how something happened— is shown below:

My sister loves to tell how a funny series of coincidental meetings led her to marry Jeff. Sally met Jeff when she substituted— very reluctantly—for someone on my bowling team who was sick. (Sally would rather have her fingernails pulled out than bowl.) The funny thing was that Jeff was also a reluctant substitute for someone who was out sick from his brother's team. A couple of days later, Sally got a flat tire on the freeway, and who do you think pulled up in a police cruiser to see if he could help? Right. It was Jeff, who just happened that day to be on patrol. Then, not even a week later, Sally was in the laundromat, where she has been going every Monday night for years because it's the least busy night, and who walks in—Jeff. That night Jeff and Sally decided they'd better start dating rather than trust to keep meeting by luck. Ten years later, they're still happily married.

Explaining a process is a very practical matter and something we do often, even daily. We tell a stranger how to get to Main Street. Our biology teacher explains how cells divide. The new sales manager explains how sales projections were met. In everyday life, the academic and business world, we are constantly giving directions, explaining how something works, or relating how something happened. Knowing how to write a good process paragraph is a useful and practical skill.

In a Nutshell

The process paragraph is any step-by-step explanation. It includes the following:

- How to do something.

- How something works.

- How something happened.

PRACTICING 1

In the blanks provided indicate what kind of process the assignment calls for. Use *A* for how to do something, *B* for how something works, and *C* for how something happened.

Example: __A__ How to use a telephone credit card

1. _____ How to build a bookcase

2. _____ Five swimming exercises you can do to develop a strong back

3. _____ The steps involved in preparing to sky dive

4. _____ How the Food and Drug Administration works

5. _____ What led up to World War II

6. _____ How to make a good cup of coffee

7. _____ What to do when you see an accident

8. _____ How Abraham Lincoln was assassinated

9. _____ How cold germs spread

10. _____ How to be a good date

How Can I Do It?

Basically, a good process explanation covers every step of a process and leaves nothing out. Writing it involves these three steps:

1. Clearly state your purpose at the beginning.
2. Cover the steps in logical order.
3. Use transitions to guide your reader.

Clearly state your purpose at the beginning.

You've learned that the topic sentence—the single sentence that sums up what the paragraph is about—usually comes first, but can come last. However, in the process paragraph the topic sentence must come first. Explaining a process without first telling the reader what you are explaining is like giving someone directions without saying to where. Here is an example of a process paragraph without a topic sentence at the beginning:

> Begin by mixing one cup of margarine or butter with one cup of brown sugar. Beat the mixture until it is pasty. Add half a cup of granulated sugar. Beat in one egg, one teaspoon of vanilla, and mix well. Stir in three cups of oatmeal, one cup of raisins, one and a half cups of all-purpose flour, one teaspoon of baking soda, and one teaspoon of cinnamon. Mix everything together until the ingredients are well blended. Drop spaced tablespoons of the mixture on a greased cookie sheet and bake at 350 degrees for approximately 10 minutes. The result will be delectable and delicious.

Yes, but what are you making? The topic sentence tells us:

> Oatmeal and raisin cookies are very easy to make. Begin by mixing one cup of margarine or butter with one cup of brown sugar. Beat the mixture together until it is pasty. Add a half a cup granulated sugar. Beat in one egg, one teaspoon of vanilla, and mix well. Stir in three cups of oatmeal, one cup of raisins, one and a half cups of all-purpose flour, one teaspoon of baking soda, and one teaspoon of cinnamon. Mix everything together until the ingredients are well blended. Drop spaced tablespoons of the mixture on a greased cookie sheet and bake at 350 degrees for approximately 10 minutes. The result will be delectable and delicious.

In the topic sentence tell your audience exactly what process you plan to explain. Just be straightforward and clear. Here are some examples of topic sentences for process paragraphs:

> Balancing a checkbook consists of five major steps.

> Planting a garden is easy if the soil is properly prepared.

> Line dancing is easier to learn than it looks.

> My father built our house over many stages.

> **PRACTICING 2**

Write a topic sentence for each of the processes listed below.

1. How to get better grades in college

_____

2. How exercise helps with weight reduction

_____

3. How you found your job (or the last job you had)

_____

> **PRACTICING 3**

Write a paragraph on one of the topic sentences in Practicing 2
above.

Cover the steps in logical order.

Most processes have a built-in logic to their steps. If, for example, you
are making a cake, before you prepare the icing you should first mix
the batter and bake it (or you'll have nothing to ice). If you are changing a tire, before you jack up the car you must first remove the spare
from the tire-well in the trunk (or the car may fall off the jack). In
short, list the steps of any process in their natural, logical order. Do
not hop around as this writer does:

> You can relax in five simple steps. Don't think of anything, espe-
> cially not events that have angered you during the day. Sit and try
> to empty your mind of all thoughts. Next, relax your muscles by
> clenching and unclenching your fist 20 times. Don't clench too
> hard—just hard enough to be purposeful. Before you do this, stand
> and stretch your arms as high as you can. Stop stretching and
> slowly lower your arms. Stretch and lower ten times. As you sit qui-
> etly, lightly breathe in and out. Concentrate only on your breathing.
> Your chair should be comfortable and away from unpleasant dis-
> tractions. Finally, close your eyes and imagine something relaxing,
> such as passing clouds, the ebb and flow of the ocean, or a flow-
> ing river. Hold this view in mind for several minutes. By the time you
> finish the fifth step, you should feel much calmer than you felt at
> the start of this exercise.

Did you have trouble following these directions? They jump around a lot.
A process explanation should never jump around; it should march from
start to finish like a well-trained soldier. Here is an improvement:

> You can relax in five simple steps. First, find a comfortable chair,
> away from unpleasant distractions. Sit and try to empty your mind
> of all thoughts. Don't think of anything, especially not events that

have angered you during the day. Second, stand and stretch your arms as high as you can. Stop stretching and slowly lower your arms. Stretch and lower ten times. Next, sit down again and relax your muscles by clenching and unclenching your fist 20 times. Don't clench too hard—just hard enough to be purposeful. Step four is to sit quietly and lightly breathe in and out. Concentrate only on your breathing. Finally, close your eyes and imagine something relaxing, such as passing clouds, the ebb and flow of the ocean, or a flowing river. Hold this view in mind for several minutes. By the time you finish the fifth step, you should feel much calmer than you felt at the start of this exercise.

One way to avoid hopping about is to jot down and number the steps you intend to explain before you actually begin writing. Process assignments are generally easier to write if you work out the steps in advance.

PRACTICING 4

Choose one of the following processes and list the steps required to complete it. Be sure the steps are in logical order.

1. How to throw a birthday party for a friend
2. How to do laundry in an automatic washing machine
3. How to study for a major exam
4. How to get over a failed love relationship
5. How to live on a limited income

_____

_____

_____

_____

_____

_____

_____

_____

Use transitions to guide your reader.

All processes consist of steps that follow one after another. First comes *this*, then comes *that*. You can help your reader follow even a complicated sequence if you use transitions. The transitions most often used are *first, second, third, next, then,* and *finally*. Transitions help your reader in two ways. First, they clearly label each separate step. Second, they connect the steps in logical order. Here is a paragraph with effective transitions:

<u>Everyone hates to iron shirts, but with a little planning, the job is quickly and easily done.</u> <u>First</u>, using an empty Windex bottle (or the like) filled with water, spray the shirt, roll it up, and place it in the refrigerator for two hours. This makes the whole shirt damp and easy to handle. <u>Next</u>, take the shirt out of the refrigerator, unfold it, and place it backside-up on the ironing board. Smooth it with your hands and iron the back until it is wrinkle-free. <u>Then</u>, turn the shirt over and do the buttonhole front. <u>Next</u>, do the button front. Now iron the arms and, <u>last of all</u>, the collar. Your shirt is now ready to wear.

Here are other transitions you can use in a process paragraph:

first	second, third	when
at first	the second, third step	while
afterward	when you have finished that step	meanwhile
after that	before	during
then	at the same time	finally
next	later	last of all

In a Nutshell

Writing a process involves three steps:

• Clearly state your purpose in the beginning.

• Cover the steps in logical order.

• Use transitions to guide your reader.

PRACTICING 5

Use your notes from Practicing 4 to write a process paragraph. Be sure to use helpful transitions.

What Do I Need to Look Out For?

To explain a process clearly, keep the following tips in mind:

■ Know the process.

■ Don't leave out any critical steps.

■ Remember your audience.

Know the process.

You cannot write about a process that you yourself don't thoroughly understand. The first step for writing a successful process paragraph is therefore simple: Know the process well. If you want to explain how to mulch a lawn, you should thoroughly understand the steps involved before attempting to explain it. If you want to write about how a vacuum cleaner works, you should master the details before you do any writing. The same advice applies if you want to explain how an accident happened—get the facts before you write a word.

> ### PRACTICING 6
>
> List five processes that you know thoroughly. They can be any of the three types of processes—how to do something, how something works, or how something happened.
>
> 1. _____
>
> 2. _____
>
> 3. _____
>
> 4. _____
>
> 5. _____

Don't leave out any critical steps.

This mistake—leaving out a critical step—is especially likely when we're explaining a process we know well. We think that a certain step is so obvious that it needn't be mentioned. What is obvious to you, however, may not be so obvious to your reader.

Here, for example, is a process paragraph about changing a tire that omits an important step:

> Changing a flat tire is a lot simpler than it looks. First, locate the jack and lug tools in the trunk. Second, jack up the car. Before the car wheels are completely off the ground, partly loosen the lugs. Third, with the wheels off the ground, remove the lugs and tire. Place the spare tire on the hub of the axle, lining up all the holes. Fourth, replace the lugs and hand-tighten. Fifth, lower the car and finish tightening the lugs with the lug tool. You're ready to travel again. Remember not to drive long on the temporary spare and never over 45 mph. Instead, drive to the nearest gas station and have your regular tire repaired.

Can you spot the omission in this common process? It is this: Before attempting to change a tire, always put the car in park and set the handbrake. Otherwise, the car could roll off the jack and crush the tire changer.

PRACTICING 7

Choose one of the familiar processes below and list the major steps in the process. Do not leave out a crucial step.

1. Preparing for a job interview
2. Washing your car
3. Curing a cold
4. Dealing with a bully
5. Preparing a healthy breakfast

_____

_____

_____

_____

_____

_____

_____

_____

Remember your audience.

A process that is easy for you to understand may be hard for someone else. For instance, an experienced angler knows how to handle a catfish to avoid the barbel—the spine on its back—that's poisonous. Those who've never fished for catfish before are unlikely to even know what a barbel is—to say nothing of its poisonous nature. The point is that you have to adjust your level of explanation to what your audience can be expected to know and not know.

Here, for instance, is a technical explanation of how a sphygmomanometer works:

> When the cuff of the sphygmomanometer is wrapped around the upper arm and fully inflated, it becomes a tourniquet, cutting off all blood flow. As the nurse then slowly releases an air valve, blood flow returns to the arm, generating Korotkoff sounds. The reading at this point, when the Korotkoff sound is first heard, is the systolic pressure. As the cuff continues to deflate, the sounds become fainter and fainter until they disappear altogether. The point of disappearance is the diastolic pressure, the pressure when the heart is at rest.

This explanation may be clear to a medical professional, but to the rest of us, who don't even know what a sphygmomanometer is, it is mystifying.

Here is how you might explain this same process to a someone with no medical training:

> A <u>sphygmomanometer</u> is a device for measuring blood pressure. It consists of an inflatable cuff and a measuring gauge that gives a digital reading. A sphygmomanometer measures a person's blood pressure by inflating the cuff around the upper arm until the blood flow is completely cut off. Air is then gradually released from the cuff. At the first sound of blood flowing again, the gauge registers the rate of flow. This is the <u>systolic</u> pressure. As the cuff continues to deflate, the gauge registers when the sound of flowing blood disappears altogether. That is the <u>diastolic</u> pressure. It is the lower of the two numbers and represents the rate of blood flow when the heart is at rest.

The point is to tailor your explanations to what your readers are likely to know and what they are likely not to know.

In a Nutshell

When writing a process, you should do the following:

- Know the process.
- Don't leave out any critical steps.
- Remember your audience.

PRACTICING 8

Write a paragraph explaining one of the following processes.

1. Folding a piece of paper into a sailboat or a hat
2. Applying make-up
3. Warming up before exercising
4. Winterizing a car
5. Barbecuing chicken

UNIT TALK WRITE ASSIGNMENT

Students were asked to explain any how-to-do process with which they were familiar. Jennifer decided to tell the class how to have a successful garage sale. Here are her informal spoken comments. In the space provided, rewrite what she says into a paragraph that follows the guidelines in this chapter. In other words, state your purpose, use a logical order for your steps, include all necessary steps, and keep your audience in mind.

Spoken Paragraph

Last weekend I helped my mom with her garage sale. We made about two hundred bucks, but I think we could've made more if we'd been better organized and had done things a little differently. If I were to make suggestions for a successful garage sale, here's what I would include—sort of in random order: First of all, have enough stuff to sell. When people see only a few items, like some clothes, a bicycle, a toilet seat, and thinly scattered junk on the lawn, they aren't going to park to take a better look. Also, make your items look good. Wash and iron the clothes. Clean and polish anything that needs it. Who do you think wants to buy a toaster filled with bread crumbs or a pot lined with scum? Display your things properly. Don't just have them laying on the ground where people have to stoop down to see them. Use card tables for objects and racks for clothing. If you don't own card tables, at least use some strong cardboard boxes from your local grocery store. Let's see what else can I say? Hmmm. Oh yes, don't forget to price all items. Experienced garage sale givers have told me that people like to see price tags—even if it's just a sign saying "All items in this box 50 cents." Just remember that people who go to garage sales are usually penny pinchers and are looking for a deal. Give it to them. By the way, get up real early on the day of the sale so that you're ready by 9:00 A.M. when the shoppers arrive. Saturday is the best day for your sale because people aren't at work and they're out doing errands and stuff. Give everyone a warm welcome. Don't make them feel like you're doing them a favor. Smile and answer their questions in a friendly way, no matter how stupid they are. I can't think of anything else, so that's it. Good luck!

Written Paragraph

_____

_____

_____

_____

_____

_____

_____

_____

Pair up with a classmate to whom you explain the steps involved in one of the following processes. Only describe the steps; do not demonstrate them. (You might want to jot down the steps on a piece of scratch paper before you begin.)

1. Tying a tie
2. Scrambling eggs
3. Improving your golf swing (or some other sport skill)
4. Packing for a weekend at a beach
5. Videotaping a movie that's on in the middle of the night

When you're finished, ask your classmate to critique your explanation.

■ Did you state the process at the beginning?

■ Did you include all the steps in their logical order?

■ Did you use transitions?

Then reverse roles and repeat the exercise with a different topic.

UNIT WRITING ASSIGNMENT

Choose one of the following options and write a process paragraph.

1. Write a how-to-process paragraph on one of the Unit Talking Assignments above.
2. Write a how-it-works process paragraph on one of the following topics:
   a. How rent control works
   b. How fast car chases help the popularity of a movie
   c. How drug use ruined a rock band
   d. How recycling newspapers helps the ecology
   e. How a famous person lost his or her popularity

3. Write a how-it-happened process paragraph on one of the following topics:
   a. How someone you know climbed the success ladder
   b. How you broke up with a girlfriend or boyfriend
   c. How you perfected your skills in something
   d. How you or someone you know accomplished a task in the face of obstacles
   e. How parents can make children feel unnecessarily guilty (or vice versa)

PHOTO WRITING ASSIGNMENT

The following photo shows a process involving several steps. Detail each step for an audience that can't see the picture. Begin by stating the process in a topic sentence. Arrange the steps in logical order, and link them with strong transitions.

Defining a Term

> "An entrepreneur is a person who takes on the risk of starting a new business."

Your neighborhood is under pressure. Ugly mini-malls and apartment buildings are springing up everywhere around it, like weeds. One particular fast-food chain wants to build practically in your backyard. Your mother protests that a proper buffer is not being maintained. The builder insists that it is.

Angry, your mother asks you to go to City Hall and research the meaning of *buffer* so she can write a letter to the developer. After doing some reading, this is what you write:

> A <u>buffer</u>, as defined in city zoning, is a strip of land that separates two properties used for different purposes, especially for business and for private residence. To qualify as a buffer, the strip of land must be at least 50 feet wide. It must also run the entire length of the boundary between the two properties. If possible, the buffer should contain mature landscaping so that the two properties are screened from each other. Otherwise, a fence should be built. The design of the fence must be agreed on by the adjoining landowners. Anything other than what is described here is not a buffer according to the city code.

You have just written a definition.

What Am I Trying to Do?

A **definition** is any writing that tries to pin down the meaning of a word. Definitions are usually necessary because a word is either unclear, technical, or its meaning is in dispute.

Here are two examples of words defined in passing because the writer thought they might be unclear to a particular audience:

> He <u>endorses</u>, or <u>supports</u>, Bob Miller for class president.

Endorses is defined in passing.

> They needed a <u>dolly</u> to move that couch. (A <u>dolly</u> is a platform on wheels used to move heavy objects.) It is not expensive to rent one.

Dolly is defined in parentheses because its meaning, which some readers might not know, is of secondary importance.

143

Here is an example of a technical word that is defined. The definition is given immediately and not in parenthesis because the term is important to the discussion, and most people won't know its meaning.

> Many reptiles, unlike mammals, are ecdytic. Ecdysis refers to periodically shedding skin, as snakes cast off their outer skin. Ecdysis is important because . . .

Sometimes a definition requires an entire paragraph, especially for words whose meanings are likely to differ among various people:

> Patriotism means love or support of country. A patriot is one who feels patriotism. But patriotism is probably the most abused word in our language. Some define patriotism in the way the well-known bumper sticker does, "My country, right or wrong," which seems to mean that to be patriotic is to support anything your country does. But this is a false patriotism. Just as it is bad parenting to put up with everything your child does, it is false patriotism to support everything your country does. The real patriot, the person who truly shows a love of country, will support his or her country when it is right but speak up when it is wrong.

When should you define a word? Often this is a judgment call. Some words are so complex that their meanings cannot be taken for granted but must be defined. Others are so clear to the world at large that defining them is unnecessary.

Here are four guidelines to help you decide on whether or not a definition is necessary:

1.   Define any word likely to be unknown to your audience. Your common sense must help you here. Some words you can simply assume your readers know.

> To hang a door properly, you need a hammer, a screwdriver, and a plumb bob. A plumb bob is a lead weight attached to a line that is used to determine perpendicularity. To hang the door, begin by . . .

Notice that the writer defines *plumb bob* but not *hammer* or *screwdriver*. Most people know what a hammer and screwdriver are; few, however, know what a plumb bob is, so the writer defines it.

2.   Define all technical words and terms when you are writing for a general audience. While a biology professor will readily know the meaning of *ecdysis*, a general audience will not. Here is another example:

> Erythromycin is a drug used for treating bacterial infections.

3.   Define slang and specialized terms when you write for a general audience.

> The Dallas Cowboys often use a nickel defense. In football the nickel defense consists of five defensive backs who protect against the pass.

4. Define any word that doesn't have the same meaning for everyone. Most people, for example, agree on the meaning of *toaster* or *car engine*. But not everyone agrees on the meaning of *courage*, *loyalty*, or *success*. Such words have to be defined.

> Faith is a word that has many meanings. In this essay, faith is used to mean a belief that rests more on spiritual outlook than on facts.

In a Nutshell

- A definition tells what a word means.

- Define any word your audience might not know, especially technical words, slang, and specialized words. Also define words that are not likely to have the same meaning for everyone.

PRACTICING 1

Circle the word in the following pairs that you think would need defining in an essay.

1. cockroach, crackpot

2. fast (referring to speed), fast (diet)

3. arson, fire

4. battery (for your car), battery (as in physical assault)

5. bummed out, upset

6. vacation, sabbatical

7. streptokinase, blood

8. sole (the fish), soul

9. gross, disgusting

10. experiment, replica plating

How Can I Do It?

In defining a word, writers generally use one or a combination of these strategies:

- Synonym

- Formal definition

■ Example

■ Saying what the word is not

■ Origin of the word

Use a synonym.

A **synonym** is a word with more or less the same meaning as another word. To cite a synonym is to use the meaning of one word to pinpoint the meaning of another. *Hope*, for example, may be defined by its synonyms—*expectation*, *optimism*, *prospect*. Synonyms are found in general dictionaries as well as in specialized synonym dictionaries. Here is an example of a definition with synonyms:

> Reputation is the name or standing a person has in a community. To have a good reputation means to be held in high esteem by people who know you or have heard about you. A reputation is a person's name. Reputation means more or less the same as character, position, standing, regard, and name. If your reputation is good, people show you respect when they meet you. If your reputation is bad, people are cautious when they meet you because they've heard bad things about you and don't know what to expect.

Note that synonyms by themselves only narrow meaning (reputation = name, standing) but do not pinpoint it. Therefore, it is often a good idea, after you give the synonym, to add some further explanation, as the writer above does.

In a Nutshell

The synonym of a word can be used to narrow its meaning.

PRACTICING 2

Using synonyms, write a one-sentence definition of the following words.

1. anticipation

_____

_____

2. deteriorate

_____

_____

3. frantic

_____

_____

4. chivalrous

_____

_____

5. autobiography

_____

_____

6. roughneck

_____

_____

7. felony

_____

_____

8. indigestion

_____

_____

9. confidential

_____

_____

10. dawdle

_____

_____

Give a formal definition.

A formal definition first states what group the word belongs to and then shows how it differs from other words in that same group. The following chart shows what we mean:

Word	**Group**	**Difference**
pizza	is a food	consisting of crust and toppings
buffer	is a strip of land	that separates two properties
penance	is an act	that shows sorrow for doing wrong

(cont.)

Word	Group	Difference
to rescue	is an act	of freeing from danger
measles	is a disease	characterized by red spots on the skin
Detroit	is a city	in Michigan

Notice that in each case the definition is a two-step process. First, the term is placed in a general group. Second, its differences from other members in that group are specified. So, *pizza* is a *food*, but it is different from other foods by having *a crust and toppings*. A *buffer* is a *strip of land*, specifically one that *separates two properties*. Likewise, *measles* is a *disease*, but one *characterized by red spots on the skin*. Dictionaries always give such formal definitions.

To give a formal definition, proceed this way: First, state the group to which the word belongs; second, tell how the word differs from others in the group. Formal definitions, in other words, always have two parts.

Anxiety is <u>a psychological disorder</u> that <u>is characterized by irrational fears</u>.

Love is <u>an emotion</u> of <u>passionate affection for someone or something</u>.

A neighbor is <u>a person</u> who <u>lives near another</u>.

The three words—*anxiety*, *love*, and *neighbor*—are first identified as belonging to the groups, *psychological disorder*, *emotion*, and *person*. Then we're told how each word differs from others in that group.

In a Nutshell

A formal definition first places the word in a group, then shows how it differs from others in that group.

PRACTICING 3

Using the chart below, choose ten words that you know well and formally define them as we did on page 147.

Word	Group	Difference
1.		
2.		
3.		
4.		
5.		

6. _____

7. _____

8. _____

9. _____

10. _____

PRACTICING 4

Give a formal definition for each of the following words. Be sure your definition has two parts—the group the word belongs to and how it differs from other words in that group. Write a complete sentence.

Example: daisy

A daisy is a flower with many white petals and a yellow center.

  1. doorbell

_____

  2. century

_____

  3. giggle

_____

  4. yogurt

_____

  5. tuxedo

_____

Give an example.

A well-chosen example can add meaning to a word. Here are some examples:

Laconic means "concise" or "brief." For instance, a trial lawyer whose opening argument is very short and to the point, without wasting a word, would be considered laconic.

Goldbricking is slang for avoiding work by coming up with excuses. For example, you're goldbricking if you say you can't work because your allergies are acting up when there's nothing really wrong with you.

An illuminating story or anecdote about a word or term can also shed light on its meaning. An example follows.

My tennis partner is a prude. Now the term prude is applied to people who are overly concerned about being proper or modest.

That's Jenny for you. She will not play mixed doubles in shorts or a tennis skirt because she says men always look at her in a "certain way" when she does. Last Friday, my brother and his buddy wanted to play a couple of sets, and Jenny was happy to join in, but she wore a jogging suit even though it was in the nineties. I think that is being prudish.

In a Nutshell

Giving an example or telling a story can add to the meaning of a word.

PRACTICING 5

Define the following terms by using a synonym or giving a formal definition. Then further clarify their meanings by giving an example or telling a story.

1. rude

_____

_____

_____

_____

2. loyalty

_____

_____

_____

_____

3. boring

_____

_____

_____

_____

4. hero

_____

_____

_____

_____

5. limber

_____

_____

_____

_____

Say what the word is not.

Many words are close in meaning without being exact synonyms. *Love* and *infatuation* are examples: Their meanings are close, but not the same. *Frugality* and *miserliness*, *pride* and *arrogance* are also close, but still different. Sometimes the best way to define a word is to show how its meaning slightly differs from another word whose own meaning is close. Here is an example:

> Jealousy is a feeling of fear at the possibility of losing a loved one. Jealousy usually comes into play in a love triangle, where two people are competing for the affections of a third. Jealousy differs from envy in that jealousy is being possessive of what you think is (or should rightly be) yours, such as a husband being jealous of his wife or a wife of her husband. Envy is wanting what someone else has, such as a person envying another's good looks or success or wealth.

In a Nutshell

Some words may best be defined by saying what the word is not.

PRACTICING 6

Define each of the following terms by stating what it is *not*, namely the similar word in parentheses.

Example: Cheap (frugal)

A person who is cheap tries to get away without paying his or her fair share. A cheap person is not the same as a frugal person. A frugal person tries to save on purchases by getting the best bargain but is still prepared to pay his or her fair share.

1. casual (sloppy)

_____

_____

_____

_____

2. annoyed (angry)

_____

_____

_____

_____

3. accidental (careless)

_____

_____

_____

_____

4. funny (silly)

_____

_____

_____

_____

5. confident (cocky)

_____

_____

_____

_____

PRACTICING 7

Expand the definitions below by giving an example or anecdote, or saying what the term is not.

Example: To be *fair* is the quality of treating everyone the same. For instance, a teacher who is fair does not give *A*'s to a student just because that student is likable. The teacher gives the grade that is deserved.

1. *Guilt* is the awareness of having done something wrong.

_____

_____

_____

2. *Greed* is a strong desire for more than you need.

_____

_____

_____

3. To feel *defeated* means to feel crushed and beaten.

_____

_____

_____

4. A *genuine* person is honest and frank.

_____

_____

_____

5. To *ooze* is to flow or leak out slowly.

_____

_____

_____

Give the origin of the word.

It can be useful in defining a word to say what it originally meant. This tactic, however, will only work for words whose origins add to their present meanings. Here is an example:

> Sarcasm comes from the Greek word sarkasmós meaning "to tear flesh." Today, sarcasm means "harsh or bitter derision" and is an especially cruel tone that one uses in criticism. The person who is sarcastic tries to wound—to tear flesh. Sarcasm is not gentle.

Not every word has an origin that can help with its present meaning. *Buffer*, for example, does not. Neither does *father*. However, as long as you're looking up a word in the dictionary, you might as well check to see if its origin can help you define its present meaning.

In a Nutshell

Occasionally, the origin of a word will help add to its present meaning.

PRACTICING 8

Give the origins of the following words. Use a good dictionary for this assignment. If there is more than one origin given, use the oldest.

1. banshee _____

2. danger _____

3. egad _____

4. game _____

5. IOU _____

6. magazine _____

7. mesmerism _____

8. origin _____

9. permanent _____

10. seduce _____

PRACTICING 9

Choose one of the words in Practicing 8 above and define it in a short paragraph. Use its origin in your definition and any other way of defining that you've learned.

PRACTICING 10

Choose one of the terms listed below and write a paragraph defining it. Begin with a formal definition, and then use any of the strategies explained in this chapter.

1. gourmet
2. failure
3. mischief
4. debate (verb)
5. sob (verb)

What Do I Need to Look Out For?

Two common problems can occur in defining. Your definition can be circular, or it can be incomplete. We'll discuss them separately and give some tips about avoiding these problems.

Circular definitions

A definition is circular if it simply repeats the word without adding substantially to its meaning. An example of a circular definition follows.

Middle-aged refers to period in the middle years of a person's life. When a person is middle-aged, he or she is between young and old, not one or the other.

This definition is circular because it adds nothing to *middle-aged* except the obvious meaning already contained in the words *middle of life*. In short, the writer does not define the word, but merely repeats it. Here is a better definition:

Middle-aged refers to the period in the middle years of human life. It is not a fixed but a variable period. Long ago, when humans lived an average of 35 years, middle-aged was, strictly speaking, anywhere between 15 and 25. But with the human life span now 78.8 years for women and 72 years for men, middle-aged is now usually defined as the years between 45 and 65. The term, middle-aged, however, does not just refer to a period of time, but more accurately to a life condition. Middle-aged people go through certain physiological and psychological changes. Their metabolism slows down; sexual energy and appetite decrease. Some men and women go through a period of self-examination and doubt known as the "mid-life crisis." Middle-aged, in sum, describes the transition that all people go through as they move from youth to old age.

PRACTICING 11

In the blanks preceding each of the following sentences, write *C* if the definition is circular. Leave the blank empty if the definition is good. Then correct and rewrite the five circular definitions in the lines provided.

1. _____ A *mask* is a cover for the face used as a disguise.

2. _____ *Stressed* is what people feel when they have too much stress in their lives.

3. _____ *Pepper* is a pungent product from the fruit of an East Indian plant used as a seasoning spice.

4. _____ A *servant* is one who serves.

5. _____ *Dissing* is an act of dissing someone.

6. _____ A *subhead* is one head lower than a main head in an outline.

7. _____ *Team spirit* refers to the team's spirits, whether they're high or low.

8. _____ The *capitol* is the building in which a state legislative body meets.

9. _____ A *barbarian* is a person who does barbaric things.

10. _____ A *monk* is a man who is a member of a religious order and lives in a monastery.

Use the lines below to correct and rewrite the circular definitions:

_____

_____

_____

_____

_____

_____

_____

_____

_____

_____

Incomplete definitions

The second problem to look out for in writing definitions is the **incomplete definition**—the definition that doesn't say enough. In particular, the incomplete definition doesn't spell out the meaning of the word in the ways we've described in this chapter. Here are some examples:

> A <u>migraine headache</u> is a severe headache.

The definition below is more complete, but still lacking:

> A <u>migraine headache</u> is a severe headache characterized by nausea, vomiting, and an extreme sensitivity to light. It can last for as long as a day.

As migraine sufferers will tell you, this definition still hardly does justice to their awful condition. Here is a better definition that is complete:

> A <u>migraine headache</u> is a severe headache that is characterized by nausea, vomiting, and extreme sensitivity to light. No one knows for sure what causes the migraine or how to prevent one. But migraine sufferers are often so stricken when an attack occurs that they can do nothing more than go to bed. A migraine often lasts from several hours to a day or longer. When my Aunt Ida has a migraine, she can do nothing more than draw the shades in her

bedroom and go to bed, where she'll stay for 24 hours, retching and feeling as if she will die. Not even the newest medications help her migraines. The only solution is isolation and bed rest.

Both errors—being circular and being incomplete—can usually be caught if you reread your work. Indeed, the best way to catch both problems is to read your work aloud, either to yourself or to another person, pretending to know nothing about the topic. Ask if you really answer the question, "What is it?" If you have doubts, rewrite the definition until you are satisfied that it fully defines your word or term.

In a Nutshell

Avoid definitions that are circular or incomplete.

PRACTICING 12

Half of the following definitions are incomplete. Identify the incomplete definitions by marking them *I*. Then rewrite them in the lines below. Use a dictionary, if you like.

1. _____ *Coffee* is a beverage.

2. _____ *Acrylics* are a type of paint that dry fast and can be mixed with water.

3. _____ A *magician* is an entertainer.

4. _____ A *chauffeur* is a person employed to drive a private car.

5. _____ *Sautéing* refers to cooking food fast in a shallow frying pan.

6. _____ The *cuticle* is part of your nails.

7. _____ A *sergeant* is a military officer.

8. _____ *Tweezers* are small metal instruments used for plucking or handling small objects.

9. _____ A *hot dog* is a type of fast food.

10. _____ *Glucose* is a type of sugar used by the cells for energy.

Now rewrite the incomplete definitions, making them clear and complete.

_____

_____

_____

_____

_____

_____

_____

_____

_____

PRACTICING 13

Read the following paragraph, then circle and label the techniques used to make the meaning of the word clear: *S* (synonyms), *N* (saying what the word is not), *E* (example), or *O* (giving the origin of the word).

Normal—a word all of us use—means "typical" or "standard." It comes from the Latin *normal*, meaning "a rule or pattern." *Normal* indicates some kind of balance, either physical or mental. For example, we say the "normal" body temperature is 98.6F° because tests show that that is the typical temperature of a well person. We also say that it is "normal" for a teenager to be rebellious because we know from developmental psychology that during the teen years many adolescents try to assert their independence. *Normal* is not the same as *average*. An "average student" is one who receives average grades. But that same student could be abnormal in some other way, say, for example, in being very tall. Someone who falls within the standards of what is expected is considered "normal." We refer to "normal" height, weight, and curiosity, meaning that these all fall within the range of the expected.

UNIT TALK WRITE ASSIGNMENT

Your assignment is to write a definition of a word. After much thought, you choose the word *asteroid.* You look up the word in your *American Heritage Dictionary,* and then you talk a paragraph to your reflection in the mirror, hoping the exercise will increase your fluency—and it does. Here is your monologue:

Spoken Paragraph

My dictionary tells me that an asteroid is a small celestial body that orbits around the sun. Most asteroids are found between Mars and Jupiter. They are much smaller than planets. At most, about 700 miles in diameter. They are very irregular in shape. I Don't think anyone knows where they came from. Actually, I already knew that because I've always been interested in planets and space. I'm a real *Star Wars* addict. But I'm not nearly as interested in the definition of asteroid as I am in the idea that one could hit Earth. NASA has decided that any news of an asteroid heading toward Earth will be kept secret because it would upset too many people. Well, I should say so. I'd just as soon not know if the end of the world is near. The thing is, asteroids move at incredible speeds, like comets, and a large one moving toward us at a humongous speed would simply create another big bang—except there wouldn't be anyone left to read about it. It's really best not to think about such a disaster. I think I have more or less explained what an asteroid is. At least I tried.

Your spoken paragraph is a good start toward developing a clear definition of asteroid. Now, use this paragraph as the groundwork for a more polished version. Be sure to make your definition complete and avoid giving circular definitions. Check your dictionary to see if there is an interesting origin of the word to include.

Written Paragraph

_____

_____

_____

_____

_____

_____

_____

_____

_____

_____

_____

_____

UNIT TALKING ASSIGNMENT

Choose a partner. Give your partner a word that you know well and ask him or her to define it. Write down your partner's definition. Then exchange places and define a word given by your partner. Collaborate on the definitions until both of you agree that the meanings of the defined words are clear.

UNIT WRITING ASSIGNMENT

Write a definition of one of the words that you worked on in the above Unit Talking Assignment. Use any of the strategies for defining that you learned in the unit: synonyms, formal definitions, examples, saying what the word is not, and the origin of the word.

PHOTO WRITING ASSIGNMENT

Use the following photo as the inspiration for defining *friendship*. Start with a formal definition, and then use synonyms or any of the other techniques taught in this chapter, including saying what the word is not, giving an example, or relating an anecdote that illuminates its meaning. Make sure that your definition is not circular or incomplete.

Classifying

"I like three kinds of jazz."

Your school is being visited by a group of computer students from Japan, and you have been asked to head up a committee to welcome the visitors and show them around campus. You tell the student government president that you need various types of students to help out. The president asks you to e-mail her about the kinds of volunteers you need. You send the following message:

> The host committee for our Japanese visitors should be made up of three types of students. To begin with, we need students who are fluent in both Japanese and English. They will serve mainly as translators. We also need some sociable students with sunny personalities to shepherd the visitors around and make them feel welcome. Third, we need computer science students who are willing to share their expertise with our visitors and show them around the computer lab. With these three types of students on our committee, I'm convinced our visitors will enjoy their stay with us.

You have just written a paragraph that classifies.

What Am I Trying to Do?

To **classify** means to sort out into types. If you say—"I've had four kinds of jobs," or "I have three kinds of friends"—whether you know it or not, you're classifying. Here is an example of a paragraph written to classify:

> <u>I have three kinds of friends in my life: close friends, just friends, and acquaintances.</u> The first type, my close friends, are people I have known most of my life who love and accept me for myself. George is the best example of this kind of friend. We've known each other since first grade. I trust George and can tell him my deepest feelings. My second type of friend, "just friends," are people I like and do things with. Missing, however, is the feeling of trust I share with George. We're friends, but "just friends," not "close friends." Finally, I have friends who are just "acquaintances." These are people I occasionally see at parties or sit next to in class. We chat and are friendly with one another if we happen to meet. But that's as far as we go. We don't plan things together. My life is richer for these three types of friends, for they provide me with a healthy variety of company.

This is a typical classification paragraph. In it the writer is trying to sort her friends into personal categories.

Her classification may be called an **informal classification**: The categories are made up; they do not already exist. A **formal classification** is classification based on categories that already exist and are not personally invented. For example, vehicles can be classified by manufacturers according to body types such as *two-door, four-door, convertible, van,* and *sports utility vehicle (SUV).* Medicine uses categories such as *internists* (general doctors for adults), *pediatricians* (general doctors for children), *cardiologists* (specialists in the heart), and *neurologists* (specialists in the brain and nervous system), to name a few of the better-known types. History courses are similarly classified into such types as *History of South America* or *History of the Renaissance.*

Imagine, for a moment, what life would be like if we were incapable of classifying. Every object or experience would strike us as utterly unique. The world we live in would soon overwhelm us with its sheer variety. Nothing would be like anything else; everything would be spectacularly different. We'd scream with discovery at the sight of a cat. Two blocks later, we'd scream just as loudly at the sight of another cat, for we would have no concept of the second cat being the same kind of animal as the first. Its uniqueness is all we would see. We'd soon be blubbering with the shock of too much novelty. In short, classification—both formal and informal—is useful because it helps us simplify the world.

PRACTICING 1

Check the topics that should be developed by classification.

1. _____ Types of houses

2. _____ Why good work habits are important

3. _____ Kinds of popular part-time jobs

4. _____ Organizing your time

5. _____ How to find information on the Internet

6. _____ Comparing Disneyland and Disneyworld

7. _____ Categorizing legal drugs

8. _____ Dividing mall shoppers into types

9. _____ The need for job retraining in large companies

10. _____ Kinds of freedom we should cherish

How Can I Do It?

Here are three tips to help you write a good classification:

1. Use a single principle.
2. Be complete.
3. State your purpose.

Use a single principle.

All classification must be made according to some ordering principle—the measure or yardstick you use for your sorting. For example, if you use *height* as the ordering principle for sorting your friends, you might come up with the categories of *tall friends*, *medium-height friends*, and *short friends*. Such a classification, however, would be silly and hardly useful. The trick is therefore to find an ordering principle that yields significant categories. For example, the student who classified her friends on page 161 used degrees of closeness as her ordering principle. This gave her the categories of *close friends*, *just friends*, and *acquaintances*. These categories are significant because they tell how people relate to each other at different levels of intimacy.

How you classify something depends on your ordering principle. For example, you might choose to classify cars by body styles—*two-door, four-door, convertible, van,* and SUV. You might also choose to classify cars by size—*subcompacts, compacts, intermediates,* and *full size*. If you choose price as your ordering principle, you might classify cars into *economy, medium-priced,* and *expensive*. You choose the single ordering principle that best suits your purpose. Once you have chosen an ordering principle, you must stick with it.

If you do not use a single ordering principle, you might end up with an illogical topic sentence like this one:

> There are five main types of car manufactured today: <u>subcompacts</u>, <u>compacts</u>, <u>intermediates</u>, <u>full size</u>, and <u>expensive</u>.

Here the writer is actually using two ordering principles: size and price. Size yields the categories *subcompacts, compacts, intermediates,* and *large;* price yields the category *expensive*. This is an illogical division since a full size or even a compact car can also be expensive.

Sometimes this kind of mixed classification occurs in an otherwise well-written paragraph, such as this one:

> My recreation consists of three types of activities: indoor activities, outdoor activities, and sports. For indoor activities, I really enjoy playing pool, especially eight-ball, and bowling. Sometimes I also like to play ping-pong. My favorite outdoor activities are playing softball on my company team, golf, and jogging. The sports I especially enjoy are pool, softball, bowling, golf, and jogging. These types of activities help me get over a dull and boring day of working.

Do you see the problem with this paragraph? It is that *sports* can be an indoor activity (pool, bowling, ping-pong, for example) or an outdoor activity (softball, tennis, football, for example). The groups are illogical, and the writer ends up being repetitious.

Here's how the student rewrote the paragraph after finding a more logical ordering principle for his recreational activities:

> <u>My recreation consists of three types of activities: sports I play with a team, sports I do by myself, and sports that I love to watch on television.</u> My favorite team sport is softball. I play on my company's team, usually as a pitcher, and enjoy the fellowship that

comes from the competition. The company also has a ping-pong team that I'm on, and sometimes I also practice with the company tag-football team. The sport I do by myself and really love, when I can afford it, is golf. I like to go to the driving range alone and hit practice balls. I like to play by myself so if I do badly, I won't feel embarrassed. I also like to run alone and try to get out at least three times a week. On weekends, especially if the weather is bad, I like to watch college basketball games and NFL football games on television. I'm also an Atlanta Braves fan and watch all their tele- vised games. Without sports, I think I would be bored, and my life would be dull.

In any classification, you must choose a single, logical principle for ordering items into types and stick to it.

PRACTICING 2

For each of the following topics, cross out the one type that doesn't fit. In the spaces provided, say why it doesn't fit.

Example: Pies

    a. Fruit pies

    b. Cream pies

    c. ~~Homemade pies~~

    d. Meat pies

Why: A homemade pie could also be any of the other three.

  1. Places to live

    a. Apartment

    b. Single-family home

    c. Condominium

    d. Downtown

    e. Two-family home

Why: _____

  2. Radio stations

    a. Oldies

    b. All-news

    c. All-talk

      d. Country and western

      e. FM

Why: _____

  3. Milk

      a. Skim

      b. Two percent

      c. Chocolate

      d. Whole milk

Why: _____

  4. Movies

      a. PG

      b. PG-13

      c. R

      d. Documentary

      e. G

Why: _____

  5. Transportation

      a. Cars

      b. Ambulances

      c. Trains

      d. Planes

      e. Buses

Why: _____

PRACTICING 3

Classify each of the following topics into at least three types. Then state your principle for classifying.

Example: Types of cars

      a. Expensive cars

      b. Medium-priced cars

      c. Economy cars

Principle of classification: price

1. Types of desserts

    a. _____

    b. _____

    c. _____

Principle of classification: _____

2. Types of athletes

    a. _____

    b. _____

    c. _____

Principle of classification: _____

3. Types of television programs

    a. _____

    b. _____

    c. _____

Principle of classification: _____

4. Types of restaurants

    a. _____

    b. _____

    c. _____

Principle of classification: _____

5. Types of music

    a. _____

    b. _____

    c. _____

Principle of classification: _____

PRACTICING 4

Write a paragraph on one of the topics from Practicing 3 above.

Be complete.

If you are classifying a subject whose parts are well known, be sure to include them all. An example of a glaring omission follows.

The military services available to young people are the Army, Navy, and Air Force.

This division omits the Marines and the Coast Guard. Here is another example:

There are seven parts of speech: nouns, verbs, adjectives, adverbs, prepositions, conjunctions, and interjections.

In fact, there are eight parts of speech. The writer has omitted pronouns, and we are left wondering why.

You don't have to worry about completeness in a personal classification of your own invention. For instance, no one can seriously challenge this classification:

High school students come in four primary types: nerds, jocks, party animals, and brains.

Obviously, this is a personal classification based on opinion.

However, in a formal classification, omitting a known category will glaringly stand out. Here is an example:

There are three types of marital status: married, divorced, and widowed. I've been two of the three and know what each feels like. I was married for three years. The first year was happy, but the next two were terrible. My wife and I fought constantly. Finally, we agreed to give up and get a divorce. I've been divorced now for two years and can't say I really like it. I feel like I failed at something that might have worked if I had tried harder. I'll probably never know what it feels like to be widowed because it's unlikely I'll ever get married again. Being married was the best of the three marital statuses; too bad it was so short for me.

This classification is incomplete: *single* is one of the marital statuses and should be mentioned.

In sum, if your classification is formal rather than personal, be careful not to leave out any categories.

PRACTICING 5

In the blanks provided, list the category that was omitted from each of the following classifications.

1. **college teachers:** instructors, assistant professor, associate

   professor, _____

2. **students:** freshman, sophomore, junior, _____

3. **student accommodations:** dorm, rented room,

   apartment, _____

   4. furniture: living room, dining room, kitchen,

   _____

   5. track distances: 100 meters, 200 meters, 400 meters,

   _____

State your purpose.

Classification is an exercise in thinking. It requires you to think logically in categories and types. Your teacher might ask you to informally classify your hobbies, relatives, or friends, or to formally classify the types of literature. All such assignments are intended to sharpen your ability to think in categories and types.

The most useful way to begin any classifying paragraph, whether formal or informal, is to state what you're going to do. Here is an example of a paragraph where the writer hides her purpose:

> Many of my boyfriends don't like to spend money. Jack is the exception. Jack never takes me anywhere without paying for both of us. If he doesn't have the money, he doesn't ask me out, but waits until he has earned it. Jack is very old-fashioned in that way. Peter always makes it clear that we're going Dutch. If I tell him I can't afford it, we don't go out. He's very modern in that way. Tony is what you would call a moocher. He wants me to pay for everything. And sometimes, if I can afford to, I do and like it because paying makes me feel in charge. Of the three, I prefer Jack if I'm broke, but don't mind either Peter or Tony when I can afford them.

This paragraph classifies the writer's boyfriends but doesn't plainly state the purpose. Here is a sharper and crisper version because it openly lists specific _kinds_ of boyfriends. Generally, if you use a word like _kinds_, _types_, or _sorts_ in your topic sentence, you're probably doing a good job of stating your purpose.

> <u>I have three kinds of boyfriends: those who are willing to pay my way on dates, those who are willing to pay only their own way, and those who expect me to pay everything.</u> Jack is the first kind of boyfriend. He never takes me anywhere without paying for both of us. If he doesn't have the money, he doesn't ask me out, but waits until he has earned it. Jack is very old-fashioned in that way. Peter is the second type. When he asks me out, he always makes it clear that we're going Dutch. If I tell him I can't afford it, we don't go out. He's very modern in that way. The third type of boyfriend can be summed up in Tony. He's what you would call a moocher. He wants me to pay for everything. And sometimes, if I can afford to, I do and like it because paying makes me feel in charge. Of the three types, I prefer Jack if I'm broke, but don't mind either Peter or Tony when I can afford them.

Always be straightforward about your purpose in your topic sentence. Your reader will thank you.

In a Nutshell

To write a good classification, follow these tips:

- Use a single principle.

- Be complete.

- State your purpose.

PRACTICING 6

Write a paragraph about the kinds of dates you've had or the kinds of company you keep. Be sure to state your purpose clearly.

What Do I Need to Look Out For?

Classifying means sorting items into either informal types, based on your own observations, or into formal categories. The errors usually made in classifying, as you might expect, are therefore errors of sorting. When you classify, be sure to do the following:

- Include at least three categories.

- Do not overlap categories.

Include at least three categories.

Generally, a classification is made up of at least three categories. For example, it makes little sense to say:

> The people in my life fall into two categories: friends and not friends.

Similarly, a vehicle is either a car or not a car, a fruit either an orange or not an orange. Neither observation says much about either cars or fruit. This topic sentence, however, with its three categories, is much more telling:

> The people in my life fall into three categories: family, friends, and acquaintances.

Make sure that your own classifications contain at least three categories.

PRACTICING 7

List at least three categories for each of the following items.

1. vacations

   a._____

   b._____

   c._____

2. stress

   a._____

   b._____

   c._____

3. communication

   a._____

   b._____

   c._____

4. home appliances

   a._____

   b._____

   c._____

5. indoor entertainment

   a._____

   b._____

   c._____

Do not overlap categories.

As we said, if you do not stick to a single ordering principle, you will produce a classification with overlapping categories. The overlapping category is such a major error of classifications that it deserves a second mention. Consider, for example, this topic sentence:

> Movies can be categorized as drama, comedy, science fiction, and children's film.

The problem here is that a children's film can be a drama, a comedy, or science fiction. In other words, the categories are overlapping.

Here is another example:

> I am a person with four basic moods: good mood, bad mood, bored mood, and morning mood.

Morning mood doesn't fit, since the writer could be in a good, bad, or bored mood in the morning. Good mood, bad mood, and bored mood are types based on how the writer feels. *Morning mood* is a type based on time of day. This mistake is the same as classifying living creatures as no-legged, two-legged, four-legged, and camels.

The primary thing you need to look out for, then, is illogical thinking about types. Be sure that you select a single principle for a classification so it yields types rather than overlapping categories. Watch out for a topic sentence like this:

> My typical day has four parts: school, work, play, and night.

In a Nutshell

When classifying, be sure to do the following:

- Include at least three categories.

- Do not overlap categories.

PRACTICING 8

Circle the overlapping category in each of the following classifications. Explain why the category is overlapping.

1. magazines: news, gossip, inexpensive, fashion, sports

_____

2. main dishes: beef, pork, chicken, stew, fish

_____

3. books: hardbacks, novels, spiral bound, paperbacks

_____

4. drinkable liquids: sodas, water, sport drinks,

Gatorade

_____

5. gasoline: high-octane, unleaded, Mobil, low-octane

_____

UNIT TALK WRITE ASSIGNMENT

Following is a conversation among students about ugly neckties. Study it and then turn the ideas into a paragraph based on classification. Begin with a topic sentence that clearly states the ways ties can be ugly. Be careful not to overlap categories. Use the lines below for your paragraph.

Conversation

Dave: It's sort of hard to say what makes a tie ugly, but I sure know one when I see it.

Melissa: I'll tell you one way ties are ugly—when they're made of weird material. Have you ever seen a tie made of wool? It looks as if it's been hand-crocheted. I mean, the knot is so thick it looks like some malignant tumor growing on the guy's neck.

Andrew: I agree. Ties should be made of smooth material—but not polyester or acrylic because they look cheap. I like ties made out of natural fabrics—like cotton.

Kiki: What about the designs on ties? I saw a tie with a picture of the Mona Lisa on it. To me that's dissing a world famous artist.

Melissa: I saw a tie once that had huge broccoli, cabbage heads, and bananas printed all over it! I wanted to barf!

Kiki: Let's not even mention ties that are sexually stupid. I mean, showing parts of women's anatomy or Santa Claus and Mrs. Claus—well, I won't say more. How gross.

Dave: Yeah—I know. But ties can be ugly even if they're made of natural material and they don't have any design at all on them. I'm talking about color. My grandmother once gave me a tie that was puke green.

Melissa: Yeah—nothing like a prune purple tie! And some of the designer ties are worst of all—combining orange bubbles with hot pink squares or dark brown stripes with neon blue rectangles.

Andrew: Hey—what's wrong with orange parrots and lavender fish? Just kidding. I have to say there's nothing like an elegant silk tie with simple stripes or squares in subdued but rich colors— you know, the kind of tie my Grandpa wears.

Written Paragraph

_____

_____

_____

_____

_____

_____

_____

_____

_____

_____

_____

_____

UNIT TALKING ASSIGNMENT

Working with a classmate, take turns finding personal categories for the following topics. Be sure you have at least three categories and that they do not overlap.

1. Roommates
2. People in a grocery checkout line
3. Sports fans
4. People you often see in a library
5. Blind dates

UNIT WRITING ASSIGNMENT

Write a classification paragraph on one of the topics you discussed in the above Unit Talking Assignment.

PHOTO WRITING ASSIGNMENT

The following picture shows a quiet neighborhood. Use it as your inspiration to write about different types of neighborhoods.

Comparing and Contrasting

"Professor Chang's class is more fun than Professor Blythe's."

Which job should you take for the summer? That is what you're wondering. You have two offers and are weighing both. You talk to friends and get so much advice that you're confused. Finally, your English teacher suggests that you write down the pros and cons of each job. You do so and come up with this:

> Both jobs—parking valet and grocery checker—have advantages as well as disadvantages. Both would give me good experience dealing with different kinds of people. Otherwise, though, each has pluses and minuses. The hours are very different. The valet job is night work, from 7 P.M. to 1 A.M. every night, including Fridays and Saturdays. The grocery checker position is strictly day work, from 9 A.M. to 5 P.M., weekdays and an occasional Saturday. If I take the valet job, I'll have no nightlife at all. The two also have very different working conditions. The valet job is an outdoor job. I will get a lot of exercise running to and from the cars. On the other hand, the grocery checker's job is indoors. I'll stand on my feet all day, with little physical activity. Finally, the jobs differ in pay. The valet job pays strictly on tips. The checker's job, on the other hand, pays a steady $5.25 per hour, with no tips. Which one do I want? I guess I should take the checker's job. I need to earn some sure money, and I don't look forward to a job that makes it hard for me to hang out with my friends.

You have just written a comparison and contrast.

What Am I Trying to Do?

A **comparison** shows similarities; a **contrast** highlights differences. Often, the two go hand in hand. In the job comparison, for example, the writer notes some similarities between the two jobs—the experience each offers as well as the chance to meet new people—before covering their differences.

We use comparison/contrast daily to make decisions and choices. You compare and contrast reviews and opinions about movies before deciding whether to see the one about a bank robbery or the one that tells a passionate love story. You buy a Honda because you think it is better made than other cars. You select one history class over another because, after comparing the instructors, you like one better. Every day we use comparison/contrast to make big and little decisions, from deciding whether to take a certain job or whether or not to buy bananas. Indeed, of all the strategies you will learn, comparison/contrast is the most useful in helping to make daily choices.

In a Nutshell

- To compare is to show similarities.

- To contrast is to show differences.

PRACTICING 1

In the spaces provided, check the assignments that call for development by comparison or contrast.

1. _____ The beauty of the Blue Ridge Mountains

2. _____ How early rock and roll and the rock and roll of the 1970s differ

3. _____ The defensive lines of two college football teams

4. _____ How to change a car tire

5. _____ Why patience pays off

6. _____ The benefits of living in the city rather than the suburbs

7. _____ How fast-food chains differ from diners

8. _____ The meaning of *poltergeist*

9. _____ How blue-collar workers differ from white-collar workers

10. _____ Women's basketball then and now

How Can I Do It?

You already have experience with comparisons and contrasts. They are a part of your daily conversations and life. You might not, however, have as much experience with writing them. Here are some tips to help you write sharp comparison/contrasts:

■ Compare things that have something in common.

■ State your purpose in the topic sentence.

- ■ Choose a pattern of comparing/contrasting and stick to it.

- ■ Use comparing or contrasting transitions.

Compare things that have something in common.

No doubt you've heard the saying that "you can't compare apples and oranges." Of course, it is nonsense. If you are buying fruit, you not only can, you should compare apples and oranges. Some things, however, are like apples and oranges in the old saying: They simply cannot be compared because they have nothing in common. So, a man may be compared to a woman because both are human beings, but a woman cannot be compared to a pin nor a man to a bicycle. Man, woman, pin, and bicycle simply do not have enough in common for a serious comparison. The same is true of a football and a chrysanthemum, or a candy bar and a lawnmower: They are simply too different to be compared seriously.

To write a serious comparison, begin with items that have enough in common to be compared. Common sense will help you make that decision. Here, for example, is an attempted comparison between a dog and stamp collecting that falls apart:

> My dog and my hobby of stamp collecting are similar in many ways and different in others. My dog spends a lot of his time roaming the woods behind our house. He likes to chase squirrels and bark at them. My hobby, stamp collecting, is also a lonesome hobby. I spend a lot of time doing it alone in my room. My dog is very energetic for he is a young dog and likes to play. Stamp collecting as a hobby, however, needs no energy. I just sit down and arrange stamps in my book. Then I look at them for their appearance. Finally, my dog usually comes when I call him. Of course, my stamp book is dead and cannot come when I call it. But I still like to take it outside, sit under a tree, and look at my stamps.

This student is trying to compare things that have nothing in common: a dog and stamp collecting.

With some refocusing, however, this comparison could work. The paragraph could be rewritten to compare two things the writer likes to do, play with his dog and collect stamps. In such a comparison the emphasis is no longer on dissimilar things—a living creature and a hobby—but on things that have something in common, namely, the writer's two favorite pastimes. Here is the rewritten paragraph:

> <u>My two pastimes, playing with my dog and collecting stamps, offer me similar as well as different pleasures.</u> When I play with my dog, I get to enjoy the outdoors. We roam the woods behind my house together, sometimes staying out for hours. I get good exercise chasing after my dog and racing him through the woods. Whereas stamp collecting gives me no exercise, it does allow me to roam in a different sense. I can look at stamps from different countries and imagine what it is like to live in them. Playing with my dog takes my mind off school and the pressures of making good

grades. Stamp collecting also takes my mind off my troubles and makes me forget whatever is worrying me. But when it comes to being affectionate, nothing can beat my dog. He gives me more love and affection than a hundred stamp albums.

Notice that with the emphasis now on pastimes, the comparison works. The writer is no longer trying to make comparisons between a dog and a stamp album, but is instead focusing on two things he likes to do: play with his dog and collect stamps.

PRACTICING 2

Check those pairs below that *can* be the subject of a comparison/contrast essay. Then state what those pairs have in common.

1. _____ A bird and chewing gum

_____

2. _____ Lions and tigers

_____

3. _____ Pot roast and fish casserole

_____

4. _____ Private elementary schools and public elementary schools

_____

5. _____ Your home and a bus station

_____

6. _____ A big chain supermarket and a corner convenience store

_____

7. _____ A used-car lot and a pretty garden

_____

8. _____ Two teachers

_____

9. _____ Swimming and sleeping

_____

10. _____ Rhinestone buttons and hiking boots

_____

State your purpose in the topic sentence.

If you are comparing/contrasting, you should plainly say so in the topic sentence. Stating your intent to compare and contrast in the topic sentence is a good focusing device for both you and your readers. For your readers, declaring your purpose in the topic sentence tells them what to expect. For you, stating your purpose at the very beginning will help keep you on track. Here is an example of a paragraph that hides its intent:

> I take both English classes and math classes at school. In math the method you use to solve a problem is as important as the answer. In English, if the answer is right, it is right; the method you use to arrive at an answer is unimportant. In math the correct answer is not as clear-cut, and often how you explain your answer determines whether it is right or wrong. In math we pay attention only to the problem we are working on, and the discussion is only about that. In English we often discuss social issues and other topics that we write about. Both classes are very interesting, but I prefer English.

This is a little vague because we have no idea what the writer is trying to do. Notice how much easier the paragraph is to read and follow if the purpose is given in the topic sentence:

> <u>English classes and math classes are similar in some ways but different in others.</u> Both are taught by the same methods—lecture, class discussion, and homework. But they differ in other ways. I take both English and math at school. In math the way you solve a problem is as important as the answer. In English, if the answer is right, it is right; the way you arrive at your answer is unimportant. In math the correct answer is not as clear-cut, and often how you explain your answer determines whether it is right or wrong. In math we pay attention only to the problem we are working on, and the discussion is only about that. In English we often discuss social issues and other topics that we write about. Both classes are very interesting, but I prefer English.

PRACTICING 3

Write a topic sentence that clearly announces a comparison/contrast paragraph for each of these topics.

Example: Running versus jogging

Running and jogging are similar in some ways, but different in others.

1. Your taste in movies versus the taste of someone else

_____

_____

2. A vegetable you love versus a vegetable you hate

_____

_____

3. Two people you know well who differ sharply

_____

_____

4. Getting carry-out versus eating in a restaurant

_____

_____

5. A class you love versus one you hate

_____

_____

PRACTICING 4

Choose one of the topic sentences from Practicing 3 above and write a comparison/contrast paragraph. After the topic sentence, discuss similarities and then differences.

Choose a pattern of comparing/contrasting and stick to it.

Comparison/contrasts may be written in one of two possible patterns. In **pattern A** you cover the items being compared/contrasted within a single paragraph. In **pattern B** you cover the same points in two separate paragraphs, one for item A, the second for item B. In either case your comparison/contrast should be done point by point.

Here is an example of what we mean by comparing point by point. Let us say that you are trying to decide on what kind of oven to buy: a microwave or a toaster oven. How would you go about comparing/contrasting them?

First, you'd probably decide what features in an oven—toaster or microwave—are important to you. Then perhaps you'd make a list to see how each kind of oven matches up on each feature. Here is one such list:

Features	**Microwave**	**Toaster oven**
expense	more expensive	cheaper
cooking time	faster, but doesn't brown	slower, but browns
cleanup	cleans easily since no burning	harder to clean

Now you have your three points.

It is only fair and logical to compare and contrast items on the same points. To mention the cooking time of the microwave but not the toaster oven would be both illogical and incomplete. In short, if you are comparing a giraffe and an elephant, you should not compare the height of the giraffe with the bellowing of an elephant. Comparison/contrasts must always be made on the same points.

Once you have the points of your comparison/contrast, you must choose which pattern you will use. The two possible patterns are diagrammed below:

Pattern A

Point 1: Expense

      microwave

      toaster oven

Point 2: Cooking time

      microwave   `SINGLE PARAGRAPH`

      toaster oven

Point 3: Clean up

      microwave

      toaster oven

Pattern B

Microwave

    Point 1: Expense   `FIRST PARAGRAPH`

    Point 2: Cooking time

    Point 3: Clean up

Toaster oven

    Point 1: Expense   `SECOND PARAGRAPH`

    Point 2: Cooking time

    Point 3: Clean up

In pattern A, within a single paragraph, you cover both the microwave and the toaster oven on all three points: expense, cooking time, and cleanup. In pattern B, on the other hand, using the same three points, you cover the microwave oven in one paragraph and the toaster oven in a separate paragraph. Here is pattern A written out:

<u>Microwave and toaster ovens are both useful to anyone trying to cook, but they differ in expense, cooking time, and cleanup.</u> A microwave oven is more expensive than a toaster oven. Sometimes it is as much as $50 to $100 more, although it is cheaper to operate. Unlike the toaster oven, the microwave saves huge amounts of time because of the speed at which it cooks. For instance, vegetables can be cooked to perfection in six minutes. A frozen dinner

can be ready to eat in ten minutes, and a cup of coffee can be reheated in 30 seconds. A toaster oven takes longer on these jobs. Finally, the microwave is easier to clean up. Because a microwave oven does not brown, it is impossible to burn food, which would then have to be scraped off the rack. The toaster oven, on the other hand, browns food and can sometimes burn it, leaving a sticky mess that's hard to clean. Since speed and ease are most important to me, I think I'll buy the microwave.

Here is pattern B:

> Microwave and toaster ovens are both useful to anyone trying to cook, but they differ in expense, cooking time, and cleanup. The microwave oven is more expensive than a toaster oven. Sometimes it is as much as $50 to $100 more, although it is cheaper to operate and saves money on electricity. The microwave is also faster than a toaster oven. For instance, vegetables can be cooked to perfection in six minutes. A cup of coffee can be reheated in 30 seconds. Finally, the microwave is easy to clean up. Because it doesn't brown, a microwave never burns food, and doesn't make a mess that's hard to clean.
>
> The toaster oven, on the other hand, is a great deal cheaper than the microwave, but it uses more electricity because it cooks more slowly than the microwave. In fact, it can cost almost 50 percent more per month to run. Also, unlike the microwave, the toaster oven browns food, which make it look more appetizing. But sometimes the food burns, leaving a sticky mess that's hard to clean. Since speed and ease are most important to me, I think I'll buy the microwave.

Which pattern to use is up to you, the writer. For a long intricate comparison, you might wish to use pattern B, separate paragraphs. In either case you must be sure to match up your compared/contrasted items on the same set of points.

PRACTICING 5

For each of the topics below, create two patterns of comparing/contrasting: pattern A, within a single paragraph, and pattern B, between two paragraphs.

1. Two restaurants

Pattern A

Point 1: _____

Point 2: _____

Point 3: _____

Pattern B

First paragraph

Point 1: _____

Point 2: _____

Point 3: _____

Pattern A	**Pattern B**
	Second paragraph
	Point 1: _____
	Point 2: _____
	Point 3: _____

2. Two places you have lived

Pattern A	**Pattern B**
	First paragraph
Point 1: _____	Point 1: _____
Point 2: _____	Point 2: _____
Point 3: _____	Point 3: _____
	Second paragraph
	Point 1: _____
	Point 2: _____
	Point 3: _____

3. Two loves you have had

Pattern A	**Pattern B**
	First paragraph
Point 1: _____	Point 1: _____
Point 2: _____	Point 2: _____
Point 3: _____	Point 3: _____
	Second paragraph
	Point 1: _____
	Point 2: _____
	Point 3: _____

4. Two pets

Pattern A	**Pattern B**
	First paragraph
Point 1: _____	Point 1: _____
Point 2: _____	Point 2: _____
Point 3: _____	Point 3: _____

Pattern A	Pattern B
	Second paragraph
	Point 1: _____
	Point 2: _____
	Point 3: _____

5. Two vacations you have taken

Pattern A	Pattern B
	First paragraph
Point 1: _____	Point 1: _____
Point 2: _____	Point 2: _____
Point 3: _____	Point 3: _____
	Second paragraph
	Point 1: _____
	Point 2: _____
	Point 3: _____

PRACTICING 6

Choose one of the topics from Practicing 5 above and write a comparison/contrast following Pattern A in a single paragraph.

PRACTICING 7

Choose another topic from Practicing 5 above and write a comparison/contrast following Pattern B, using two paragraphs.

Use comparing or contrasting transitions.

Transitions help your reader follow the point-by-point comparison/contrast you are drawing. Without transitions, the points you're comparing and contrasting may blur into one another. Here is an example:

Reggae and soca are musical forms that differ in rhythm, beat, and message. Reggae originated in Jamaica. Its best-known singer is still Bob Marley. Soca originated in Trinidad with its annual carnivals. The rhythm of reggae is steady, pulsating, and not particularly fast. Soca rhythms can be hypnotically fast, allowing for wild dancing in the streets at carnival time. Reggae has a regular, predictable beat that is best described as a background washboard scraping. Soca's beat can be fairly modulated as in the soca song "Dollar Wine," or erratic, as in that soca favorite "Hot, Hot, Hot." Reggae preaches a message of social justice and Rastafarianism. Soca has no message beyond its flirtatious calls to dance. Reggae is beloved by the ghetto youth and soca by the fun-loving middle class.

Notice how much easier the paragraph is to read with the transitions (underlined) added.

Reggae and soca, both of which come from the same part of the world, are musical forms that differ in rhythm, beat, and message. Reggae originated in Jamaica. Its best-known singer is still Bob Marley. Soca, on the other hand, originated in Trinidad with its annual carnivals. The rhythm of reggae is steady, pulsating, and not particularly fast. In contrast, soca rhythms can be hypnotically fast, allowing for wild dancing in the streets at carnival time. Reggae has a regular, predictable beat that is best described as a background washboard scraping. Not so with soca. The beat can be fairly modulated, as in the soca song "Dollar Wine," or crazily erratic, as in that soca favorite "Hot, Hot, Hot." But where the two musical forms differ most is in their message. Reggae preaches a message of social justice and Rastafarianism. Soca, on the other hand, has no message beyond its flirtatious calls to dance. Partly because of these differences, reggae is beloved by the ghetto youth and soca by the fun-loving middle class.

The transitions used in comparison/contrasts are common ones. Here is a list of those most frequently used:

although

and, also, additionally

as well as

both, neither

but

conversely

however

in contrast (to)

in the same way

just as . . . so

like

on the other hand

similarly

too

unlike

whereas

while

yet

Use these words generously in your own comparison/contrasts and you'll make your writing easier for a reader to follow.

In a Nutshell

To write good comparisons, be sure to do the following:

- Compare things that can be compared.
- State your purpose in the topic sentence.
- Choose a pattern of comparison and stick to it.
- Use transitions.

PRACTICING 8

Underline the transitional words that show contrast or comparison in the following paragraph.

American men are different from Italian men. For one, Italian men often cry to express their sadness. Their culture encourages this outlet in them. On the other hand, American men don't cry because they think crying is unmanly and for sissies. However, American men, for the most part, respect women's rights. Most American men wouldn't consider whistling at a woman passing in the street. Italian men don't hesitate to whistle at a passing woman, to show their appreciation for her good looks. Finally, American men tend to share more in household chores, even though many wives think they could do more. Italian men, on the other hand, are notoriously unwilling to share household chores, which they consider "women's work." Italian men probably suit Italian women best, who know what to expect from them. But some American women would find the Italian man too difficult to live with.

What Do I Need to Look Out For?

Incompleteness in a comparison or contrast is the most common error by far in paragraphs and essays. **Incompleteness** is covering one side of the comparison/contrast but failing to cover the other. Here is an example:

> My favorite aunt and uncle, Aunt Ida and Uncle Ralph, are alike in looks but vastly different in personalities. Aunt Ida is tall and slender. She wears a size 6 dress and weighs no more than 100 pounds. But her personality is very fiery. She is never afraid to try new things and is always experimenting in the kitchen. Aunt Ida took sailplane flying lessons in her sixties. She soloed on her sixty-seventh birthday and got her license a week later. She said she learned to fly because she used to be afraid of heights and wanted to conquer her fear. She's very brave, and I admire her a lot. Uncle Ralph is just as tall and thin but doesn't have her spunk.

The student who wrote this paragraph obviously spent too much time on *Aunt Ida* and too little on *Uncle Ralph*. We get a clear picture of what Aunt Ida is like, but no picture at all of Uncle Ralph. The comparison/contrast, in short, is incomplete, filling in one side but ignoring the other.

Here is how the student corrected this oversight:

> My favorite aunt and uncle, Aunt Ida and Uncle Ralph, are alike in looks but vastly different in personalities. Aunt Ida is tall and slender. She wears a size 6 dress and weighs no more than 100 pounds. Uncle Ralph is also tall and thin. He's very wiry and weighs only slightly more than Aunt Ida. Their personalities, however, are quite different. Aunt Ida is very fiery. She is never afraid to try new things. She is always experimenting in the kitchen, and when she was in her sixties, she took sailplane flying lessons. She soloed on her sixty-seventh birthday and got her license a week later. Uncle Ralph, on the other hand, is far from fiery. He is as calm as a slow-moving river. Nothing ever gets him upset. He's happy eating the same things for breakfast, lunch, and dinner, day after day. He thought Aunt Ida was foolish to start flying in her sixties, but he never said anything because he respects her wishes. The two of them, although very different, have been happily married now for 30 years.

In a Nutshell

Cover both items of a comparison/contrast more or less equally.

PRACTICING 9

Write a paragraph in which you compare and contrast one of the pairs listed below. Be sure to give equal emphasis to both sides.

1. Your father and your brother
2. Your mother and your sister
3. Your father and you (if you are a male)
4. Your mother and you (if you are a female)
5. Two of your best friends

UNIT TALK WRITE ASSIGNMENT

Listen to Eddie explaining the difference between a grunge and a slob. Then, in the space provided, turn his spoken words into a well-developed contrast paragraph. Use what you have learned in this unit. Begin with a topic sentence in which you announce what you intend to contrast. Make your points of contrast clear and use Standard English.

Spoken Paragraph

Don't call me a "slob"; I ain't no slob. I'm a grunge. You mean you don't know the difference between a grunge and a slob? You guys are hopeless. Look, a slob is a person who looks crude and sloppy. He couldn't care less about what he wears or what style it is. He's basically gross—know what I mean? O.K., a grunge is something different. A grunge just seems sloppy, but he is not. You have to work for the grunge look. A grunge may get his outfit at a thrift shop, a flea market, or at a Salvation Army store, but he puts hisself together with lots of care. He sort of copies Billy Corgan—you know, the guy that plays guitar for the Smashing Pumpkins. Like, here's a typical grunge outfit: A faded tight plaid shirt with the three top buttons left open, beige or gray plain pants, combat boots for sure, and a worn leather jacket. No jewelry—just maybe a tattoo on the chest. A partially shaved head if your parents let you, which, of course, mine wouldn't. Now, you see, a slob is a different animal completely. The typical slob wears huge, long shorts that hang below the knees, a torn, oversized dirty tee shirt, filthy tennis shoes, and a beat up baseball cap worn backward on dirty hair. Nothing fits, and everything has spots. The slob isn't trying to make a statement; he's just too lazy to look in style. It takes work to be a grunge. It doesn't take anything to be a slob. Now, I'm a grunge, not a slob, see?

Written Paragraph

_____

_____

_____

_____

_____

_____

_____

_____

_____

_____

_____

_____

_____

UNIT TALKING ASSIGNMENT

Get together with a classmate and discuss your opinions on one of the
following subjects. List the points on which you agree and disagree.

1. Your attitude toward money
2. The importance of regular exercise
3. Football versus soccer as spectator sports
4. When to go casual and when to dress up
5. Being strict or lenient with children

UNIT WRITING ASSIGNMENT

Using the outline you created for the Unit Talking Assignment above,
write a comparison/contrast of your views with those of your classmate. Be sure to treat both sides fairly and to use transitions that
stress the contrast.

PHOTO WRITING ASSIGNMENT

Note the sharp contrast shown in the following photo. Find appropriate points of contrast and develop a comparison/contrast paragraph.

UNIT 14
Arguing

"**People should make an attempt to get involved in local politics.**"

You're in college and doing fine. But you wish you had your own computer so you didn't have to go to the computer lab every time you had to write a paper. It's a great lab and the student tutors are really helpful, but sometimes the lab is completely booked when you're free, and you have to go really early in the morning or late at night if you want to meet your deadlines. You must get a computer. But how? You're broke. Even though you work every weekend delivering pizza, you simply can't afford one. You write your parents and ask for a loan, and your mom, ever the practical one, asks you to put your request in writing. She says she'll work on your dad if you make a strong case for needing a computer. You sit down and begin to write:

> A computer is the most useful, practical purchase I could make because it would help me become a better student in several ways. First, instead of having to share a crowded computer lab with hundreds of other students, I could write in the quiet of my own room where I can really concentrate. I'd write better papers and do it faster. Second, during peak hours at the lab, students can schedule only a maximum of two hours. There have been times when I'd have revised a paper further, but couldn't get the computer time. If I had my own computer, I would always have the time to write the best possible paper and therefore get a better grade. In fact, having my own computer would probably raise my overall gradepoint average. Not having to get to the lab early in the morning or late at night would leave me with more time to read and study. Finally, doing well in school, I'd probably be motivated to take extra classes and I'd graduate ahead of time. Then I'd be able to pay off the loan earlier. Truly, a computer is just the tool I need to become a better, more efficient student.

What you did was write an argument, trying to persuade your parents to lend you money to buy a computer.

What Am I Trying to Do?

An **argument** is an attempt to persuade someone—a listener or reader—to accept your opinion on a certain subject. Also referred to as *persuasion*, argumentation is part of daily life. We use it to press home our opinions on trivial as well as important topics.

In a way, all writing is argumentation, an attempt to get someone else to see things your way. If you are describing an onion, you are trying to get the reader to see the onion as you do. If you are narrating a horrifying event, you are trying to get your reader to feel your horror.

Argument or persuasion is all around you—from the friend who tries to talk you into letting him use your car, to the teacher who urges you to do better work. Indeed, hardly a day passes when we don't use argumentation. It may be a sports argument, say, that Rod Carew in his prime was a better hitter than any of today's players, or that Nolan Ryan was a better pitcher than Tom Seaver, or that Greg Maddux is the best righthander in baseball. It may be about funding a community arts program or about whether you or your sister does more daily chores. Arguments, serious or lighthearted, are part of everyday life.

In a Nutshell

Argumentation is an attempt to persuade someone to your point of view.

PRACTICING 1

Put an *A* before each of the following statements that should be developed as an argument.

1. _____ Student parking should be free; we shouldn't have to buy parking stickers.

2. _____ There's a right and a wrong way to do strength training.

3. _____ "Love" means different things to different people.

4. _____ We should cut back on military spending and put the money into education.

5. _____ There are advantages to living in the country, but I'll take the city any day.

6. _____ I can always count on my sister to cheer me up.

7. _____ Changing a tire is not as hard as it looks.

8. _____ Free medical care is a right, not a privilege.

9. _____ Television does more good than harm.

10. _____ My boss is demanding but fair.

How Can I Do It?

To write a good argument, you must do the following:

- Evaluate your position.

- Give your reasons.

- Cite evidence.

- Refute the opposition.

Evaluate your position.

Writing an argument means taking a position on some issue. Before you try arguing, make sure that you have a sound position and know the facts.

For example, consider this situation: Your student council is thinking of closing the only sandwich shop on campus and installing in its place sandwich-dispensing machines. The council's argument is that the shop is little-used and that the machines will save money. Your view is that the shop serves the evening students well, especially those on tight schedules who can't get to the main cafeteria, some distance away on the north campus. Before dashing off a letter to the student government opposing the machines, you should ask yourself these four questions:

1. *Have I defined the problem clearly?* In other words, what exactly is the student government proposing—to close the shop for good or just temporarily, as an experiment to see how well the machines are received? What kind of vending machines will be installed in place of the shop? What kind of food will they offer? How much will the machine food cost? What savings will the student body realize from closing the shop? In other words, you need to know what you're up against before you can begin to argue.

2. *Have I gathered enough information to form an opinion?* You oppose the closing of the shop because you and other evening students like eating there and hate vending-machine food. In this particular case, beyond learning the details of the proposed closing, you don't need a lot of additional information. Say, however, that someone asks your opinion on a massive tax cut proposed by a presidential candidate. How could you give an opinion without having information on the effect such a cut might have on the economy? You can't. You need to gather information before you make up your mind one way or the other.

3. *Does my opinion reflect an honest search for truth, or is it simply self interest?* Although we sometimes argue a position out of self interest, it alone is not a strong argument. Indeed, looking out only for yourself can hurt someone else. Better by far is an argument based on the public good. So you need to show that many students will also be inconvenienced by closing the sandwich shop, not just you.

4. *Have I tested my position in discussions with others who disagree with it, or do I have a closed mind?* Bouncing your ideas off someone who disagrees with you is a good test of the strength of your arguments. Ideally, if you see that the other side has a stronger and more logical case than you do, you should be willing to change your opinion.

Here is a paragraph that reflects a position not carefully evaluated:

> I am against closing the sandwich shop on the south side of campus and replacing it with vending machines. I leave work at 5:30, and it takes me almost an hour to get to campus. Having a sandwich at the shop with other students gives me a half-hour to unwind before my evening class. It would be a great personal inconvenience to me if the shop were closed because I don't have time to get to the main cafeteria, which is on the north side of the campus. Moreover, I don't like machine-vended food. I think it tastes stale. I think the shop should not be closed. If it is, I will have to go without dinner.

Notice that the argument is completely self-centered. Here is a better argument, based on an evaluated position:

> Closing the sandwich shop and replacing it with vending machines, as the student government proposes, will inconvenience many evening students. The projected savings assumes that students will patronize the new machines. Many, however, will not. I have spoken with at least 30 students who say they'd rather skip a meal than eat machine-vended food. Machine-vended food, no matter how quickly it is restocked, does not taste as good as freshly prepared food. Going to the cafeteria is not an option. It is on the north campus and too far away for students rushing to get to evening classes after work. If the shop is losing money, as the student government says, perhaps a slight increase in price could be considered as an alternative to closing the shop altogether. Most evening students on the south campus are prepared to pay a little more to keep the sandwich shop open.

This is a better argument because it is based on a well-defined problem and enough information. Moreover, it reflects a concern for the public good rather than only one person's narrow interests.

PRACTICING 2

Choose one of the topics below and, in the space below, apply to it the four evaluation questions.

1. Colleges should require a physical education course for graduation.
2. Everyone should be forced to retire at age 67.
3. Liquor advertisements on billboards should be illegal.

4. All adopted children should be told who their natural parents are.
5. College athletes should be paid to play.

1. Have I defined the problem clearly?

_____

_____

_____

2. Have I gathered enough information to form an opinion?

_____

_____

_____

3. Does my opinion reflect an honest search for truth, or is it simply a personal interest?

_____

_____

_____

4. Have I tested my position in discussions with others who disagree with it, or do I have a closed mind?

_____

_____

_____

Give your reasons.

All arguments turn on a *should*. You think something *should* be this way or that way for certain reasons. Then you support your arguments with those reasons. To be convincing, your reasons must be logical and reasonable. A *logical* reason is one that makes sense. A *reasonable* reason is one that is fair.

Here are some examples of illogical arguments—that is, arguments that make no sense—along with their corrections:

Illogical: We should pass laws to limit the budgets of political campaigns because campaign ads on television are on almost more than the regular programs during an election.

Logical: We should pass laws to limit campaign budgets so that every candidate will have an equal chance—rich or poor.

Illogical: Pooper-scooper laws should be revoked because concrete walkways need fertilizing.

Logical: Pooper-scooper laws should be revoked because they make it difficult for the elderly to walk their pets.

It is illogical to argue that political campaign budgets must be limited because of the frequency of televised campaign ads. The logical argument is that budgets must be limited to put everyone on equal footing. It is illogical to do away with pooper-scooper laws because concrete walkways need fertilizing (they don't, and neither does shoe leather). It is logical to argue that these laws might make it difficult for the elderly to walk their pets.

Here are some examples of unreasonable arguments—that is, arguments that are unfair—along with their corrections:

Unreasonable: Libraries should stay open all night because sometimes I can't sleep and would like to borrow a book.

Reasonable: Libraries should offer more flexible opening hours to accommodate busy working people.

Unreasonable: Weed killers should not be sold because weeds need to live, too.

Reasonable: Weed killers should not be sold because they seep into the soil and poison the groundwater.

It is unreasonable to expect libraries to stay open all night because one patron cannot sleep. It is entirely reasonable to expect libraries to have hours that are convenient to working people. It is unreasonable to argue that weed killers should not be sold because they deprive weeds of life (that's the point). It is reasonable to make this same argument if the weed killers are contaminating the groundwater.

Similarly, a reason may be logical but unreasonable. It is logical for you to argue that you won't do household chores because you're not your parents' slave (you're right, you aren't), but it is unreasonable (everyone in a household should share the chores; neither are your parents your slaves).

To back up an argument with reasons, you first state your position and then your reasons for supporting it. This is what you basically do:

> Topic sentence
> > Reason 1
> > Reason 2
> > Reason 3—if there is one

Here is this pattern in practice:

Our college library is good but its collection of books is small, so students find it hard to get the books they need for their classwork. Therefore, students should be allowed to check out books for only one week instead of the present two. This restriction would allow more students access to the small supply of books. It would also be fairer than the present system, which allows some students to monopolize the books while others can do nothing but wait. When the library has built up its collection, the two-week loan period could be reinstated.

The reasons given are both logical and reasonable. It is logical—that is to say, it makes sense—to shorten the checkout time until more books become available. The argument is also reasonable because it proposes sharing the books among all students rather than permitting a lucky few to monopolize the collection. Your own reasons, when you give them in your arguments, must also be logical and reasonable.

In a Nutshell

The reasons behind your arguments must be both logical and reasonable.

PRACTICING 3

Read the two arguments below. Which one gives more logical and reasonable reasons? Explain your choice.

A.

Dieting is utterly stupid. People spend hundreds of dollars a month on the latest diet fad. They do that because when it comes to dieting, people are copycats. So, there goes another sucker who will lose 20 pounds in one month and gain it all back within six months. I have several friends who have spent hundreds of dollars to go on fad diets, only to admit in the end that the diet did not work. My grandmother, who is from Austria, tells me that in her day nobody dieted; yet, people were not nearly as fat as we are in this country. She says that Americans should walk more; then they wouldn't be so neurotic about dieting. She may be right. Every newspaper advertises some weight clinic, some exercise gym, or some appetite-suppressant pill. I say, eat reasonably, exercise some, and leave the rest to nature.

B.

Following a fad diet plan does not lead to long-term weight loss. I recently read an article in *Reader's Digest* indicating that 85 percent of people who go on diets regain their weight within three to five years. That is why my doctor takes a reasonable approach to dieting. She says that if you need to lose weight, just give up 100 calories a day permanently, and within a year you will have lost 20 pounds. Or, if you want to lose a little faster, just eat an apple at noon instead of lunch. The point is to lose weight slowly and without dramatically altering your eating habits. Also, my doctor believes you must exercise to lose weight. But exercising does not have to involve jogging or working out at an expensive gym. Just park a distance away from where you are driving, walk up stairs whenever possible, and take short breaks to walk down the hall or across the building at work. In other words, my doctor believes that making small but important lifestyle changes leads to long-term weight loss, not going on some extreme diet. I think she's right.

PRACTICING 4

Give at least two logical and reasonable reasons in support of the following topics.

1. Playing a boom box should be banned on public transportation.

Reason 1: _____

Reason 2: _____

Reason 3: _____

2. Smokers should be allowed to smoke in restaurants.

Reason 1: _____

Reason 2: _____

Reason 3: _____

3. Uniforms should be worn in all public high schools.

Reason 1: _____

Reason 2: _____

Reason 3: _____

4. General elective courses should be optional, not mandatory.

Reason 1: _____

Reason 2: _____

Reason 3: _____

5. Students should take a year off between high school and college to do community service work.

Reason 1: _____

Reason 2: _____

Reason 3: _____

Cite evidence.

Aside from reasons, the next important support of your argument is evidence. Evidence consists of the following:

- Examples

- Facts

- Testimony

- Personal observation

Examples

An **example** is a part used to represent the whole. You say that Larry has a bad temper. Someone asks, "What do you mean?" You say, "Larry became completely irrational, yelling and cursing, when he learned the movie was sold out." This scene gives one example that supports your point about Larry's temper.

The following paragraph likewise uses an example in support of its topic sentence.

> <u>Students should be careful about blind dating because it can be risky.</u> For example, my best friend, Marla, went out on a blind date. Her date got drunk, even though he was under the drinking age. On the way home, he nearly wrecked the car. Fortunately, he was pulled over and taken into custody, and she was driven home in a police cruiser.

To use examples, all you have to do is introduce them with a suitable phrase such as *for example*, *for instance*, or *take the case of*, and then you spell out the example you have in mind. Naturally, any example you use should support your point.

Facts

A **fact** is a statement that is true or can be verified. For instance, the fact that George Washington was born on February 22, 1732, can be confirmed by checking the encyclopedia or any biography of the first president. Some facts are simply accepted by everyone because they have never been proven untrue. That sooner or later all humans die is one such fact.

Here is an example of an argument supported by facts:

> <u>Students who want to save money and live well should sell their cars and ride public transportation.</u> Gasoline in my city is now $1.50 per gallon. My insurance was $890 per half-year, and it cost another $800 per year to license my car. Just selling the car saved me over $2,500 per year in fixed costs. Meanwhile, it costs $1.50 to ride the train to school, with no charge for parking, either.

Facts add believability to a paragraph. Of course, you must always be sure that your facts are indeed facts and not opinions. Ask yourself, can a reader look up this statement and confirm its truth? If not, the statement is an opinion, not a fact.

Testimony

Testimony is expert opinion that backs up your topic sentence. The expert may be someone who is recognized in the field or who has had personal experience with your topic. Here is a paragraph that uses both types of testimony—personal experience and expert opinion:

> <u>Wearing a helmet while riding bicycles on campus should be mandatory.</u> Campus Police Officer Jane Johnson reports that she has investigated at least five serious accidents just this semester in which the rider suffered a severe head injury. In one case, Officer Johnson says, the rider was so seriously injured that he had to leave school. Last week I witnessed a bicycle accident on the road that runs before Old Main. The rider skidded on a slick patch of pavement and hit her head against a tree. I found out later she suffered a concussion that would have been prevented if she'd been wearing a helmet.

Personal observation

Personal observation usually consists of descriptive details and examples based on your experience. Some topics are strictly personal and must be supported mainly by your own observation. Here is such a paragraph that uses both:

> <u>My parents are so unhappy in each other's company that they should get a divorce.</u> My father and mother never talk. When he comes home from work, he heads straight for his room (they have separate bedrooms). When she comes home, she heads for the television set. They do almost nothing together. For example, they bowl on separate teams on different nights; she eats alone in the kitchen; he eats in his room. They do not even spend holidays together. At Christmas he goes to his brother's house, and she to her sister's. For years they used us children as an excuse for staying married, but we're all grown up now with our own families. There's no reason for them to prolong their misery.

The details this writer uses are not available in any library, but come solely from observation and memory.

In a Nutshell

- Cite evidence to support your arguments.

- Evidence includes examples, facts, testimony, and personal observations.

PRACTICING 5

Decide where you stand on each of the arguments stated below. Then present what you consider one good piece of evidence—an example, fact, testimony, or personal observation—to use in support of the argument.

Argument: We should have stricter laws against trapping wild animals such as bears, foxes, wolves, and mountain lions.

Evidence: *Trapping is an exceedingly cruel way to kill animals.*
Death is not instantaneous. The animal often starves to death.

Type of evidence: *Fact*

1. **Argument:**   Many professional sports have become too expensive for the average fan.

Evidence: _____

_____

_____

Type of evidence: _____

2. **Argument:**   Television programs used to be better than they are today.

Evidence: _____

_____

_____

Type of evidence: _____

3. **Argument:**   Teachers should state their attendance and grade policies in their class syllabus at the beginning of each term.

Evidence: _____

_____

_____

Type of evidence: _____

4. **Argument:**   Textbooks are too expensive.

Evidence: _____

_____

_____

Type of evidence: _____

5. Argument: Teachers should take student evaluations
seriously.

Evidence: _____

_____

_____

Type of evidence: _____

PRACTICING 6

Choose one of the topics from Practicing 5 above and, after adding
more evidence, write a well-supported argument on it.

PRACTICING 7

Choose one of the arguments listed below and write an argument
in support of it, using reasons and evidence as your backing.

1. Parents should find alternative ways of punishing children
   rather than spanking them.
2. Because of the many recent crashes, airlines should adopt
   strict measures to assure the safety of passengers.
3. Despite criticism by many grown-ups, Halloween must be
   preserved as a part of childhood.
4. Whenever possible, disabled children should be placed in
   regular classrooms.
5. High school proms have become a shameful waste of money
   for the students and their parents.

Refute the opposition.

A good argument does not ignore its opposition. Instead, it tries to
refute it—to show that the opposition's case is weak. The best way to
do this is simply to state the opposing side and then immediately
respond. For example, in an argument for gun control, you might
acknowledge that some people think gun ownership is a constitutional
right. Then you would immediately go on to point out that gun control
only *regulates* gun ownership, but does not *abolish* it.

Or, if you are arguing that watching violent movies leads to violent
behavior, you might mention the contrary view, namely, that watching
violent movies may actually get rid of violence by harmlessly venting
it. Then you would refute this view.

It is a good idea to refute the opposition because it shows that you
are aware of opposing viewpoints and have thought through both sides.
Your reader, who may be thinking, "Yes, but what about this or that?"
finds, with a jolt, that not only have you thought about *this* and *that*,
but that you've answered them.

Here is an example of how to refute the opposition to an argument
in favor of coed dorms:

Now there are those who say that coed dorms will promote sexual activity between students. But the women's and men's dorms are presently located right next to each other and have no restrictions on visiting. Students already have ample opportunity to have sexual relations, and many do. What they do not presently have is the opportunity to just live with each other in the same building (not the same room) and interact like dormmates and friends, rather than like lovers. There are also those who object to unmarried men and women sharing a building on religious grounds. So don't live in the coed dorms if you feel that way. Live in one of the unisex buildings. But don't stop those who don't share your particular morals from living as they please.

This student raises the question of sex in coed dorms as well as religious opposition, and answers both objections.

In a Nutshell

Always mention the opposing view and refute it.

PRACTICING 8

For each argument listed below, state what you think would be one opposing point of view.

1. Obscene literature should be banished from public libraries.

Opposing point of view: _____

_____

2. U.S. citizens should simply pay a flat 10 percent tax.

Opposing point of view: _____

_____

3. Everyone should be tested for the AIDS virus.

Opposing point of view: _____

_____

4. Employers should pay for workers' child daycare.

Opposing point of view: _____

_____

5. The physical education requirement for graduation from college should be eliminated.

Opposing point of view: _____

_____

What Do I Need to Look Out For?

Arguments are based on logic and reasonableness. When an argument fails, it is usually because the writer has stated the case illogically. Other pitfalls that you should look out for in writing an argument follow.

- State your position clearly.

- Don't argue the unarguable.

- Watch out for some common fallacies.

State your position clearly.

Don't be timid in expressing your point of view. We're not suggesting that you be obnoxious in making your arguments, only that you be committed. Consider the following examples:

Committed topic sentence:	Coed dorms should be established on campus for those students who wish to live in them.
Uncommitted topic sentence:	Coed dorms are being tried on many campuses.
Uncommitted topic sentence:	Coed dorms seem okay.
Uncommitted topic sentence:	Coed dorms might or might not work, depending on your point of view.

These uncommitted topic sentences do not take a stand. The first mainly gives information, the second waffles, the third is wishy-washy. Oddly enough, an uncommitted topic sentence makes your job as a writer horribly difficult. It is easier to write about anything when you take a definite stand than when you try to tiptoe around the subject, just as it is easier to take a trip when you know where you want to go.

PRACTICING 9

Mark *C* if the sentence is committed and *U* if it is uncommitted. Then, in the spaces below, rewrite the uncommitted topic sentences.

1. _____ Political candidates should be limited in the amount of money they can spend on a campaign.

2. _____ It's probably not a good idea to drive without insurance.

3. _____ Playing a team sport teaches valuable lifelong lessons.

4. _____ Giving a tax break for daycare seems like a good idea.

5. _____ Maybe something should be done about the potholes on State Street.

6. _____ If you want to succeed, you must do two things: Get a good education and work hard.

7. _____ We need garbage pickup twice a week, not just once.

8. _____ Assisted suicide may or may not be a good idea, depending on your beliefs.

9. _____ It should be just as hard to get married as to get a divorce.

10. _____ Statistics show that cars with airbags are safer.

Rewritten topic sentences:

_____

_____

_____

_____

_____

_____

Don't argue the unarguable.

An issue is arguable if it is expressed in such a way that it can be settled by reasons and evidence. You should always word an issue in a way that makes it arguable. Here are some examples:

Unarguable: Bungee jumping is a truly loathsome sport.
Arguable: Bungee jumping is a dangerous sport.

Unarguable: Tattooing is ugly.
Arguable: Tattooing may be "cool" when you're young, but it has a social cost later.

Unarguable: Smoking should be banned because it is a sin.
Arguable: Smoking should be banned because it is unhealthy.

You cannot prove that a sport is *loathsome*, but you can use statistics to prove that it is *dangerous*. *Ugly* is a personal opinion that cannot be documented by evidence, but evidence can be cited to show the social consequences of a tattoo. No one can prove with evidence or reasons that an act is a *sin*, but the health hazards of smoking have been amply proven.

To sum up, be sure the point you want to argue is arguable, that is, provable by evidence and reasons.

PRACTICING 10

Check the topic sentence in each pair that is arguable, and state why the other is unarguable.

Sample

   a. _____ The Volvo sedan is the best car on the market.

   b. __X__ The Volvo is the safest car on the market.

   "Best" cannot be proved by evidence and reasons, but "safest" can.

1. _____ **a.** Marriage is a rotten institution.

    _____ **b.** Many marriages end in divorce.

    _____

    _____

2. _____ **a.** Since the present movie-rating system has not accomplished what it set out to do, it should be abolished.

    _____ **b.** The present movie-rating system could be vastly improved if the movie industry would listen to the public's concerns about violence, sexual diseases, and family problems.

    _____

    _____

3. _____ **a.** Birds make by far the best pets in the world.

    _____ **b.** Birds can be excellent companions for elderly people who are lonely and forced to be indoors.

    _____

    _____

4. _____ **a.** Having school year-round would help ease the space crunch so that more classes could be offered.

   _____ **b.** Having school year-round would make our educational system the best in the world.

   _____

   _____

5. _____ **a.** Modern art is pure garbage, with its wild colors splattered across canvasses.

   _____ **b.** Before you can criticize modern art, you should learn something about it.

   _____

   _____

PRACTICING 11

Rewrite the following topic sentences to make them arguable.

1. Baseball is the greatest sport in the world.

   _____

2. *Titanic* is the best movie of all time.

   _____

3. *Mamma Mia's* is the best restaurant in town.

   _____

4. Investing in the stock market is a pastime for idiots.

   _____

5. Women are superior to men in every possible way.

   _____

Watch out for some common fallacies.

A **fallacy** is a misleading or unsound argument. Here are some common fallacies:

■ Climbing on the bandwagon

■ Attacking the opponent instead of the issue

- Over generalizing

- Citing nonexperts as experts

Have you ever heard (or perhaps said), "But, Mom, everyone is going to Florida for spring vacation!," or "But, Dad, everyone is getting a motorcycle!" **Climbing on the bandwagon** is arguing that an idea is right just because everyone is doing it. Here is an example of the bandwagon fallacy:

> The laws against drinking before the age of 21 should be repealed. The fact is that alcohol is widely available to teenagers. In fact, every 18-year-old I know drinks, and regularly.

Attacking the opponent instead of the issue is a common tactic that many of us occasionally use. It varies in degrees of ugliness and is so common in political campaigns as to be a joke. Here is a sample of it:

> To vote for Smith is to throw away your vote on a draft-dodging, pot-smoking radical-liberal from the 1960s.

No mention is made anywhere of what Smith stands for or what policies Smith would try to enact. Only Smith the person (of 30 years ago, no less) is attacked.

The third fallacy, **over generalizing**, draws a hasty conclusion from too few instances. For example, if you conclude from one bad experience with a used-car dealer that *all used-car dealers are crooks*, you're over generalizing. Here is an over generalization made in a paragraph arguing that students are better off living in dorms than renting a room in the neighborhood:

> Another problem is that the rental rooms available in this neighborhood are all dirty, shabby, and roach-infested. I know because I've lived in one.

To conclude that since one rented room was bad that all are likewise bad is to over generalize.

Finally, there's the fallacy of **citing nonexperts as experts**. Television commercials and other advertisements are guilty of this fallacy when they get an actor who plays a doctor on TV to endorse a particular brand of aspirin. An actor is an actor, not a medical expert. Similarly, consider this sentence below:

> Jimmy is right about our math teacher being no good; Jimmy's the best athlete on campus.

Being a good athlete doesn't make Jimmy an expert on math teachers. Indeed, Jimmy may be the best athlete but the worst judge of math teachers. Skill in one area does not necessarily make anyone an expert in another. Be sure that the experts you quote are really experts in the subject on which you are quoting them.

In a Nutshell

When you write an argument, be sure to do the following:

• State your position clearly.

• Argue only the arguable.

• Avoid common fallacies.

PRACTICING 12

Identify the fallacy in each of the following arguments.

1. Everyone knows that playing football builds character.

Fallacy: _____

_____

_____

2. Switching from gas to electric cars is the only way to save the environment.

Fallacy: _____

_____

_____

3. Because religious cults always drive their members to suicide, our government should make them illegal.

Fallacy: _____

_____

_____

4. If John Smith, who plays a doctor on "ER," endorses Bayer aspirin, that's good enough for me.

Fallacy: _____

_____

_____

5. Bob Jones would make a bad student body president because he barely has a *C* average.

Fallacy: _____

_____

_____

UNIT TALK WRITE ASSIGNMENT

An argument can take many turns and styles. Some arguments are complex and legalistic, such as the argument against prayer in schools; some arguments are simple and emotional, such as the one below. Students in an English class paired up to talk out their arguments on the subject "Something You'd Like to See Changed." After carefully studying this student's argument, rewrite it into an acceptable Standard English paragraph. Pay attention to the tips offered in this chapter. Feel free to add information to develop the paragraph. Use the blank space provided.

Spoken Paragraph

Call them "rubbernecks," "gawkers," "looky-loos," or whatever you want, but they drive me crazy because they're a menace on the freeway. They slow you down. So, here I am late to work, and all of a sudden the lanes going south slow down and almost come to a dead halt. The snake of cars is not moving. "What's going on?" I mutter to myself. I settle for this snail's pace. I play some nice rap music on the radio. I discover what the delay is all about. Someone's changing a tire in the emergency lane. I don't understand this gawker's effect. I know that one person slowing down can cause hundreds of drivers to slow down even more. One expert says that in our county alone drivers lose a total 1.6 million hours a year to gawking. That's over 6,000 hours every working day. I wish somehow we could all keep driving when we see accidents that are being tended to. I'm sure psychologists would have something to say about why we gawk at disasters. It's probably because somewhere in our deepest nature we are the most curious animals that have ever lived. But on the freeway, we should not gawk at accidents, strange sights, or any other distractions. It's unsafe and it wastes time. I say, "Stop the gawking!"

Written Paragraph

_____

_____

_____

_____

_____

_____

_____

_____

_____

_____

_____

_____

_____

_____

_____

_____

_____

_____

_____

UNIT TALKING ASSIGNMENT

Break into groups of six. Then choose one of the topics that follow and decide which two students will be for, which two will be against, and which two will be judges. Take ten minutes for the pro and con teams to discuss their positions and come up with reasons and evidence. Present the arguments to the judges, who will critique them according to what you have learned in this chapter.

1. Should we continue ROTC programs on campus?
2. Should teaching assistants be given so much authority in running classes?
3. Should college classes be graded pass/fail rather than with a letter grade?
4. Should we have a volunteer military?
5. Should the college placement office be responsible for getting graduates jobs?

UNIT WRITING ASSIGNMENT

Choose one of the topics from the above Unit Talking Assignment and argue your stand on it. Be sure to make your reasons logical and fair, to use strong evidence, to refute the opposition, and to avoid fallacies.

UNIT PHOTO ASSIGNMENT

The following photo shows a beautiful forest during the fall. Write an essay in which you argue against cutting down trees without replacing them in our forests. Begin by evaluating your position, using the questions on page 211. Be sure your topic sentence is clearly committed. Finally, give logical and fair reasons, cite solid evidence, refute the opposition, and avoid fallacies.

PART IV

Writing Good Essays

This part of *Writing Talk* teaches you how to write an essay. We discuss the essay as a written form and why students are asked to write it. We focus on particular elements of the essay, specifically the thesis statement and the part it plays in the overall essay. We show you how to write and organize the three major parts of the essay—the introduction, body, and conclusion—and give practical advice on writing each part. Finally, each unit ends with an actual student essay in major and minor stages of revision.

What Is an Essay?

> "Writing essays is good preparation for the kind of business writing you will have to do later in life."

An **essay** is a related group of paragraphs written to entertain, inform, or persuade. Recall from Unit 2 that all writing more or less serves one of these broad purposes. So far you have been writing paragraphs. The essay is merely a collection of paragraphs about the same subject, with a more definite beginning, middle, and end.

Writing essays will teach you some important lessons. You will learn how to organize your thoughts on a subject, put them down clearly on paper, and back them up with facts, examples, testimony, reasons, and personal observations. Writing essays will also give you practice in expressing yourself in Standard English—the universal language of business. Mastering Standard English will help you do well in college and get a good job.

Finally, the classroom essay is usually between 300 and 500 words long, about the size of a memo—the workhorse of business writing. If you go into virtually any kind of business, sooner or later you will find yourself writing memos. Writing essays, in sum, is good preparation for the kind of business writing you will have to do later in life.

An **essay consists of three parts**: the introduction, the body, and the conclusion. We will deal with each part separately.

The Introduction

The **introduction** of an essay—the opening paragraph—**has two main purposes**: to grab the reader's attention and to introduce the thesis statement, or main point, of the essay.

blueprint

To grab the reader's attention, you need a catchy opening, something that will make a reader perk up and want to read on. Here are some examples of opening sentences. Which ones make you want to read on?

It's midnight, and you're relaxing on the front porch of your home, when suddenly a thunderous explosion rattles your house.

The automobile, owned by most Americans, is a self-propelled vehicle used for travel on land.

The word <u>cannibal</u> comes from the <u>Carib</u> West Indians, a ferocious and warlike people, who skinned their enemies and ate them.

We should all try to be balanced in our political, religious, and social views.

The first and third sentences grab your attention. They make you want to read on to find out more about the explosion and the Caribs' gruesome diet.

Another function of the introduction is to present the **thesis statement**—a single sentence that sums up what the essay is about. Usually, the thesis statement is the last sentence of the first paragraph. Here are some examples of thesis statements:

The entertainment industry should start giving an Oscar to the best benefit show.

The qualities I like best in a teacher are fairness, knowledge, wit, and compassion.

Religious symbols, such as crosses and menorahs, should be kept out of our public parks.

People usually go into debt for three reasons: unemployment, lack of budgeting, and running credit cards to the limit.

If the topic sentence is a shrimp (statement of small purpose), the thesis statement is a jumbo shrimp (statement of a bigger purpose). The thesis statement, in fact, is like a big topic sentence. It gives the point of the entire essay, whereas the topic sentence gives the point of a paragraph. Basically, that is the only difference between them.

In a Nutshell

The introduction to an essay should grab the attention of the reader and introduce the thesis statement.

PRACTICING 1

Underline the thesis sentence in the following opening paragraphs. Then, in the spaces provided, evaluate how well the opening grabs the reader's attention. If you think the opening is dull, write a more catchy one.

1. Atlanta during the 1996 Olympics was very hot. Several days in a row during the first week of competition the temperature topped 90F° with humidity of over 80%. Fortunately, the first week was taken up with mainly swimming.

There's no question, as the games once again proved, that sultry weather affects athletic competitions.

_____

_____

_____

2. There was a sudden lurch, a roar, and then the small Japanese car became airborne. I woke up in the back seat to find myself flying in a Toyota. I glanced at Nicky, who was strapped into the seat beside me, and saw terror in her eyes. Someone screamed just before we hit the bottom of the ravine and began to roll. The most terrifying night of my life was the night I almost died in an accident.

_____

_____

_____

3. Why is one place considered ugly and another pretty? Who decides what is pretty and what is not? Chaney Trail in the Angeles Crest Mountains is an ugly recreation area because it has been torn to pieces by off-road bikers.

_____

_____

_____

4. The water was warm and inviting, and some 20 feet below the float was the faint shadow of a shimmering reef. Overhead, the sky stretched in a clear vault of spotless blue. A seagull circled and glided onto the top of a small wave, without making a ripple. I was at my favorite holiday place, Silver Sands in Jamaica.

_____

_____

_____

5. "Four of the things I'd be better without: Love, curiosity, freckles, and doubt." So wrote Dorothy Parker, the American writer. She was right about three—curiosity, freckles, and doubt—but wrong about love. Love is indispensable in life.

_____

_____

_____

The Body

The **body** of an essay consists of all the subideas that prove your thesis statement. Each subidea is expressed in a separate paragraph with its own topic sentence.

Here are some examples of thesis statements and the topic sentences of the three paragraphs that make up the body of the essay. Notice that all the topic sentences that follow are already nested in the thesis statements.

Thesis statement:	Before you leave on vacation, take these easy steps to prevent a home burglary.
First topic sentence:	Ask a neighbor to pick up your morning newspaper from the front of your house.
Second topic sentence:	Leave on some lights in the house.
Third topic sentence:	Let friends and neighbors know that you will be gone.
Thesis statement:	It took a while, but after my father's death, I discovered how to deal with grief: accept it, hold on to hope, and keep busy.
First topic sentence:	I simply accepted what had happened.
Second topic sentence:	I held on to the hope that life still offered some goodness.
Third topic sentence:	I kept busy with schoolwork and some social life.
Thesis statement:	A brisk 30-minute walk every day will increase your cardiovascular fitness, tone up your muscles, and help you to relax.
First topic sentence:	A daily, brisk 30-minute walk will help your cardiovascular fitness.
Second topic sentence:	A daily, brisk 30-minute walk will also tone up your muscles.

Third topic Finally, a daily, brisk 30-minute walk will help
sentence: you to relax.

In a Nutshell

The body of the essay consists of paragraphs that prove your thesis.

PRACTICING 2

Write three topic sentences for each of the following thesis statements.

1. Whenever I become discouraged about achieving my goals,
   I think of three people who have overcome serious physical
   handicaps.

First topic sentence: _____

_____

_____

Second topic sentence: _____

_____

_____

Third topic sentence: _____

_____

_____

2. Horror movies are gory, nerve-racking, and fun.

First topic sentence: _____

_____

_____

Second topic sentence: _____

_____

_____

Third topic sentence: _____

_____

_____

3. Being very short (or very tall) is a special challenge as you grow up.

First topic sentence: _____

_____

_____

Second topic sentence: _____

_____

_____

Third topic sentence: _____

_____

_____

4. There are three steps to making up your bed properly.

First topic sentence: _____

_____

_____

Second topic sentence: _____

_____

_____

Third topic sentence: _____

_____

_____

5. People who are fanatic patriots are dangerous.

First topic sentence: _____

_____

_____

Second topic sentence: _____

_____

_____

Third topic sentence: _____

_____

_____

The Conclusion

The **conclusion** of your essay summarizes your opinions and leaves the reader with a final thought. A good conclusion does not leave the reader dangling. Rather, it ends the essay gracefully and with a sense of finality. Below are conclusions for the burglary essay and for the essay on overcoming grief:

> Taking these three steps may not guarantee that your house will not be burglarized, but at least you will know that you've done your best to prevent a burglar from stealing your treasures.

> Of course, I still get sad sometimes when I think of my dad. But I now cherish the memories of him, as he would want me to do. I also know that Dad would want me to live my life to the fullest, just as he did.

These conclusions are good because they do not merely parrot back the thesis sentence. Instead, they sum up what the writer has said in the body of the essay and add, as a finishing touch, a final thought.

PRACTICING 3

Which of the pair of conclusions that follow do you think is better? Say why in the lines provided.

1. From an essay about a crotchety uncle:
   a. So that is why I say my Uncle Charlie is crotchety.
   b. From cigar smoking to reciting poetry when he's had too much to drink, Uncle Charlie is my most crotchety and colorful relative. Maybe that's why I love him so much.

   It gives more detail and doesn't leave the reader hanging

2. From an essay about maintaining a rose garden:
   a. Gertrude Stein was obviously not a gardener. Only a nongardener would say that "a rose is a rose is a rose." Those of us who work with roses know better. We know that every rose species is uniquely lovely and special. If you start your own rose garden, you will learn that, too.
   b. In conclusion, that is why I say that a rose is not a rose is not a rose, for the reasons given above. Those reasons also show that Gertrude Stein didn't know anything about roses.

   Gives more detail

3. From an essay on why Monopoly is such a popular board game:
   a. Bankruptcy, property repossession, a sudden turn-around because of dumb luck: These are all part of the thrill that explains Monopoly's success. Try it. In no time at all, like me, you'll find yourself hooked.
   b. Monopoly, in sum, is popular because it is like life. As I said in paragraph one, it is an unpredictable game. As I also pointed out in my second paragraph, it is an old game that many people remember playing as children. And as I said in paragraph three, it is a game where you can become very rich or broke. That is why people like Monopoly.

   _____

   _____

4. From an essay on the joys and risks of riding a motorcycle:
   a. So you can see, riding a motorcycle brings a sense of freedom, but it also brings many risks.
   b. It's all included in motorcycle riding—the delight of feeling your hair blown by a breeze at 60 miles per hour to the sudden possibility of a broken leg because of an uncaring driver. The risks are there, but they add to the joy.

   _____

   _____

5. From an essay on handgun ownership:
   a. So these are the reasons I oppose handguns. The chances of shooting someone you love are too high. The chances of being shot by your own gun are also too high. Plus, as I said in paragraph two, handguns are only for shooting people, and that's murder. So why would I want to own a handgun?
   b. My opposition to handguns is based on very practical reasons. Instead of protecting homeowners, the handgun is more likely to imperil them. Statistics clearly show that handguns in the home are mainly used against other family members in tragic accidents or by home-owners in suicides or suicide attempts. The toll is even higher when there are children in the household. Hand-guns do not make a home safer. In fact, they have the very opposite effect. Given that grim fact, why would anyone want one in the home?

   _____

   _____

The Whole Essay

The essay has a predictable form that consists of three principal parts. Here it is in visual form:

Title of Essay

Introduction   _____

                        _____

                        _____

Thesis statement   _____

       Topic sentence: _____

                        _____

Body   _____

                        _____

                        _____

       Topic sentence: _____

                        _____

Body   _____

                        _____

                        _____

       Topic sentence: _____

                        _____

Body   _____

                        _____

                        _____

Conclusion   _____

                        _____

                        _____

                        _____

The following essay is by Laura Unterman, a student. It follows the five-paragraph format illustrated above.

In the Land of the Walls, Deserts, and Shwarma

Thesis statement

It is a land of breathtaking beauty, a three-thousand-year-old history grafted onto a rich and lively culture, and this summer I found myself there, in Israel. By car, boat, and on foot, I crisscrossed this ancient land during the sweltering, Middle Eastern summer. When I left, three memories in particular stayed with me, and probably will forever: the Western Wall, the Negev Desert, and the food.

First topic sentence: the Wall

<u>The Western Wall, the only structure remaining from Jerusalem's great temple, evokes powerful emotions.</u> Jews from all over the world come to it to pray. I couldn't believe the emotional outpourings I witnessed. One woman cried as she gently kissed the Wall. A man was so deep in prayer that he was oblivious to being pushed and jostled by others trying to touch the Wall's rough stone surface. People gathered in groups and prayed out loud. Others were lost in silent meditation. As I observed, I came to realize how important the Western Wall is to not just the Israelis, but to Jews all over the world.

Second topic sentence: the Negev Desert

<u>The Negev Desert of Israel is a place of piercing beauty.</u> I spent two weeks there, hiking, camping, and rock climbing. When I first saw the Negev, I was startled. I had expected an endless expanse of sand. Instead, I saw rock formations in hues of brown, red, yellow, and orange, and mountains so perfectly formed they seemed to be the painstaking product of God's own hand. The sky was a crisp blue, and the air was clean and sharp. The plants had a strange and delicate beauty. Even the animals native to the Negev seemed different—almost otherworldly. I will never forget the beauty of the Negev.

Third topic sentence: the Food

<u>My third memory of Israel is as powerful and exotic as my experience with the land and its monuments: It is of delicious food.</u> My budget was tight, and I had to scrimp on everything, but still I delighted in falafel and shwarma—two of the most popular fast-food dishes in Israel. Falafel is a vegetarian dish served in pita bread. Shwarma is pita bread stuffed with lamb or chicken. Both are freshly prepared, hot and delicious, and add a spicy zest to the day's adventures.

Conclusion

The Western Wall, the Negev Desert, and the Middle Eastern food—these are the memories I still have of my summer in Israel. The Wall moved me; the desert awed me; the food left me licking my chops. My total self—mind, soul, and body—were all separately enriched and nourished by this trip.

Laura's essay shows all the characteristics of a good five-paragraph essay:

1. The **introduction** catches our attention with its crisp summary of the experience. It ends with the **thesis statement** *When I had left, three memories in particular stayed with me, and probably* *will forever: the Western Wall, the Negev Desert, and the food.* Notice that the subideas that will become the topic sentences of the three paragraphs are nested in this thesis statement.

2. The **body** of the essay consists of three paragraphs that prove the thesis statement:

Topic sentence 1. The Western Wall, the only structure remaining from Jerusalem's great temple, evokes powerful emotions.

Topic sentence 2. The Negev Desert of Israel is a place of piercing beauty.

Topic sentence 3. My third memory of Israel is as powerful and exotic as my experience with the land and its monuments: It is of the delicious food.

3. The **conclusion** of the essay gives a sense of finality by returning to the three memories and summarizing the effect each had on the writer. It concludes that each experience enriched and nourished the writer in a different way.

PRACTICING 4

Read the student essay below and answer the questions that follow.

Greatness Misunderstood

"Aww, he's just a nut with a crackpot idea." This is how most people respond to someone who suggests something new. People resist change, even change for the better. But history shows that greatness has often been misunderstood and that breakthrough ideas are seldom welcome when they first appear.

One perfect example of misunderstood greatness is Wilbur Wright. When he tried to sell his flying machine to the U.S. government, the officials in charge were highly skeptical. They didn't know anything about the machine since Wright had developed it almost entirely in secret. The government demanded proof—drawings, formulas, and statistics—showing that flying was possible. It demanded budgets detailing the costs of building a flying machine. These bureaucratic demands almost killed Wright's project, but in the end his diligence prevailed and he proved that people could fly.

Brigadier General William (Billy) Mitchell, an American army officer and pilot during World War I, is another example of misunderstood greatness. It was his persistence that forged the airplane into a weapon. Mitchell argued strongly for an independent air force. When his superiors wouldn't listen, he directed the sensational sinking of several war ships in a prearranged bombing—to prove the power of strategic bombing. This stunt led to his court martial in 1925, his suspension for five years, and his resignation from the army in 1926. As a civilian, he continued to argue for a separate air force. Finally, his superiors realized the wisdom of his ideas and, during World War II, the U.S. Air Force was created. Imagine what the Nazis would have done to the world had Mitchell not won his argument, and you can easily grasp the importance of his persistence.

My last example of misunderstood greatness is Frank Lloyd Wright, the father of modern architecture. His idea of beauty was simple geometric forms and vast openness inside buildings. To escape the deadening influence of European architecture, he broke every conventional rule. He was the first to hang cantilevered houses over cliffs. He used cement, glass, and steel to create buildings of astounding beauty. He designed and built the Mile-High Illinois Building, a tripod one-mile high with 528 stories and a taproot foundation that slopes down into solid bedrock. Today his basic designs are evident in buildings everywhere. Yet his work was initially scorned and laughed at.

The lesson to be learned from Wilbur Wright, General Billy Mitchell, and Frank Lloyd Wright is that greatness does not always win the popularity contest. Yale President Kingman Brewster once said, "There is a correlation between the creative and the screwball. So we must suffer the screwball gladly."

1. How does the writer get our attention in the introduction?

_____

_____

_____

_____

2. What is the thesis statement of the essay?

_____

_____

_____

_____

3. What are the topic sentences in the body paragraphs?

First topic sentence: _____

_____

_____

Second topic sentence: _____

_____

_____

Third topic sentence: _____

_____

_____

4. Is the conclusion abrupt, or does it seem to give a sense of finality to the essay? Explain your answer.

_____

_____

_____

_____

In a Nutshell

An essay consists of three parts:

- An introduction with its thesis statement.

- A body of paragraphs, each with a topic sentence that proves the thesis statement.

- A conclusion that gives the essay a sense of finality.

The Title

Put yourself in your instructor's shoes. You have 25 essays to read and grade by tomorrow. Many of them are written, if not on the same, then on similar topics. You come across two: One is titled, *How I Spent My Vacation Last Summer*, the other, *Cooking Beans and Burritos in the Bronx*. Which do you think you'd rather read?

Chances are you'd go for the beans and burritos because it has a splash of color in the title, especially in contrast to the drab *How I Spent My Vacation Last Summer*. What was the beans and burritos essay all about? How one student spent her summer vacation—working for a Mexican restaurant.

The point is that you should use some imagination and make your title sparkly and bright. A title that's plainly descriptive and drab won't attract a reader. Here are some examples. Which of these titles would make you more inclined to read the essay?

About a tightfisted relative:
Aunt Viola
At Heart, A Squirrel

About the benefits of exercise:
Exercise Is Good
The Real Fountain of Youth

About a bad airplane trip:
A Bad Airplane Trip
Turbulence at 35,000 Feet!

About a rotten date:
   A Date I Didn't Like
   A Night in Purgatory

Our own votes are for the squirrel, the fountain, the turbulence, and purgatory.

Movie producers, newspaper headline writers, and magazine editors all spend considerable time writing catchy titles and captions. So should you. Of course, your title mustn't mislead the way tabloid titles often do (a tabloid headline, "Bigfoot in Brooklyn," could mean that someone there was spotted wearing a size 19 shoe).

PRACTICING 5

Without knowing anything about the essays, underline the title in each pair that makes you want to read the whole work.

   1. Cutting Up at the Box Office / Today's Horror Movies

   2. The Convertible / The Breeze and I

   3. The Danger in Your Back Pocket / Credit Cards

   4. Acne Is Bad / The Teenager's Burden

   5. Divorce Hurts / Divorce

UNIT TALK WRITE ASSIGNMENT

Students were asked to write an essay on something from their youth that had a lasting influence on them. Several paired off to talk out their ideas before beginning to write. The following is what one student said.

Read this student's spoken essay and then use it to write a plan for a complete essay. Begin with an attention-getting introduction and clearly stated thesis statement. Then write three topic sentences. Finally, write a conclusion. You will need to add material to create three topic sentences. Use the essay form provided.

Spoken Paragraph

During one of my high school math classes when we were having a test, I watched a couple of students exchanging answers on pieces of torn paper. At first I thought how helpful it would be to set up that kind of communication with a friend so that I could get a decent grade. After all, math is hard and when you're nervous, you make mistakes that you wouldn't usually make. Having a buddy pass me answers to compare with my own would sure save time, and I wouldn't have to study so hard. But then I remembered a story my mom used to read to me when I was a little boy. It's the story of "The Turtle and the Hare." You know, it's a famous story about a bragging hare—by the way, a hare is just a rabbit—who could run like crazy compared with his turtle friend, who just crawled along at a terribly slow pace. The hare used to tease the turtle mercilessly about being so disgustingly slow. One day the turtle challenged the hare to a race. The hare looked at the turtle with a snobby, sarcastic attitude and accepts the challenge, thinking, "You slow poke; you'll lose big time. I'll beat you all to pieces." Of course, the hare immediately jumps far ahead of the turtle. Part way through the race, he stops to sit down on a tree stump and enjoy the scenery. "What a stupid, slow animal that turtle is! How nervy of him to challenge me to a race!" he says to himself. Then the hare takes a nap. Behold, when he wakes up, the plodding turtle has reached the goal and won the race. This story has been with me all of my life, whenever I've been tempted to take shortcuts or to avoid honest work. I keep hearing my mother's voice telling me, "Slow and steady wins the race."

Written Essay

Introduction: _____

_____

_____

_____

Thesis statement: _____

_____

_____

_____

Topic sentence, first paragraph: _____

_____

_____

Topic sentence, second paragraph: _____

_____

_____

_____

Topic sentence, third paragraph: _____

_____

_____

_____

Conclusion: _____

_____

_____

_____

UNIT TALKING ASSIGNMENT

Choose a classmate and brainstorm an attention-grabbing introduction to an essay about the importance of legible handwriting. Try out several approaches. When you have settled on the best introduction, write it below. Then write a thesis statement, three topic sentences for the body paragraphs, and at least one ending sentence for the conclusion.

Introduction: _____

_____

_____

_____

Thesis statement: _____

_____

_____

_____

Topic sentence, first paragraph: _____

_____

_____

_____

Topic sentence, second paragraph: _____

_____

_____

_____

Topic sentence, third paragraph: _____

_____

_____

_____

Conclusion: _____

_____

_____

UNIT WRITING ASSIGNMENT

Write one of the essays you just partially created above—about not taking shortcuts or the importance of legible handwriting. When you finish, write an attention-getting title.

PHOTO WRITING ASSIGNMENT

Study the following picture, and brainstorm ideas for an essay about it. On a separate sheet of paper, write a thesis statement that will serve as the main idea of the essay. Now write down three topic sentences that will support the thesis statement. Finally, write the essay. Be sure the introduction makes the reader want to read on, and the conclusion gives the whole essay a sense of finality. When you are through, write an attention-getting title.

The Thesis Statement

> "The thesis statement is where you take a stand on the topic."

The **thesis statement** is a single sentence in the opening paragraph that sums up what the essay is about. Every essay should have a thesis statement that functions like a road sign, telling the reader where the essay intends to go.

A thesis statement has three practical aims:

1. It tells in a single sentence what your essay is about: *Fast driving causes accidents and increases air pollution.* We know that this essay intends to discuss the consequences of fast driving, not an encounter with a bear in a campground.

2. It helps you organize your essay: *To do well on an essay exam, you must know the material, understand the question, and organize your answer.* This thesis statement suggests three subtopics for the essay's paragraphs—how knowing the material, understanding the question, and organizing the answer will help you do well on essay exams.

3. It reflects your feelings on the topic: *Affirmative action gives everyone an equal chance.* The writer obviously believes in affirmative action.

The thesis statement is where you take a stand on the topic. If you feel that smoking is your right and you're tired of being nagged about it, say so in your thesis statement. Make your stand strong, definite, and clear.

The most common faults of thesis statements are as follows:

■ Too narrow

■ Too broad

■ Uncommitted

■ Unclear

We'll discuss each fault separately.

The Too-narrow Thesis Statement

An essay discusses the idea expressed in the thesis statement. It is, however, possible to box yourself in with a too-narrow thesis statement that leaves you with little or nothing to discuss. Here are some examples, along with their revisions:

Too narrow: Hamburger is food.
Discussible: Hamburger is highly popular food.

Too narrow: My cat is declawed.
Discussible: A declawed cat makes a good indoor pet.

Too narrow: Kites are flown on Los Angeles beaches.
Discussible: Kite flying is a popular sport on Los Angeles beaches.

Your thesis statement should have at least one or two key words in it. If it doesn't, it is probably too narrow. **Key words** are words that add a discussible edge to the thesis statement. For example, in the thesis statement *Hamburger is highly popular food*, the key words are *highly popular*. That is what you must discuss and prove—the popularity of hamburgers. In the thesis statement *A declawed cat makes a good indoor pet*, the key words are *good indoor pet*. You must discuss and prove that a declawed cat does make a good indoor pet. Finally, in the thesis statement *Kite flying is a popular sport on Los Angeles beaches*, the key words are *popular sport*. That kite flying is a popular sport on Los Angeles beaches is what you must prove. You might discuss county-sponsored kite flying contests. You might describe the flocks of kites swarming the beaches on weekends. These details will go a long way toward proving your thesis statement that kite flying is popular.

The point is, your thesis statement must not be too narrow or it will leave you fumbling for something to say. One way to avoid narrowness is to be sure that your thesis statement contains *key words* that lend it a discussible edge.

PRACTICING 1

Indicate which one among the following pairs of thesis statements is more discussible. Say why.

1. I get a haircut every week. /My haircut reflects my personality.

   You can discuss how it reflects your personality

2. Flying is the safest way to travel. / I like to fly.

   You could give reasons it is safest

3. Housepainting is my job. / Housepainting is a tedious job.

Give more detail about it

4. Dancing is good aerobic exercise. / I can dance.

Describe the different types of dancing

5. I love Chinese food. / Chinese food is easy to make and healthful.

You could tell how to make it.

PRACTICING 2

Insert key words to make the following thesis statements discussible. Indicate in the spaces provided what the inserted words oblige you to discuss and prove.

Example: Joe is my friend.

Revision: Joe is my trustworthy friend.

What I have to do: Find examples that show Joe's trustworthiness.

1. Volkswagen has introduced a new bug.

Revision: *Volkswagen has introduced a new style bug.*

What I have to do: *research the new bug.*

2. I photographed my grandfather.

Revision: *I photographed my grandfather's activities.*

What I have to do: *tell what activities he has photographed.*

3. Our family has a reunion every year.

Revision: *Our family has a different type of reunion every day.*

What I have to do: *tell how there different*

4. I like to watch MTV.

Revision: *I like to watch the different shows on MTV.*

What I have to do: *List the shows*

5. I lift weights.

Revision: *I lift several weights.*

What I have to do: *tell what weights you lift.*

The Too-broad Thesis Statement

A thesis statement is too broad if it commits you to a topic too big to cover in a brief essay. The solution to a too-broad thesis statement is to pare it down to a more manageable size. Here are some broad thesis statements with their more manageable revisions:

Too broad: I have 30 cousins in my family, each with a distinct personality.

Narrowed: My twin cousins, Jane and Jean, differ greatly in personality, politics, and career goals.

This broad thesis statement would require you to write at least 30 paragraphs—one per cousin. A short essay consists typically of five paragraphs. The revised thesis statement, on the other hand, limits you to cover only two cousins, a much more manageable topic.

Too broad: The detective story is an important type of world literature.

Narrowed: Sherlock Holmes was one of the first popular detectives in the detective story.

Whole books have been written about the detective story, making this a topic too vast for a short essay. The revised topic is more manageable, allowing you to focus on one popular fictional detective.

Too broad: Building your own home requires you to be an expert in many different trades.

Narrowed: If I were going to build my own home, it would be a log cabin.

To do justice to the first topic, you need to discuss architecture, carpentry, plumbing, roofing, plastering, cabinetry, and painting, to mention only a few of the trades involved in home construction. Your essay would quickly balloon into 50 paragraphs or more. The more manageable thesis statement only requires you to give reasons why you'd build a log cabin rather than a regular house.

PRACTICING 3

Narrow the following thesis statements so they can be covered in a short essay.

1. Adolescence is difficult.

Teenagers are difficult _____

_____

2. Sports are an important part of American life.

Basketball, Football & Baseball are important part of American life.

3. Nature is beautiful, but it can also be dangerous.

The forest are beautiful, but can be dangerous.

4. Newspapers play an important role in our society.

Evansville Courier play an important role in our society.

5. Drugs are a major social problem in the United States.

Meth, and pot are a major social problem in the U.S.

The Uncommitted Thesis Statement

A thesis statement is uncommitted if it does not plainly state the writer's opinion on the subject, but instead tries to wriggle out of taking a stand. Here is an example of what we mean:

> Isn't it strange that only men are supposed to face the enemy with a gun in foreign countries, while women keep complaining that they want equal rights?

The writer is probably trying hard to be tactful because the issue is controversial—the military double standard that exists for men and women. This kind of politeness, however, is often the cause of bad writing. Just as it is hard to say something sensible on a subject you know nothing about, it is hard to write an essay if you have no opinion on the topic. This writer needs to either choose a less controversial topic or express an opinion clearly.

Here is the revised thesis statement:

> It is unfair for women to insist on equal rights but not have to bear arms the way men have to in war.

Here is another example:

| **Uncommitted:** | One wonders what makes some parents abuse their children. |
| **Good:** | Parents who abuse their children should be held accountable for their acts in court. |

Sometimes an uncommitted thesis statement is due to simple carelessness. Some examples follow.

| **Uncommitted:** | Parachuting is something else! |
| **Good:** | Few sports can rival parachuting for the sense of thrill and freedom it provides. |

| **Uncommitted:** | Bicycle riding is fun. |
| **Good:** | Cycling is a convenient, healthful, and inexpensive way to get around. |

| **Uncommitted:** | I love chess. |
| **Good:** | Chess is a popular sport among college students because it is cheap, engrossing, and can be played almost anywhere. |

Each of these uncommitted thesis statements gives an opinion, but supplies no key words. Remember that a good thesis statement always includes one or two key words that point the way to developing the rest of the essay. The rewritten thesis statements all do just that; the one on parachuting, for example, promises paragraphs on the thrill and freedom of parachuting. Likewise, the cycling example promises a paragraph each on the convenience, healthfulness, and low cost of cycling. Finally, the chess example promises paragraphs proving that chess is a low-cost, high-interest game that can be played anywhere.

PRACTICING 4

The following thesis statements are uncommitted. Rewrite them to express an opinion clearly.

1. People today don't seem to care how they speak to each other in public.

   _____

   _____

2. Perhaps the college should do a better job of trying to keep the campus looking spick-and-span.

   _____

   _____

3. I don't want to criticize our library, but the books do seem somewhat disorganized, and the magazines I'm looking for are hardly ever on the shelves.

_____

_____

4. It would be wonderful if football fans would behave somewhat differently than they do over disputed calls.

_____

_____

5. I love weddings.

_____

_____

The Unclear Thesis Statement

The unclear thesis statement is one that is badly written. It may be wordy, fuzzy, or pompous. The solution to the unclear thesis statement is not simple rewriting. It is rethinking how you feel about the topic, perhaps through some of the methods taught in Unit 3—talking writing, freewriting, brainstorming, and clustering.

Here are some examples of unclear thesis statements along with their clearer versions:

Unclear: In my opinion, which may not be agreed upon by everyone in society, the reason the United States is a great leader in the political world is that everyone is treated equal as to chances by men and women.

Clear: One of the reasons the United States is considered a great land of opportunity is that men and women have an equal chance to succeed.

Unclear: Walking is an ideal exercise of which old and young make no difference as far as being able to improve a physical condition that is not particularly good.

Clear: Walking is an ideal exercise for both young and old people who are not in top physical condition.

The unclear thesis statement is sometimes the result of trying to impress rather than to communicate. Here is an example:

The culinary art that I mastered from due hours of observation of my grandmother's methods instilled in me the rare disciplines of patience, cleanliness, and timing in all endeavors.

This writer tried to pretty up a simple but important idea, namely, that he learned patience, cleanliness, and timing from watching his grandmother cook. After some discussion with classmates, he tried again and came up with this better thesis statement:

Learning how to cook from my grandmother taught me the importance of patience, cleanliness, and timing.

Your aim as a writer is to express yourself, not to impress the reader. If you really want to impress your readers, speak your heart and mind on the page. Nothing else is quite as impressive.

PRACTICING 5

Revise the following thesis statements to make them clearer.

1. Characters in children's stories, including the so-called hero, need uplifting in tone and stature to evoke admiration from children, and probably ought not to be puny weaklings.

   _____

   _____

2. Decisions as to money that I must repay are hard for me to make without encountering feelings of guilt.

   _____

   _____

3. Arizona is a state of splendid, great, stupendous, and magnificent beauty, especially the area that comprises and includes the Grand Canyon.

   _____

   _____

4. The house of my grandfather has not been maintained, and the surrounding greenery, especially in the front, looks as if it has suffered neglectful treatment from the lawn mower.

   _____

   _____

    5. A course in business can promote, abet, and assist anyone, even homemakers who need to make ends meet in the most judicious way, and should be a requirement for graduation.

_____

_____

In a Nutshell

The thesis statement should:

- Tell what the essay is about.

- Narrow a subject.

- Suggest subtopics for its paragraphs.

- Reflect your feelings on the subject.

The thesis statement should not be:

- Too narrow.

- Too broad.

- Uncommitted.

- Unclear.

The Good Thesis Statement

Without question, the thesis statement determines how good your whole essay will be:

> ■ If your thesis statement is too narrow, your essay will be boring because it lacks a discussible edge.

> ■ If your thesis statement is too broad, your essay will be either superficial because you didn't deliver what you promised or too long because you did.

> ■ If your thesis sentence is uncommitted, your essay will drift, not clearly making a point (because you don't have one).

> ■ If your thesis statement is unclear because of bad writing, the point of your essay will be fuzzy; if your thesis statement is unclear because of pompous writing, your reader may not even bother to continue reading.

A good thesis statement, in short:

■ Has a discussible edge.

■ Presents a manageable topic.

■ Gives the writer's committed opinion.

■ Is clearly written.

Here, for example, are two thesis statements:

> My fishing trip was a disaster.

> Thunderstorms, vicious mosquitoes, and bad food made my fishing trip a disaster.

Which of the two do you think is a better thesis statement? We cast our vote for the second.

The first thesis statement is not altogether bad, but it would be harder to develop than the second. It hinges on one key word: *disaster*. In writing about how your fishing trip was a disaster, you'd probably eventually come up with the topics of thunderstorms, vicious mosquitoes, and bad food. Therefore, in addition to writing, you'd also have to be looking—for topics.

In the second thesis statement you can concentrate on the writing. Your topics of *thunderstorms*, *vicious mosquitoes*, and *bad food* are already nested in the thesis statement. You know exactly what to write about and in what order. The second thesis statement is a good thesis statement for these reasons:

■ **It is not too narrow.**	It gives three reasons why the fishing trip was a disaster; one reason would *not* have been enough.
■ **It is not too broad.**	The three topics—*thunderstorms*, *vicious mosquitoes*, and *bad food*—can be nicely covered in a short essay. You don't have to write a book.
■ **It is committed.**	We know exactly the writer's opinion of the fishing trip—it was a disaster.
■ **It is not unclear.**	The language is plain and straightforward with no wordiness or pompousness.
■ **It has key words that suggest a structure for the essay.**	The writer knows what support to provide and in what order.

PRACTICING 6

Mark *G* beside the good thesis statement in each pair and then explain why it is good.

1. _____ **a.** Last Thanksgiving was an awful holiday.

   _____ **b.** Last Thanksgiving was an awful holiday because I quarreled with my sister, burned the turkey, and fell off a ladder.

Reason: _____

_____

2. _____ **a.** Stephen King writes readable books.

   _____ **b.** Stephen King's books are so good because they are about normal people who get into supernatural situations.

Reason: _____

_____

3. _____ **a.** Recharging the cartridges of laser printers saves money, recycles a useful part, and helps the environment.

   _____ **b.** Recharging the cartridges of laser printers is worthwhile.

Reason: _____

_____

4. _____ **a.** *Consumers Reports* magazine helps me make buying decisions, brings me up to date, and informs me of product recalls.

   _____ **b.** *Consumers Reports* magazine helps me.

Reason: _____

_____

5. _____ **a.** I enjoyed my vacation in Destin, Florida.

   _____ **b.** Destin, Florida, is a great undiscovered vacation spot with something for everyone.

Reason: _____

_____

UNIT TALK WRITE ASSIGNMENT

Spoken Opinions

The subject is prayer in public schools. Here are four different opinions, offered informally and in spoken form, by four students. Use these ideas—as well as your own—to write a good thesis statement. It should have a discussible edge and committed opinion. It should also have key words that will suggest the structure for an essay. Use Standard English.

1. Why would anyone not want prayer in the schools? Prayer is wonderfully comforting, and it is part of all religions. Prayer is universal. I don't know what I'd do without prayer. When my mother was very sick, I prayed for her, and she recovered.

2. Catholics pray holding beads in their fingers. Buddhists pray surrounded by incense. Shintoists clap their hands to pray. Muslims bow towards Mecca to pray. You could go on and on, describing how people around the world pray. Prayer belongs in schools because it belongs everywhere.

3. Praying in school is wrong because it forces students to pray in a certain way, which not all students may believe in. Why can't we just pray at home or in our house of worship? God will hear us.

4. I'm against prayer in schools. One-minute prayers are allowed, and the next thing you know, they're required. No one says you can't pray now—just do it silently. But don't tell me I have to pray in school using someone else's prayers.

Thesis Statement

_____

_____

_____

_____

_____

_____

_____

_____

UNIT TALKING ASSIGNMENT

Pair up with a classmate. Each person should choose a topic from the list below and write a thesis statement. Exchange thesis statements with your partner and take turns critiquing them. Be sure the thesis statement is not too narrow, too broad, uncommitted, or unclear, and that it includes key words.

1. What to do about stalkers
2. Spike Lee's movies (or some other director)
3. How to avoid losing your temper
4. Cultural diversity on campus
5. Should final examinations be abolished? (yes or no)

UNIT WRITING ASSIGNMENT

Write an essay using the thesis statement you wrote for the Unit Talking Assignment immediately above.

PHOTO WRITING ASSIGNMENT

Study the following picture. Then write a thesis statement about how you think the person in the picture is likely to feel 20 years from now about doing this act. Create a committed thesis statement, and write a five-paragraph essay.

Organizing Your Essay, from Beginning to End

> "The beginning of your essay is what your reader sees first and where you make an important first impression."

Every essay has three parts: a beginning, middle, and end. The beginning, called the **introduction**, consists of an opening paragraph and includes the thesis statement. The **body**, or middle of the essay, includes paragraphs that support and prove the thesis. The **conclusion**, or end, consists of a final paragraph that brings the essay to a close.

Even in essays that are otherwise not alike, these three parts still play the same role. We will discuss the role of each part and give advice for writing catchy introductions, solid supporting paragraphs, and effective conclusions.

The Introduction

Here is what a typical introduction looks like:

- Opening sentences (grabbers)

- Transition

- Thesis statement

To illustrate how all three parts work in the introduction, we're going to build a typical introductory paragraph from scratch. This is the model we will use as our pattern:

Introduction

   Grabbers: three to six sentences that pull in the reader.

   Transition (if necessary): sets the stage for the thesis.

   The thesis: single sentence that sums up the essay.

An example of an opening paragraph that contains all these necessary parts follows.

Grabbers	Bang! The explosion shattered the stillness of the house. An object whizzed through the wall, smashed through a picture hanging on the wall, and flew over the streets of New York. I sat stunned in my chair, unable to move. Then I got up to investigate. In the next room my little brother, six years old, sat sobbing on the
Transition sentence (underlined)	floor. Beside him was my mother's handgun that had just gone off accidentally. <u>This incident taught me a lesson.</u> Handguns are dangerous
Thesis statement	to own because they provide little protection, can be used in the heat of a quarrel, and often cause deadly accidents.

We'll discuss each separate part in some detail.

Opening sentences (grabbers)

The opening sentences, or grabbers, pull the reader in. This is the readers' first bite of your offering, and how it tastes will really make a difference in how they receive your essay. If you begin with the usual humdrum fare, your readers might chew on, but only reluctantly. Here are some techniques to help you write catchy grabbers.

1. Begin with a quotation or catchy saying.

Beginning with a quotation allows you to use someone else's clever words to get your essay started. Standard reference works such as *Bartlett's Familiar Quotations* or *The Oxford Dictionary of Quotations* are good sources of quotations. Other books, magazines, and newspapers are also rich sources. For example, one student opened her essay on books that she loves with this quotation:

> "When I am dead, I hope it may be said, 'His sins were scarlet, but his books were read.'" So wrote the English writer Hilaire Beloc. He didn't need to worry. His books are read. In fact, he happens to be one of the writers whose books I love. . . .

In this example, a student uses a catchy saying to open an essay about being in charge of your life:

> "You get what you tolerate." I heard my father say this a hundred times, but I didn't realize what it meant until one day when I was complaining about my girlfriend Jenny's lack of consideration. Suddenly I understood. I had a part in how she was treating me. I was letting myself be a doormat. That day I learned a valuable lesson: I never have to be a victim in life.

Here are some tips for opening with quotations or sayings:

- Don't use this opening all the time: Anything in excess soon becomes stale.

- Identify the person you quote unless he or she is so famous as to be immediately recognizable (e.g., Martin Luther King, Jr., Abraham Lincoln, William Shakespeare).

- Make sure your quotation is short—a sentence or two at the most.

- Choose a quotation that's spicy and insightful, something with a real zing to it.

2. Describe a personal experience.

We all like to hear about personal experiences and tend to get pulled into them quickly. The paragraph about the handgun, for example, opens on a personal experience. Here is another such introduction, about the difficulty of parking on campus:

Grabbers	The rain was pouring down in huge, shimmering sheets. I could barely see where I was driving. When I turned into the campus parking lot, I moved my head as close to the windshield as possible in order to see, but I could barely make out the outlines of parked cars. After I had circled the student parking lot three times, I finally found a spot up in what we call "monkey heaven"—a narrow parking area behind the
Transition sentence (underlined)	technical building—blocks away from the science building. <u>I learned that night what every student who drives to school here knows.</u> Because of overcrowding and the scattered layout of the buildings, our campus desperately
Thesis statement	needs a multilevel parking structure located in a central position and open to all students.

This opening is sometimes referred to as opening "in the middle of things" because it places the reader right in the middle of a dramatic situation. Then it ties in the experience with the point of the thesis statement.

Here are some tips for opening with a personal experience:

- Make the opening situation dramatic.

- Keep it brief.

- Connect it with a transition sentence to the thesis statement.

3. Ask a question.

Asking a question gets to the point of your thesis statement immediately. Here is an example:

Do you suddenly change into a monster the moment you get behind a steering wheel? Many people do. They live the calm life of

Dr. Jekyll until they slide behind the wheel of a car, and then they turn into an ugly Mr. Hyde. Such, for example, is the case of my Aunt Matilda, who drives a taxi for a living. My Aunt Matilda has two contrasting personalities, the one when she is out of a car and another uglier one when she is behind the wheel of her taxi.

Although the thesis statement itself should never be worded as a question, a question is a zippy opening because it pulls in readers by addressing them directly. Plus, it immediately raises the topic of your thesis statement.

4. Give a startling fact or statistic.
Facts and statistics make punchy grabbers. Here are some examples:

From an essay on how we celebrate Memorial Day:	In 1868, General John A. Logan, Commander in Chief of the Grand Army of the Republic, did a wonderful thing. He created Memorial Day.
From an essay on having a car stolen:	In 1991, over 200,000 people were arrested for car theft, according to the Information Please Almanac. I was one who had a car stolen that year. . . .
From an essay on suffering through the flu:	It killed 20,000,000 people in 1918, 500,000 in the United States. I'm talking about the flu. . . .

Here are some tips for opening with facts:

■ Be sure your facts are indeed facts and not opinions.

    Fact: The Washington Post is published in Washington, D.C.

    Opinion: I think the Washington Post is a great newspaper.

■ Use only specific, not general, facts.

    General fact: It is sad to realize that many people die from heart problems caused by smoking.

    Specific fact: Every year in the United States, 170,000 people die from heart problems caused by smoking.

One way to check that your opening sentences are real grabbers is to read them aloud as if you were using them to start a conversation. Or, better yet, read them aloud to a friend. Does your friend want to hear more? If the answer is no, you have a little more work ahead. If you make three or four false starts, that's fine. Keep trying. Eventually, you will write a snappy introduction that will grab your reader.

In a Nutshell

An essay consists of three parts:

- Introduction.
- Body.
- Conclusion.

The introduction, in turn, also consists of three parts:

- Grabber sentences that pull the reader in.
- A transition sentence that ties in the grabbers to the thesis statement.
- The thesis statement.

PRACTICING 1

Write a grabber for each of the following topics.

1. A time you said "yes" when you should have said "no"

_____

_____

_____

_____

_____

2. A memorable Halloween experience

_____

_____

_____

_____

_____

3. Being surprised

_____

_____

_____

_____

_____

4. Earliest childhood memories

_____

_____

_____

_____

_____

5. A very good friend

_____

_____

_____

_____

Transition sentence

After the grabber comes the **transition**, a sentence that ties your introduction to the thesis statement. Sometimes a transition is necessary, but sometimes it is not, depending on the wording of your grabber. In this paragraph, for example, which we quoted earlier, the transition is clearly necessary:

Grabbers	Bang! The explosion shattered the stillness of the house. An object whizzed through the wall, smashed through a picture hanging on the wall, and flew over the streets of New York. I sat stunned in my chair, unable to move. Then I got up to investigate. In the next room my little brother, six years old, sat sobbing on the
Transition sentence (underlined)	floor. Beside him was my mother's handgun that had just gone off accidentally. <u>This incident taught me a lesson.</u> Handguns are dangerous to own because they provide little protection,
Thesis statement	can be used in the heat of a quarrel, and often cause deadly accidents.

In the following paragraph the grabber ties in so naturally with the thesis statement that a transition is unnecessary:

My hands were trembling. A cold sweat washed over my brow. When the teacher told us to begin, I was in such a state I could hardly turn the page. I tried to begin by answering the first question, but before I could write, I had to stop my knees from knocking. I was sure that everyone in the room could hear my quaking. <u>Test taking is always an ordeal for me because of my fear of doing poorly, my nervousness, and my tendency to overprepare.</u>

The grabber leads so naturally to the thesis statement at the end that a transition is unnecessary.

In your own opening paragraphs, your ear and common sense will tell you whether you need a transition. Read the paragraph aloud. If the grabber seems to flow naturally into the thesis statement, you need no transition. However, if the grabber seems to need tying into the thesis statement, use a transition sentence.

Thesis statement

The thesis statement ends the introduction. In Unit 16 we discussed the thesis statement at length. We said it was a single sentence in the opening paragraph that sums up what the essay is about. Every essay must have a thesis statement. It is like a road sign, telling your reader where your essay intends to go. The thesis statement is usually the last sentence of the opening paragraph. If you wish to refresh yourself on the thesis statement, review Unit 16.

In summary, when you write your own opening paragraph, be sure to include a grabber, a transition sentence (if your ear tells you that one is necessary), and a thesis statement.

In a Nutshell

In addition to the grabber, the introduction also contains two other parts:

- A transition sentence (if necessary).

- The thesis statement.

PRACTICING 2

Choose one of the five topics listed below and write an introduction to pull in your audience. Your introduction should include a grabber, transition sentence (if necessary), and thesis statement. Keep your work. You will need it for Practicing 4.

1. The first time you did something
2. A disappointment with your family
3. Evaluating a current movie (good or bad)
4. Working in a group
5. A difficult experience

The Body

In writing the body of your essay, you will use the strategies learned in Part III of this book. Which strategy you will use depends on your thesis statement. Some essays, in fact, may require paragraphs developed by different strategies. For example, if you are writing an essay on anger, you might define anger in one paragraph, give examples of it in another, and explain the process you use to control your own temper in a third. Other essay assignments—for example, to compare two people—may require you to focus on one strategy only—comparing/ contrasting.

Indeed, many thesis statements have topics that lead naturally to one particular strategy over another. If you were asked, for example, to tell a love story, you would naturally use narration, not argumentation, to develop an essay on that topic.

Here is a table listing the various strategies you might use in developing an essay. The second column lists the unit that covered the particular strategy. The last column gives an example of a topic that might be developed by that strategy. Use the table to review any strategy you're unsure of as you prepare to write your own essays.

Strategy	Unit	Uses	Example topic
Narration	7	To tell a story	My appendicitis operation
Description	8	To describe	My beloved cat, Fluffie
Illustration	9	To give examples	The stresses of college life
Process	10	To explain anything step by step	How to make good compost
Definition	11	To pinpoint the meaning of a word	What is romance?
Classification	12	To sort into types	Four types of teachers
Comparing and contrasting	13	To find similarities and differences between two things	Baseball versus football
Argumentation	14	To debate a point	Drinking on campus should be banned

Using the strategies to develop paragraphs that support the thesis statement is just one technique that you would use in writing the body of your essay. Here are other techniques you would also practice:

- Stick to the thesis statement.

- Link your paragraphs.

- Write solid paragraphs.

Stick to the thesis statement.

The best way to stick to the thesis statement is to underline its key words. In Unit 16 we defined *key words* as words that add a discussible edge to the thesis statement. These, in effect, are the ideas that the body of your essay must support and prove. For example, let us say that this is your thesis:

> Driving at night is <u>harder</u> to do than driving at day because of the <u>problems</u> caused by <u>poor visibility,</u> <u>fatigue,</u> and the occasional <u>drunk driver</u>.

By underlining the key words, you know exactly what three ideas you must cover in the body of your essay: (1) problems caused by poor visibility, (2) problems caused by fatigue, and (3) problems caused by drunk drivers.

Stick to the topics you promised to cover in your thesis. Not to do so is like being a server at a restaurant and bringing stew when you promised pancakes. If you need a refresher course on sticking to the topic, review Unit 6.

Link your paragraphs.

In Unit 6 we also discussed how to link sentences *within* a paragraph to help your reader follow your train of thought. Paragraphs, too, must be linked or your reader might get lost. In the following section we will discuss how to link the paragraphs of an essay.

1. Repeat key words from the thesis statement.
Here is an example:

Thesis statement:	Driving at night is <u>harder</u> than driving during the day because of the <u>problems</u> caused by <u>poor visibility, fatigue,</u> and the occasional <u>drunk driver</u>.

Here is how repetition would be used in the topic sentences of the paragraphs:

Topic sentence of first paragraph:	Driving at night is harder because of the problems caused by poor visibility.
Topic sentence of second paragraph:	Driving at night is harder because of the problems caused by fatigue.
Topic sentence of third paragraph:	Driving at night is harder because of the problems caused by the occasional drunk driver.

2. Use transitional words and sentences.
Transitional words like *first, second, third,* and *finally* help the reader to see the relationship between paragraphs. Other expressions are *nevertheless, in contrast, in addition, another point is, an example that comes to mind is,* and *therefore.* These words may be combined with an opening sentence—either the topic sentence or a new one written just for the transition—to link two paragraphs. Here are some examples:

Opening sentence of first paragraph:	<u>First,</u> driving at night is harder because the visibility is poor.
Opening sentence of second paragraph:	<u>In addition,</u> fatigue is a problem for the night driver.
Opening sentence of third paragraph:	<u>Finally,</u> the night driver must cope with the occasional drunk.

Here is how a specially written transition sentence could be used to link paragraph three to the previous paragraphs:

> The problems faced by night drivers don't end here, however. In fact, the worst problem may be drunk drivers.

3. Repeat words and ideas.

This is the "step back, then step forward" approach. First you step back to the ending of the preceding paragraph, then you step forward to the topic of the new paragraph.

Here is an example. This is the first paragraph from the essay on night driving. Notice how the opening sentence of the next paragraph first steps back and then steps forward into the new topic:

> First, driving at night is harder because the visibility is poor. It is, of course, harder to see at night because of darkness. Added to the darkness is the uneven glare from roadside lighting, which makes visibility even poorer. But the worst problem of all is that many drivers do not dim their lights for an oncoming car. Nothing can blind a driver quicker than the dazzling lights of an inconsiderate oncoming motorist. On two-lane highways, many accidents are caused by this temporary blindness. My uncle, for example, ran his car off the road and into a ditch because a semitruck blinded him with its bright lights. The driver of the truck didn't even stop and may not even have known that he or she had caused an accident.

Step back:	But even the blinding lights of oncoming trucks don't cause as many nighttime traffic accidents as
Step forward:	an even more common problem—fatigue. Fatigue is . . .

Write solid paragraphs.

If an essay can be said to have a meat-and-potatoes section, it is the body, where you prove your thesis. In the body of the essay your evidence and supporting details must be solid. Use all the techniques about paragraph writing that you've learned in this book. If you need to review a topic, use the following table.

To review this topic	**See this unit**
The importance of Standard English	1
Questions to ask about your audience	2

To review this topic   ## See this unit

In a Nutshell

To write the body of your essay, follow these tips:

• Stick to your thesis statement.

• Link your paragraphs.

• Write solid paragraphs.

Here are some ways to link paragraphs:

• Repeat key words from the thesis statement.

• Use transitional words and sentences.

• Repeat words and ideas.

PRACTICING 3

For each thesis statement below, name the strategy you would use to develop it into an essay.

1. Seat belts have repeatedly proven their value in saving lives.

Strategy: _____

2. There is a right way to read a book.

Strategy: _____

3. Saving money, even a little at a time, can bring surprising benefits.

Strategy: _____

4. My old neighborhood and my new neighborhood are as different as night and day.

Strategy: _____

5. My first day at camp was the most horrible day of my life.

Strategy: _____

6. There are three types of animal lovers.

Strategy: _____

7. Forsythia in bloom is the loveliest of all flowering bushes.

Strategy: _____

8. It's easy to plan a wedding if you begin early.

Strategy: _____

9. The hardest job I ever had was selling brushes door-to-door.

Strategy: _____

10. Bikes should be banned from the pedestrian pathways on campus.

Strategy: _____

PRACTICING 4

Return to Practicing 2 and the introduction you wrote for an essay. Now write a three-paragraph body that will prove your thesis statement. Be sure that you stick to your thesis statement. Save your work; you will need it for Practicing 5.

The Conclusion

The conclusion to your essay is a final, short paragraph that wraps up the essay. This is your "goodbye" to the reader. Unlike the introduction, which has a three-part form—grabber, transition (if necessary), and thesis statement—the conclusion has no special subsections. In some essays, the conclusion may be as long as the introduction; in others it may be only a sentence or two. Your aim in the conclusion is to tie up all loose ends and leave the reader with a sense of completion.

Even though conclusions vary, there are some well-known ones that are best avoided because they add nothing but filler to an essay. The first is the *so-as-you-can-see* ending. Here is an example:

So, as you can see from what I've written, the proposal to raise the parking fees on campus is bad for the reasons I've given.

If you've given the reasons, you don't need to say that you've given them. Just giving them is enough.

Another stale ending is the *in-conclusion-my-thesis-statement-proves-that* or *states-that* ending. Your thesis statement by now has already been proved. You don't need to rehash it.

> In conclusion, my thesis statement states that family vacations are seldom fun for teens because they deny teens the company of their friends, force them to do things they're not interested in, and usually stick them with baby-sitting. For these very reasons, I am against family vacations if teens have to go on them.

Here are three good ways to end an essay:

1. Give one final thought.

In this conclusion you add one last insightful comment on the topic. Here is an example:

Thesis statement:	Garage sales have become popular because they allow people to get rid of their clutter, earn a little extra money, and meet their neighbors and other people.
Conclusion:	Over the years the garage sale has grown up. Aside from all their other functions, garage sales have become a huge recycling enterprise that operates on the principle, "One person's junk is another's treasure." Garage sales, in fact, ease the pressure on the landfills. Plus, garage sales are fun!

The final thought is that garage sales, in addition to everything else, are also fun.

2. Suggest an action.

Here is an example from an essay on ways to increase your vocabulary:

Thesis statement:	You can increase your vocabulary in three simple steps: Jot down each word you read or hear whose meaning you don't know and look it up later; write down the definition and memorize it; use the new word as soon as possible.
Conclusion:	It pays to increase your word power. You are judged not only by the clothes you wear, which show the outer person, but by the words you use, which show the inner. But if you don't have the time to follow my suggestions, there is one thing you can do that's fun and that will help you build a bigger vocabulary: Work the crossword puzzles in your local newspaper. You might not do well

at first, but eventually these puzzles will increase your vocabulary and give you an appreciation for the power of words.

The suggestion—that working crossword puzzles will help increase your vocabulary—is the final shot of this ending paragraph.

3. Ask a thought-provoking question.

A thought-provoking question leaves your reader thinking about a point raised by your essay. It is a natural impulse in most of us to want to answer a question, or at least to think about how we would answer it. We are therefore left thinking. An example follows.

Thesis statement:	Test taking is always an ordeal for me because of my fear of doing poorly, my nervousness, and my tendency to overprepare.
Conclusion:	At the end of every test, I always feel as if I've tried my hardest but been hampered by my nervousness. I also know that no matter whether I was nervous or not, some tests have an important effect on my life. An SAT result, for example, might determine where I can go to college. Yet, I can't help thinking I would do better on tests if they didn't make me so nervous. And I can't help wondering: Is it fair for society to put so much stock in a single event, especially one where my nervous nature might cause me to do worse than I otherwise would?

We are left to puzzle over this question: Indeed, is it fair?

In a Nutshell

In your conclusions avoid these endings:

- The *so-as-you-can-see* ending.

- The *in-conclusion-my-thesis-statement-states* ending.

Among the various ways of ending an essay are these:

- Give one final thought.

- Make a suggestion.

- Ask a final question.

> **PRACTICING 5**
>
> Complete the essay you started in Practicing 2 and continued in Practicing 4. Write a forceful conclusion, using one of the methods suggested above.

The Whole Essay

No matter what kind of essay you write or on what topic, it will consist of the three parts we just discussed—the introduction, body, and conclusion. Keep in mind what the shell of an essay looks like.

Title of Essay

Introduction _____
_____
_____

Thesis statement _____

      Topic sentence: _____

_____
Body _____
_____
_____

      Topic sentence: _____

_____
_____
Body _____
_____
_____

      Topic sentence: _____

_____
_____
Body _____
_____
_____

Conclusion _____
_____
_____
_____

You can use this shell for writing an essay on any topic. Before you begin writing your essay, copy down this shell and use it as your model to be filled in with different words, depending on your topic.

Here is this pattern used in an actual student essay:

Title of essay	Sweating It Out

Introduction (Grabbers)

My hands were trembling. A cold sweat washed over my brow. When the teacher told us to begin, I was in such a state I could hardly turn the page. I tried to begin by answering the first question, but before I could write I had to stop my knees from knocking. I was sure that everyone in the room could hear my quaking.

Thesis statement

<u>Test is taking always an ordeal for me because of my fear of doing poorly, my nervousness, and my tendency to overprepare.</u>

First paragraph: developed by narration

I have a tremendous fear of doing poorly when I sit down to take a test, and no matter how hard I try, I can't seem to shake the feeling. But I know exactly where I got it from and how it began. I was in first grade and taking a test that would determine who got into the "Discovery Program," which was for gifted kids only. Our teacher was a substitute, and she cracked a joke about how the test would show who among us were horses and who were donkeys. We all wanted to be horses, not donkeys, but as I took the test, I kept saying to myself, "This is going to make you look like a donkey." And it did. I didn't get into the program, but my best friend did. I was so ashamed that when I was given another chance to take the test in third grade, I begged my mother not to make me.

Second paragraph: developed by definition of _nervousness_

My nervousness is another reason I don't test well. By <u>nervousness</u> I don't mean "fear." I think I have as much courage as anyone my age. I have done the usual stupid things and taken my share of risks. The nervousness I'm talking about is a raw physiological reaction to situations where I feel stress. My palms sweat; my heart races; I become confused and feel as if the ground itself might swallow me up. Yet this feeling comes over me in situations that pose no physical risk, like meeting a new girl, for example. My doctor told me that I'm adrenaline sensitive. When I asked him what that meant, he said it meant that I was a nervous person. And I am. I just can't help the extreme way that my body reacts to stress.

Third paragraph: developed by comparison/ contrast

Finally, I have a tendency to overprepare for a test. When I compare myself and the way I prepare for a test with the way my best friend, Jason, prepares, I see right away that I'm overdoing it. For a psych test we had last week,

Jason read the chapter through twice and skimmed it once, the night before the test. In contrast, I read it six times, all the way through. Some sentences and paragraphs I knew by heart. Even the morning of the test I was still hitting the books whereas Jason was talking about baseball. Then the test began, and I broke out in a cold sweat and became confused—from knowing too much, I think. I did all right, but no better than Jason, who didn't work as hard but who managed to stay cool.

Conclusion: ends with a question

At the end of every test, I always feel as if I tried my hardest but was hampered by my nervousness. Yet, I also know that no matter whether I was nervous or not, some tests have an important effect on my life. An SAT result, for example, might determine where I can go to college. Yet I can't help thinking I would do better at tests if they didn't make me so nervous. And I can't help wondering: Is it fair for society to put so much stock in a single event, especially one where my nervous nature might cause me to do worse than I otherwise would?

UNIT TALK WRITE ASSIGNMENT

What follows is a student's rambling talk about an old-fashioned institution—the milkman. Search through this spoken material to extract the following ingredients for an essay: a grabber to introduce the essay, a thesis to control the essay, three topic sentences to form the body of the essay, and a final sentence to conclude the essay. Use the space below to write the skeleton of your essay.

Spoken Paragraph

Rats! Out of milk again. Now I've got to stop everything I'm doing and run to the store. What a bummer! How I wish we had Mr. Garrett to deliver milk, cream, cheese, orange juice, and eggs directly to our house. When I visit my grandmother in California, I enjoy the fact that she has a friendly milkman who takes good care of his route customers. Mr. Garrett delivers dairy products every Tuesday and Thursday morning. The guy is on such friendly terms with his customers that he actually steps into their kitchens to check the refrigerator's stock. Then he might say, "Mr. B, you have plenty of fresh milk until Thursday. No need to add any." Then he leaves, but not before telling one of his funny jokes. He's like a member of every family on his route. Even watch dogs don't bite him. They just jump on him with friendly yelps because they're so tickled to see him. He has been known to jump into the middle of a roughhouse fight between neighborhood kids, separating them while he reminds them that their mothers wouldn't like how they're behaving. I heard he even prayed with a couple on his route who planned to get a divorce. With someone like Mr. Garrett watching your fridge and making sure you're stocked, you never have to bother with last-minute runs to the market. By the way, if Grandma wants an extra order, like chocolate milk or ice cream, she just leaves a note on the door, and, like magic, Mr. Garrett fills her order. I sure do wish they'd bring back the old-fashioned personal milkman.

Written Essay

Title of Essay

Introduction: _____
_____
_____

Thesis statement: _____
_____
_____

Body:
(First topic sentence) _____
_____
_____

Body:
(Second topic sentence) _____
_____
_____

Body:
(Third topic sentence) _____
_____
_____

Conclusion: _____
_____
_____
_____

UNIT TALKING ASSIGNMENT

Join with three other classmates and plan an essay on one of the following topics.

1. Are our thoughts as important as our action?
2. Being tolerant of others
3. Moral responsibility
4. The pleasures of being alone
5. An emotional experience

Use the essay shell given in this unit. Working together, write:

■ A thesis statement.

■ An attention-grabbing opener.

■ Three topic sentences for the body of the essay.

■ A suitable conclusion.

UNIT WRITING ASSIGNMENT

Write a complete essay on the group topic you chose and developed in the Unit Talking Assignment above. Or, if you prefer, choose one of the other topics and develop it into an essay.

PHOTO WRITING ASSIGNMENT

Study the following picture of a football game. Then write an essay in which you argue that playing a team sport teaches important values, such as self-discipline and working toward a common goal. Ask yourself these questions as you develop your essay:

■ Do I have an attention-grabbing opener?

■ Did I place my thesis statement at the end of the first paragraph?

■ Do the three body paragraphs support the thesis statement?

■ Does my ending wrap up the essay?

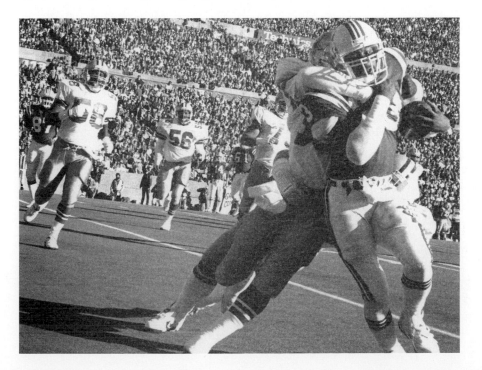

Revising, Editing, and Proofreading

"Revising means, literally, seeing again."

Writing a good essay requires us to play two roles. First, we must be writers, putting words down on the page. Then we must become readers, putting ourselves in the reader's shoes to evaluate what we have written.

This is what you did as a writer:

You wrote a thesis statement.

You wrote an attention-getting introduction.

You supported your thesis statement, beginning each paragraph with a topic sentence.

You wrote the first draft.

Now, to improve and correct your work, you must take the role of reader. Here is what you must do:

- Revise what you have written.

- Edit your revised essay.

- Proofread your essay before you hand it in.

So far, we have mainly discussed your role as a writer. In this unit we will focus on your role as a reader. Naturally, there is some carryover from one role to the other. For example, as you pore over your work from the reader's viewpoint, you will occasionally become the writer again to correct or improve it.

Revising

Revising means, literally, "seeing again." It is during this stage that you have the chance to make your writing better. Indeed, most writers do their best work during revision. Here is where you shift paragraphs, add details, scrap sentences, cut deadwood, substitute words—in short, do anything necessary to improve the writing.

However, don't revise immediately. Instead, after you have completed your first draft, put it aside for a while—if you can—to let it "settle." Then pick it up a few days later and give it a fresh look. Don't worry if you're not satisfied with it. Most writers feel exactly the same way about their first drafts—dissatisfied. In any case, no matter how rough your draft seems, at least you now have something to work with.

One good way to start the revision process is to read your paper aloud—to someone else or to yourself. Reading your paper aloud gives you a sense of how it sounds. Here is a checklist you can use:

REVISING CHECKLIST

1. ✔ Do I have a clear thesis statement that controls my essay? (Unit 16) yes

2. ✔ Do I get my reader's attention in the introduction? (Unit 17) yes

3. ✔ Do my body paragraphs have clear topic sentences? (Units 4 and 17) yes

4. ✔ Do I support my thesis statement by using the strategies effectively? (Units 7–14) yes

5. ✔ Do I stick to the point I make in the thesis statement? (Unit 6) yes

6. ✔ Do I link the paragraphs of my essay? (Unit 6) yes

7. ✔ Is my purpose clear (to entertain, inform, or persuade)? (Unit 2) yes

8. ✔ Have I taken my audience into account? (Unit 2) yes

9. ✔ Have I used Standard English throughout? (Unit 1) yes

10. ✔ Do I close my essay with a sense of finality? (Unit 17) yes

---

Notice that the Revising Checklist tells you the units that you need to review if you're unsure how to answer a particular question. Don't be reluctant to go back and review an earlier unit. Indeed, the advice in these units is more likely to sink in only after you actually try to apply it to your own writing. You learn to ride a bicycle in much the same way: not by reading, but by doing.

Revising, like writing, is a uniquely personal process. It can be done in many different ways. Some students like to scribble on their papers, circling words that need deleting or improving, rewriting passages that are muddled, using arrows to add or move sections. A few students hate messiness and revise by writing a second draft on a clean sheet of paper. Still other students go immediately to their computers to work on screen, moving sentences and paragraphs around and adding inserted material. No matter what your style, it is a good idea to double-space your first draft. The added space on the page makes rewriting *much* easier.

Using talk skills to revise your work

Talking can help with revision. Start by reading your work aloud to a partner or friend. Reading aloud forces you to pay attention to every word and not skip any words or sentences. It also helps you to tell how your writing sounds to someone else. Does it sound choppy? Or, do you have a sentence that goes on and on—and on?

To use talk skills to revise, do the following:

- Read your essay aloud to a friend.

- Ask your friend what you can do to improve it.

- Apply every question on the Revising Checklist to your first draft.

- Make changes as you or your friend think of them.

- If you don't understand a question on the Revising Checklist, review the unit where it is discussed.

If you are working with someone in your class, you will have to take turns going over each other's material. Be patient with each other. The mutual give-and-take will help you both learn how to revise.

If you must work alone, follow the same steps given above. If you feel funny about reading your work aloud, do it in private. Reading your work aloud lets you use your speaker's ear to help judge the writing. Finally, don't be afraid to scribble mercilessly over your first draft. Scratch out and rewrite sentences to your heart's content. First drafts are supposed to look beaten up. If yours is clean and nice, ask yourself honestly: Am I being too easy on myself?

PRACTICING 1

Here is the first draft of an essay that needs to be improved. Read it carefully and then complete the Revising Checklist.

My girlfriend Tiara doesn't get along with my friends. After puzzling over the possible reason, I have decided that Tiara is so needy for attention that her stunning looks can't save her from the annoyance people feel in her presence. Now, Tiara makes heads turn because she looks exotic. She is from the Middle East and has huge black eyes, creamy skin framed by silky black hair, with a figure to die for. But here is a typical example of what she does. We're in the same geology class, and last Saturday, the teacher organized a field trip to Red Rock Canyon, a desert area filled with unusual geological formations. Who knows how long these rocks have been there and how many winds and rain storms washed over them? Time has ravished many spots of nature. We were to meet at 9:00 A.M. in front of the library to board a college bus that would take us to our destination. At 9:10 Tiara was nowhere in sight, so the driver waited another fifteen minutes. As the bus was ready to pull out, there she came running, with a mane of newly dyed bright purple hair flying in the wind and wearing short shorts, an orange tube top, and flimsy little sandals. "Wait for me!" She shouted happily, and, of course, we did. People who make other people wait are rarely popular. Resentment was written all over the faces of those she had inconvenienced. Worse yet, on the trip she couldn't walk with those flimsy sandals and she kept skinning her legs and knees. Needless to say, she also spent a lot of time pulling up her tube top. By the end of the day, everyone was so disgusted with her.

Now apply the Revising Checklist. Go over the essay point by point. Note problems in the space provided.

Revising Checklist	**Responses**
1. Do I have a clear thesis statement that controls my essay? (Unit 16)	**1.** _____ _____ _____ _____
2. Do I get my reader's attention in the introduction? (Unit 17)	**2.** _____ _____ _____ _____

is my neighbor ~~m~~rs. ~~l~~illy Hammond who graduated from ~~k~~ent ~~l~~aw
~~s~~chool several years ago and ~~past~~ ~~she passed~~ her bar exams, but could not
afford to rent an office for her legal practice. ~~Turning~~ ~~She turned~~ her back bedroom into an office and ~~dealing~~ ~~dealt~~ with her clients at home. She likes
the arrangement, both financially and personally, because she saves
money, ~~And~~ a can be home for her children.

My retired computer science teacher, who runs a business from
his house. ~~Advising~~ He advises people who need help with their computers. He
just left some flyers around the ʌNeighborhood, letting people know
that the can help them set up their computers, also show them how to use
a new computer program, and get glitches out of older programs. I
am told that this man is making good money through his home-
based business.

PRACTICING 6

Here are two more paragraphs for you to edit, using the Editing
Checklist as a guide.

The T-shirt is one of the best fashion inventions of all time, it
allows the wearer, whether male of female, to be comfortable. I
happen to be male and love to dress informal but yet attractive. It
use to be that I felt dressed up only when I wore a white shirt with
a tie. Now, I just wear a black cotton T-shirt under a sport coat of
any color except Navy. Its' such a relief to sit at a movie or in a
restuarant without feeling that your neck is getting a rash from the
stiff shirt or that your being strangled by a tie noose.

I've seen women devoted to T-shirts as well. In fact, this
summer I spied several girls wearing long T-shirts as dresses that
walked along the shopping mall of our city. Looking relaxed yet
attractive. Some of these T-shirts were striped to give a naval look
others had gold letters stitched on them, such as "DKNY," which
apparently stands for "Dona Karen of New York," a well-known
designer. Quite a few revealed colored patches of cats, birds, dogs,
or flags. But what they all had in common was a sense of comfort.
I think T-shirts as a proper fashion statement should be promoted,
and I'll risk a fashion arest to say so.

PRACTICING 7

Edit the essay that you wrote and revised for Practicing 4. Use the
Editing Checklist on pages 273 and 274.

Proofreading

Proofreading means giving your paper one final check for errors you might have missed. Don't rush. Proofreading is crucial to catch any errors that escaped your eye during both revising and editing—accidentally omitted words, misspellings, and punctuation slipups. In fact, you might ask a classmate to exchange papers for proofreading. At this stage, a writer is often too close to the paper to spot errors easily seen by a stranger's eyes. Indeed, writers often see what they *intended* to write rather than what they actually wrote. If you can't find someone to proofread your work and have only yourself to rely on, we advise you to read slowly, one word at a time.

If you are writing on a computer, be sure to use a spell-check program on your essay. Bear in mind, however, that the spell-check process is not foolproof. A word may be spelled correctly but still misused. For instance, a spell check will not catch the error in the sentence *We baked to dozen cookies.* No spell-check program knows the difference between *to*, *too*, and *two.*

In a Nutshell

After you've produced a first draft, you should put your paper through the following steps:

- Revising.

- Editing.

- Proofreading.

Student Essay in Progress

In this section we present a student essay in progress. We include:

■ The first draft with its revisions

■ The second draft with its editing

■ The final draft, all proofread

First draft with notes for revising

Having Good Manners   *needs attention-getting opening*

unclear
(When they are young parents teach their kids about   *Explain what manners are*

manners.) Parents always want their kids to have good

manners. When people have good manners there polite

need clear plan of evelopment -
1. business
2. friends
3. family

make thesis clear

use consistent point of view

and aren't rude. People use thier manners all of the time everyday. (Having good manners is important to make friends and to get a job.) If (you) don't have good manners then no one will like you. Having good manners can be as simple as saying thank you and please. When you are at work, you must be polite to your boss and the other people around you. If somebody is trying to get a job then they need to dress nicely and act polite. Nobody will hire a guy whose slopy and rude.

organize ideas more clearly

explain why - give examples

If you want to have any friends then you need good manners. If your friends throwing a party, you should tell them if you are coming or not. Throwing a party is fun, but it is also takes lots of planning. You had to figure out who to invite and what kind of food to have. (Then knowing how much stuff to buy.) When people dont say if they are coming then you don't know how much to buy.

give more examples

off topic of manners

Fragment

unclear

People with bad manners are (geeks.) They dont have any friends and no one likes them. You should have good manners all of the time. (Even at home.) When someone calls at home, you should take a message and not forget. That is rude. It is a bummer to live with rude people even if their your family. That is why we need manners.

Slang

Be more specific

Fragment

give examples

re-write conclusion Focus on why manners are important.

Edited first draft

The Importance of Good Manners

Keep your elbows off of the table. Don't slurp your soup. Say "please." Most of us have heard our parents say these phrases many times before. Did our parents simply enjoy enforcing these rules, or do good manners actually have a purpose in life? As we grow, manners, or the socially correct way of acting, become more and more important. Good manners are necessary to succeed in

business, social, and family situations.

In the work place, good manners can make the difference

and staying unemployed. *to set up an* *one*

between getting a job ~~or not~~. When calling up for ~~an~~ interview, ~~you~~

should be polite and professional to the person answering the

ing

phone. ~~Another example of good manners is to~~ arrive at the

is another way to impress the boss.

interview on time and well dressed. Wearing jeans or shorts is

not appropriate *it is polite to*

~~sloppy~~. Several days after the interview ~~you can~~ send a letter

his or her *Having good manners like these will*

thanking the interviewer for ~~their~~ time.

impress people in business situations, and can increase one's success in the work place.

Manners are important in social situations such as parties. ~~If~~

When a friend *also* *with a party invitation, one*

~~someone calls to invite you to a party~~, ~~you~~ should check the date

accept or decline *Responding promptly to an*

and ~~respond quickly~~. ~~Calling back about the~~ invitation is an

one

example of good social manners. When attending the party, ~~you~~

A

should not bring people along who weren't invited. ~~Guest~~ who

five or six other *be*

shows up with ~~a whole bunch of~~ people will probably not get invited

again *ing*

~~anymore~~. When ~~you~~ leaves the party it is polite to thank the host

he or she *s* *Friends will feel appreciated when they are*

and ask if ~~they~~ needed any help cleaning up. *treated this way.*

It is easy to forget about using *with family members but manners become very important*

Good manners ~~are vital for a happy home life when dealing with~~ *when*

people live together *We can be considerate to relatives by* *ing*

~~your family members~~. ~~One example is~~ to remember to relay phone

It can be upsetting

messages. ~~I get really mad~~ when messages are forgotten or

written down wrong. Another problem can result from borrowing

One

items without asking or returning them. ~~You~~ should always ask

permission to borrow something, like clothes or even toothpaste.

Being polite and returning borrowed items quickly will keep family

members happy. Another way to ~~to~~ respect family members with

entering

good manners is to knock on doors before ~~barging~~ in a room

This type of

because everyone appreciates having some privacy. ~~Behavoir like~~

~~this~~ will improve relationships and keep the house peaceful.

using

Many people believe that ~~to use~~ good manners is not

is

important, or an old fashioned way of behaving. However, parents realize that manners are important and they teach their children

how be polite so that they can achieve many things. ~~S~~itting up *(Although)*

straight and ~~saying~~ "thank you" may ~~be~~ a lot of trouble, ~~but~~ good *(remembering to)* *(seem like)* *(using)*

manners will ~~lead to success.~~ *(keep employers, friends, and family happy.)*

Final draft

The Importance of Good Manners

"Keep your elbows off of the table." "Don't slurp your soup." "Say 'please.'" Most of us have heard our parents say these phrases many times. Did our parents simply enjoy enforcing these rules, or do good manners actually have a purpose in life? As we mature, manners, or the socially correct way of acting, become more and more important. Good manners are necessary to succeed in business, social, and family situations.

In the work place, good manners can make the difference between getting a job and staying unemployed. When calling to set up an interview, one should be polite and professional to the person answering the phone. Arriving at the interview on time and well dressed is another way to impress the boss. Wearing jeans or shorts is not appropriate. Several days after the interview it is polite to send a letter thanking the interviewer for his or her time. Having good manners will impress people in business situations, and can increase one's success in the work place.

Manners are also important in social situations such as parties. When a friend calls with a party invitation, one should check the date and either accept or decline. Responding promptly to an invitation is an example of good social manners. When attending the party, one should not bring people along who weren't invited. A guest who shows up with five or six other people will probably not be invited again. When leaving the party it is polite to thank the host and ask if he or she needs any help cleaning up. Friends feel appreciated when they are treated this way.

It is easy to forget about using good manners with family members, but manners become very important when people live together. We can be considerate to relatives by remembering to relay phone messages. It can be upsetting when messages are forgotten or written down wrong. Another problem can result from borrowing items without asking or not returning them. One should always ask permission to borrow something, like clothes or even toothpaste. Being polite and returning borrowed items quickly will keep family members happy. Another way to respect family members with good manners is to knock on doors before entering a room because everyone appreciates having some privacy. This type of behavior will improve relationships and keep the house peaceful.

Many people believe that using good manners is not important, or is an old-fashioned way of behaving. However, parents realize that manners are important and they teach their children how to be polite so they can achieve high goals. Although sitting up straight and remembering to say "thank you" may seem like a lot of trouble, using good manners will keep employers, friends, and family members happy.

UNIT TALK WRITE ASSIGNMENT

What follows is a spoken paragraph expressing one participant's views from a panel discussion on fathers (or in some cases mothers) who don't make child support payments. It is your job to rewrite these spontaneously expressed ideas into a brief essay that includes an introduction, a body, and a conclusion. You will probably need to draw upon your own experiences and reading to write three solid body paragraphs. Use the space below and additional paper for this assignment since you will need to do several drafts.

Spoken Paragraph

I'm embarrassed to admit this, but my own dad hasn't give my mom a penny toward our support for the last two years. He lives in Montana, and my mom got tired of dinging him all the time. Sure, she could get a lawyer on him, but she doesn't have that kinda money. In fact, she has to work extra hours in order to pay our bills. It's hard on her as a single parent and it leaves us kids home alone a lot more. Even Saturdays and Sundays when she waitresses. Parents who neglect to support their children don't have any idea how furious and bitter children get about this. They see the parent as a loser or a real jerk. Of course, some times I suppose the parent could be out of a job or in some kind of financial mess. But still, if you had the kids, you have to support the kids. You don't just walk away. You ought to have to make up any back payments. I heard where one father moved to a different state so it would be easier for him to hide from making child support payments. How can any parent be so stone hearted that he doesn't give a rip about his own flesh and blood. No wonder some kids don't talk to their fathers for the rest of their lives. I guess the only way to make sure that parents fulfill their obligations to their children is to send them to jail when they don't. Did you hear about the bill that's before Congress now? About making it a felony for parents to cross state lines in order to not pay child support? Some states already have laws to imprison delinquent parents, but they aren't always enforced. We should start enforcing these laws, too. I happen to know several cases where the kids are getting no support—zero, zilch. I say, if you're old enough to have kids, you're old enough to be responsible and pay for them. Period.

Written Essay

_____

_____

_____

_____

_____

_____

_____

_____

_____

_____

_____

_____

_____

_____

_____

_____

UNIT TALKING ASSIGNMENT

Get together with a classmate and brainstorm on one of the following topics. Circle any usable ideas from the brainstorming session, and save the list for the next assignment.

1. How a modern invention has changed our lives
2. The importance of preserving our national parks
3. A recent fad that you consider good or bad
4. A controversial issue that's been in the news

UNIT WRITING ASSIGNMENT

Use the brainstorming ideas gathered from the Unit Talking Assignment above to write an essay. Be sure that you have a clear thesis statement, topic sentences opening every body paragraph, paragraphs developed with strong evidence, and a strong conclusion. Then revise and edit your essay. Use the Revising and Editing Checklists. Carefully proofread before you submit the final draft to your instructor.

PHOTO WRITING ASSIGNMENT

The following photo shows a Boy Scout troop. Write an essay about any youth program, such as scouting, 4-H, summer sport camp, or a church retreat in which you were involved, saying how it affected you for good or ill. Use the Revising and Editing Checklists to revise and edit. Your teacher may ask you to hand in all three drafts—the first draft, the revised draft, and the edited and proofread final draft.

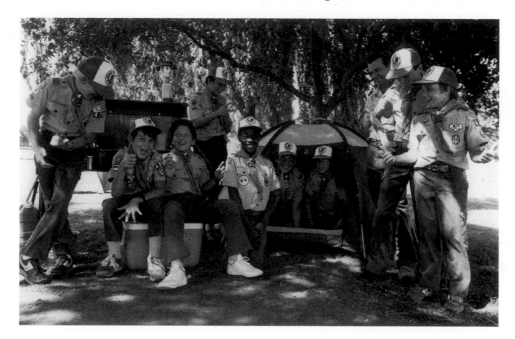

Sentence Basics

This part of *Writing Talk* covers the fundamentals of understanding and writing clear, correct sentences. Unit 19 discusses the basics of sentence structure, and Unit 20 focuses on basic sentence types and gives tips on how to write with sentence variety.

The Sentence

A sentence is a group of words that expresses a complete thought. This completeness is what your speaker's ear uses to recognize a sentence. If someone said to you, "match," you'd probably reply, "What?" meaning, "What do you mean?" If, however, someone said, "If I had a match, I would light the fire," you might reply, "Oh, let me find one." You respond differently because the second statement is complete enough for you to understand it.

Subject and Verb

To be complete, every sentence must have a subject and a verb. In its simplest form, the **subject** is someone who does something:

> The bird sang.

> Dick shouted.

> Mary fell.

Naturally, the subject of a sentence can also be *something* rather than *someone:*

> The car stopped.

> The bell rang.

> Jealousy destroys.

The word that tells what the subject does or did is called the **verb.** From these examples, we know that the bird *sang,* Dick *shouted,* and Mary *fell.* We also know that the car *stopped,* the bell *rang,* and jealousy *destroys.*

Each of these examples is called a kernel sentence. A **kernel** sentence is the smallest sentence possible. Here are some other kernel sentences:

> Jump!

> Hurry!

> Watch out!

These kernel sentences are commands. The subject (you) is implied:

> (You) jump!

> (You) hurry!

> (You) watch out!

Every sentence—no matter how long and complex—contains a kernel sentence. For example:

> The bird sang.

Although we can add words to it, making it longer and more detailed, its kernel will still be *the bird sang*. Here are some examples with added words:

> Early in the morning, <u>the bird sang.</u>
>
> <u>The bird,</u> spreading its yellow wings, <u>sang.</u>
>
> Despite black clouds and thunder rolls, <u>the bird sang.</u>
>
> <u>The bird sang</u> as if his heart were broken.
>
> Perched on a tree limb, <u>the bird sang</u> until noon.

When we read a sentence, we know who did what or what happened and to whom. Therefore, to find the subject of a sentence, simply do this: First identify the verb. Then ask "Who?" or "What?" in front of it. The answer will be the subject. So, for example, in the sentence *The bird sang*, we know that the verb is *sang*. If we ask "Who sang?" the answer is the subject, *the bird*.

PRACTICING 1

Underline the subject once and the verb twice in each of these sentences.

1. The man ate.

2. The clouds drifted.

3. The baby giggles.

4. The bomb exploded.

5. Knives cut.

PRACTICING 2

Underline the kernel sentence in each of these sentences.

1. Greg leaped into the air.

2. Gathering yellow pansies, Marcia lifted the basket.

3. The townspeople voted for the incumbent mayor.

4. The soccer players, victorious grins on their faces, left the field.

5. As the whole family sat down to dinner, she announced her divorce.

6. My hometown named our largest park after Ben Jones, who won a medal in the 1972 Olympics.

7. Jimmy cornered me in the drugstore.

8. Some hideous person stole three of our bikes.

9. Mr. Hightower ran down the road in his underwear.

10. Rain or smog, we walk at 6:00 every morning.

Prepositional Phrases

Sometimes it's easy to spot the subject of a sentence, but sometimes it isn't. For example, what is the subject of this sentence?

One of Mary's friends gave her a surprise party.

If we apply the test of asking "Who?" before *gave*, we find that *one* is the subject. Because the prepositional phrase *of Mary's friends* comes before the verb *gave*, you might mistake *Mary's friends* for the subject.

A **preposition** is a word that shows the relationship between two things; a **prepositional phrase** is a group of words beginning with a preposition. A preposition always has an **object**—usually a noun or pronoun that follows it. The preposition and its object make up the prepositional phrase. Here is an example:

Ginger placed the napkin in the napkin ring.

Preposition   Object

Here the preposition is *in*, and the object is *napkin ring*. Remember this formula:

Preposition	+	Object	=	Prepositional phrase
on		the table		on the table
to		the sea		to the sea
of		the college		of the college
from		the store		from the store

Below is a list of the most common prepositions:

about	at	beyond	in
above	before	by	inside
across	behind	despite	into
after	below	down	like
against	beneath	during	near
along	beside	except	of
among	besides	for	off
around	between	from	on

out	to	under	upon
outside	toward	underneath	with
over	through	until	within
past	throughout	up	without
since			

One way to avoid mistaking a preposition for the subject of a sentence is to cross out all the prepositional phrases in any sentence whose subject you're trying to find. Here are some examples:

The captain ~~of the baseball team~~ encouraged the players.

The top ~~of the mountain~~ could not be seen.

PRACTICING 3

Create a prepositional phrase for each of the following prepositions. Then write a complete sentence using the prepositional phrase.

1. on

_____

_____

2. under

_____

_____

3. without

_____

_____

4. from

_____

_____

5. near

_____

_____

6. between

_____

_____

7. behind

_____

_____

8. off

_____

_____

9. like

_____

_____

10. throughout

_____

_____

PRACTICING 4

Cross out the prepositional phrase(s) in each of the sentences below. Then identify the subject by circling it.

1. (Tom) went ~~up the block~~ and ~~down the street.~~

2. ~~After the lecture,~~ (we) went ~~into the Orange Room~~ ~~for coffee.~~

3. (She) ran ~~out the door~~ ~~without her keys.~~

4. (I'll) have a chocolate (sundae) ~~with fudge sauce~~ and ~~nuts~~ ~~on top.~~

5. (She) backed ~~into the driveway~~ ~~without her glasses.~~

6. (We) turned ~~into the left lane~~ and ~~stopped~~ ~~at the next light.~~

7. ~~From the other side~~ (we) watched.

8. (Fred) walked ~~around the tent~~ and ~~into the woods.~~

9. (We) waited ~~in the lobby~~ ~~for Nick and Steffie,~~ ~~but they were already in their seats.~~

10. ~~During the night,~~ (snow) drifted ~~against the door.~~

Action Verbs and Linking Verbs

Verbs tell us who did what action in a sentence. However, what about a verb like *is*? What action does *is* describe? In fact it describes no action because *is* is a linking verb.

Indeed, there are two main kinds of verbs: action verbs and linking verbs. **Action verbs** describe an action. They tell us that the subject did a particular something. Here are examples:

Jack **answered** the question.

The dog **chewed** the bone.

Jerry **served** the drinks.

A **linking verb** connects the subject to other words that say something about it. Here are some examples:

My family **is** poor.

Grandpa **looks** happy.

The cheese **smells** bad.

The linking verb *is* connects the subject *family* to the word *poor,* which is the family's condition. Likewise, *Grandpa* is linked to *happy* by the linking verb *looks,* and *cheese* to the word *bad* by the linking verb *smells.* Linking verbs are said to be *linking* because they *link* the subject to other words that tell us something about the subject.

Some common linking verbs

am	sound
are	look
has been	appear
is	seem
was	taste
were	smell
feel	

PRACTICING 5

Circle the linking verb in each of the following sentences.

1. Addictions are dangerous.

2. Missy is a tiny parakeet.

3. Harry Pendergast was my dad's banker.

4. Her car looked old and battered.

5. Most people appear honest.

6. Does the apple pie taste delicious?

7. College freshmen often feel insecure.

8. The sky looks overcast.

9. Cheeseburgers are popular everywhere.

10. My cousin has been my best friend.

Helping Verbs

Verbs sometimes need additional words to express the past, present, and future. These additional words are called **helping verbs**. In the sentences below the **complete verb** is underlined.

The teachers <u>are meeting</u> at noon.   **(Present)**

The teachers <u>will meet</u> at noon.   **(Future)**

The teachers <u>had met</u> before noon.   **(Past)**

The teachers <u>were meeting</u> when   **(Past)**
the fire alarm rang.

The teachers <u>have been meeting</u>   **(Past)**
all week.

By tomorrow, the teachers   **(Future)**
<u>will have met</u>.

Here, for example, are some of the many forms of the verb *eat*. Notice the many different helping verbs.

Eats	should have been eating	would have eaten
ate	can eat	should have eaten
is eating	would have been eating	must have eaten
was eating	will be eating	having eaten
may eat	had been eating	did eat
should eat	have eaten	had eaten
will eat	has eaten	does eat
will have eaten		

Occasionally, words that are not part of the complete verb will come between the helping verb and the main verb. Here are some examples:

She has <u>definitely</u> registered.

Many students had <u>already</u> taken the course.

A flashlight would <u>certainly</u> help.

PRACTICING 6

Underline the complete verb in the following sentences.

1. She <u>will be going</u> to Emory University next year.

2. The seamstress <u>should have charged</u> more.

3. Marie <u>is sweeping</u> the porch right now.

4. We <u>will remember</u> her generosity.

5. As always, Mother was cooking enough for an army.

6. The renters should have signed their lease.

7. The horses were galloping toward the barn.

8. They could have waited for Heather.

9. He may be in his room.

10. They must have decided to get rid of the photos.

PRACTICING 7

Underline only the complete verb in the following sentences. Do not underline words that come between the helping verb and the main verb.

1. We must always tell the truth.

2. She has often driven Aunt Betty to the doctor.

3. The stock market should have quickly rallied.

4. Women cannot always accomplish the physical feats that men can.

5. The smart person will never repeat idle gossip.

6. They had really hoped she would leave the next day.

7. The groundhog could have quickly disappeared down the hole.

8. Jessica had trustingly answered the question.

9. The new coach has just arrived.

10. The souvenir shop will not return your money.

Verbals

Verbals are words that look like verbs, but do not act like verbs. Verbals are of three kinds: gerunds, participles, and infinitives. We'll look at each separately.

Gerunds

Gerunds are words that end in *-ing* and act as nouns. How can you tell if an *-ing* word is a gerund or a verb? Easy: Look for the helping verb. For an *-ing* word to be a verb, it must have a helping verb. Look at these sentences:

We were studying.   (*were* + *-ing* = verb)

Studying is hard.   (*Studying* = subject = gerund)

Apply the test for a subject by asking "Who?" or "What?" before the verb. What *is hard? Studying*. In other words, *studying* = subject = gerund.

> **PRACTICING 8**

Write *V* when the *-ing* word is used as a verb, and circle the helping verb. Write *G* when the *-ing* word is used as a gerund.

1. _____ We have been driving around the city.

2. _____ Both girls were licking an ice cream cone.

3. _____ Lending money to friends can cause disappointment.

4. _____ Jack is organizing his backpack.

5. _____ Getting all As would be terrific.

6. _____ He is losing his battle against staying thin.

7. _____ Walking is good exercise.

8. _____ Driving a car is a necessity in the United States.

9. _____ He has been bothering his girlfriend.

10. _____ Avoiding work is no solution.

Participles

Participles are words that look like verbs but act like adjectives, meaning that they describe. Present participles end in *-ing*. Past participles end in *-ed*. Here are some examples:

Ginny is marrying Jack.	(*is marrying* is a verb telling what Ginny is doing)
Henry is a marrying man.	(*marrying* is a present participle describing the man Henry)
We chopped the onions.	(*chopped* is a verb telling what we did to the onions)
The chopped onions will add flavor.	(*chopped* is a past participle describing the onions)

PRACTICING 9

Underline the participle in each of the following sentences.

1. The banging shutter woke us up.

2. Running water damaged our roof.

3. The sandwich tasted like a piece of soaked cardboard.

4. Why are detergents always "new and improved"?

5. Several bored teenagers hung around the music store.

6. Liz had difficulty combing her tangled hair.

7. I was frightened out of my wits.

8. Tell everyone to get out of the blistering heat.

9. Have you received your marching orders yet?

10. The right front fender is dented.

Infinitives

Infinitives consist of *to* plus a verb. Infinitives *never* act as verbs. They always serve some other function. Study these examples:

Suzy preferred to suffer alone.   (*to suffer* **tells what Suzy preferred. The verb is** *preferred.***)

He wanted a place to study.   (*to study* **tells what kind of place; the verb is** *wanted***)

She vowed to get their respect.   (*to get* **tells why she vowed; the verb is** *vowed***)

Be careful not to confuse an infinitive with the preposition *to* followed by a noun or a pronoun.

Infinitive: Jennifer decided to skip the party.
Preposition: Jennifer went to the party.

PRACTICING 10

Underline only the infinitives in the following sentences. Do not underline if *to* is a preposition.

1. How do you plan to win?

2. I plan to offer the job to Jim.

3. Don't forget to visit your elderly aunt.

4. We prefer to walk in the garden.

5. Many students try to cram for tests.

6. He hesitates to drive at night.

7. I ran to see what had happened to her.

8. They did not want to risk their reputations for him.

9. Just cut some string and bring it to me.

10. Peter's pulse began to quicken.

PRACTICING 11

Underline the verb and circle the infinitive in the following sentences.

Example: The wind <u>began</u> (to blow.)

1. We are expecting to settle in Kentucky.

2. All the mothers preferred to stay with their children.

3. Her brother likes to tease her.

4. All of us would like to speak fluent English.

5. Try to keep all the tickets in one envelope.

6. He will certainly have to apologize.

7. To be happy is not my main goal in life.

8. He insisted on his right to leave the country.

9. I plan to cook dinner on Monday.

10. Bullets, real and psychological, aim to kill.

Compound Subjects and Verbs

A sentence with more than one subject is said to have a **compound subject**. Here are some examples:

Mary and Madeline shopped.

The woman and her dog ran.

My roommate and I argued.

A sentence may also have more than one verb—called a **compound verb**. Here are some examples:

Mary walked and shopped.

The woman waved and yelled.

My roommate huffed and puffed.

Compound subjects and verbs may occur in the same sentence:

Mary, Helen, and Isa walked and shopped.

The woman and her friend waved and yelled.

My roommate and I argued, made up, and laughed.

PRACTICING 12

Underline the compound subjects in the following sentences.

1. My boss and his daughter came to my birthday party.

2. Politeness and civility seem to be characteristics of the past.

3. Spaghetti, a green salad, and fresh bread are my favorite meal.

4. A fool and his money are soon parted.

5. Museums, churches, and castles invite tourists to visit them.

6. Bears, wolves, foxes, and other wild animals should be protected.

7. Newspapers and magazines are great to read on the airplane.

8. Looks plus talent are a good combination.

9. Love and marriage go together like a horse and carriage.

10. Action and freedom are an important part of U.S. history.

PRACTICING 13

Underline the compound verbs in the following sentences.

1. The crook staggered and disappeared.

2. Expensive gifts often displease and embarrass.

3. The French king captured the throne and governed the people.

4. She arched her brows and smiled.

5. We stood in line and talked.

6. Shawna made breakfast and walked the dog.

7. Michael jumped from the car and ran into the house.

8. The vine climbed and curled along the fence.

9. She delicately peeled and ate the orange.

10. Ronnie slept and snored all night.

UNIT TALK WRITE ASSIGNMENT

Listen to this informal conversation between two friends who confide their fears in one another. From this dialogue, develop an essay of at least three body paragraphs defining courage. You may use examples from your own life and memory or from the dialogue between Ted and Bob. After you have completed and edited your essay, underline several examples of verbal forms that you have used (gerunds, participles, and infinitives).

Spoken Dialogue

Ted: Yesterday I had a real scary experience.

Bob: Oh, yeah? What happened?

Ted: I was flying home from San Francisco, and the plane got into some heavy turbulence. It scared the daylights out of me.

Bob: Yeah, I know what you mean. I don't like to fly, either.

Ted: You ever notice how some things scare some people and other things don't? The woman in the seat beside me, for instance, slept through the whole thing. She was even snoring. I couldn't believe it.

Bob: Yeah, like my dentist was telling me the other day, he's got a patient who falls asleep in the chair every time. Can you believe that? Sleeping in a dentist's chair? I could never do that.

Ted: Me, neither. Dentists scare the heck out of me.

Bob: Me? I can't stand tight places. When I broke my wrist last year, I had to have an MRI. I panicked in the tube. I thought I would pass out. It felt like I was in a coffin. Yet the technician was telling me that some people find the experience quite relaxing.

Ted: I'm afraid of running water. I can dive and swim in a lake or in the ocean without any problems. But put me in a river, and I freak.

Bob: Yeah? I'm okay in a river or in the ocean or in a lake. Just don't take me into the deep woods. I'm likely to go bananas.

Ted: I wonder why? I'm not afraid of woods. Just of running water.

Bob: Not me. I think I could go over Niagara Falls if I had to.

Ted: Must be something to do with our early childhood experiences.

Bob: I guess.

Ted: Kinda makes you wonder, doesn't it? Like, I mean, what's courage anyway?

Bob: Yeah? Like, for instance, me getting into a river, which is a thing I'm not afraid of, doesn't take any courage. But climbing into an MRI tube, now that's a whole different story.

Ted: That would be a piece of cake for me. I'd probably fall asleep in there. But put me on a riverbank, and I begin to shake like a leaf.

Bob: Shoot! That's not scary. That doesn't take any courage.

Ted: It does, for me. Like, going into the deep woods, for me anyway, doesn't take any courage. I've never had an MRI, but I'm not afraid of tight places, and I'm sure one wouldn't bother me in the least. None of that takes courage for me. But if you ever see me standing in a river, when I get out give me a medal, cause that took guts.

Bob: So maybe courage is, like, not rescuing someone from a burning building but, like, I mean, doing what you're afraid of—facing up to your fears.

Ted: That's deep, man. So maybe the soldier who charges a machine gun nest and blows away the enemy, is only doing it because he's not afraid of it. Him doing that is like you going over Niagara Falls.

Bob: Yeah. Or like you getting an MRI.

Ted: Who knows. This is too deep, and I gotta get to class. See you later, Buddy.

Bob: Hang in there.

Written Paragraph

_____

_____

_____

_____

_____

_____

_____

_____

_____

_____

_____

_____

_____

_____

_____

_____

_____

UNIT TEST

In the following paragraph, underline all subjects once and verbs (including helping verbs) twice. Circle the gerunds, participles, and infinitives.

I love to visit Lucinda's *Bonjour Café.* Everyone should have a private oasis of that kind—a warm, comforting place. *Bonjour Café* is not an elegant restaurant like restaurants uptown with thick carpets, damask drapes, and someone to check your overcoat. It is just a cozy, clean little shop with a display cabinet full of fresh pastries and a coffee machine for making great capuccino. The motley clientele includes all kinds of old people from the retirement home across the street, small business owners renting in the neighboring mall, and people simply wanting to interrupt their day with a fresh, home made lunch. Lucinda owns and operates the shop. She is the reason it attracts such a faithful clientele. Lucinda's warm hospitality and her French effervescence are a strong magnet. She goes out of her way to be kind to those frail oldsters limping in on walkers, and she never forgets to ask people about the good or bad events in their lives. My closest friends and I love to meet at *Bonjour* for lunch or for an afternoon snack. Lucinda will be there to welcome us like long lost members of her family.

UNIT TALKING ASSIGNMENT

Choose a partner to whom you ask the questions below and who must write down an answer in a complete sentence. Exchange roles and have your partner ask you the same questions to which you write your answers in complete sentences. Exchange papers. Circle the subject and underline the verb in your partner's paper, while your partner does the same to yours. Do you agree on all the subjects and verbs? In case of disagreement, ask your instructor.

1. Where would you like to spend your next vacation?
2. Why have you chosen this destination?
3. Whom would you choose as a companion?

4. What characteristics make him or her a good companion?
5. How would you describe the place?
6. How expensive or inexpensive is it?
7. What activities would you pursue?
8. How long would you stay?
9. How would this place enrich you?
10. How would you sum up your attitude toward this place?

UNIT WRITING ASSIGNMENT

Use the sentences you wrote in the Unit Talking Assignment to write about your ideal vacation spot. You may wish to add some additional sentences.

PHOTO WRITING ASSIGNMENT

Write an essay imagining what you would do if your neighborhood were being evacuated because of a hurricane or tornado. What thoughts would be uppermost in your mind? What possessions would you take with you? Who might be with you? Where would you seek shelter? After you have completed the assignment, including revising and editing, go back over the essay and underline all participles once, gerunds twice, and infinitives three times.

Building Sentences

Every sentence must have a subject and a verb: To this rule, there is no exception. Not every construction with a subject and verb, however, is a sentence. It could be a *dependent clause*.

Dependent and Independent Clauses

A **clause** is a group of words with both a subject and a verb. If a clause makes sense on its own and is a complete sentence, it is called an **independent clause**. The following are independent clauses and, therefore, complete sentences:

> He cleaned his glasses.
>
> They took the bus home.
>
> We are saving money for a vacation.

What about the following?

> When he cleaned his glasses
>
> If you take the bus
>
> By saving money for a vacation

Each of the above clauses has a subject *(he, you, who)* and a verb *(cleaned, count, are saving),* but none makes complete sense. These are **dependent clauses**—a group of words with a subject and verb that must be connected to an independent clause to make sense.

> John could see the crack—when he cleaned his glasses.
>
> If you take the bus, get off at Maple Street.
>
> By saving money for a vacation now, you won't go into debt.

Your ear for language is the best judge of whether a clause makes sense or not and is therefore independent or dependent. Many dependent clauses begin with a telltale sign—one of these words:

who   which

whom   that

whose

These words are called ==**relative pronouns**==. They get that name because they show how a dependent clause is *related* to a main clause. A dependent clause may also begin with one of these words, called ==**subordinating conjunctions**==: ◀

after	if	so that	whenever
although	in order that	than	where
as if	now that	that	wherever
because	once	though	whether
before	provided that	unless	while
even if	rather than	until	why
even though	since	when	

all of these words

Typically, it is these linking words that make a clause dependent. In fact removing the subordinate conjunction changes a dependent clause into an independent one. Here are some examples:

Dependent: Until you forgave him.

Independent: You forgave him.

Dependent: Because you served on the jury.

Independent: You served on the jury.

PRACTICING 1

In the blanks provided, write *D* if the clause is dependent and *I* if the clause is independent.

1. __D__ Who spoke with a high, nasal voice.

2. __I__ He imagined himself walking down the street.

3. __I__ The cover was torn and dirty.

4. __D__ Although no one spoke.

5. __D__ Rather than covering up the mistake.

6. __I__ They stood there with their hats on.

7. __D__ Since it is such a beautiful day.

8. __D__ That she decided to become a nun.

9. __D__ If war could have solved the problem.

10. __I__ The temptation is to rush.

PRACTICING 2

In each blank, write an independent clause to complete the sentence.

1. _That is the girl_____ , who won first prize.

2. If you agree, _you will come with me_____ .

3. _Over in that room is_, where I collapsed from fatigue.

4. Now that he's graduated, _he is going to college_ .

5. _I fell_____ while watering the lawn.

6. Before you give him the gift, _make his guess what it's_

7. I'll try to finish the story while _you get ready._ .

8. _He makes me mad_ whenever he opens his mouth.

9. Let's ask him whether _he is going or not_____ .

10. We finally found a piece of land where _we can build a house._

Three Basic Sentence Types

There are three basic sentence types: simple, compound, and complex. All three sentence types are commonly used in writing and talking. We will discuss each separately.

The simple sentence

A **simple sentence** consists of a single independent clause. First graders routinely write simple sentences such as these:

I like Billy.

Peggy is mean.

I like green beans.

But the simple sentence, in spite of its name, is not always short, crisp, and childlike. It can be expanded if given more than one subject or verb. Here are some examples:

Simple sentence with plural subject:	The hens and chicks scratched for bugs.
Simple sentence with one subject and three verbs:	Too many people speak without thinking, read without understanding, and work without goals.

Another way to expand the simple sentence is to add **modifiers,** words that describe and explain the subject or verb. Here are some examples:

Simple sentence:	The chicken scratched for bugs.
First expansion:	The chicken, a big, beautiful Rhode Island Red, scratched for bugs.
Second expansion:	The chicken, a big, beautiful Rhode Island Red, scratched for bugs in the dusty barnyard.

PRACTICING 3

Expand the simple sentences below by adding subjects, verbs, or modifiers.

1. The bed is old.

The big bed is old
The bed is big an and falling apart.

2. The wife took the stand.

The old mans wife took the stand & testified

3. The old man sat on the bench.

The old man sat on the bench and fed the birds

4. A book can be a good friend.

A good book can be a good friend to someone like you

5. My cousin throws money away.

My cousin throws money away like he will never run out

6. Foolish friends are a burden.

Friends are a burden when they act foolish

7. To face reality is sometimes difficult.

To Face reality is sometimes difficult when you don't want to.

8. The two cars crashed.

The two cars that crashed where my friends

9. My aunt tells wonderful stories.

My aunt tells wonderful stories about you.

10. All the foods I like are fattening.

All the foods I like to eat are fattening

The compound sentence

A **compound sentence** consists of two or more simple sentences joined by a coordinating conjunction. There are seven **coordinating conjunctions**: *and, but, for, or, nor, so,* and *yet.* A comma is placed immediately before the conjunction. The simple sentences in a compound sentence should express ideas of equal importance. Here are some examples:

Simple: Comic strips entertain. Sermons inspire.

Compound: Comic strips entertain, and sermons inspire.

Simple: Jason must get some sleep. He will get sick.

Compound: Jason must get some sleep, or he will get sick.

Simple: He was athletic. He didn't practice. He lost the match.

Compound: He was athletic, but he didn't practice, so he lost the match.

Notice that a comma comes immediately before the coordinating conjunction that joins the sentences.

PRACTICING 4

Use a coordinating conjunction to join each pair of simple sentences into a compound sentence. Don't forget the comma.

1. The dog fetched the bone. Those watching enjoyed the sight.

   The dog fetched the bone, for those watching enjoyed the sight.

2. I telephoned my grandmother. I congratulated her on her 75th birthday.

   I telephoned my grandmother, and I congratulated her on her 75th birthday.

3. I have dieted for one month. I have not lost any weight.

   I have dieted for one month, but I haven't lost any weight

4. The doctor made a house call. He had forgotten his medical bag.

   The doctor made a house call, but he had forgotten his medical bag.

5. John will straighten out the living room. It will look good for company.

Jon will straighten out the living room, and it will look good for company.

6. Give me a big hug. I need to feel loved.

Give me a big hug, for I need to feel loved.

7. The moon is bright and golden. We should go for a walk.

The moon is bright and golden, so we should go for a walk.

8. I have studied all day. I still don't feel ready for the test.

I have studied all day, yet I still don't feel ready for the test.

9. Everyone has left. The room is empty.

Everyone has left, so the room is empty.

10. I drank some strong coffee. Now I can't sleep.

I drank some strong coffee and now I can't sleep.

The complex sentence

The **complex sentence** consists of one independent clause joined to one or more dependent clauses. Unlike the compound sentence, which connects two equal ideas, the complex sentence emphasizes one idea over the other. The less important idea is said to be *subordinate*. Naturally, the more important idea is expressed in the independent clause:

> Alica's heart is broken because her sweetheart left.

Alicia's broken heart is the main idea; the less important idea is why it is broken—because her sweetheart left.

Common sense and your ear for language will help you decide which of two ideas is more important and therefore belongs in the independent clause. Here are, for example, two sentences:

> I hung out the American flag. I went to the post office.

If you want to emphasize *going to the post office*, you will put it in the independent clause:

> After hanging out the American flag, I went to the post office.

If you want to emphasize *hanging the American flag*, you will put it in the independent clause:

> Before I went to the post office, I hung out the American flag.

Bear in mind the words that signal a dependent cause. You may wish to review the relative pronouns on page 301 and subordinating conjunctions on page 302 before you do the exercises.

PRACTICING 5

Join the following sentences into complex sentences using a relative pronoun or subordinating conjunction. Be sure to express the most important idea in the independent clause.

1. I congratulated Henry. He was pleased.

_____

_____

2. We are at a crossroads. We shall succeed or fail.

_____

3. I bought a Chevrolet. It has more room than a Honda.

_____

_____

4. We need a curfew on our street. The noise pollution is terrible.

~~We need a curfew on our street, because so~~

~~the noise pollution is terrible~~

5. She acts very mature. She is the youngest.

~~She acts very mature, for one to~~

~~the youngest,~~

6. Anger causes suffering. Indifference is even worse. He put down the heavy box. He rang the doorbell.

~~Anger causes suffering and Indifference~~

_____

7. Skydiving is exciting. It is extremely dangerous.

_____

_____

8. Children often feel responsible for their parents' divorce. They suffer guilt.

_____

_____

9. Moving away can be difficult. It often means losing old friends.

_____

_____

10. I love suspense movies. They keep me awake at night.

_____

_____

PRACTICING 6

Write a series of sentences on one of your favorite activities—something you really enjoy. Each sentence should be of the specific type listed below.

1. Simple sentence with more than one subject:

_____

2. Simple sentence with more than one verb:

_____

3. Simple sentence with modifiers:

_____

4. Two compound sentences:

   a. _____

   _____

   b. _____

   _____

5. Three complex sentences:

   a. _____

   _____

b. _____

_____

c. _____

_____

PRACTICING 7

Exchange papers with a classmate and discuss the sentences you wrote in Practicing 6. Help each other make any necessary corrections.

Sentence Variety

Writers seldom write in only one sentence type for the same reason that good cooks season their food with more than just salt. Any sentence pattern that is overused will quickly seem boring. Variety is the key to a good writing style and can be achieved easily if you use a mix of simple, compound, and complex sentences. The following is a ho-hum passage:

> Rap music started during the 1970s. It comes from African chanting. It also comes from chatting. Rap music means "chat music." It contains. . . .

This passage consists of a string of simple sentences. Notice how it is immediately improved when the sentences are varied:

> Rap music, which started during the 1970s, comes from African chanting. It also comes from chatting. Rap music means "chat music," and it contains. . . .

This sort of sentence variation is exactly what you instinctively do in your everyday talking. It is what you must also try to do in your writing.

PRACTICING 8

Rewrite the following paragraph to eliminate the choppy effect of too many simple sentences. Read the sentences aloud to determine the relationship between them. Then reduce the number of simple sentences by combining some into compound and complex sentences.

Hairdressers often function as therapists for their clients. They listen to all kinds of personal confessions. I have my hair cut once a month. I am always surprised by what I overhear. Once I heard a women literally broadcast her husband's affair. She told the entire salon. She was speaking above the noise of the blow drier. She was not aware of how loud she was. I have pondered why such intimacy exists between hair dressers and clients. For one thing, hair dressers are service oriented. They are kind to their clients. Also, hair dressers do not belong to most clients' normal social groups. Hairdressers can be objective. They can be uninvolved listeners. Many hair dressers understand human nature. They offer good advice. They offer practical advice. They can help with personal problems.

UNIT TALK WRITE ASSIGNMENT

When we talk, most of us pay little conscious attention to sentence variety. But the more sophisticated we become in language, the more we are likely to naturally vary our sentences. The following spoken comments—about keeping a neighborhood looking attractive—lack sentence variety. In the space provided, rewrite the passage to add sentence variety by using coordinating or subordinating clauses. Be sure to use Standard English.

Spoken Paragraph

I don't believe in neighborhood yard police. Every hedge doesn't have to be clipped like every other hedge on the street. Home owners create a home that reflects their taste. But, gee whiz, some yards look trashy. Some yards look like second-hand car lots. One guy up the street keeps a truck on his front lawn. He keeps two motorcycles. He keeps all kinds of weird looking motors. He lets his grass grow tall. He lets his grass get dry. He lets it get brown. I believe in individual freedom. His yard goes too far. Here are some rules I would suggest. They are general. They are easy. Keep all vehicles inside the garage. Keep the garage door down. Trim hedges weekly. Mow the lawn weekly. Water the lawn when the weather is hot. Get rid of all weeds. Get rid of dry tree limbs. If you have children, keep their toys inside when they aren't using them. Keep their bicycles inside when they aren't using them. Mend broken fences. Paint fences when necessary. A peeling fence is super ugly. A fence with broken slats is super ugly. Follow these simple rules. They will make a big difference. People should keep up their own property. Then the combined properties will make a pretty neighborhood. The neighborhood won't look like a shanty town.

Written Paragraph

_____

_____

_____

_____

_____

_____

_____

_____

_____

_____

_____

UNIT TEST

1. Write a simple sentence with modifiers about the clothing you are wearing today.

   _____

2. Write a complex sentence beginning with *Although*. Be sure to place a comma following the dependent clause.

   _____

   _____

3. In the spaces provided tell whether the sentence is simple (*S*), compound (*C*), or complex (*X*).

   a. _____ Before we arrive home, let's count the money.

   b. _____ Think hard, and you will find the answer.

   c. _____ This pottery, which is made by Hopi Indians, is expensive.

   d. _____ When I receive your letter, I'll answer it.

   e. _____ This is a dull, gray morning, but the sun is peeking through the clouds.

4. In the paragraph below, underline all **independent** clauses.

Parents must preach what they practice. They must not preach morality that they themselves ignore. For instance, Peggy's parents constantly tell her to be more frugal and to quit buying clothes that sit unused in her closet. I find that rather ironic since Peggy's mother wears a different outfit every day and buys only from Neiman Marcus, Saks Fifth Avenue, or some other expensive store. How can Peggy absorb the message of frugality from a spendthrift mother? Then there are my friend Ray's parents. Because they want him to become a lawyer, they criticize him if he ever gets a C. They don't let him go out more than once on a weekend. "You won't get into law school," they say. But I never see Ray's parents without a glass of beer or Scotch in their hands. They drink all the time. Now what kind of hypocrisy have we here? We have parents who preach a gospel of hard work and deprivation while they party. One basic principle of child rearing is this: Parents must preach only those moral principles that they themselves observe.

5. Rewrite the following paragraph to eliminate the choppy effect of too many simple sentences.

Train watching is an old tradition. It is an American tradition. We do not use trains the way people do in Europe. In Europe people regularly use trains for transportation. They travel from city to city by hopping on a train. But here in the United States, trains are relatively rare. Perhaps that is why people love to watch trains. Retired men especially love to watch trains. They love to watch trains arrive. They love to watch trains depart. My home town is Glendale, California. My home town has a strong tradition of train watching. Every morning a group of men gathers at the Metrolink Station. They gather soon after dawn. These men have little in common. What they do have in common is their love for trains. To them watching trains is wonderful entertainment. Watching trains is cheap, too. They watch freight trains. They watch passenger trains. Every train has its special attraction. When it rains, these men sit in their cars. They watch from the driver's seat. That isn't as much fun. They would rather stand at the rail. They would rather talk about the trains. They would rather talk about the trains' exotic destinations. The men have a nice camaraderie. There is another perk to being a train watcher. The train engineer gives an extra toot on the whistle as a train passes. He acknowledges this special band of spectators.

UNIT TALKING ASSIGNMENT

Get together with two or three classmates to talk about what really bugs you (for example, your boss at work, drivers who don't signal a turn, a roommate who is sloppy, textbooks that are utterly boring). When one student is speaking, the others should write down some of the sentences. When everyone has discussed his or her "bug," take turns presenting and classifying the written sentences as simple, compound, or complex.

UNIT WRITING ASSIGNMENT

Using the ideas you accumulated during the Unit Talking Assignment above, write about some specific aspect of your life or society that annoys you. Make a special effort to use sentence variety.

PHOTO WRITING ASSIGNMENT

Write an essay discussing the advantages or disadvantages of being an identical twin. To support your view, use your imagination to describe situations in which twins might be involved. You may want to add some humor to your essay. After you have completed the assignment, including revising and editing with a view toward sentence variety, find one example of each type of sentence—simple, compound, and complex. Write and label each sentence at the bottom of your paper.

The 20 Most Common Sentence Errors

(continued)

This part of *Writing Talk* deals with sentence errors that we all make occasionally. The errors are not arranged in any particular order, and run the range from fragments to misspellings. If you find yourself routinely making any of these errors, review the appropriate material and work the exercises.

Sentence Fragments

A **sentence fragment** is only part of a sentence. It is a "wannabe" sentence that lacks either subject, verb, or sense. Sometimes the omission occurs because the writer is "on a roll" and flying across the page. It's fine to write fast and get all your thoughts down in a hurry, but then you must always proofread for errors.

Here are some examples of fragments:

Lost his wallet.   **(Missing subject)**

Mary's job.   **(Missing verb)**

Despite his charm.   **(Missing sense)**

A fragment can spring from one of several causes. If you learn to recognize these, you will be able to avoid fragments in your own writing.

Fragments Caused by a Missing Subject

When you include the verb but forget to write the subject, the result will be a fragment. Here are some examples:

Lenny made a date with Fern. Then never showed up.

After the party they had double milk shakes. Also apple pie.

In these examples the writer mistakenly thought that the subject of the first sentence also applied to the second group of words. It does—but the second thought must be formally joined to the first by a conjunction such as *and* or *but*. If you forget the conjunction, you must write the two thoughts as separate, complete sentences.

Lenny made a date with Fern, but he never showed up.

or

Lenny made a date with Fern. Then he never showed up.

After the party they had double milk shakes and apple pie.

or

After the party they had double milk shakes. They also had apple pie.

317

PRACTICING 1

Correct the following fragments caused by a missing subject. You can either join the fragment to the sentence before or rewrite it as a separate sentence.

1. The children were excited. And ran into the gym.

The children were excited as they ran into the gym

2. Murphy found out that he was adopted. Then searched for his biological mother.

After Murphy found out he was adopted, he searched for his biological mother.

3. Grandma put on the rented ice skates. Stood up and let go of the railing. And started to skate as if she were still a teenager.

Grandma put on the rented ice skates. She stood up & let go of the railing, and she started to skate as if she were still a teenager.

4. He locked the door. Or at least thought he did.

He locked the door, or at least he thought he locked it.

5. The courtship was passionate. But burned out in two months.

I thought the courtship was passionate, but it was burned out in two months.

Fragments Due to -ing Words

Some fragments are triggered by an *-ing* word such as, say, *puffing*. Here are some examples:

He sat there with contentment. Puffing on his cigar.

I remained at my desk. Playing with some yellow silly putty.

Why beginning with an *-ing* word often leads to a fragment is something of a puzzle. Possibly, the writer mistakes the *-ing* word for a full verb, but it isn't.

To correct a fragment due to an *-ing* word, either join it to the sentence that went before (use a comma to set off the first part of the sentence), or rewrite it as a separate sentence:

He sat there with contentment, puffing on his cigar.

I remained at my desk, playing with some yellow silly putty.

or

He sat there with contentment. He puffed on a cigar.

I remained at my desk. I played with some yellow silly putty.

PRACTICING 2

Correct the *-ing* fragments by rewriting the sentences below.

1. The lions slept in the sun. Sn~~oring~~ contentedly.

Snored.

2. Max and I stood at the bus stop. ~~Waiting~~ for my Uncle Joe.

To wait

3. Dad loves soy sauce. ~~Pouring~~ it on everything.

He pours

4. Judy loves to create romance. ~~Using~~ candlelight for every dinner she cooks.

She uses.

5. I am a registered Democrat. ~~Voting~~ often, however, for Republican legislation.

I vote

Fragments Due to "To" Clauses

A third common type of fragment is triggered by *to* clauses. Two examples follow:

We are trying to save money. To pay our bills.

Melany read the newspaper. To see if the Trojans had won the game.

As before, you can correct this type of fragment by either joining it to the sentence before or rewriting it as a separate and complete sentence:

We are trying to save money to pay our bills.

or

We are trying to save money. We want to pay our bills.

Melany read the newspaper to see if the Trojans had won the game.

or

Melany read the newspaper. She wanted to see if the Trojans had won the game.

Note that you could also move the *to* clause to the beginning of the combined sentence. If you do this, put a comma after the *to* clause.

To pay our bills, we are trying to save money.

To see if the Trojans had won the game, Melany read the newspaper.

PRACTICING 3

Correct the following *to* fragments by either joining them to the sentences before or rewriting them as separate sentences.

1. The students went on a trail hike. To clean up the environment.

   _____ ,to _____

   _____

2. The hog was created as a scavenger. To clean the earth.

   _____ we _____

   _____

3. He wanted desperately to persuade her. To quit calling him "Snooky."

   _____ She _____

   _____

4. She stood outside the office waiting for enough nerve. To speak to her professor.

   _____ , to _____

   _____

5. Try to get some spirit and loyalty. ~~To cheer~~ the team on.

_____ Cheer ____

_____

_____

Fragments Due to Dependent Words

You have learned about fragments caused by omitted subjects, *-ing* words, and *to* clauses. You have also learned two main ways of correcting fragments—by joining the fragment to the sentence before or by rewriting the fragment as a separate sentence.

We come now to a fourth kind of fragment. This one is triggered by misused relative pronouns and subordinate conjunctions. *This fourth type of fragment is corrected in only one way: by joining it to the sentence before.* Here is a list of relative pronouns that can cause fragments:

who

whom

whose

which

that

Here are examples of fragments caused by unconnected relative pronouns:

We looked at the flat tire. <u>Which</u> was beyond repair.

We have a week to pay our landlord, Mrs. Smith. <u>Who</u> has been most patient.

Here are the corrections:

We looked at the flat tire, which was beyond repair.

We have a week to pay our landlord, Mrs. Smith, who has been most patient.

As you can see, both fragments were corrected by joining them to the sentence before. Indeed, both were caused by the writer's use of a period instead of a comma.

Similarly, a fragment can be caused by the misuse of a subordinate conjunction. As with relative pronouns, this type of fragment can only be corrected in one way—by joining it to the sentence before. Here is a list of subordinate conjunctions:

after	although	as if
because	before	even if
even though	if	in order that
now that	once	provided that
rather than	since	so that

(cont.)

than	that	though
unless	until	when
whenever	where	wherever
whether	while	why

Here are some examples of fragments caused by unconnected subordinate conjunctions:

<u>Although</u> his desk is messy. He runs a well-organized program.

<u>Wherever</u> he lives and works. Discord breaks out.

To correct such fragments, simply join them to the neighboring sentence:

Although his desk is messy, he runs a well-organized program.

Wherever he lives and works, discord breaks out.

Note that if the dependent clause comes first, it is separated from the independent clause by a comma:

Incorrect: Since it was raining. We brought along our umbrellas.
Correct: Since it was raining, we brought along our umbrellas.
Or: We brought along our umbrellas since it was raining.

PRACTICING 4

Rewrite the following fragments by joining them to a neighboring sentence.

1. Even though the old roof is leaking, We are not getting a new one.

   We are not getting a new roof, even though the old one is leaking.

2. She bought a new watchband, Which looks very expensive.

   Her new watch band looks very expensive.

3. Ask him about his family. If you see pictures of children on his desk.

   If you see pictures of children on his desk, ask him about his family.

4. Find out more about his background. Before you hire him.

   Before you hire him, find out about his background.

5. Purchase one good outfit each season, Rather than a dozen cheap ones.

Purchase one good outfit each season, rather than a dozen cheap ones.

Fragments Due to Added Details

Details added to a sentence can also cause a fragment. Beware of the words listed below. They often lead to added-detail fragments.

especially	including
except	not even
particularly	such as
in addition	for example

Here are three examples of fragments caused by added details:

No one knew exactly what they were feeling. Not even the boss.

They won several prizes. Including a trip to Hawaii, a new car, and a refrigerator.

Abraham Lincoln saw violence as the supreme threat to America. Particularly war.

To correct a fragment caused by added details, simply attach the details to the previous sentence, adding any words necessary. Use a comma to set off the added details.

No one knew exactly what they were feeling, not even the boss.

They won several prizes, including a trip to Hawaii, a new car, and a refrigerator.

Abraham Lincoln saw violence as the supreme threat to America, particularly war.

If the additional detail fragment is long, you can make it into a separate sentence:

Fragment: Fred tends to antagonize people because he acts like a real jerk. For example, never being on time, talking only about himself, interrupting others, and talking with his mouth full.

Corrected: Fred tends to antagonize people because he acts like a real jerk. For example, he's never on time, talks only about himself, interrupts others, and talks with his mouth full.

PRACTICING 5

Correct the following fragments caused by added details by joining them to the sentence before.

1. Rick is so paranoid he's put three locks on his door. In addition to installing a security system.

   _____

   _____

2. She can't stand to be touched. Except by her own sister.

   _____

   _____

3. I suffer from allergies all year round. Ragweed, treemold, and dust.

   _____

   _____

4. We gave her some excellent suggestions for staying out of debt. Including creating a budget.

   _____

   _____

5. A major problem of our industrialized world is job boredom. Such as the boredom of factory assembly jobs.

   _____

   _____

UNIT TEST

The following paragraph contains fragments. Correct each error by one of the methods you have learned.

I often wonder how old people manage to stay happy, Especially, when their health fails. One afternoon, I expressed this wonderment to my 85-year-old great grandmother, Because, I felt it was important to find an answer. She was in her wheelchair, Having suffered a broken hip last year. I sat in a chair next to her, Thinking about how frail she had gotten. Though I didn't really know exactly what words to use, I finally took courage and asked, "Grandma, how do you handle being confined to a wheelchair? When you were always so active?" She thought for an instant, then she said, "Getting old is not for sissies, Not even for people who are not sissies, Especially if you have lost your health and mobility. But, as long as I have my mind, I can enjoy something every day, For instance, your visit right now, It's such fun to hear about your college life. Particularly the classes you are taking and the friends you are making." What she was really telling me was that people have, to make the best of their situation, Which is true at any age, Not just when you're old. I felt inspired by her attitude.

Run-on Sentences

A **run-on sentence** is actually two sentences written as one. There are two main types of run-on sentences: the fused sentence and the comma splice.

The **fused sentence** consists of two sentences joined—or fused— without any punctuation between them:

> We drove to Las Vegas it is an exciting city

Here is how the sentence should be written:

> We drove to Las Vegas. It is an exciting city.

The second type of run-on sentence is the **comma splice**—two full sentences separated by a comma instead of a period:

> We took a day trip to Hoover Dam, it's so impressive.

Here is the sentence, corrected:

> We took a day trip to Hoover Dam. It's so impressive.

PRACTICING 1

In the blanks provided write *FS* if the run-on sentence is fused and *CS* if it is spliced. Then correct the error.

1. _____ Stop talking to me I have no time for this.

_____

2. _____ You must be on time, he will be angry if you aren't.

_____

3. _____ Golf is a very hard game it is probably the hardest game of all.

_____

4. _____ It was a lovely evening, there wasn't a cloud in the sky.

_____

5. _____ Take the bus save gas money.

_____

Correcting Run-on Sentences

There are four ways to correct run-on sentences. Take, for example, this one:

> I'm in a good mood you are in a better mood.

To correct it, you can do one of the following:

- Put a period at the end of the first sentence:

   I'm in a good mood. You are in a better mood.

- Put a semicolon at the end of the first sentence:

   I'm in a good mood; you are in a better mood.

- Put a coordinating conjunction at the end of the first sentence (note that a comma goes before the conjunction):

   I'm in a good mood, but you are in a better mood.

- Use a subordinating conjunction (note that a comma is placed between the two clauses):

   I'm in a good mood, though you are in a better mood.

   or

   Though I'm in a good mood, you are in a better mood.

PRACTICING 2

Correct the following run-ons in all four possible ways.

1. He missed his plane he had to take a later flight.

Insert a period: _____

_____

Insert a semicolon: _____

_____

Insert a coordinating conjunction and comma: _____

_____

_____

Insert a subordinating conjunction and comma: _____

_____

_____

2. I like to play chess I'm no good at the game.

Insert a period: _____

_____

Insert a semicolon: _____

_____

Insert a coordinating conjunction and comma: _____

_____

_____

Insert a subordinating conjunction and comma: _____

_____

_____

3. I'll go to the bookstore we can drive your car.

Insert a period: _____

_____

Insert a semicolon: _____

_____

Insert a coordinating conjunction and comma: _____

_____

_____

Insert a subordinating conjunction and comma: _____

_____

_____

PRACTICING 3

Correct the following run-on sentences using one of the four possible ways.

1. Jennifer is a lucky person she should play the lottery.

_____

_____

2. The political season is upon us, there are daily ads on television for the candidates.

_____

_____

3. Worms are beneficial to the soil they are everywhere.

_____

_____

4. Shoplifting is not just a nuisance crime it is paid for by honest shoppers.

_____

_____

5. Speeding is a common traffic offense it is not as bad as reckless driving, though.

_____

_____

6. My landlord is very punctual he's always on time to collect the rent.

_____

_____

7. Don't sneeze on me, I don't want your cold.

_____

_____

8. I'm madly in love with my neighbor she doesn't even know I exist.

_____

_____

9. Men are vainer than women they just hide it better.

_____

_____

10. Many people read for pleasure, on the other hand, more people read for business.

_____

_____

UNIT TEST

The following long paragraph contains fused sentences and comma splices. Correct each error in any way you choose.

One summer I worked as a lifeguard at the local pool, I found the job surprisingly difficult. Chief among my difficulties was keeping the roughhousing kids in line, especially the teenagers, I found that frequently they would defy my authority. Since I was a teenager myself, it was a constant struggle to control them, I had to really put my foot down. One day an incident occurred that taught all of us a lesson. Some boys were horsing around in the deep end, dunking each other and splashing I told them to stop but they wouldn't listen they kept right on, churning up the water and disturbing other swimmers I yelled at them repeatedly. Finally, I said to myself, that's it, this has to stop and it has to stop right now. I got off my lifeguard stand and went down to the pool deck to really let them have it when I thought I saw the vague outline of a submerged swimmer. I screamed at the boys to stop their splashing they screamed right back at me. I dove in they started to splash me, too, but in spite of all the foam I swam to the bottom, found an unconscious swimmer, and brought him to the surface. While someone called the paramedics, I worked on the boy the other teenagers suddenly become very serious they stopped all the horsing around. By the time the paramedics arrived, I had pumped most of the water out of the victim's lungs he was conscious and talking. He said he had had a seizure because of all the splashing he had been unable to attract attention and get help. For the rest of the summer, those boys never gave me any more trouble I think they realized that they had almost caused someone to drown.

Lack of Subject-Verb Agreement

Subjects and verbs must agree in number: that is the one rule of subject-verb agreement. A singular subject always takes a singular verb; a plural subject always takes a plural verb. Most of the time, this rule is plain and easy to follow, as in the following sentences:

> Peggy admires Fred.

> The workers admire Fred.

Peggy, a singular subject, takes the singular verb *admires. Workers,* a plural subject, takes the plural verb *admire.*

We are also likely to come across sentences like these:

> Jack don't want company.

> There is pickles in the refrigerator.

He, a singular subject, is incorrectly paired with the plural verb *don't. Pickles,* a plural subject, is incorrectly paired with the singular verb *is.*

Subject-verb agreement errors are typically caused by some common words and grammatical situations. Here they are, in no particular order:

- *Don't, was,* and *wasn't:*

  Incorrect: He don't remember his promise.
  Correct: He doesn't remember his promise.

  Incorrect: You was right again.
  Correct: You were right again.

- *Each, every, either/or,* and *neither/nor:*

  Incorrect: Each of us are to blame for the mistake.
  Correct: Each of us is to blame for the mistake.

  Incorrect: Either of the shirts are the right size.
  Correct: Either of the shirts is the right size.

- Prepositional phrase between a subject and verb:

  Incorrect: One of the three television sets are broken.
  Correct: One of the three television sets is broken.

- Sentences beginning with *there/here*:

  Incorrect: There is too many potatoes to peel.
  Correct: There are too many potatoes to peel.

  Incorrect: Here is the best solutions to the problem.
  Correct: Here are the best solutions to the problem.

- Questions:

  Incorrect: Where is the warm blankets?
  Correct: Where are the warm blankets?

- Compound subjects joined by *and*, *or*, *either/or*, or *neither/nor*:

  Incorrect: The doctor and nurse was talking.
  Correct: The doctor and nurse were talking.

  Incorrect: The doctor or the nurse were upset.
  Correct: The doctor or the nurse was upset.

- The indefinite pronouns *each*, *everyone*, *anybody*, *somebody*, and *nobody*:

  Incorrect: Each of the passengers wish to get off here.
  Correct: Each of the passengers wishes to get off here.

- *Who*, *which*, and *that*:

  Incorrect: Larry is one of those people who gives cheap gifts.
  Correct: Larry is one of those people who give cheap gifts.

We'll take up these situations one by one.

Do, Don't, Was, and Wasn't

Subject-verb disagreements are often caused by the words *do* and *don't*, *was* and *wasn't*. Here are the correct forms of *to do*:

Singular	**Plural**
I do	We do
You do	You do
He, she, it does	They do

Here are examples of agreement errors made with *do* and *don't*:

Incorrect: She do her assignments on time.
Correct: She does her assignments on time.

Incorrect: He don't realize what time it is.
Correct: He doesn't realize what time it is.

Was and *wasn't* are also often involved in many subject-verb agreement errors. Here are the correct forms:

Singular	**Plural**
I was	We were
You were	You were
He, she, it was	They were

Here are some examples of errors commonly made with this verb:

Incorrect: You was in the kitchen.
Correct: You were in the kitchen.

Incorrect: They was eating taffy apples.
Correct: They were eating taffy apples.

PRACTICING 1

Underline the correct verb in parentheses.

1. They (was, were) sitting in the bleachers.

2. That answer (doesn't, don't) make sense.

3. (Wasn't, weren't) you already up by 6:30 this morning?

4. Donna, you (was, were) supposed to get dessert.

5. Matthew (doesn't, don't) always act on principle.

Each, Every, Either/Or, and Neither/Nor

The words *each*, *every*, *either*, and *neither* all take a singular verb. Here are some examples:

Each dog, cat, and owner was (not *were*) listed by name.

Every skirt and blouse is (not *are*) being ironed and folded.

Neither of the senators votes (not *vote*) for more college funds.

Either of the photos is (not *are*) flattering to her.

Don't be confused by the prepositional phrase—for example, *of the photos*—that usually follows *each*, *every*, *either*, or *neither*. Cross it out and the verb choice will be clear.

Either/or and *neither/nor* are also trouble-spots. Here are some examples:

Incorrect: Neither the pitcher nor the catcher were any good this season.

Correct: Neither the pitcher nor the catcher was any good this season.

Incorrect:	Neither the teacher nor the student were in the wrong.
Correct:	Neither the teacher nor the student was in the wrong.

If one subject joined by *either/or* or *neither/nor* is singular and one is plural, the verb should agree with the nearer subject.

Incorrect:	Either the coyotes or our dog bark all night.
Correct:	Either the coyotes or our dog barks all night.

Incorrect:	Either our dog or the coyotes barks all night.
Correct:	Either our dog or the coyotes bark all night.

PRACTICING 2

Underline the correct verb in parentheses in the following sentences.

1. Neither of the sandwiches (has, have) mayonnaise.

2. Each of the contestants (hold, holds) a little flag.

3. Every house on the block (is, are) blue.

4. Either the criminal or the victims (is, are) being interviewed now.

5. Neither the cherries nor the apricots (has been, have been) picked.

Phrases Between a Subject and Its Verb

A prepositional phrase that comes between a subject and verb can cause an agreement error. Here is a list of common prepositions:

about	beside	inside	to
above	besides	like	toward
across	between	near	under
after	beyond	of	underneath
against	by	off	until
along	despite	on	up
among	down	out	upon
around	during	outside	with
at	except	over	within
before	for	past	without
behind	from	since	
below	in	throughout	
beneath	into	through	

Here is a typical agreement error caused by a prepositional phrase coming between a subject and verb:

Only one of his many movies have won an Oscar.

The prepositional phrase *of his many movies* comes between the subject *one* and the verb *have*. However, the subject is still *one*, and *one* is always singular. Cross out the prepositional phrase and the subject is immediately clear:

Only one ~~of his many movies~~ has won an Oscar.

PRACTICING 3

Cross out all prepositional phrases in the sentences that follow. Circle the subject and underline the correct verb.

1. The bicycles leaning ~~against the ladder~~ (is, are) for sale.

2. The sheets ~~on the bed~~ (look, looks) like silk.

3. That box ~~of cans and bottles~~ (go, goes) to the recycling center.

4. ~~Out of season~~, a pound of cherries (costs, cost) more than $5.00.

5. The vase ~~on the piano~~ (is, are) filled with pink silk flowers.

Sentences Beginning with There/Here

Subject-verb agreement errors can easily occur in sentences that begin with *there is, there are, here is,* and *here are.* Here are some examples:

Incorrect: There <u>was</u> three women sitting in the back row.
Correct: There <u>were</u> three women sitting in the back row.

Incorrect: Here <u>is</u> the black buttons to sew on my coat.
Correct: Here <u>are</u> the black buttons to sew on my coat.

In all these examples the writer is confused by *there* or *here,* which strike the ear as singular. Neither *here* nor *there,* however, is the subject of the sentence. If you're confused by such sentences, reword them to make the subject come before the verb, and the mistake will quickly become visible.

Two women were sitting in the back row.

The black buttons to sew on my coat are here.

PRACTICING 4

Underline the correct verb in parentheses. Circle the subject.

1. Here (is, are) Linda Palmer's application.
2. There (is, are) the Colorado Rockies.
3. There (is, are) times in life that try my soul.
4. Here (is, are) the books you requested.
5. There (was, were) two clouds on either side of the rainbow.

Questions

Most sentences that we write or speak are statements, such as these:

> The stars are out.

> The apple is green.

In these, and in most statements, because the subject comes before the verb, it is easy to spot an agreement error.

On the other hand, when we ask a question, the verb typically comes before the subject:

> Where are the stars?

> What color is the apple?

With the subject following the verb in a question, it is easy to make an agreement error, such as this one:

> When is Keith and Samantha leaving?

To use the correct plural verb *are* requires a speaker or writer to guess that a plural subject—*Keith and Samantha*—lies ahead. Sometimes we guess wrong.

If you're in doubt about the subject-verb agreement in a question, simply reword it as a statement. So, for example, we have:

> Keith and Samantha (is/are) leaving soon.

It is now evident that the plural *are* is the correct verb since *Keith and Samantha* refer to two people.

PRACTICING 5

Underline the correct verb form in the following questions.

1. Who (is, are) those men standing on the corner?
2. When (do, does) Simone and Mary arrive?

3. Where (is, are) the knives and forks?

4. How many raffle tickets (has, have) Marvin sold?

5. Why (was, were) the fans cheering?

Compound Subjects Joined by And, Or, Either/Or, or Neither/Nor

Sentences that look like this can give writers trouble:

singular noun + and + singular noun

Here are some examples:

The bride and groom looks happy.

Luck and hard work is a winning combination.

Cobwebs and dirt covers the window.

In all these sentences the writer was fooled by what seemed to be a singular subject. However, just as one plus one make two, one singular subject plus another singular subject joined by *and* always make a subject plural. The sentences should therefore read:

The bride and groom <u>look</u> happy.

Luck and hard work <u>are</u> a winning combination.

Cobwebs and dirt <u>cover</u> the window.

Although two singular subjects joined by *and* always take a plural verb, two singular subjects joined by *or* require a singular verb:

Steak and chicken <u>are</u> on the menu.

    but

Steak or chicken <u>is</u> on the menu.

Burt and Gus <u>are</u> driving to Florida.

    but

Burt or Gus <u>is</u> driving to Florida.

Two plural nouns joined by *or* take a plural verb:

Usually the class presidents or vice-presidents sit on stage.

What happens when a sentence has two subjects, one singular and one plural, joined by *or*? In that case the verb agrees with the *nearer* subject:

The vice-presidents or <u>the president sits</u> next to the guest speakers.

but

The president or the <u>vice-presidents sit</u> next to the guest speakers.

The same rule applies with two subjects joined by *either/or* and *neither/nor*: The verb agrees with the nearer subject:

Either the coach or the <u>co-captains unfurl</u> the flag.

but

Either the co-captains or <u>the coach unfurls</u> the flag.

PRACTICING 6

Complete the following sentences using a correct singular or plural verb form.

1. Neither Heidi nor her pals _____.

2. Cash or credit cards _____.

3. Either the drummer or the guitarists _____.

4. Two sweaters or one coat _____.

5. Either chocolate or butterscotch _____.

PRACTICING 7

Underline the correct verb in parentheses in the following sentences.

1. Her limpid blue eyes and golden hair ((have), has) enormous appeal.

2. Wages and salaries ((are), is) the same thing.

3. Chocolate chip cookies and ice cream (is, (are)) a favorite food of Flora's.

4. A solid education and a strong character (was, were) required of all applicants.

5. My parents and my boyfriend (urges, urge) me to finish college.

The Indefinite Pronouns Each, Everyone, Anybody, Somebody, and Nobody

Indefinite pronouns are so called because they refer to no specific—or definite—person. The following indefinite pronouns always take a singular verb:

another	everyone	nothing
anybody	everything	one
anything	nobody	somebody
anyone	none	
everybody	no one	

Here are some examples:

Everybody <u>has</u> (not have) the duty to protect our freedoms.

Everyone <u>opposes</u> (not oppose) the new mall.

Nobody <u>wishes</u> (not wish) him more luck and happiness than we do.

Another <u>makes</u> (not make) a different point entirely.

PRACTICING 8

Underline the correct verb in parentheses.

1. None of the sardines (<u>has,</u> have) been eaten.
2. Everyone (<u>has,</u> have) a mind with which to decide.
3. One of the paramedics (<u>comes,</u> come) from Guadalajara.
4. Somebody (<u>is,</u> are) hiding behind that bush.
5. None of the restaurants (<u>is,</u> are) open.

Who, Which, and That

Who, which, and *that* are often used to replace nouns in dependent clauses. When they are so used, they should agree with the *closest* preceding noun. An example follows.

Incorrect: My mother is one of the reporters who covers City Hall.

Correct: My mother is one of the reporters who cover City Hall.

The closest noun that went before *who* is not *mother* but *reporters*. It is *reporters* that therefore determines the case of the verb.

In fact the sentence is a blend of two smaller sentences:

My mother is one of the reporters. The reporters cover City Hall.

The *who* stands for *reporters,* not for *mother.*
Here are other examples:

Leon or Ray is one of the climbers who <u>are</u> going to attempt the pinnacle.	(*climbers,* not Leon or Ray, is the closest noun before *who*)
Among my greatest fears and worries is encountering a snake that spits poison.	(*snake,* not *fears* or *worries,* is the closest noun before *that*)

PRACTICING 9

Circle the closest noun preceding *who, which,* or *that* in the following sentences. Then underline the correct verb.

1. She is among those scientists who (believe, believes) in Martians.

2. Fabio is one of several students who (merit, merits) an award.

3. The barn is one of the buildings that (need, needs) painting.

4. Patsy is among the seniors who (is, are) dissatisfied.

5. The trunk and suitcases, which (look, looks) sturdy, fall apart easily.

UNIT TEST

The following paragraph contains subject-verb agreement errors. Rewrite the paragraph, making all required corrections.

One of my strongest wishes are to have a flower garden filled with roses, pansies, sweet peas, and other colorful blossoms. But no one realize more than I do that tending a flower garden is constant work. Once you decides to plant a flower garden, you have to take care of it regularly. You has to pull out the weeds that quickly grows, and you has to water regularly. It don't matter if you are tired and prefer watching T.V.; the garden call you when it need tending. There's the various weather problems to consider as well. For instance, a hot sun or strong winds ruins flowers. A heavy, pelting rain destroys blooms, too. Children and animals is another problem. They has little awareness of flowers and will trample them as they runs or plays. Aunt Bee is among my relatives who has a spectacular flower garden. Either she or her two sons works in it every single day to keep it beautiful. Nobody know better than they how much work a garden takes. Until I am sure that I have plenty of time to devote to a flower garden, I guess I'll just enjoy gardens that has been grown by my friends and relatives.

Incorrect Verb Forms

Verbs are either regular or irregular. Regular verbs form the past tense by adding *-d* or *-ed*. They also form the past participle by adding *-d* or *-ed*. The past participle generally refers to actions in the distant, rather than the immediate, past. It requires a helping verb, either *have*, *has*, or *had*. Here are some examples of common regular verbs:

Present tense	Past tense	Past participle
charge	charged	have, has, or had charged
live	lived	have, has, or had lived
bake	baked	have, has, or had baked
hike	hiked	have, has, or had hiked
heave	heaved	have, has, or had heaved

Here are some examples of these words in sentences:

Past:	He lived in California for a year.
Past participle:	He has lived in some exotic places.
	He had lived in New York many years ago.

Past:	They baked the cake yesterday.
Past participle:	They have baked many cakes.
	They had already baked the birthday cake.

Don't let your ear fool you into dropping the *-d* or *-ed* endings of past tense verbs. Although this is a common mistake we all occasionally make in everyday speech, you must not make it in your writing.

Dropped ending:	They were suppose to do better.
	They were not use to the heat.

Correct:	They were supposed to do better.
	They were not used to the heat.

PRACTICING 1

Change the underlined regular verb in each sentence to the past participle. Remember to use *has*, *have*, or *had*. Write out the entire sentence.

1. They <u>decide</u> not to go.

   _____

2. Maxine <u>bought</u> a new computer.

   _____

3. Her mother <u>worked</u> as my father's accountant.

   _____

4. The dog <u>sniffs</u> at the fire hydrant.

   _____

5. We <u>row</u> every day on the lake.

   _____

Omitting the Helping Verb in a Past Participle

In some slangy talk it is common to drop the helping verb in a past participle—an act your ear might even excuse. However, dropping the helping verb, whether your ear approves or not, is always wrong in writing. Here are some examples:

Dropped verb: I seen that movie.

Written form: I <u>have</u> seen that movie.

Dropped verb: We been around the block twice.

Written form: We <u>have</u> been around the block twice.

Dropped verb: Why Harry brought flowers?

Written form: Why <u>has</u> Harry brought flowers?

PRACTICING 2

Rewrite each sentence below in the lines provided, inserting the helping verb where it belongs.

1. He been a cocky kid since he was young.

   _____

2. She said she given enough for one day.

   _____

3. The refrigerator frozen the food.

   _____

4. You eaten yet?

_____

5. They fallen from a high place.

_____

> ### PRACTICING 3

The paragraph that follows contains errors in the use of past participles. First underline each error; second, rewrite the paragraph with the correct past participles.

My budget fallen on hard times lately. No matter how hard I try, it been real hard to make ends meet. If I work a full shift, I clear $120 per week. Last year this use to be enough to pay my bills, but this year it isn't. It costs me about $60 per week for rent. That leaves me with about half of what I take home. For food, I use to budget $20 per week, but this year for some reason, that simply isn't enough. I'm more likely to spend at least $30 for food, and that means eating a lot of junk. Last year I could occasionally go out for a hamburger, but not this year. So after rent and food, I have about $30 left for everything else. I'm suppose to pay car insurance and tuition and everything on that. That means, if I want to go to a movie, which costs about $7, or nearly a third of my weekly pay that's left, I really have to think hard. I ask myself, what could happened that I'm so broke this year? I think it's because everything gone up. What used to cost $5 last year, now costs about $7. Gasoline gone up, too, and it seems I'm buying more gas. Maybe my car become a gas guzzler. I don't know. All I know is that I can barely make ends meet.

Irregular Verbs

Verbs are **irregular** if their past tense is not formed by adding *-d* or *-ed*. For example, if the rule for changing tenses were applied to *bring*, its past tense should be *bringed*. It isn't—it's *brought*. *Bring* is therefore an irregular verb.

Below is a list of irregular verbs that many of us use every day. Remember, the past participle always requires the use of the helping verbs *have, has,* or *had.*

SOME COMMON IRREGULAR VERBS

Present	Past	Past participle
arise	arose	arisen
be	was	been
bear	bore	borne
become	became	become
begin	began	begun
break	broke	broken
bring	brought (not *brung*)	brought
build	built	built
burst	burst (not *busted*)	burst
catch	caught	caught
buy	bought	bought
choose	chose	chosen
cling	clung	clung
come	came	come
dive	dove	dived
do	did (not *done*)	done
draw	drew	drawn
drink	drank	drunk
drive	drove	driven
fall	fell	fallen
eat	ate	eaten
feed	fed	fed
feel	felt	felt
fight	fought	fought
fly	flew	flown
forgive	forgave	forgiven
freeze	froze	frozen
get	got	gotten
go	went	gone
grow	grew	grown
hang (clothes)	hung	hung
hang (execute)	hanged	hanged
have	had	had
hold	held	held
hurt	hurt (not *hurted*)	hurt
know	knew	known

Present	Past	Past participle
lead	led	led
lay	laid	laid
lie	lay	lain
lose	lost	lost
make	made	made
mean	meant	meant
meet	met	met
pay	paid	paid
put	put	put
read	read	read
ride	rode	ridden
ring	rang	rung
rise	rose	risen
run	ran	run
say	said	said
see	saw (not *seen*)	seen
seek	sought (not *seeked*)	sought
sell	sold	sold
set	set	set
shake	shook	shaken
shine	shone	shone
shrink	shrank	shrunk
sing	sang	sung
sink	sank	sunk
sleep	slept	slept
speak	spoke	spoken
spend	spent	spent
spin	spun	spun
spit	spat	spat
spring	sprang (not *sprung*)	sprung
stand	stood	stood
steal	stole	stolen
sting	stung	stung
stink	stank (not *stunk*)	stunk
strike	struck	struck
strive	strove	strove
swear	swore	sworn
swim	swam (not *swum*)	swum
swing	swung	swung
take	took	taken
teach	taught	taught

(cont.)

Present	Past	Past participle
tear	tore	torn
tell	told	told
think	thought	thought
throw	threw	thrown
understand	understood	understood
wake	woke	woken
weave	wove	woven
wear	wore	worn
win	won	won
wring	wrung	wrung
write	wrote	written

PRACTICING 4

Complete the following chart. Refer to the list of irregular verbs beginning on page 348, if in doubt.

	Present	Past	Past participle
1.	seek	_____	_____
2.	sell	_____	_____
3.	steal	_____	_____
4.	ring	_____	_____
5.	fly	_____	_____
6.	teach	_____	_____
7.	hurt	_____	_____
8.	strive	_____	_____
9.	hang (execute)	_____	_____
10.	spit	_____	_____

PRACTICING 5

In the following sentences, the past tense is used incorrectly. Write the correct form in the spaces provided.

1. His mother <u>waked</u> him up to go to work. _____

2. She <u>weared</u> that blouse yesterday. _____

3. I <u>throwed</u> the ball to the pitcher. _____

4. They <u>selled</u> themselves short. _____

5. I could have <u>ate</u> the whole cake. _____

6. The worker <u>striked</u> for better pay. _____

7. I've <u>fighted</u> that battle before. _____

8. Because of the yeast, the bread had <u>raised</u>. _____

9. I found out I <u>payed</u> too much for the battery. _____

10. She <u>swinged</u> in the park all morning. _____

Problems with irregular verbs

Two problems are common with the everyday use of irregular verbs:

- Using the simple past instead of the past participle.

  Incorrect: She has wove two rugs.

  Correct: She has woven two rugs.

  Incorrect: They have tore the book.

  Correct: They have torn the book.

- Using an incorrect form of the past participle.

  Incorrect: He had brung his rollerblades to school before.

  Correct: He has brought his rollerblades to school before.

  Incorrect: She has broke the remote control.

  Correct: She has broken the remote control.

Beware of these two common errors.

PRACTICING 6

Some of the underlined past participles that follow are correct, some are incorrect. If the participle is correct, write *C* in the blank; if it is incorrect, write the corrected participle in the blank.

1. I have <u>wore</u> that many times. _____

2. They couldn't have <u>sang</u> any worse. _____

3. The president has <u>saw</u> to the problem. _____

4. They have <u>drug</u> the boat through the mud flat. _____

5. Because of the freezing weather, the pipes have

   <u>busted</u>. _____

6. In another move or two, he will have <u>sprang</u> the

    trap. _____

7. Because she washed my jeans in too hot water, they have

    <u>shrunk</u>. _____

8. She has <u>wrote</u> him three times. _____

9. I have <u>drew</u> my own conclusions. _____

10. You have <u>ran</u> away from home for the last time. _____

Problem Verbs

A few verbs seem to give the entire English-speaking world trouble.
They are *lie/lay*, *sit/set*, and *rise/raise*.

Lie/lay

Here are the principal parts of these two verbs:

Present	Past	Past participle
lie	lay	lain = to rest in a horizontal position like a sleeper
lay	laid	laid = to set down something, as you might do a book

To lie	To lay
I like to lie on the grass.	She lay (what?) the tile in the bathroom.
The dog is lying on the grass.	She is laying (what?) the tile in the bathroom.
Yesterday I lay on the grass.	Yesterday she laid (what?) the tile in the bathroom.
I have lain on the grass too long.	She must have laid (what?) the tile in the bathroom.

PRACTICING 7

Underline the correct verb in parentheses.

1. (Lie, Lay) the portable phone on the desk.

2. I have been (lying, laying) plans in my dreams.

3. He was (lain, laid) to rest with all military honors.

4. She was tired and went to (lie, lay) down.

5. She complains that all he does is (lie, lay) around watching

    television.

Sit/set

Here are the principal parts of *sit* and *set*:

Present	Past	Past participle
sit	sat	sat = to rest on one's bottom
set	set	set = to place something somewhere

To sit	**To set**
He sits at the head of the table.	The child sets (what?) his toys by his bed.
She is sitting by the window.	He is setting (what?) the toys in a row.
The crew sat in the cockpit.	Last night he set (what?) the bear next to the giraffe.
They have always sat in the front row.	Did he set (what?) the toys on the table?

PRACTICING 8

Underline the correct verb in parentheses.

1. They (sat, set) in the bleachers, hoping to catch a fly ball.

2. I'm (sitting, setting) the groceries on the counter.

3. (Sit, Set) yourself down on the sofa and listen to me play the piano.

4. She (sat, set) the socket wrench set on the bench.

5. (Sit, set) with me under a tree and listen to the bird sing.

Rise/raise

Here are the principal parts of *rise* and *raise*:

Present	Past	Past participle
rise	rose	risen = to get up or move up on your own
raise	raised	raised = to lift up someone or something

To rise	**To raise**
Let us rise and be counted.	You should not raise (what?) your hopes too much.
I am rising early to greet the dawn.	She is raising (what?) the hem two inches.
Everyone rose when the anthem. was played.	They raised (what?) the flag.
The audience has risen.	She has raised (what?) an objection.

> ### PRACTICING 9

Change the underlined word(s) by substituting *rise* or *raise*. Do not change the tense of the original.

1. <u>Lift</u> the banner above your head. _____

2. The moon <u>came up</u> over the ocean. _____

3. The entire team had <u>stood up</u> to watch the home run.

   _____

4. Victory <u>pulled up</u> their spirits. _____

5. He <u>got up</u> late today. _____

Lie/Lay, Sit/Set, Rise/Raise: Does It Really Matter?

Even if students don't ask the question, "Does it really matter if I say *lie* or *lay*?" they often think it. The answer is, yes, it does matter.

True, if you commanded *Lay down*! instead of *Lie down*! your dog would probably obey just as quickly. "If I'm understood when I incorrectly say *lay* instead of *lie*, or *lie* instead of *lay*, what does using the correct form matter?"—that is what many students wonder. Being understood, however, is no substitute for being correct. Furthermore, being correct is what makes you understandable.

Language does change, and as the years roll by, we predict that one day *lie* and *lay* will have the same meaning in grammar books. Until that day comes, these differences do matter. For example, you might scribble this memo to your boss: "Dear Boss, I lay the contract on your desk before I left." Upon reading it your boss might mutter, "No, you didn't. You laid it there. If you can't get that right, how can I trust you with this important contract? I'm giving the account to Nancy." In other words, these little differences are important because they matter to people.

Of course, they don't matter if you work for a dog.

UNIT TEST

The paragraph below contains errors in the past tense and past participles of irregular verbs. Find and correct all the errors.

When I began working at Gary's Restaurant, I was lead to believe that I would soon be given a rise in pay. Mrs. Smith, my supervisor, even complimented me when I was hired, telling me that I brung a lot of experience to the company. Now as I set here writing this letter, I cannot help but feel that I was misleaded. I don't want to rise this point and belabor it, but when the pipes in the kitchen busted, I was the one who saved the food in the walk-in. Furthermore, in my six months of employment here, I have never shrinked from doing my duty. Whatever my supervisor told me to do, I always did it as well as I understanded the request. Nobody has ever wringed work out of me. I'm always the first to volunteer. I have wrote this letter because I feel not only mistreated, but also misleaded. As I drived to work today, I thinked to myself that Gary's is a good place to work. But now my confidence has been shook. Now that I have spoke my honest opinion, I hope that I will get the pay increase I deserve. I hope by this letter I have not fell out of favor. But as I have always been brung up to believe, honesty is the best policy.

Incorrect Forms of <u>Do</u>, <u>Be</u>, and <u>Have</u>

Even if you've spoken English all your life, verbs can still be troublesome. Part of the problem is that we don't speak and write verbs the same way. In speech we sometimes drop the tense endings of verbs when we shouldn't, as in this sentence:

> She laugh all the time.

Or, we add an ending when we shouldn't:

> They laughs all the time.

In the first sentence, since *she* is singular, the verb must also be singular—*laughs*. In the second sentence, since *they* is plural, the verb must also be plural—*laugh*.

You can make these mistakes in everyday speech—we all occasionally do—and be forgiven. You should not, however, make them in writing. The standards for grammar are stricter in writing than in speech, meaning that you must always write verb tenses correctly.

Present Tense Endings

In Standard English you must use the correct endings with verbs. You cannot use a plural ending with a singular subject, or a singular ending with a plural subject. Here are the correct endings for regular verbs in the present tense:

PRESENT TENSE—SINGULAR

Incorrect	Correct
I walks	I walk
you walks	you walk
he, she, it walk	he, she, it walks

PRESENT TENSE—PLURAL

Incorrect	Correct
we walks	we walk
you walks	you walk
they walks	they walk

Present tense problems

There are two kinds of problems that commonly occur with verbs in the present tense:

- Dropped *-s/-es* endings for *he*, *she*, and *it*.

  Incorrect: He take the train to work.
  Correct: He takes the train to work.

  Incorrect: She make pancakes for breakfast.
  Correct: She makes pancakes for breakfast.

  Incorrect: It hurt my feelings.
  Correct: It hurts my feelings.

- Unnecessary *-s/-es* for *we*, *you*, and *they*.

  Incorrect: We visits Gram every weekend.
  Correct: We visit Gram every weekend.

  Incorrect: You always smiles, even in sad times.
  Correct: You always smile, even in sad times.

  Incorrect: They both plays the accordion.
  Correct: They both play the accordion.

Problems with dropped and added endings occur, as we said, because we are less precise in our speech than we must be in our writing. If you make such errors regularly in your speech, your ear may not be particularly helpful in catching them. In that case you should simply memorize the correct endings.

PRACTICING 1

In the blanks provided write *C* if the verb is correct and *NC* if it is not.

1. _____ Bernice and I drives in the same car pool.

2. _____ We try to pay our electricity bill.

3. _____ Our neighbor keep trying to win the lottery.

4. _____ Jeremy buy Melinda's affection.

5. _____ She repeat herself constantly.

PRACTICING 2

In the passage that follows, strike out any incorrect verb and write the correct form above it.

Most of my friends likes to watch soccer. During the World Cup

season, we sits in front of my TV all day long to watch the

competition. My friend Danny always support the team from Brazil,
but I cheer for the Italian team with Baggio, who wear a braid down
his back. That seem cool to me. The penalty kicks excites everyone
the most. Then we screams and yells at the top of our voices. If the
kicker make a goal, we goes crazy. If the goalie intercept the ball,
we explodes. Soccer get you involved, no matter what side win.

Past Tense Endings

Here are the correct endings for regular singular verbs in the past
tense:

PAST TENSE—SINGULAR

Incorrect	Correct
I walk	I walked
you walk	you walked
he, she, it walk	he, she, it walked

Here are the correct endings for regular plural verbs in the past
tense:

PAST TENSE—PLURAL

Incorrect	Correct
we walk	we walked
you walk	you walked
they walk	they walked

With both singular and plural verbs, we can be careless in our
speech and drop the *-ed* ending. In writing, however, you must *always*
use the *-ed* ending with regular verbs in the past tense.

Incorrect: I pick up the mail yesterday.
Correct: I picked up the mail yesterday.

Incorrect: He drop several hints.
Correct: He dropped several hints.

PRACTICING 3

In the blank at the end of each sentence, write the past tense of the
underlined verb.

1. The mechanical teddy bear <u>dance</u> a jig. _____

2. Studies <u>suggest</u> that TV violence is bad. _____

3. Despite my pleadings, Betty <u>continue</u> to smoke.

    _____

4. Some countries <u>remain</u> neutral during the war.

    _____

5. He <u>manage</u> to turn the tiny argument into a major

    problem. _____

6. Beverly <u>challenge</u> her opponent. _____

7. Jack and Jill <u>decide</u> to go up the hill. _____

8. I secretly <u>open</u> the door to the safe. _____

9. The strange voice on the telephone <u>ask</u> my name.

    _____

10. They <u>litter</u> the grass with cans and wrappers. _____

Problems with -ing Verbs

Verbs ending in *-ing* describe an action that is either happening now or is ongoing. All *-ing* verbs need a helping verb.

He is eating in the kitchen.

He was eating in the kitchen.

He has been eating in the kitchen.

He had been eating in the kitchen, but now he eats in the dining room.

Two kinds of problems can occur with *-ing* verbs:

- *Be* or *been* is used instead of the correct helping verb.

    Incorrect: She be eating in the kitchen.
    Correct: She is eating in the kitchen.

                              or

                     She has been eating in the kitchen.

    Incorrect: She been studying in the library.
    Correct: She was studying in the library.

                              or

                     She has been studying in the library.

■ The helping verb is completely omitted.

Incorrect: They bragging too much.
Correct: They are bragging too much.
                 They were bragging too much.
                 They have been bragging too much.
                 They had been bragging too much.

PRACTICING 4

Rewrite the following sentences to correct the misuse of *be* or *been*, or to insert the missing helping verb.

Example: The birds be chirping outside my window.

The birds are chirping outside my window.

1. My car be needing a lube job.

_____

2. She forcing her son to give up college.

_____

3. My father buying a house near the train station.

_____

4. How your mother be coming along with her knitting?

_____

5. Marcy hoping that she can marry next year.

_____

6. They be ignoring all of his advice.

_____

7. Margaret sitting under an elm tree when the lightning struck.

_____

8. Every young person be searching for a way to feel important.

_____

9. Dylan expecting to inherit some money from an uncle.

_____

10. Schwarz be waiting for him in the adjoining room.

_____

Difficult Verbs

Verbs can be hard to master. Few are harder than the three verbs we probably use more than any others in the language: *be*, *have*, and *do*.

To be

To be is commonly used both as a verb on its own and as a helping verb. Here is a listing of the forms of the verb *to be*:

PRESENT TENSE—SINGULAR *TO BE*

Incorrect	**Correct**
I be, I ain't	I am, I am not
you be, you ain't	you are, you are not
he/she/it be, he/she/it ain't	he/she/it is, he/she/it is not

PRESENT TENSE—PLURAL *TO BE*

Incorrect	**Correct**
we be, we ain't	we are, we are not
you be, you ain't	you are, you are not
they be, they ain't	they are, they are not

PAST TENSE—SINGULAR *TO BE*

Incorrect	**Correct**
I were	I was
you was	you were
he, she, it were	he, she, it was

PAST TENSE—PLURAL *TO BE*

Incorrect	**Correct**
we was	we were
you was	you were
they was	they were

As you can see—indeed as you already know from repeated use—*to be* is an irregular verb. As both a verb and a helping verb, it is often incorrectly spoken. All of these sentences below, for example, are wrong, even if your ear tells you otherwise.

I ain't staying in New York.

The lake be dangerous because the wind be blowing hard.

You was rude to step in front of her.

If these are forms that you commonly use in your daily speech, be especially careful not to trust your ear with *to be*. Instead, you should memorize its correct forms.

Here is how these sentences should be written:

> I am not staying in New York.

> The lake is dangerous because the wind is blowing hard.

> You were rude to step in front of her.

PRACTICING 5

The following passage contains several errors in the use of the verb *to be*. In the space provided, rewrite the passage, correcting all errors. (Hint: you should find eight errors.)

Today I be sad. It be the third anniversary of my dad's death. Believe me, even after three years, it ain't easy to lose your dad. He been my best friend. We went fishing and camping together every year. We was simply best buddies. Last summer I hiked where my dad and I had hiked along a lake high up in the Sierras. I be feeling sick with my heavy heart. My mom tried to comfort me by reminding me that I have some great memories. But that can't make up for the present loss. Right now, I wish he and I was sitting down to plan one of our famous outings. But it can't happen. He be gone forever.

_____

_____

_____

_____

_____

_____

_____

_____

_____

_____

To have

To have, like *to be*, is commonly used both as a verb and a helping verb. Also like *to be*, it is an irregular verb. Here are its main forms:

PRESENT TENSE—SINGULAR *TO HAVE*

Incorrect	Correct
I has	I have
you has	you have
he/she/it have	he/she/it has

PRESENT TENSE—PLURAL *TO HAVE*

Incorrect	Correct
we has	we have
you has	you have
they has	they have

PAST TENSE—SINGULAR *TO HAVE*

Incorrect	Correct
I has	I had
you has	you had
he/she/I have	he/she/it had

PAST TENSE—PLURAL *TO HAVE*

Incorrect	Correct
we has	we had
you has	you had
they has	they had

To have is so often misused in daily speech that you should be cautious about trusting your ear to judge its correctness. These sentences below, for example, are all incorrect:

> She have two nieces and two nephews.

> Benny have a nifty new Honda convertible.

> They has a party yesterday.

Here are the correct forms:

> She has two nieces and two nephews.

> Benny has a new Honda convertible.

> They had a party yesterday.

> **PRACTICING 6**

Fill in the correct form of the verb *to have* in the following sentences.

Example: She <u>has</u> to be on time.

1. Judith _____ a free ticket to the game.

2. You _____ to take him to the bus.

3. The Baxters _____ two beautiful daughters.

4. He _____ my raincoat, and I must _____

   it tomorrow.

5. I _____ got to live alone, and Mother _____

   to understand why.

6. _____ they mentioned the problem?

7. Where _____ Pete been?

8. She _____ embarrassed me too often.

9. Everyone _____ to follow the regulations.

10. We _____ two computers, but our neighbors

   _____ only one.

To do

The verb *to do*, like *to be* and *to have*, is used both as a verb and a help-ing verb. Here are its correct forms:

PRESENT TENSE—SINGULAR *TO DO*

Incorrect	**Correct**
I does	I do
you does	you do
he/she/it do	he/she/it does

PRESENT TENSE—PLURAL *TO DO*

Incorrect	**Correct**
we does	we do
you does	you do
they does	they do

PAST TENSE—SINGULAR *TO DO*

Incorrect	Correct
I done	I did
you done	you did
he/she/it done	he/she/it did

PAST TENSE—PLURAL *TO DO*

Incorrect	Correct
we done	we did
you done	you did
they done	they did

Ear Alert

The main problem with *to do* is that it is used in informal speech differently than it is in writing. So, again, do not trust your ear. All these sentences below, for example, are incorrect:

He don't have the sense to come in out of the rain.

I does whatever I'm told.

She done her homework early.

Here are the correct forms:

He doesn't have the sense to come in out of the rain.

I do whatever I'm told.

She did her homework early.

or

She has done her homework early.

PRACTICING 7

Use the correct form of *to do* in the following sentences.

1. He _____ admire his parents' high standards.

2. She _____ whine considerably, _____ she?

3. _____ you belong to a study group?

4. How _____ you get the wallpaper off the wall?

5. Melissa rarely _____ poorly on math exams.

6. I _____ object to his superior attitude.

7. _____ Mr. Smith understand that the payment is due today?

8. Where _____ they dispose of their trash?

9. _____ not interfere in our argument.

10. _____ it matter whether or not he believes you?

UNIT TEST

Fill in the blanks with the correct form of the verb in parentheses.

1. Yesterday Julie (insist) _____ that we go with her.

2. Melvin (be) _____ the grump of the year.

3. They both (be) _____ good readers.

4. Last May, Elvira (decide) _____ to buy a blond wig.

5 Miranda (do) _____ follow him around too much.

6. David still (eat)_____ too many sweets.

7. She (hide) _____ her spy novels so I can't get them.

8. If you (be) _____ satisfied, then pay the workmen.

9. The roof (have) _____ a terrible leak.

10. (Do) _____ she always tease you so unmercifully?

11. Jessie (have) _____ told us some crazy gossip.

12. City Hall (have) _____ the duty to build safe bridges.

13. If she (swim) _____ to the island, she (be) _____ strong.

14. You have (do) _____ the most work.

15. The door (have) _____ to be sanded down and painted.

The paragraph that follows contains incorrect forms of the *do, be,* and *have* verbs. Rewrite the paragraph to correct these errors. (You should be able to find 22 errors.)

If I be a waitress, I would try to be cheerful, efficient, and polite. So many waitresses nowadays doesn't offer good service. If I be a waitress, I would approach the customer with a smile and a warm greeting. I wouldn't just grab my notebook and ask, "What would you like to order?" The other day at Benny's coffee shop, where my best friend and I be going for breakfast, the waitress at our table ask us abruptly, "What can I get you?" I be surprised at such a cold attitude, and my friend have a hard time giving her order for pancakes. After she be taking our order, the waitress walk over to another customer and talk, talk, talk without even placing our order with the kitchen. I be real offended. We was in a hurry, and this waitress deliberately ignore our needs. Well, finally she brought our order, but when she place it on the table, she spill some coffee and made noise banging the dishes because she be so rough. Most polite waitresses wish you a pleasant meal or enjoy, but not this one. She just disappear until we call her over to get our check. I have no idea why she do her job so poorly. If I be a waitress, I be trying hard to please my customers.

Passive Voice

English has two voices; the active and the passive voice. The **active voice** stresses *who* did an act. The **passive voice** stresses *to whom* or *to what* an act was done. Most of us usually speak in the active voice because it is simpler and more direct.

Active voice: The cashier gave us our change.

Passive voice: Our change was given to us by the cashier.

Because it hides the doer, the passive voice is often preferred by writers who wish to avoid naming names. Here is a case in point.

The tax return was lost.

Who lost the tax return? The active voice would have told us:

Bill lost the tax return.

In writing you should mainly use the active voice. It is livelier and stronger than the passive voice and more like everyday talk. The passive voice is occasionally used in scientific reporting, where what was done is more important than which researcher did it:

The chemical mixture was heated.

It is also occasionally used in instances where an act is more important than its cause:

The fishing village was destroyed by a tidal wave.

Here the important fact is the destruction of the village. That it was destroyed by a tidal wave is secondary.

PRACTICING 1

Read the paired sentences aloud and write *A* in the blank beside the sentence in the active voice.

Example: __A__   **a.** Louise made the coffee.

_____   **b.** The coffee was made by Louise.

1. _____ **a.** The package was advertised by the travel agent.

   _____ **b.** The travel agent advertised the package.

2. _____ **a.** Initiative is crushed by bureaucracy.

   _____ **b.** Bureaucracy crushes initiative.

3. _____ **a.** Mrs. Stanhope spoke to the letter carrier.

   _____ **b.** The letter carrier was spoken to by Mrs. Stanhope.

4. _____ **a.** The people were misled by the cult.

   _____ **b.** The cult misled the people.

5. _____ **a.** The boat was stopped by the Coast Guard.

   _____ **b.** The Coast Guard stopped the boat.

6. _____ **a.** I enjoyed the lecture.

   _____ **b.** The lecture was enjoyed by me.

7. _____ **a.** The play was staged by the Drama Club.

   _____ **b.** The Drama Club staged the play.

8. _____ **a.** An invasion of ants interrupted the picnic.

   _____ **b.** The picnic was interrupted by an invasion of ants.

9. _____ **a.** The developer obtained the building permit.

   _____ **b.** The building permit was obtained by the developer.

10. _____ **a.** A strong case was made by the prosecuting attorney.

    _____ **b.** The prosecuting attorney made a strong case.

PRACTICING 2

Rewrite the sentences below to change verbs to the active voice from the passive voice.

Example: The marshmallows were enjoyed by the Boy Scouts.

Answer: The Boy Scouts enjoyed the marshmallows.

1. An ace was served by the tennis champion.

   _____

2. The home was inspected by the building inspector.

   _____

3. The movie was enjoyed by everyone.

_____

4. The sugar water was relished by the humming birds.

_____

5. A screenplay was written by my neighbor.

_____

6. The candidate was backed by women's groups.

_____

7. Jogging is done by many people for exercise.

_____

8. The statue was removed by the protestors.

_____

9. The law was passed by the Senate.

_____

10. The taxicab was summoned by the doorman.

_____

PRACTICING 3

Rewrite these sentences to put them in the active voice.

1. A bad fall was suffered by the polevaulter.

_____

2. The car was fixed by the mechanic.

_____

3. Encouragement was given to the class by the dean.

_____

4. New soles were put on the shoes by the shoemaker.

_____

5. The order was placed by Jim.

_____

6. A standing ovation was given to the player.

_____

7. The plane was guided in by the air controller.

_____

8. The poor homeowners were robbed by the slick-talking con man.

_____

9. The wonderful tarts were made by him.

_____

10. An incentive was offered by the sales manager.

_____

11. A lively tune was played by the band.

_____

12. Our snow was shoveled by our neighbor's son.

_____

13. The oven was cleaned by me.

_____

14. The syllabus was handed out by the professor.

_____

15. A safety flare was shot off by the lifeguard.

_____

UNIT TEST

Rewrite the following paragraph in the active voice.

Last summer our house was painted by me. The job took about two weeks. First, the exterior was washed using warm water and a mild detergent. Then all the chinks and pores in the walls were sealed with putty. It was not an easy job. After the putty had had a chance to dry, the exterior could be painted. A latex paint was used because it is easy to apply and cleans up with water. A whole week was needed to finish this part of the job. I was very careful to apply the paint evenly because I did not want to have to apply two coats. A color was used that was very close to the original color. Our house is a two-story house, which meant that a ladder was needed to do the second story. This was the hardest part of the job. It meant working 35 or 40 feet high, which was not easy. The paint can had to be balanced on the top rung of the ladder while I worked. Plus it was very hot, and I had to keep coming down to drink water. But when the job was finished, a great deal of satisfaction was felt by me. I had to pat myself on the back. Even my dad said that a good job was done.

Shift in Tense

If you begin a sentence in the present tense, you must end it in the present tense. If you begin in the past tense, you must end in the past tense. For example, look at this sentence:

> Larry blew a tire, and then just keeps on driving.

The problem with the sentence is that it begins with a verb in the past tense and ends with a verb in the present tense. Larry is made into a time-traveler—hopping from the past to the present in one breath. To be correct, the sentence must read:

Larry blew a tire, and then just **(All past tense)**
kept on driving.

> or

Larry blows a tire, and then **(All present tense)**
just keeps on driving.

Your tense use must be consistent. You must not shift tenses unless there is a logical reason. Yet because we mix up our verb tenses all the time in everyday speech, your ear might mislead you into making the same mistake in writing. Be alert to this possible error. Make sure your verbs in a written sentence all use the same tense.

PRACTICING 1

Correct the shifts in verb tense in these sentences.

1. The teacher writes the assignment on the board, and then left the room with no comment.

_____

_____

2. When I warned her that the road was slippery, she simply pays no attention.

_____

_____

3. He memorizes the entire Bill of Rights, but failed the test anyway.

_____

_____

4. When clouds covered the moon, the lovers leave the park.

_____

_____

5. I had barely started my laundry when the washing machine floods all over the floor.

_____

_____

6. She grabbed the pen on the desk and hurriedly signs the contract.

_____

_____

7. The night before her wedding, Annie had dinner with her best friends and weeps for two hours.

_____

_____

8. When the first snow falls, the men in the neighborhood got out their shovels to clear the walkways.

_____

_____

9. All of us lustily sang "I've Been Workin' on the Railroad," and then we eat three huge pizzas.

_____

_____

10. He climbed to the top of the hill and builds a fire.

_____

_____

PRACTICING 2

Correct the shifts in verb tense in these sentences.

1. Mary recognized the car and is yelling, "There goes the thief!"

_____

_____

2. For twenty years he has kept the secret and never tells a soul.

_____

_____

3. We stop recruiting volunteers and had started to work.

_____

_____

4. Tom envied Lud and wants to take over his job.

_____

_____

5. The clouds looked menacing, so we pull up our stakes and leave the camp.

_____

_____

6. I look out the window and saw three fire engines.

_____

_____

7. They paid for her tuition and gave her spending money, but she never shows an ounce of gratitude.

_____

_____

8. He is a carpenter and has received good benefits.

_____

_____

9. Although I felt dizzy, I manage to cross the stream on the rope bridge.

_____

_____

10. Most of the stories are old, but we listened with fascination.

_____

_____

> **PRACTICING 3**

Complete the sentences below, using the correct verb tense.

1. She set the table, while he _____

2. People gathered around the accident and then the fire truck

   _____

3. Before the curtain rose, the actor _____

4. When the wind howls outside our windows, _____

5. We made reservations for 7:00, which _____

6. They did apologize, so _____

7. Francis walks two miles every day, but _____

8. They applauded the mayor and then _____

9. December was mild, but January _____

10. He leaves the cap off the toothpaste, and _____

UNIT TEST

Rewrite the following paragraph to correct all shifts in tense.

My mother is so funny. Once she watched a TV program about regular car maintenance. Then, for weeks afterward, she gives our family long harangues about getting the oil changed regularly and replacing a weak battery. "Won't you feel silly if you were in a busy intersection and your car stalled?" she must have asks me every night. And practically all day Saturday, there she is in the garage, checking some hose or gasket or belt. She visited every neighbor and points out the dangers of ignoring an oil leak or bad brakes. "Watch out for uneven tire wear," she preaches to everyone. My father was embarrassed that Mom is so forward about telling our neighbors how to run their lives. He tells her that if she wanted to take good care of her car, fine, but that she should allow the neighbors to make their own decision about their own cars.

Shifting Point of View

Writing is easier to read if it uses the same point of view through-out. You may choose a first person, second person, or third person point of view:

First Person	**Second Person**	**Third Person**	
I	you	he, she, it, one	SINGULAR
we	you	they	PLURAL

Here are some examples:

Incorrect: When a <u>person</u> sees an accident, <u>you</u> should imme-diately offer assistance.

Correct: When <u>you</u> see an accident, <u>you</u> should immediately offer assistance.

or

When <u>one</u> sees an accident, <u>one</u> should immediately offer assistance.

Here is a paragraph containing many shifts:

How <u>we</u> wake up in the morning affects how <u>you</u> view the rest of the day. If <u>you</u> start the day off badly, <u>we'll</u> be in a bad mood for the rest of the day. Start off strong and cheerful, and <u>one</u> will be facing the day with a positive outlook. On the other hand, if <u>we</u> wake up in a so-so mood, chances are good that <u>your</u> so-so mood will carry over through the rest of the day and make it so-so. There's no mystery in this: It's simply a matter of common sense. The mood <u>you</u> wake up in sets the tone for the rest of <u>one's</u> day.

Here is the correction using *you*. *You*, *we*, or *one* would all be correct as long as you don't shift from one pronoun to another.

How <u>you</u> wake up in the morning affects how <u>you</u> view the rest of the day. If <u>you</u> start the day off badly, <u>you'll</u> be in a bad mood for the rest of the day. Start off strong and cheerful, and <u>you</u> will be facing the day with a positive outlook. On the other hand, if <u>you</u> wake up in a so-so mood, chances are good that <u>your</u> so-so mood with carry over through the rest of the day and make it so-so. There's no mystery in this: It's simply a matter of common sense. The mood <u>you</u> wake up in sets the tone for the rest of <u>your</u> day.

PRACTICING 1

Correct the shifts in point of view in the following sentences by crossing out and rewriting words when necessary.

1. When I went to San Francisco, we had a wonderful time.

2. They stood in line all day, which is what you have to do if you want to get tickets.

3. In spite of my attempt to do the right thing, you could see there was no way to win.

4. A person should study hard if you want to be a success in college.

5. The counselor at the school is a sympathetic person that one can share your troubles with.

6. If one intends to drive for a long time, you should try to get enough sleep the day before.

7. To overcome your bad habits, we should all practice will power.

8. For someone to succeed in a new job, we must be willing to watch and learn.

9. One's love of ice cream can easily overcome your desire to stay on a diet.

10. I don't play the lottery because you know you can't win.

PRACTICING 2

Complete each of these sentences using a pronoun. Do not shift point of view.

1. When you go out on a blind date, _____

2. If a person exercises, _____

3. Even though I'm a big baseball fan, _____

4. If you pay attention to the big things _____

5. I made several phone calls, but _____

6. You should floss twice a day if _____

7. A person who likes poetry _____

8. If someone wants to save money grocery shopping, _____

9. A person who likes Chinese food should _____

10. Should you feel restless, _____

PRACTICING 3

Rewrite the following sentences to correct the shifts in point of view.

1. If you like to read, one should try the local library.

   _____

   _____

2. One should not talk too much if you don't know the subject well.

   _____

   _____

3. When you go on a trip, one should always have your insurance paid up.

   _____

   _____

4. A person can get good bargains if you shop at outlet stores.

   _____

   _____

5. Someone can make new friends in a city if you join a health club.

   _____

   _____

6. One only has to listen to know that you can't take anything they say at face value.

   _____

   _____

7. Broccoli will help one's digestion, but carrots will help your night vision.

   _____

   _____

8. As you walk into the room, one can hear the people babbling away.

_____

_____

9. When I bought my blender, you could never tell that it would come in so handy.

_____

_____

10. One must try hard at everything one does, or you'll never know if you could succeed.

_____

_____

UNIT TEST

Rewrite the following paragraph to correct the shifts in point of view.

As part of freshman orientation week, some colleges organize a hike in the mountains or even an overnight camping trip. Now, to me that sounds like a good idea. Imagine how we could bond while you're fighting off mosquitoes, building a fire, or sharing our dried food inside your tents. Starting one's freshman week with a lecture, an English placement test, and an explanation of the campus rules we're supposed to follow is dull by comparison. But a one or two-day hike by a lake or in the Sierras encourages students to make new friends quickly while you enjoy a few hours of hiking, cycling, trail exploring, or even canoeing. Then you could gather around a campfire at night while the freshman ask questions of the older students, who can reassure us that college is fun as well as hard work. I think such an orientation would give me confidence as we face college life.

Unclear or Missing Referent

If writing were baseball, the pronoun would be a relief pitcher whose job is temporarily to relieve nouns, who are the starters. In both speech and writing, the **pronoun** is a word used in place of a noun.

The **referent** of a pronoun is the noun it replaces. Consider this sentence:

> Elaine works, but she is getting her degree at night.

The pronoun is *she*; its referent—the word it refers to—is *Elaine*.

Most of the time, the referent of a pronoun is perfectly clear from the context of a sentence. However, sometimes it isn't. Sometimes a referent is either unclear or altogether missing.

Unclear Referents

Here is an example of an unclear referent:

> Peggy told Denise that she had made a grave error.

In the above sentence the referent of the pronoun is unclear. We do not know whether Peggy or Denise made the grave error. Here is the same sentence rewritten to avoid the unclear referent:

> Peggy told Denise, "You have made a grave error."

> or

> Peggy told Denise that Denise had made a grave error.

Sometimes the unclear referent is not a person, but an action, feeling, or episode.

Unclear: The service was slow, and the food was cold when it arrived, which really upset Herbert.

Was Herbert upset because the service was slow, because the food was cold, or both?

Clear: Not only was the service slow, but the food was cold, both of which upset Herbert.

Another example follows:

Unclear: The population of the United States is aging, which means that in the future, young people will have much more contact with older people. Many people think this is a good thing.

What does *this* refer to? We do not know. It could refer to the fact that more of the U.S. population is older rather than younger, that young and old will interact more in the future, or both.

Clear: The population of the United States is aging, which means that in the future, young people will have much more contact with older people. Many people think such increased contact will benefit both young and old.

Note that sometimes to get around an unclear referent, you may need to rewrite one sentence into two.

PRACTICING 1

Rewrite the following sentences so that the pronouns refer clearly to only one referent.

1. Marty decided to move to Costa Rica and study medicine, which his parents couldn't understand.

   _____

   _____

2. She scraped the handrails and the stairs and painted them.

   _____

   _____

3. It was hot, the line was long, and the clerk was slow, which really tried Jack's patience.

   _____

   _____

4. My father told my brother that he was a good father but a bad husband.

   _____

   _____

5. Betty was a good friend of Mary's until she moved to New York.

   _____

   _____

6. Alexa held a lipstick in one hand and blush powder in the other, putting it on as we laughed about the new styles.

_____

_____

7. Ben told Richard he had been a loyal friend.

_____

_____

8. Stanley and Merle's room was a chaotic mess because he left everything on the floor or on the bed.

_____

_____

9. We have made great progress in cleaning up our environment, but we still have a long way to go. This surprises many people.

_____

_____

10. Mom and Aunt Lottie went shopping even though she had a bad cold.

_____

_____

Missing Referents

In both speech and writing we often use pronouns with missing referents. This is especially true of the pronouns *they* and *it*. Here is an example:

> Although my grandfather and father were farmers, I have no interest in it.

What is *it*? We have a fuzzy idea that by *it* the writer means *farming*, but the word *farming* does not appear in the sentence.

Usually the best way to rewrite such a sentence is to omit the pronoun and provide the missing noun.

> Although my grandfather and father were farmers, I have no interest in farming.

Here are some more examples:

Missing: Between games, they announced the score.

Who is this mysterious *they* in the sentence?

Clear: Between games, the announcer called out the score.

Incorrect: It says to yield to the driver approaching from your right.

Correct: The sign says to yield to the driver approaching from your right.

Now we know the identity of the unnamed *it*.

The requirement that every pronoun have a specific and clear referent is not picky. In everyday talk we do not observe such exactness in pronoun use because we can always ask "What?" and get an answer. In writing, however, there's no second chance. Every pronoun must therefore have a specific referent.

PRACTICING 2

Rewrite the following sentences to clarify the pronoun reference.

1. It says the shirt comes in plum, mango, and lime green.

_____

_____

2. My boyfriend is a great cook, but I have no interest in it.

_____

_____

3. They did not allow us to touch the Indian weavings.

_____

_____

4. I deposited the money in my bank, but they haven't posted the correct balance.

_____

_____

5. We were in the middle of registering when they informed us that the class was closed.

_____

_____

6. They refused to give me a refund even after I wrote a strong letter.

_____

_____

7. If you don't have a ticket, they won't let you in.

_____

_____

8. See; it says this is a dead-end street.

_____

_____

9. They say one should not beg a lover to stay faithful.

_____

_____

10. It has an alarm that goes off when you open the door from the outside.

_____

_____

PRACTICING 3

Rewrite the following sentences to correct the pronoun errors.

1. Maggie treated Jeanne and her mother to dinner.

_____

_____

2. When Vladimir lent money to Gorsky, he did not know he would go bankrupt.

_____

_____

3. It says the police caught the burglar.

_____

_____

4. Fred insisted to Woody that his wife was not to blame.

_____

_____

5. There is a big difference between the politicians of the past and those of today. They lack nobility.

_____

_____

6. We found a pressed rose in the book that my grandmother gave my grandfather.

_____

_____

7. They allow you to make three separate payments.

_____

_____

8. The nurse told Emma that her name was unusual.

_____

_____

9. They say that gelatin is good for your nails.

_____

_____

10. If your Persian cat will not eat raw fish, boil it.

_____

_____

UNIT TEST

Rewrite the following paragraph to eliminate all the pronoun reference problems.

My friend, Lucy, loves her cat, Fluffy, so much that she purrs constantly. When she takes her to the veterinarian, she orders a limousine so she can hold her and pet her, and so she can feed her little pieces of shrimp, which I think is a bit extreme. Once Lucy told a neighboring woman that she was noble because she loved cats. They say that women who love cats make good mothers. It wouldn't surprise me. Now, I admire cats because they have such independent spirits, but I do not intend to get one. The other day Lucy's cat held a real mouse in one paw and a toy mouse in the other, eating it as she frisked and pranced. As long as cat owners outnumber cats, they will not be a problem.

ERROR 10
Lack of Pronoun Agreement and Sexism

A pronoun and its referent (the noun it replaces) must agree in number. Singular nouns require singular pronouns. Plural nouns require plural pronouns. Here are some examples:

The bride put on *her* veil.

The attendants picked up *their* flowers.

In the first sentence the singular noun *bride* requires the singular pronoun *her*. In the second sentence, the plural noun *attendants* requires the plural pronoun *their*.

Although pronoun agreement is often not a problem, it can be when we try to find a pronoun to replace an indefinite pronoun.

An **indefinite pronoun** is a pronoun that refers to no one in particular. Here is a list of common indefinite pronouns (they are always singular):

Indefinite pronouns

one	nobody	each
anyone	anybody	either
everyone	everybody	neither
someone	somebody	

Study these sentences:

Incorrect: Each of the men carry a bottle of water.

Correct: Each ~~of the men~~ carries a bottle of water.

(*Each* requires a singular pronoun. Remember, cross out the prepositional phrase if you are confused about the subject.)

Incorrect: Either Harriet or Jo Ray will give me their paycheck.

Correct: Either Harriet or Jo Ray will give me her paycheck.

(*Either* requires a singular pronoun.)

Ear Alert

In both speech and writing, to avoid being sexist, we often use the plural *their* to refer to many indefinite pronouns that are singular. We say, for example, and it sounds perfectly right to our ear:

Someone put their keys on the table.

Technically speaking, this use is wrong. *Their* is plural; *someone* is singular. On the other hand, the singular pronoun *his* is sexist:

Someone put his keys on the table.

It is sexist because *someone* could be a female, a possibility the pronoun ignores.

The best way to correct an agreement problem is by rewriting the sentence. You can change the wrong pronoun either to singular or plural. Here is an example:

Incorrect:　Everyone who donates $50 will get their name on a plaque.

Correct:　If you donate $50, you will get your name on a plaque.

Correct:　People who donate $50 will get their names on a plaque.

Here is another example:

Incorrect:　Did everyone have their coffee?

Correct:　Did you have your coffee?

Correct:　Did every diner have coffee?

PRACTICING 1

Correct the agreement errors in the following sentences both ways that you've learned—by changing to the singular and to the plural.

1. Is everybody bringing their date to the party?

Singular: _____

Plural: _____

2. Everyone should help themselves to dessert.

Singular: _____

Plural: _____

3. Nobody knows for certain what their future holds.

Singular: _____

Plural: _____

4. If anyone needs help, they should ask me.

Singular: _____

Plural: _____

5. Would everyone who saw the accident give me their names?

Singular: _____

Plural: _____

6. If everyone did what they were told, the world would be a better place.

Singular: _____

Plural: _____

7. If someone tries hard, they will be sure to succeed.

Singular: _____

Plural: _____

8. If someone has a problem with a coworker, they should try to work it out privately.

Singular: _____

Plural: _____

9. Will everyone please tell us their names?

Singular: _____

Plural: _____

10. Neither Dennis nor Derrick sent in their money.

Singular: _____

Plural: _____

Sexism in Writing

You have just learned how to avoid the sexist use of indefinite pronouns. Sexism in writing is even worse when a singular pronoun automatically assigns the male sex to professionals:

Every police officer should wear his badge at all times.

The use of *his* in the above sentence suggests that every police officer is a man, which is both sexist and untrue. On the other hand, using *his or her* is correct but clumsy. Another solution is to make the whole sentence plural, using the neutral pronoun *their*. The possible nonsexist choices follow.

Incorrect:	Every policy officer should wear his badge at all times.
Correct:	Every police officer should wear his or her badge at all times.
Correct:	Police officers should wear their badges at all times.

Their includes both men and women, and it is not as clumsy as *his or her*.

On the other hand, sometimes we are quick to assume that some professions are dominated by women. For example, we may refer to nurses, secretaries, and grade school teachers as *she*. This is also sexist because both men and women can be nurses, secretaries, and grade school teachers. Here is an example of this type of sexism in writing:

Incorrect:	A teacher should be a good role model for her students.
Correct:	A teacher should be a good role model for his or her students.
Correct:	Teachers should be good role models for their students.

If you are facing a pronoun agreement problem that you simply cannot rewrite in the plural, then use *his or her*. If the choice is between being sexist or being clumsy, we think it is better to be clumsy.

PRACTICING 2

Rewrite the following sentences to correct the sexist bias.

1. When a plumber is finished working, he shouldn't leave a mess for the customer.

   _____

   _____

2. A hair stylist should always keep her station clean.

   _____

   _____

3. A good secretary keeps her boss organized.

   _____

   _____

4. A flight attendant should be sure her uniform is clean and pressed.

_____

_____

5. You could call a lawyer and find out what he thinks.

_____

_____

6. A social worker visits her clients regularly to check their progress.

_____

_____

7. A criminal who breaks the law repeatedly should serve his full jail term.

_____

_____

8. A reporter must check his facts carefully.

_____

_____

9. An anthropologist in the field should take care of his digging tools.

_____

_____

10. If your doctor doesn't give you an itemized bill, ask him for one.

_____

_____

PRACTICING 3

Rewrite the following sentences to correct the agreement errors and sexism.

1. Everyone should call their mother at least once a month.

_____

_____

2. Neither Nicole nor Sally turned in their homework.

_____

_____

3. A professor should be available to help her students.

_____

_____

4. Either my dog or my cat will get their shots today.

_____

_____

5. Everyone knows that they should not walk on the grass when it is wet.

_____

_____

6. A good boss plans her day efficiently.

_____

_____

7. Nobody in their right mind would do such a thing.

_____

_____

8. An architect needs his blueprints to present his ideas.

_____

_____

9. Everybody wanted their refund by mail.

_____

_____

10. An obstetrician should be considerate of his pregnant patients.

_____

_____

UNIT TEST

Rewrite the following paragraph to correct all pronoun agreement and sexism errors.

One problem I have with our neighborhood grocery store is that they hide flawed fruits and vegetables behind fruits and vegetables that are perfect. For instance, the other day, I was in the mood for a juicy nectarine. So, I drove to Tim's Market. In the back of the store, I spied a bin heaped with gorgeous yellowish red nectarines. With glad anticipation I gently palpated the top row of the heap to confirm that each of the globes were perfectly ripe—just ready to be eaten in heavenly juicy bites. Everyone around me were also admiring the fabulous display. No one indicated that they suspected anything wrong with the fruit. But when I started lifting off the top nectarines, I found that the nectarines in the layers underneath were bruised, small, or hard. Each of these nectarines were of inferior quality. None were like the large, attractive, ripe fruit adorning the top layer. It seems to me that when someone owns a grocery store, they should not pretend that all the fruit they sell is top quality. Damaged fruit and vegetables should be placed in a special bin to be sold at a lower price. Every grocery owner should respect his clients enough to be truly honest in his marketing strategies.

Trouble with Comparisons and Superlatives

Adjectives and adverbs are **modifiers**, words that describe and explain. **Adjectives** describe a noun or a pronoun by narrowing it down to a specific type, such as in the following cases:

I envy that thin girl.	**(Which girl? The *thin* one.)**
She feels lonely.	**(How does she feel? She feels *lonely*.)**
The apples look ripe.	**(How do the apples look? They look *ripe*.)**

Adverbs describe verbs, adjectives, and other adverbs in the following ways:

- They tell *how*.

- They tell *when*.

- They tell *where*.

- They tell *to what extent*.

Many adverbs end in *-ly,* but not all. These are all adverbs: *neatly, roughly, slowly, totally, considerably, really, yesterday, nearby.* Here are some more examples:

She ran very quickly.	**(*Very* tells *how* she ran—describes the adverb *quickly*.)**
We're leaving soon.	**(*Soon* tells *when* we're leaving—describes the verb *leaving*.)**
He stood here.	**(*Here* tells *where* he stood—describes the verb *stood*.)**

They are terribly late.   **(*Terribly* tells *to what extent* they are late— describes the adjective *stubborn*.)**

Comparisons

Adjectives and adverbs are often used to make comparisons between two things. The rules for making comparisons are straightforward:

- For an adjective or adverb of one syllable, add *-er*.

  The bread is warm.   **(One-syllable adjective)**
  The rolls are warmer.

  He swallowed hard.   **(One-syllable adverb)**
  She swallowed harder.

- For an adjective or adverb of more than one syllable, add *more*.

  The book was shocking.   **(Adjective of more than one syllable)**
  The movie was more shocking.

  Our camp rebelled openly.   **(Adverb of more than one syllable)**
  Their camp rebelled even more openly.

- For an adjective or adverb that ends in *y*, drop the *y* and add *-ier* in the comparative.

  She's lucky at love.
  She's luckier at cars.

  Jerry is funny.
  Mary is funnier.

PRACTICING 1

Write the comparative form of each word listed below.

Example: long *longer*

             beautiful *more beautiful*

1. messy _____

2. blunt _____

3. furious _____

4. desirable _____

5. cold _____

6. goofy _____

7. mean _____

8. clumsy _____

9. intelligent _____

10. happy _____

Double comparisons

A common mistake often heard in everyday speech is the **double comparison**, using both *-er* and *more*.

Incorrect: Phoenix is more hotter than San Francisco.
Correct: Phoenix is hotter than San Francisco.

Incorrect: Bunny is more quieter than Lisa.
Correct: Bunny is quieter than Lisa.

PRACTICING 2

Rewrite the following sentences to correct the comparisons.

1. Wayne has the more relaxeder attitude.

_____

2. The sooner you leave, the more faster you will get there.

_____

3. Her hairdo is attractiver than Joyce's.

_____

4. This story is more sadder than I expected.

_____

5. She was at peace and more serener than before.

_____

6. Squirrels are much more quicker than rabbits.

_____

7. Where freedom is concerned, Americans are more luckier than most other citizens.

_____

8. When can we afford a more better car?

_____

9. He traveled frequentlier than he had told me.

_____

10. The ocean was dangerouser than it looked.

_____

Superlatives

The comparative form of adjectives and adverbs is used to express a difference between two things.

> The first bell is loud.
> The second bell is louder.   **(Comparative)**

To express differences among three or more things, you must use the **superlative** form of an adjective or adverb.

> The first bell is loud.
> The second bell is louder.   **(Comparative)**
> The third bell is loudest.   **(Superlative)**

> The salmon is fresh.
> The swordfish is fresher.   **(Comparative)**
> The trout is freshest of all.   **(Superlative)**

The rules for changing adjectives and adverbs into the superlative form are simple:

- For an adverb or adjective of one syllable, add -*est*.

dark	darker	darkest
light	lighter	lightest
short	shorter	shortest

He was the shortest of all the basketball players.

Notice that some adjectives or adverbs double the final consonant: gladder/gladdest, sadder/saddest, dimmer/dimmest, bigger/biggest.

- For an adjective that ends in *y*, drop the *y* and add -*iest*.

funny	funnier	funniest
fancy	fancier	fanciest
petty	pettier	pettiest

Marty was the craziest of them all.

■ For an adjective or adverb of two or more syllables, add the word *most*.

wonderful	more wonderful	most wonderful
fortunate	more fortunate	most fortunate
interesting	more interesting	most interesting

Loons make the most dreadful sound at night.

PRACTICING 3

In the blanks provided, write the correct superlative forms of the words below.

1. merciful _____

2. skinny _____

3. sweet _____

4. carefully _____

5. pushy _____

6. smoothly _____

7. thoughtful _____

8. hideous _____

9. unusual _____

10. thick _____

Problems with superlatives

When you use superlatives, watch out for these common errors of every-day speech:

■ Use the superlative only when you are speaking of *more than two* things.

Incorrect: She is the most qualified of the two applicants.
Correct: She is the more qualified of the two applicants.

Incorrect: This is the funniest of the two scenes.
Correct: This is the funnier of the two scenes.

■ Do not use both an *-est* or an *-iest* ending and *most*.

Incorrect: That is the most kindest gesture imaginable.
Correct: That is the kindest gesture imaginable.

Incorrect: She has the most sunniest disposition.
Correct: She has the sunniest disposition.

PRACTICING 4

Rewrite the following sentences to correct the errors in forming the superlative.

1. Isn't this place the most wonderfulest you could ever imagine?

_____

_____

2. Both models on the cover are the beautifulest.

_____

_____

3. This is the most hardest math assignment I have ever been given.

_____

_____

4. Older people can give you the most wisest counsel of all.

_____

_____

5. Of the three, she is the most youngest.

_____

_____

6. Have the judges given out the gold medal to the most worthiest of the three athletes?

_____

_____

7. Many people find Irish storytellers the interestingest of all English language writers.

_____

_____

8. Miami's the most hottest city imaginable in the summer.

_____

_____

9. Our choir has the most talentedest singers.

_____

_____

10. The biggest cities are bound to harbor the corruptest criminals.

_____

_____

PRACTICING 5

For the following sentences, first decide if a comparative or superlative form is needed. Then write the correct form.

Example: It was the (beautiful) _most beautiful_ rainbow I'd ever seen.

1. She was the (fanatic)_____ person I have ever met.

2. Of the two dogs, the boxer was the (friendly) _____ .

3. The Arco Building seemed the (high) _____ building I had ever seen.

4. Of all the office managers, she was the (efficient) _____ .

5. A ripe peach is (sweet) _____ than a ripe plum.

6. Of the two candles, the red one was the (pretty) _____ .

7. Uncle George was the (ambitious) _____ member of my dad's family.

8. Consider the three routes, then take the (fast) _____ .

9. We were asked to relate the (embarrassing) _____ moment of our childhood.

10. The bridge is (slippery) _____ than the road when it rains.

UNIT TEST

On a separate sheet rewrite the passage that follows to correct all incorrect comparatives or superlatives.

When there is a choice at the grocery store, I always ask for a plastic bag rather than a paper one. First of all, plastic bags are usefuller than paper ones because you can use them as small garbage can liners or as handy travel bags. Second of all, plastic bags are more stronger than paper ones. If a paper bag gets the least bit damp, it tears, and all of its contents spill out—sometimes causing the embarrassingest situation imaginable. People rush to your aid thinking, "This shopper is more clumsy than a clown." Besides, plastic bags preserve trees because to make paper bags you have to cut down trees. I show off that I am more ecologicaler than shoppers with paper bags when I exit from the grocery store. Using plastic instead of paper grocery bags is one of the most easiest ways to be environmentally conscious.

Dangling or Misplaced Modifiers

A **modifier** is a word or phrase that describes. Modifiers are adjectives, adverbs, or words or phrases that function as adjectives or adverbs. What a modifier describes in a sentence depends not only on what it says, but also where it is put.

> Snapping violently, the tourists ran from the alligator.

Here *snapping violently* is a modifier. Because of its place in the sentence, however, it modifies *tourists* rather than *alligator*. Such a modifier is said to dangle.

Dangling Modifiers

A **dangling modifier** is a word or phrase at the beginning of a sentence that mistakenly modifies the word immediately following. When a modifier begins a sentence, *the word it modifies must come immediately after.* Otherwise, the modifier will be unconnected to the word the writer meant it to modify. In short, it will dangle. Here are some examples:

Dangling: Dipping below the horizon, I watched as the sun set.

Dangling: Confused and upset, the crowded store caused the little girl to lose her mother.

Dangling: Screeching, we looked for our binoculars as the owl flew by.

To correct these sentences, place the word being modified immediately after the modifier and rewrite as necessary.

Correct: Dipping below the horizon, the sun set as I watched.

Correct: Confused and upset, the little girl lost her mother in the crowded store.

Correct: Screeching, the owl flew away as we looked for our binoculars.

Sometimes correcting a dangling modifier results in the passive voice. In this case, restructure the sentence completely. Here is an example:

Dangling:	Hiding under a rock, I found a little lizard.
Correct but passive voice:	Hiding under a rock, a little lizard was found by me.
Correct and active voice:	I found a little lizard hiding under a rock.

PRACTICING 1

Rewrite these sentences to correct the dangling modifiers.

1. Fluttering wildly, I caught the butterfly in my net.

_____

_____

2. Newly polished, the guests marveled at the gleaming silverware.

_____

_____

3. Hurrying through the grocery store, my shopping bag seemed especially heavy.

_____

_____

4. Old and broken, she left the couch behind when she moved.

_____

_____

5. Drooping pitifully, I watered the plant.

_____

_____

6. Drenched from the recent rain, he still watered the lawn.

_____

_____

7. Weeping on stage, the audience was enthralled by the actor.

_____

_____

8. Pounded by waves and sinking at the stern, I watched the ship go down.

_____

_____

9. As an athlete, weight training is very important.

_____

_____

10. Wearing my new glasses, the stars in the sky looked beautiful.

_____

_____

Misplaced Modifiers

A modifier tends to modify the nearest noun. For example, notice how the meaning of the following sentence changes as we move the modifier *only*:

She went into the pool wearing her only bikini.	**(She owned only one bikini. *Only* is modifying *bikini*.)**
She went into the pool wearing only her bikini.	**(She wore nothing but a bikini. *Only* is modifying *wearing*.)**

A **misplaced modifier** is too far from the word it is meant to modify and, as a result, it doesn't convey the correct meaning or it gives the sentence an unintended, funny meaning. Here are some examples of misplaced modifiers with unintentional meanings:

Misplaced: The fisherman caught a bass with a chuckle.

Misplaced: I climbed a tree with new shoes on.

Misplaced: She bicycled to Burlington to visit her grandmother wearing a bike helmet.

Because of a misplaced modifier, we have *a bass with a chuckle, a tree with new shoes,* and *grandmother wearing a bike helmet.* A misplaced modifier is corrected by rewriting the sentence. You must reword the modifier or move it closer to the word it modifies. Here are possible corrections:

With a chuckle, the fisherman caught a bass.

With new shoes on, I climbed the tree.

Wearing a bike helmet, she bicycled to Burlington to visit her grandmother.

To avoid the confusion of misplaced modifiers, always place a modifier immediately in front of the word it is meant to modify. This is especially true of one-word modifiers such as *almost, even, hardly, nearly, only,* and *often.* Because these words limit what follows, it is important where they occur in a sentence. Remember the bikini example at the beginning of this section. Another example follows.

He just baked a cake.   **(He did it a moment ago.)**

He baked just a cake.   **(He didn't bake bread.)**

PRACTICING 2

First underline the misplaced modifier in each sentence below. Then rewrite the sentence so that the modifier is correctly placed.

Example: I put money in the bank <u>with a smile</u>.

With a smile, I put money in the bank.
_____

1. Jonathan gave his dog a bone with a pat on the head.

_____

_____

_____

2. At the ceremony, he retired with honors in his uniform.

_____

_____

_____

3. The pool table seemed tilted to the customers.

_____

_____

_____

4. We saw huge fir trees skiing down the slope on both sides.

_____

_____

_____

5. Josephine barbecued ribs for 20 people on the grill.

_____

_____

_____

6. The jogger ran past the dog wearing a funny hat.

_____

_____

7. Spaghetti is most delicious when it is eaten on a patio with meatballs.

_____

_____

_____

8. She almost handed out candy to the trick-or-treaters for two hours.

_____

_____

_____

9. We saw the ocean waves sitting on a deck.

_____

_____

_____

10. The young lovers admired the moon going on a stroll.

_____

_____

_____

UNIT TEST

Underline the dangling and misplaced modifiers in the following paragraph. Then rewrite the sentences correctly in the spaces below. You should find six errors.

My favorite place during the summer is the beach. Relaxing on the sand, the waves roll in peacefully. Seagulls look for crabs overhead. When I'm on the beach, my mind is full of nothing but relaxation and pleasant dreams playing in the sand. Buzzing noisily, I ignore the hordes of flies. Occasionally, I wade into the surf and enjoy watching the waves up close with my shoes on. Thinking neither of work nor school, the beach is pure pleasure. In fact, when I'm on the beach, I think of nothing at all, except how lovely it is to be there.

_____

_____

_____

_____

_____

_____

_____

_____

_____

_____

_____

_____

_____

_____

_____

Omitted Commas, Part I

Punctuation marks are the traffic signs of writing. They are the visible marks that tell the reader when to slow down, when to speed up, and when to stop. In spoken sentences punctuation is heard as pauses, upbeats, and downbeats.

The Comma (,)

You hear the comma as a half-pause. Sometimes the comma just makes listening or reading easier, but sometimes it is crucial to meaning. Here is an example:

> Still, water was important to many primitive tribes.

> Still water was important to many primitive tribes.

The difference in the meanings of these two sentences depends on where the comma is placed. In the first sentence, *still* means "nonetheless" or "nevertheless." In the second sentence, *still* serves as an adjective describing water.

In this section we will cover two hard-and-fast rules of comma usage.

Commas with coordinating conjunctions

Place a comma in front of coordinating conjunctions (*and*, *but*, *or*, *for*, *nor*, *so*, *yet*) that link independent clauses (see Unit 20).

> He dated Mabel, but he did not fall in love with her.

> I am obsessed with neatness, and my girlfriend is, too.

> He wrote me three letters, so I finally answered him.

Do not use a comma before *and* if it is not followed by an independent clause.

Incorrect: He read a magazine, and watched TV.

Correct: He read a magazine and watched TV.

PRACTICING 1

Finish the following sentences by adding another independent clause and a coordinating conjunction. Remember to use a comma.

Example: The clouds were beautiful.

The clouds were beautiful, but they brought heavy rain.

1. The earth is mother to us all, and we should care of it. all take
2. I love movies, especially the newest one that came out
3. On July 4 we always have a picnic, so you should come
4. Make a fresh pot of coffee, but don't make it so strong.
5. Love is what makes the world happy, so keep it that way.
6. Fred plays the violin in private, but he wants someone to listen to him
7. We're good friends, and nothing can seperate us.
8. Many people are utterly sincere, but when it comes to times like this their not.
9. The dew was on the rose, yet it still looks pretty
10. Jane should stop feeling sorry for herself, but she won't listen

Commas with introductory words, phrases, and clauses

Use a comma after introductory words, phrases, and clauses.

Words: Therefore, we beg you to be patient.
              Well, I am not the least bit surprised.
              Derrick, I'll take full responsibility.

Phrases: Seen from the top of the hill, the church was small.
              Having expressed my view, I withdrew from the argument.
              By the way, you owe me $10.00.

Use a comma after a dependent clause only if it comes at the beginning, but not at the end, of a sentence:

If at first you don't succeed, try again.

                                but

Try again if at first you don't succeed.

When I get a raise, I'm getting a new suit.

                                but

I'm getting a new suit when I get a raise.

PRACTICING 2 ✳

Insert commas where needed. Mark "C" for correct if no comma is needed.

_____ 1. No, they cannot enter without paying a fee.

_____ 2. If he is a great man, then many men are great.

_____ 3. Although he had a headache, Clarence continued to run.

__C___ 4. Take a left on Elm Street and then a right at the first light.

_____ 5. She made a budget, but she is not sticking to it.

_____ 6. Nevertheless, high heels are bad for your posture.

__C___ 7. I have two job interviews tomorrow and one on Monday.

_____ 8. When we live by the sword, we perish by the sword.

_____ 9. First of all, finding happiness should not be your primary goal.

_____ 10. He hates to give speeches, but he always accepts when it's for a good cause.

PRACTICING 3 ✗

Insert commas where needed. In the spaces provided, state the rule that makes the comma necessary.

Example: Ted, your dad is looking for you.

Rule: _A comma follows an introductory word._

1. Because I am a woman, I believe that mothers influence sons.
Rule: ~~comma follows~~ dependant clause ~~before~~

2. Serena, please pass the salt and pepper.
Rule: follows an introductory word

3. She accepted the gold trophy, and he accepted the blue ribbon.
Rule: _____

4. If we had known the consequences, we would have stayed at home.
Rule: follows a dependant clause

5. Additionally, he stole her wallet.

Rule: _____

6. The lightening bolt flashed across the sky, and rain poured from the heavens.

Rule: _follows an Independant Clause_____

7. From where I sit, I have observed some fascinating people.

Rule: _____

8. Although he hates routine, he orders his coffee at 7:00 A.M. every morning.

Rule: _____

9. Are they planning to pick you up, or are you driving alone?

Rule: _____

10. If you hate your job, your health is bound to be affected.

Rule: _____

UNIT TEST

Correct the passage that follows by placing commas where they belong.

Parents and grandparents who don't learn to use the Internet are behind the time and their situation will only get worse. From a common sense point of view, computer literacy is a modern requirement. If you think about it, learning to use computers today is equivalent to learning to drive a car fifty years ago. The schools in my home town, sponsor several media literacy classes, and our local community college offers special workshops in using the Internet. These classes teach older adults basic skills, and how to connect with the World Wide Web. They even receive tips on how to supervise their children's use of the Internet. My mother, has not yet taken advantage of these classes. Therefore, she knows nothing about the technology her children use every day. However, our neighbor took a computer course and enjoyed it very much. If this neighbor's enthusiasm influences my mother to sign up for the class, I'll be thrilled. She might then become technologically literate and part of the twenty-first century.

Omitted Commas, Part II

In Error 13 you learned two rules for using commas:

1. Place a comma in front of coordinating conjunctions (*and, but, or, for, nor, so, yet*) that link independent clauses.
2. Use a comma after introductory words, phrases, and clauses.

In this section you will learn two more hard-and-fast rules for using commas: (1) Use commas to separate items in a series, and (2) place commas around words that interrupt the flow of a sentence.

Use commas to separate items in a series.

We can talk, daydream, play cards, or read.

They swam, played football, and threw the Frisbee.

The soft, furry leaves feel like velvet.

We will research the facts, gather support, and publicize our cause.

Do not, however, use commas unnecessarily with words in a series.

Do not use a comma before "and" if only two items are mentioned.

Incorrect: He reads novels, and poetry.
Correct: He reads novels and poetry.

Do not use a comma between modifiers unless you can insert the word "and" between them.

Incorrect: She carried beautiful, red roses.
Correct: She carried beautiful red roses.

You wouldn't say *She carried the beautiful and red roses*, so you shouldn't use a comma. You would, however, use a comma between the modifiers of this sentence:

A fresh, brisk breeze blew off the ocean.

You could insert an *and* between the modifiers, and the sentence would still sound right:

A fresh and brisk breeze blew off the ocean.

Do not use a comma before the first item in a series or after the last.

Incorrect: We went, to sightsee, to shop, to dine out, and to enjoy, ourselves.

Correct: We went to sightsee, to shop, to dine out, and to enjoy ourselves.

Incorrect: She put, her shoes, her handbag, and her suitcase, in the trunk of the car.

Correct: She put her shoes, her handbag, and her suitcase in the trunk of the car.

PRACTICING 1

Insert commas as necessary to separate items in a series.

1. They jumped over rocks, trees, and bushes.

2. We can do the job with a little luck, a little effort, and a little perseverance.

3. I love you more than chocolate, marshmallows, apple pie, and fudge brownies.

4. You need paper, pencil, and your textbook.

5. Bright, sparkling, water gushed from the beautiful old fountain.

6. They ate pasta, bread, and peanuts to get ready for the race.

7. I have a dog, a cat, a bird, and a snake.

8. Do you prefer yams, bananas, or plantains?

9. My mother, my father, my sister, and my brother live with me.

10. I like to watch baseball, football, tennis, and soccer on television.

PRACTICING 2

Strike through the unnecessary commas in the following sentences.

Example: The old lady put down her coat, and hat.

1. She runs, lifts weights, and eats plenty of fresh vegetables, to keep fit.

2. I love my house, and my garden.

3. My neighbors include, a Jamaican, an American, and an Armenian.

4. My ugly/blue car is in the garage.

5. Pack sandwiches, fruit, drinks, and cookies/ for the picnic.

6. I love Beethoven/ and Chopin.

7. Among my uncle's favorite foods/ are ice cream, apples, peaches, and apricots.

8. The brand/ new Jeep belongs to my roommate.

9. The card games we like include/ canasta, gin, poker, and hearts.

10. The band played blues/ and rock and roll.

Place commas around words that interrupt the flow of a sentence.

In talking it is natural to pause before and after words that interrupt the flow of thought. In writing, this pause is signaled by a comma. Interruptions include the following:

1. Expression.

   You understand, of course, that the position is temporary.

2. Descriptive phrase.

   The lighthouse, tall and majestic, stood among the rocks.

   Mr. Golub, our mail carrier, is always very pleasant.

3. Prepositional phrase.

   The ice, on which the skaters glided, shone in the moonlight.

4. Unessential clauses that begin with *who, whose, which, when, where,* or *that.*

   Elaine, who went to Oakland Community College, now lives in Detroit.

A clause containing information that is *not* essential to understanding a sentence is enclosed by commas.

Ms. Jones, who works at Benson's, witnessed the accident.

(Because Ms. Jones is named, the information in the clause is not essential to identify her as the woman who witnesses the accident.)

On the other hand, the clause containing information *essential* to understanding the sentence is not set off by commas.

The woman who works at Benson's witnessed the accident.

Now the information in the clause is essential to identify who witnessed the accident—*the woman who works at Benson's*, since we don't know her name.

Commas needed:	The poet read "Daddy," which I'd never heard.
Commas not needed:	The poet read a poem that I'd never heard before.

Most of the time, relative clauses with *which* need commas while relative clauses with *that* do not.

Commas needed:	The horse *Anchovy*, which I often ride, is in the stable.
Commas not needed:	The horse that I often ride is in the stable.

PRACTICING 3

Underline the words that interrupt the flow of the sentence, then place commas around them.

Example: My uncle who now has gray hair is also my best friend.

My uncle, who now has gray hair, is also my best friend.

1. The beloved teacher, who had taught for 50 years, finally retired.

2. The divorce, which no one expected, was final last week.

3. He realized, of course, that he would never make his plane.

4. My mother, a champion rug hooker, never took lessons in her art.

5. The old cat, purring furiously, rubbed up against my leg.

6. The police officer, who is also our crossing guard, always looks out for the small children.

7. Mr. Smith, by the way, is a champion chess player.

8. Self-confidence, a key ingredient in success, can be developed.

9. The garden, around which we strolled, is very well cared-for.

10. You are, nevertheless, mistaken on that point.

PRACTICING 4

Insert the omitted commas in the following sentences. Use all four rules that you have learned in Errors 13 and 14. Then, in the spaces provided, state the rule. If no comma is needed, state the rule that makes it unnecessary.

1. I spoke to him repeatedly, but he wouldn't listen.

Rule: _____

2. You need a walking stick, a backpack, and a compass for the hike.

Rule: Series _____

3. Of course, it is your right to decline.

Rule: Introductry material _____

4. My uncle Harry, who wears a hearing aid, was at my graduation.

Rule: clause intruption of flow _____

5. Peter, will you answer the bell?

Rule: Introductry _____

6. I wore my new blue blazer.

Rule: _____

7. They had, however, other plans.

Rule: clause intruption of flow _____

8. She heard my voice and came into the room.

Rule: _____

9. My best friend, who is also my accountant, went with me.

Rule: clause intrupte flow _____

10. Because you're so nice, I wanted to give you a gift.

Rule: Introductry _____

UNIT TEST

Rewrite the following paragraph to add commas where needed.

Even with a plan it's easy to get derailed. For example when I started college my goal was to become a pediatric nurse. I concentrated on getting good grades so I studied hard working long hours into the night. My science classes required a tremendous amount of reading memorizing and hours of lab work. But in the spring of 1998 I enrolled in a drama class as an elective. I was chosen to be in the school musical and I started to hang out with other drama students. They were all one big bad influence. They spent their days and evenings in the auditorium instead of the classroom. Being young and naïve I took to these devil-may-care people faster than you can say "ambisol." As a result my career goals crashed burned and went up in smoke. I neglected reading assignments cut class and skipped labs. All I did was hang around with my new theater friends pretending we were headed for Broadway and fame. When my mother noticed my grades slipping she warned me that my new friends were bad for me but of course I didn't listen. Fortunately the school newspaper panned my performance and I came to my senses. I also realized that I was hurting my mother the person I loved most. So I quit drama and started studying. I am now back to my original hopes and dreams bolstered by diligence and determination.

Apostrophe Problems

The apostrophe (') has two uses, to show possession and to indicate a contraction.

Use the apostrophe to show possession.

The chart below shows how apostrophes are used to show possession or ownership. For a singular noun, always add 's. However, to form the possessive of a plural noun ending in s, add only the apostrophe. If the plural does not end in s, add 's.

Singular (always add 's)	Plural
dog's tail	dogs' tails
boss's desk	bosses' desks
woman's hat	women's hats
Genevieve Smith's home	the Smiths' home

PRACTICING 1

Make the following nouns possessive. First decide if the noun is singular or plural. Then decide if you need only an apostrophe or 's.

1. The Browns barbecue

2. The cat dish

3. The doctors offices

4. The person mood

5. The children games

6. The car windshield

7. The Moses Ten Commandments

8. The politicians photograph

9. The churches towers

10. The barnyard smell

Use the apostrophe to show an omission in a contraction.

Apostrophes are used to show omitted letters in contractions, such as *don't (do not)* or *isn't (is not)*. Contractions are commonly used in informal writing. Here are some common contractions:

cannot	can't
could have	could've
could not	couldn't
did not	didn't
do not	don't
has not	hasn't
have not	haven't
he is	he's
I am	I'm
I would	I'd
it is	it's
let us	let's
she is	she's
should have	should've
should not	shouldn't
they are	they're
they are not	they aren't
was not	wasn't
who is	who's
will not	won't
would have	would've
would not	wouldn't

In speech we can hear these contractions. What we cannot hear is exactly where the apostrophe goes—where the letter was actually omitted.

wouldn't, not would'nt   **(The apostrophe marks the omission of the *o*.)**

they're, not theyr'e   **(The apostrophe marks the omission of the *a*.)**

Remember to put the apostrophe exactly where the letter is missing.

Do not use apostrophes unnecessarily.

Only use an apostrophe with a possessive.

Incorrect: The mother's are having a bakesale for Oakton School.

Correct: The mothers are having a bakesale for Oakton School.

To test whether a noun is possessive or not, turn it into an *of* phrase.

The baby's blanket is wet.

(baby's blanket = blanket of baby= possessive)

The quiz answers' are on the sheet.

(answers' are = the are of the answers = not possessive)

Do not use apostrophes with the pronouns his, hers, its, ours, yours, or theirs.

Incorrect: The scarf is hers'.

Correct: The scarf is hers.

Incorrect: Put the CD back in it's case.

Correct: Put the CD back in its case.

It's is a contraction—short for *it is*. If you unravel the contraction, you get:

Put the CD back in it is case.

which makes no sense.

PRACTICING 2

Rewrite the following sentences to use contractions whenever possible.

Example: They did not obey the rules.

They didn't obey the rules.

1. You should not rollerblade without knee pads.

   you shouldn't rollerblade without knee pads

2. I could not have cared less.

   couldn't

3. Lou will not take out the garbage.

   won't

4. He ~~was not~~ at all impressed with their answer.

wasn't

5. They said they ~~had not~~ seen him.

haven't

6. If he ~~could have~~ attended the meeting, he would have.

could've

7. Why ~~have you not~~ finished your homework?

haven't you

8. If you ~~did not~~ owe me $10 dollars, I ~~would not~~ be so skeptical.

didn't   *wouldn't*

9. I am afraid ~~it is~~ too late for apologies.

it's

10. ~~Who is~~ going to carry in the cake?

who's

PRACTICING 3

Insert apostrophes where needed.

1. Despite health warnings, people's desire for junk food continues.

2. Were wondering how long he's going to defy the law.

3. According to him, its someone else's fault.

4. Ten artist's are displaying their paintings at John Kellers new gallery.

5. She's afraid of lightning, but he isnt.

6. Africa's wild life attracts many photographers.

7. The story's ending puzzled many readers.

8. My cousin inherited Aunt Ida's old piano.

9. The governments leader's would only meet in neutral territory.

10. Marv's tattoos have become infected.

PRACTICING 4

Every sentence below has one apostrophe error. It may be missing an apostrophe (or *'s*) in a possessive or in a contraction. Sometimes the error is an unnecessary apostrophe. Add apostrophes (or *'s*) where they are needed. Strike out all unnecessary apostrophes.

1. Lets fetch Grandpa's coat so he won't be cold.

2. Wasn't he the biggest coward you've ever seen?

3. Put the trophy in it's place on the mantle.

4. Don't be so sure that the bracelet is her's.

5. The contract is asking for two weeks vacation per year.

6. Put an apple and two cookies's in his lunch box.

7. Its my opinion that students' shouldn't get an A on a late paper.

8. The Rodmans' and the Joneses' attended the game.

9. It's not up to me to give you a pass.

10. Most of the actors' faces had been made up to look old.

UNIT TEST

The passage that follows contains ten misplaced or missing apostrophes. Rewrite the passage to correct these errors.

The best taste in the world belongs to chocolate. Whether dark cocoa or light milk chocolate, it's creamy texture delights my pallet. But chocolate is addicting, and once I start eating it, I ca'nt stop. Lately Ive read that doctors attitudes have changed toward chocolate. Doctors used to warn that chocolate caused tooth decay, headache's, and all manner of other illnesses. But now some medical researchers have found that chocolate is a mood elevator and even an aphrodisiac. I think it was my mothers fudge that started me on the road to being a chocolaholic. No one elses fudge could compare with her's. I used to sit in my room with a large square of Mom's fudge on a porcelain saucer, and I felt so comforted and queenly as I bit into one nutty piece after another. You woul'dve thought I was in heaven. Other desserts are lovely, but they just dont compare with good chocolate.

Trouble with Quotation Marks

Your ear may tell you when a pause means a comma, but sometimes your ear is of little use in identifying the correct punctuation. For certain punctuation marks, you must simply learn the rules. In this unit you will learn how to use quotation marks correctly.

Use quotation marks to indicate a person's exact words.

One of the two main written uses for quotations marks (" ") is to indicate a person's exact words—called a direct quotation. Direct quotations can be reported in a number of different ways, all requiring quotation marks.

> He remarked, "This is rather difficult."

> "This is rather difficult," he remarked.

> "This," he said, "is rather difficult."

> "This is difficult," he remarked. "And it doesn't get any easier."

Begin every quotation with a capital letter.
Do not, however, use a capital letter for the second part of a divided quotation that is *not* a full sentence.

> "I work at the zoo," she said, "because I love animals."

Here the second part of the divided quotation is not a full sentence, so a comma is used after *said*, but no capital letter.

> "Give me the money," his father said. "I'll put it in the bank for you."

Here the second part of the divided quotation is a full sentence. A period follows *said* and the second part of the quotation begins with a capital letter.

Do not use quotation marks in indirect quotations.
An indirect quotation—rewording what someone has said—does not require quotation marks. Often an indirect quotation word is announced by the words *that, what,* or *if.* Some examples follow.

Direct quotation:	Peter said, "Go ahead and start without me."
Indirect quotation:	Peter said that we should go ahead and start without him.
Direct quotation:	The butler asked, "Shall I serve tea, Madam?"
Indirect quotation:	The butler asked if he should serve tea.

PRACTICING 1

Add the required quotation marks.

Example: I'm betting on your horse, said the gambler, because he's the fastest.

"I'm betting on your horse," said the gambler, "because he's the
fastest."

1. Whatever you do, don't look back, said the guide.

2. I'm a man of the ocean, said the sailor. That's why I hate land.

3. Why was I ever born? the teenager asked.

4. To do the dishes, his mother replied. That's why you were born.

5. Alexander wondered, Where have all the flowers gone?

6. I do not, she said, always fall asleep during the sermon.

7. I don't eat anything with eyes, explained the vegetarian.

8. Jumping through the hoop, the tiger seemed to be saying, I'm tired of this.

9. I shower only on Sunday, the old gentleman remarked. I never shower on Monday.

10. The auctioneer cried, Going, going, gone!

PRACTICING 2

Place quotation marks only around the exact words of the speaker; leave the sentence unchanged if the quotation is indirect.

1. John wondered what had happened at the party.

2. Let me guess, Josephine said. You must be the new mail carrier.

3. Tony asked his editor if she had gone crazy.

4. As a matter of fact, the editor replied, I have—from deadlines.

5. The police recommended that we file a report.

6. Happy birthday, we all shouted, and many happy returns.

7. She suggested that we stay for cake and coffee.

8. Walter explained that only one replacement would be hired.

9. Are you here to apply for the job? he asked. Please fill out this application.

10. It's getting late, she said. Are you nearly finished?

Using other punctuation with quotation marks

Commas and periods always go inside the quotation marks.

"The food is very spicy," said Hal.

"Eat slowly," she suggested, "and drink plenty of water."

Question marks and exclamation points go either inside or outside, depending on the sentence.

Inside: "Why are you asking?" the lawyer wondered.
Outside: Who just asked, "Why are you asking"?

In the first example the spoken words make up a separate question; in the second example the spoken words are part of the question.

"Duck!" Paul screamed.

Paul keeps screaming, "Duck"!

In the first example the spoken words make up a separate command; in the second the spoken words are part of the command.

PRACTICING 3

The sentences that follow use other punctuation marks in connection with quotation marks. In the spaces provided, write *C* if the sentence is correctly punctuated and *NC* if it is not. Correct the sentence if it is incorrectly punctuated.

Example: ___C___ "What are you doing?" he asked.

1. _____ The acrobat cried, "I missed you"!

2. _____ "How much is your rent?" he asked.

3. _____ The gentleman grumped, "So you say", adding, "but I know better."

4. _____ Who said, "Give me liberty, or give me death"?

5. _____ "Find yourself a job"! she bawled.

6. _____ "Give me a break!" he cried.

7. _____ Who just said, "I'm tired of this movie?"

8. _____ "Sir," she remarked bitterly, "you are no gentleman".

9. _____ "I will not"! she snapped.

10. _____ They asked, "Now, what's the matter"?

Use quotation marks to indicate titles of short works.

Use quotation marks to indicate the titles of short works, such as magazine articles and short stories. Underline or italicize the titles of long works.

Shorter works	**Longer works**
magazine article—"Outlet Shopping"	magazine—*Consumer Reports*
newspaper article—"City Council Approves New Train Station"	newspaper—*The Cleveland Press*
book chapter—"The Child from Ages 2 to 6"	book—*Child Development*
poem—"America"	poetry collection—*The Collected Poems of Allen Ginsberg*
song—"Buffalo Soldier"	movie—*Shane*
editorial—"Stand Up for Your Rights"	television series—*Frasier*

PRACTICING 4

Use quotation marks or underlining as required.

Example: Stay Young is an essay that appears in an anthology titled Readings for Writers.

"Stay Young" is an essay that appears in an anthology titled Readings for Writers.

1. Chapter 3 is entitled Purpose and Thesis.

2. My favorite Bob Marley song is No Woman No Cry.

3. Running in the Family is an amusing book.

4. My uncle's favorite book is A Passage to India.

5. Did you see the movie Titanic?

6. I read an interesting editorial in the Atlanta Constitution; it was called "Enough Already."

7. The Jamaica Journal is an informative magazine about Jamaica.

8. I love the television series The Nanny.

9. Saving Private Ryan is a realistic but gory movie.

10. His favorite play is Death of a Salesman.

UNIT TEST

Add the missing quotation marks where needed. Some sentences are correct.

My aunt and I have a private book club between us. Every week, we try to read a book together and then discuss it afterwards. Sometimes we choose a book that's too big to be read in a week, and it takes us longer. The last book we read together was The Nightmare Years by William L. Shirer. My aunt's favorite chapter in that book is chapter 4, which is entitled The Year Off in Spain, 1933. I like the way he writes, said my aunt. I especially like his plain style. I agree, I replied, because he gets right into his subject quickly and without any fussiness. What do you mean by fussiness? my aunt wondered. I explained that I meant Shirer is not a pretentious writer. He's always down-to-earth and to the point, I added. My aunt agreed with me. She said she found that trait also in his most famous book, The Rise and Fall of the Third Reich, which we had read last year. He writes that way, said my aunt, because he used to be a newspaper reporter for the Chicago Tribune. He learned his writing trade in the newsroom. When we're finished reading this book, we intend to read Berlin Diary, Stranger Come Home, and The Rise and Fall of Adolf Hitler, which are other books by Mr. Shirer.

Incorrect Capitalization, Part I

Because capital (uppercase) and lowercase letters sound the same, your ear cannot help you with capitalization: *Penny*, the name, sounds the same as *penny*, the noun, meaning "a one-cent coin." To learn capitalization, you must know the rules. Here are the first set of rules (you will learn additional rules in the next section, Error 18):

- Capitalize the first word in a sentence or direct quotation.

- Capitalize names of individual persons and the word *I*.

- Capitalize family relationships used as names.

- Capitalize the names of nationalities, religions, races, tribes, and languages.

- Capitalize after a colon if what follows is a full sentence.

- Capitalize the names of the days of the week, months of the year, holidays, and religious occasions.

- Capitalize the names of specific places, including monuments.

- Capitalize the names of companies, clubs, political groups, and other official organizations.

Here are these rules of capitalization, one by one.

Capitalize the first word in a sentence or direct quotation.

Children often feel insecure.

Ralph Sockman said, "The test of courage comes when we are in the minority; the test of tolerance comes when we are in the majority."

"The fault," she insisted, "is in us."

Notice that in the third example, *the* is capitalized because it begins a new sentence; however, *is* remains lowercase because it is part of the first sentence.

PRACTICING 1

Correctly capitalize the following sentences.

1. Jessica complained vigorously. she said she felt deprived.

2. "can you give me a map?" she asked. "my sense of direction is terrible."

3. Carmen laughed, "he'll be fine if you just leave him alone."

4. I want to be remembered as a helpful person. helpful people are saints.

5. Run for your life! don't stay under the tree.

Capitalize names of individuals and the word I.

Give the note to Miss Ehrlich, not to Captain Douglas.

Our family doctor is Ruth Kazan.

Notice that nicknames are also capitalized.

He was known by his buddies as Big Shoulder Beans.

PRACTICING 2

Capitalize the names of individuals in the following sentences.

1. All Americans revere abraham lincoln.

2. I hate it when my dad's college pals call him shorty.

3. Laurence bradley, carolyn costaldo, and jose guiterrez are scheduled to talk at Career Day.

4. The greatest Sioux leader was sitting bull.

5. Many cities have named streets after the great civil rights leader, martin luther king.

Capitalize family relationships used as names.

Here comes Uncle Joe, drunk as a lord.

After Grandpa Justin had lunch, we went to the park.

Please don't give Mom so much trouble.

Notice that you do *not* capitalize *mother*, *father*, *grandmother*, *grandfather*, *uncle*, *aunt*, *cousin*, and so forth when these terms are preceded by *my*, *your*, *our*, or any other possessive word.

Ask Grandma if she'd like more tea.

but

As your grandma if she'd like more tea.

His aunt raises golden retrievers.

but

Auntie Meg raises golden retrievers.

PRACTICING 3

Capitalize wherever necessary. Write *C* in the blank if the sentence is correct.

1. _____ My mother grew up on a farm in West Texas.

2. _____ I was so mortified that I never wanted to see aunt

   Ruby again.

3. _____ Her grandmother could ride a horse like a cowboy
   in a rodeo.

4. _____ My uncle Frank never mentions his brother, Norm.

5. _____ If you take dad to the airport, remind him to call

   mom.

Capitalize the names of nationalities, religions, races, tribes, and languages.

I love Chinese, Vietnamese, and Italian food.

The Baptist, Methodist, and Catholic churches are sponsoring a community picnic on Sunday.

Denise Chavez writes about the Mexican-American community in New Mexico.

Native Americans of the Southwest include the Zunis, Navajos, Apaches, and Utes. Most people in Montreal speak both French and English.

PRACTICING 4

Fill in the blanks as indicated.

Example: In high school, I took (language) Spanish_____ .

1. My best friend is (nationality) _____ .

2. Someone who is bilingual speaks two languages fluently,

   such as _____ and _____ .

3. People who live in Canada are _____ , and people

   who live in Mexico are _____ .

4. There are many Protestant denominations, including

   _____ , _____ , and _____ .

5. The (races) _____ , _____ , and

   _____ must learn to appreciate each other's

cultures.

Capitalize after a colon if what follows is a full sentence.

Here is a command I can respect: "Love your neighbor as yourself."

                                          but

The following ingredients are needed: eggs, flour, sugar, and milk.

PRACTICING 5

If the sentence is capitalized correctly, leave it alone. Write over any lowercase letters that should be capitalized.

                                  W
Example: Dear Sir: ~~we~~ regret that the table you ordered is still not in stock.

1. Please enclose the following papers: the bank statement,

   the tax return, and the application.

2. The poem begins as follows: "despair is a green snake with black wings."

3. Follow these directions: Dig a trench, hammer some stakes into the ground, and set up the tent.

4. Here are the virtues I am anticipating: loyalty, courage, and faith.

5. This is what I advised him: continue to take your medicine and see what happens.

Capitalize the days of the week, months of the year, holidays, and religious occasions.

Labor Day always falls on Monday.

My favorite time to snow ski is in January or February.

Halloween is becoming a very popular holiday.

Every Easter, I attend church services at sunrise.

Note that the seasons of the year are not capitalized.

I love the fall when all the leaves take on brilliant hues.

In the spring, people's thoughts turn to love.

PRACTICING 6

In the spaces provided, mark *C* if the sentence is properly capitalized and *NC* if it is not. Then correct the errors.

1. _____ Many Americans celebrate palm sunday as well as passover.

2. _____ Next Summer I plan to visit Guadalajara.

3. _____ I attend night school on tuesdays and wednesdays.

4. _____ Does school close on Martin Luther King Day?

5. _____ Every Christmas I eat candy until I'm sick.

Capitalize the names of specific places, including monuments.

Last summer we visited Mount Rushmore.

Some day I want to visit the Leaning Tower of Pisa in Italy.

Who engineered the Golden Gate Bridge?

I attend New York University and hope to graduate this year.

Follow Anderson Blvd. all the way to Stocker Road.

Park right in front of Brown's Bakery Shop.

Do not capitalize the names of places that are not specific:

He walked down the street toward the bakery shop.

but

He bicycled down Maple Street to Brown's Bakery Shop.

PRACTICING 7

Correct the capitalization errors in these sentences.

1. The hurricane hit miami and tampa before heading up the coast to south carolina.

2. Thousands of people visit yellowstone national park and mount rushmore each year.

3. My mother was born in the small town of haskell, texas; my father came from limerick, ireland.

4. First I have to stop at wagner's drug store and then at five star cleaners, which is right next door.

5. New orleans is on lake pontchartrain, which empties into the gulf of mexico.

Capitalize the names of companies, clubs, political groups, and other official organizations.

You can still get "full serve" at some Standard Oil stations.

"Bonjour" is the name of our French Club.

My brother switched from the Republican Party to the Democratic Party.

I belong to the National Organization for Women.

The Federal Bureau of Investigation (FBI) is headquartered in Washington.

PRACTICING 8

Underline the words that should be capitalized in the following sentences.

1. Our college uses national-international student progams (NISP) for its international study programs.

2. Belonging to the sorority alpha sigma alpha has helped me make friends on campus.

3. Several of my friends work at pacific bell telephone company.

4. Our next-door neighbor has been elected to the house of representatives.

5. She works at flossmore general hospital.

UNIT TEST

Correct all the capitalization errors in the following essay.

I love santa fe, new mexico. When you drive through the center of town, you would never guess that this is a state capital. The small town square is bordered on all sides by fabulous shops displaying authentic indian jewelry, rugs, and pottery. At the center of the square is a pretty little park where you can watch tribal dances and listen to hispanic music. One side of the square is called "governor's mansion." Along its front is a portal, where craftspeople from the various pueblos of the area display their wares. They sell hopi kachina dolls, zuni fetishes, navajo silver jewelry, and acoma pots. When I visit santa fe, I always stop by the wheelwright museum because it has a wonderful gift shop, where

I can buy antique hopi kachinas. I also love to drive out to the little town of susuque for some delicious mexican tamales, smothered in red salsa and accompanied by freshly mashed guacamole. There's a picturesque little catholic church with a classic black steeple standing at the side of the road. If I have the time, I like to hike in bandalero state park or take a drive to some of the famous rock formations, like ship's rock or camel rock. All houses in santa fe are made of adobe so that when you drive up hyde park road toward the ski lift, you might actually think you're in a foreign country like iraq or in some mexican village. The new mexico sky in santa fe is gorgeous—filled with giant white puffy clouds that are a magical backdrop for lightning storms at night. Santa fe may not be as wild and exciting as chicago or new york city, but it is stunning in its rustic and artistic charms.

Incorrect Capitalization, Part II

In the last section, Error 17, you learned these rules for capitalizing correctly:

- Capitalize the first word in a sentence or direct quotation.

- Capitalize names of individual persons and the word *I*.

- Capitalize family relationships used as names.

- Capitalize the names of nationalities, religions, races, tribes, and languages.

- Capitalize after a colon if what follows is a full sentence.

- Capitalize the names of the days of the week, months, holidays, and religious occasions.

- Capitalize the names of specific places, including monuments.

- Capitalize the names of companies, clubs, political groups, and other official organizations.

Now you will learn these other capitalization rules:

- Capitalize names of commercial products.

- Capitalize titles of books, magazines, essays, poems, stories, plays, articles, films, television shows, songs, and cartoons.

- Capitalize titles used in front of a person's name.

- Capitalize specific college courses.

- Capitalize areas of the country.

- Capitalize historical eras and events.

- Capitalize abbreviations of familiar organizations, corporations, people, countries, time, and titles.

■ Capitalize the opening and the first word of the closing of a letter.

Capitalize the names of commercial products.

I use Tide because it works as well as any other laundry detergent.

Do not capitalize types of products.

We need paper towels, spaghetti sauce, and peanut butter.	**(These are merely types of products, not brand names.)**

but

Post oatmeal is good for you.	**("Post" is a brand name, but "oatmeal" is a type of food.)**

PRACTICING 1

Capitalize the names of commercial products in the following sentences.

1. I love hershey's chocolate.

2. My favorite milk additive is carnation.

3. I always use gillette shaving cream.

4. The most popular car of the 1960s was the volkswagen.

5. To repel mosquitoes, off works really well.

Capitalize titles of books, magazines, newspapers, essays, poems, stories, plays, articles, films, television shows, songs, and cartoons.

Book:	Have you read *Hearts* by Hilma Wolitzer?
Magazine:	I subscribe to *Discover* magazine.
Newspaper:	*The Washington Post* is a respected newspaper.
Essay:	Her essay is entitled "Affirmative Action and Women: Off the Cuff Comments."
Poems:	I love Lorena Bruff's poem, "The Cello."
Story:	"A Worn Path" is a moving short story.
Play:	She was wonderful in *King Lear*.
Article:	Read the article called "Shakespeare in the Bush."
Film:	*Civil Action* is a powerful movie.
Television Show:	I always watch "60 Minutes" on Sunday night.

Song:	Bob Marley's "War" uses the words of a speech as its lyrics.
Cartoon:	I miss "The Far Side" cartoons.

Notice how words are capitalized in titles. The beginning word is always capitalized. The first word after a colon is also always capitalized. Certain words are not capitalized, however, unless they come at the beginning.

Do not capitalize:

- The article *a*, *an*, or *the* unless it is the first word

- The coordinating conjunctions *and*, *but*, *yet*, *or*, *nor*, *so*, and *for*

- Short prepositions such as *of*, *from*, *by*, *in*, *up*, and *out* (capitalize prepositions of five or more letters, such as *about*, *among*, *between*, *behind*, *through*, *though*, and *without*)

PRACTICING 2

Correctly capitalize the titles in the following sentences.

1. I read an article in science fiction digest entitled "UFOs appear in farmer's field."

2. Paul Laurence Dunbar wrote a poem called "we wear the mask."

3. Two of my favorite television shows are "wheel of fortune" and "mad about you."

4. *A farewell to arms* can be found in the book, *collected short stories of ernest hemingway.*

5. First she sang "fly me to the moon" and then "moon over miami."

Capitalize titles used in front of a person's name.

President Bill Clinton, Governor Zell Miller, Secretary of State Madeline Albright, General H. Norman Schwarzkopf, Jr., Attorney General Janet Reno, Mrs. Miller, Mr. Planter, Ms. Lowery

but

Bill Clinton, the president of the United States; Zell Miller, governor of Georgia; Madeline Albright, secretary of state; H. Norman Schwarzkopf, Jr., retired general; and Janet Reno, attorney general of the United States

PRACTICING 3

In the blank in front of each sentence, write *C* if the sentence is correct and *NC* if it is incorrect. Correct by writing above the word.

1. _____ Warren Christopher was once the Secretary of State.

2. _____ My congratulations to Mr. Smith and miss james.

3. _____ One day a woman will be President of the United States.

4. _____ Richard Nixon was once vice president.

5. _____ They said that Congresswoman McKinney would speak.

Capitalize specific college courses.

I aced the exam in Algebra 100.

but

All my life I've hated algebra.

I am taking Introduction to Psychology.

but

Classes in psychology are very popular.

Language courses are always capitalized.

I'm taking French 100.

I'm planning on studying Chinese.

PRACTICING 4

Capitalize the names of specific college courses.

1. The hardest class I ever took was introduction to speech.

2. Last semester I got an A in anthropology and a B in spanish.

3. He says he is taking religion 101.

4. I made a fool of myself in introduction to acting.

5. My favorite class is introduction to prison literature.

Capitalize areas of the country.

People in the Midwest sometimes talk like Canadians.

We decided to move to the South.

I'll never live on the West Coast.

Do not capitalize compass directions or areas of the country used as adjectives.

Go south for two blocks, then turn north.

My mother speaks with a western clip.

PRACTICING 5

Fill in the blanks with an area of the country or a compass direction. Capitalize correctly.

Example: Her favorite aunt lives on the <u>East Coast</u> .

1. On the _____ side of the mountains, was a valley.

2. We drove all night, always heading _____ .

3. Thirteen years ago I moved from the _____ Coast

   to the _____ Coast.

4. If I could choose, I'd live in the _____ .

5. Go _____ on Berkford, and then turn _____

   on Nancy Creek.

Capitalize historical eras and events.

In the Age of Reason humans tried to make sense of their world.

I wish I had lived during the Medieval Period.

Poetry from the Romantic Age was largely about nature.

Many Americans were hurt during the Depression.

The Battle of the Bulge was the last great battle of World War II.

PRACTICING 6

Mark *C* beside the sentence in each pair that is correctly capitalized.

1. _____ **a.** Custer was killed in the battle of little big horn.

   _____ **b.** Custer was killed in the Battle of Little Big Horn.

2. _____ **a.** The Civil War pitted American against American.

   _____ **b.** The civil war pitted American against American.

3. _____ **a.** In the Victorian age people were very prudish.

   _____ **b.** In the Victorian Age people were very prudish.

4. _____ **a.** The modern age is characterized by many good novels.

   _____ **b.** The Modern Age is characterized by many good novels.

5. _____ **a.** World War I was settled by the Treaty of Versailles.

   _____ **b.** World war I was settled by the treaty of versailles.

Capitalize abbreviations of familiar organizations, corporations, people, countries, time, and titles.

Organization:	FAA, NCAA, MADD
Corporation:	GE, AT&T, MCI
People:	JFK, FDR, LBJ
Countries:	U.S.A. or USA, U.K, or UK
Time:	12:00 A.M., 2:30 P.M.
Titles:	Benjamine Stein, Sr.; Felicia Baquero, M.D.; Theodore Munch, Ph.D.; Carolyn Wu, D.D.S.

PRACTICING 7

Complete the following sentences with an appropriate abbreviation.

1. The abbreviation for the Soviet Union was _____ .

2. The Boy Scouts of America is sometimes abbreviated

   _____ .

3. The Food and Drug Administration, or _____ , is
   an important government agency.

4. Alcoholics Anonymous is known as _____ , and the
   Automobile Association of American is known
   as_____ .

5. John Chavez is both a medical doctor, or _____ and
   a doctor of philosophy, or _____ .

Capitalize the opening and the first word of the closing of a letter.

Dear Madame,

My dear Joseph,

Dear Dr. Pevitts,

Sincerely,

Sincerely yours,

Best regards,

Love and kisses,

PRACTICING 8

Write a letter about yourself as part of your application to be
admitted to college. Capitalize correctly.

UNIT TEST

Correct all the capitalization errors in the following letter.

april 1st, 1999

Dear Peter,

this is a hard letter to write since I do not convey bad news well.
I have signed up for three classes, all of which I like. I'm enrolled
in introduction to freshman composition, economics 101, and us
history from the revolutionary war to the civil war. I expect to do well

in all of them because I am determined to study hard and get good grades. What's the bad news? Well, it is this: the girl you like so much—the one from the south who speaks in such a charming way—is in all my classes. What's more, on her own and without any prompting whatsoever from me, she has decided to sit right next to me in every class. I told her that you would not like that, especially since you come from the northeast and have a very jealous nature. You know what she said? She said she didn't care if you were secretly a cia agent from Washington, d.c., she intended to sit where she pleased. What can I do? I'm just a kid from the west coast who is used to free spirited california girls. I told you you should've stayed at citrus college rather than transferring to riverside university, but you wouldn't listen. Now, because of your thoughtlessness, I'm stuck with the prettiest girl in town.

yours sincerely,

John

P.S. I don't work for the fbi, but this is a fib. Happy april fools' day!

Misspelled Words, Part I

Before the existence of dictionaries, words were spelled entirely by ear or by whim. *Slow* might be spelled *sloe, slo,* or *slough*. With the appearance in the eighteenth century of the first English dictionary, however, spelling gradually became standardized to the point that children today compete in spelling bees.

Even if we never get skilled enough at spelling to enter a spelling bee, we can all become better spellers by observing some simple rules.

Tips for Improving Your Spelling

1. Sound out words. For instance, the word *government* contains an "n" if you say it aloud slowly. The word *find* has a final "d" sound and should not be spelled *fine*. Saying a word aloud can definitely help you to spell it correctly.

2. Make up your own memory tricks for remembering the spelling of problem words. For example, *cemetery* is spelled with all *e*'s because it is so eerie; the *principal* is your pal; *dessert* has two *s*'s because it is doubly good.

3. Use a dictionary. Looking up words regularly will help make you familiar with any quirks in their spellings. Ask your teacher to recommend a good dictionary.

4. Keep a list of words you often misspell and refer to it when you proofread your writing.

5. If you write with a computer, the first rule of spelling is simply this: Use the spell checker that comes with your writing program. Most programs have spell checkers built into them. However, even sophisticated spelling checkers go only so far. Although they catch such misspellings as *heighth* for *height* and *occassion* for *occasion*, they don't tell you if you've incorrectly used *its* for *it's* or *their* for *there* or *they're*.

Rules for Spelling

Spelling in English is not always as clear-cut as we would like. Nearly every rule has an exception. Nevertheless, learning the rules and the exceptions will make you a better speller.

As you go over the rules, bear in mind the difference between vowels and consonants.

Vowels: *a, e, i, o, u,* and sometimes *y*
Consonants: all other letters of the alphabet

Using ie and ei

Remember the age-old rule: "*i* before *e* except after *c* or when sounded as *ay* as in *neighbor* or *weigh*."

niece

relieve

believe

but

ceiling

receive

deceive

EXCEPTIONS

either	leisure	species
caffeine	neither	their
financier	seize	weird
foreigner	science	
height	society	

PRACTICING 1

Underline the correct spelling of each word-pair in parentheses.

1. (Neither, Niether) Fred nor Mark is going to the club brunch.

2. They bought (their, thier) tickets in advance.

3. What is that (wierd, weird) sound?

4. A good (neighbor, nieghbor) is as valuable as silver or gold.

5. What do you like to do in your (leisure, liesure) time?

6. Drinks that contain salt are just as bad as those that contain (caffeine, caffiene).

7. You cannot live a serene life if you flout the rules of (soceity, society).

8. She has always done well in (sceince, science) courses.

9. If you (believe, beleive) that, I have a bridge to sell you.

10. She left a (breif, brief) e-mail message for me.

Changing y to i

When you add an ending to a word that ends in a consonant plus *y*, change *y* to *i*. Keep the final *y* when it is preceded by a vowel.

try + ed = tried

worry + er = worrier

silly + ness = silliness

buy + er = buyer

sway + ing = swaying

EXCEPTIONS

horrify	horrifyingly
lady	ladylike
carry	carrying
cry	crying (but crier)
worry	worrying
study	studying

PRACTICING 2

Combine the following words with the ending shown to the right and place the correct word in the blank provided.

Example: study + es = <u>studies</u>

1. testify + es = _____

2. merry + ily = _____

3. muddy + ed = _____

4. mortify + es = _____

5. lazy + ily = _____

6. bury + ing = _____

7. obey + ing = _____

8. fry + ed = _____

9. lonely + ness = _____

10. beauty + ful = _____

The final silent e

When you add endings that start with a vowel, such as *-al*, *-able*, *-ence*, or *-ing*, drop the final *e*. When you add an ending that starts with a consonant, such as *-ment*, *-less*, or *-ly*, keep the final *e*.

Here are some examples for you to study:

bride	+	al	=	bridal		
like	+	able	=	likable		
emerge	+	ence	=	emergence		
take	+	ing	=	taking		
manage	+	ment	=	management		
love	+	less	=	loveless		
polite	+	ly	=	politely		

EXCEPTIONS

argue	+	ment	=	argument
courage	+	ous	=	courageous
judge	+	ment	=	judgment
manage	+	able	=	manageable
nine	+	th	=	ninth
notice	+	able	=	noticeable
true	+	ly	=	truly

PRACTICING 3

Place a *C* to the left of the word that is spelled correctly.

Example: _____ pleasureable   _C_ pleasurable

1. _____ likeable   _____ likable

2. _____ management   _____ managment

3. _____ desperately   _____ desperatly

4. _____ arguement   _____ argument

5. _____ dosage   _____ doseage

6. _____ movable   _____ moveable

7. _____ managing   _____ manageing

8. _____ useable   _____ usable

9. _____ judgement   _____ judgment

10. _____ supposing   _____ supposeing

Doubling the final consonant

In one-syllable words

To add *ed*, *ing*, *er*, or *est* to a one-syllable word, double the consonant if it is preceded by a single vowel.

pin	+	ed	=	pinned
trim	+	ing	=	trimming
thin	+	er	=	thinner
sad	+	est	=	saddest

PRACTICING 4

Add the indicated endings to the words listed below and spell them correctly in the blanks provided.

Example: set (ing)   *setting*_____

  1. dip (ed) _____

  2. stop (ing) _____

  3. dig (ing) _____

  4. flop (ed) _____

  5. knit (ed) _____

  6. run (er) _____

  7. slam (ed) _____

  8. drop (ing) _____

  9. blab (ed) _____

  10. big (est) _____

In multi-syllable words

To add *ing* or *ed* to words of more than one syllable, double the final consonant if the following is true:

■ The stress is on the final syllable:

com-mit′

be-gin′

oc-cur′

■ The last three letters consist of a consonant/vowel/consonant:

commit

begin

occur

Therefore:

commit	+	ed	=	committed
begin	+	ing	=	beginning
occur	+	ed	=	occurred

Now, consider these words:

travel = traveling   **(Do not double because the accent is on the first syllable: *tra′-vel*.)**

benefit = benefited   **(Do not double because the accent is on the first syllable: *be′-ne-fit*.)**

repeat = repeating   **(Do not double because the last three letters do not fit the consonant/vowel/consonant pattern.)**

PRACTICING 5

In the blanks on the right, add *ed* and *ing* to the following words.

	ed	**ing**
Example: admit	admitted	admitting
1. prefer	_____	_____
2. unwrap	_____	_____
3. expel	_____	_____
4. remit	_____	_____
5. defer	_____	_____

PRACTICING 6

Add *ed* and *ing* to the following words.

1. travel   + ed _____   + ing _____

2. suspect   + ed _____   + ing _____

3. profit   + ed _____   + ing _____

    4. label   + ed _____   + ing _____

    5. defect   + ed _____   + ing _____

Forming plurals

Most words form their plurals by simply adding *s*.

Singular	Plural
sled	sleds
egg	eggs
sister	sisters
rag	rags

However, there are a few exceptions that you should master.

Words ending in -s, -ss, -z, -x, -sh, or -ch

Words ending in *-s, -ss, -z, -x, -sh,* or *-ch* form their plurals by adding *-es*, an extra syllable for easier pronunciation.

Singular	Plural
lens	lenses
kiss	kisses
buzz	buzzes
box	boxes
wash	washes
church	churches

PRACTICING 7

Form the plurals of the following words.

    1. fox _____

    2. crash _____

    3. beach _____

    4. buzz _____

    5. dash _____

    6. mix _____

    7. bush _____

    8. quiz _____

    9. kiss _____

    10. bus _____

Words ending in -o

If a word ends in an *-o* preceded by a vowel, add *-s*.

rodeo	rodeos
patio	patios
zoo	zoos
radio	radios
video	videos

If a word ends in an *-o* preceded by a consonant, add *-es*:

hero	heroes
potato	potatoes
echo	echoes
buffalo	buffaloes

EXCEPTIONS

alto	altos
grotto	grottos
memo	memos
motto	mottos
photo	photos
piano	pianos
solo	solos

PRACTICING 8

Write a sentence for each of the following words using the plural form.

1. potato _____

2. video _____

3. motto _____

4. echo _____

5. radio _____

6. tomato _____

7. zoo _____

8. hero _____

9. piano _____

10. solo _____

Words ending in -f
Most words ending in -*f* (or -*fe*) change the *f* to a *v* and add -*es*

Singular	Plural
half	halves
calf	calves
leaf	leaves
wife	wives

EXCEPTIONS

roof	roofs
safe	safes
chief	chiefs
proof	proofs

PRACTICING 9

Form the plurals of the following words.

1. leaf _____

2. roof _____

3. half _____

4. safe _____

5. wharf _____

6. chief _____

7. thief _____

8. knife _____

9. calf _____

10. hoof _____

Irregular plurals
Some words form irregular plurals.

Singular	Plural
woman	women
foot	feet
ox	oxen
mouse	mice

PRACTICING 10

Form the plural of the following words.

1. goose _____

2. man _____

3. mouse _____

4. louse _____

5. woman _____

Words that do not change

Some words have the same spelling for singular and plural.

Singular	**Plural**
deer	deer
fish	fish (or fishes)
sheep	sheep
species	species
series	series
moose	moose

PRACTICING 11

Turn the following words into plurals and then write a sentence using the plural.

Example: deer *deer*_____

_We saw a herd of deer at the saltlick._____

1. fish _____

_____

2. mouse _____

_____

3. moose _____

_____

4. series _____

_____

5. sheep _____

_____

PRACTICING 12

Circle the word in each pair that is correctly spelled.

1. halfs, halves
2. measurless, measureless
3. admited, admitted
4. expeled, expelled
5. pianos, pianoes
6. benefitted, benefited
7. mouses, mice
8. biggest, bigest
9. tomatoes, tomatos
10. slopy, sloppy

11. heros, heroes
12. writing, writting
13. likable, likeable
14. permited, permitted
15. occurring, occuring
16. recieve, receive
17. argument, arguement
18. hieght, height
19. coppying, copying
20. wives, wifes

UNIT TEST

Rewrite the following passage to correct all misspelled words (there are 14).

Scuba diving terrifys me. Although I have recieved a diploma admiting me to the elite group of certified scuba divers, I have never conquered my fear when under water. Niether my fearless brother nor my athletic sister has ever been able to releive my nervousness. Once I put on my scuba diving suit and grab my gear in readyness for a diving expedition, all I can think about is getting back home. I don't mind the cold water; I don't mind the tight divving suit. My bigest problem is the foriegn world that greets me under water. For instance, there are the slimmy sea weeds brushing against my face and making me afraid that they will start wraping around my neck or around the valves of my oxygen tank. I don't even enjoy seeing the multi-hued fishes swiming because I'm so scarred that among them might be a hidden shark. As for the darkness at depths of more than thirty feet, I just want to get back up to the world above the sea waves. Beleive me, I'm always utterly grateful to climb back on board the boat and head back to shore.

Misspelled Words, Part II

English spelling is difficult. Words are often not spelled the way they sound. *Raccoon* sounds like it should have a "k" but doesn't. *Threw* sounds like *through* but is spelled differently. *Though*, *cough*, and *through* look like rhyming words but actually are not pronounced at all alike. Given that English has a vocabulary of over 400,000 words, it's a wonder that we spell as well as we do.

Some words—called **homophones**—sound exactly alike but have different spellings and meanings. Other words are not exact homophones but are similar enough to be confused often. Study the following examples:

altar (a raised platform in church)	alter (to change)	**HOMOPHONES**
it's (it is)	its (pronoun: *Its engine was throbbing.*)	
accept (to receive with consent: *They accept our offer.*)	except (excluded: *Everyone cried except Peter.*)	**CONFUSING WORDS**
advice (noun: *I gave my advice.*)	advise (verb: *I advise you to leave.*)	

Homophones and Frequently Confused Words

Learn the meaning and spelling of these homophones and frequently confused words. Errors in spelling can change the meaning of writing. *Angel* spelled correctly will still confuse your reader if you really meant *angle*.

accept—to take or receive/ **except**—excluding, other than, but for

> They accept our thanks.
> I work every day except Sunday.

access—a means of approach / **excess**—more than the usual

> She had access to my room.
> Drinking to excess is not good.

advice—recommendation (noun) / **advise**—to caution, to warn (verb)

> The lawyer's advice is to do nothing.
> I advise you not to move.

affect—to influence, to change / **effect**—to bring about (verb); consequence, result (noun)

> Watching too much television affected my sanity.
>
> The new supervisor effected some good changes.
>
> It will have an effect on my pocket book.

altar—a raised platform in a church / **alter**—to change

> They exchanged wedding vows at the altar.
>
> The coach should alter the pitcher's motion.

bare—without covering or clothing / **bear**—to bring forth, to endure (verb); an animal (noun)

> The playing field was bare of any grass.
>
> Every year the mares bear foals.
>
> I can't bear going to the dentist.
>
> As I hiked past the river, I spotted a bear.

capital—value of goods, money; a principal city / **capitol**—a building in which legislators meet

> Investors should not squander their capital.
>
> Nashville is the capital of Tennessee.
>
> The capitol was a scene of heated debate.

cite—to quote / **site**—place or scene / **sight**—ability to see

> He loves to cite Shakespeare's words.
>
> The site for the monument was chosen by a committee.
>
> He claims to have the gift of second sight.

course—a path; subjects taken in school / **coarse**—rough in texture

> The obstacle course took us over mountains.
>
> I'm taking a course in literature.
>
> The sheets felt coarse.

desert—a dry land (noun); to abandon (verb) / **dessert**—something sweet served at the end of a meal

> We're going to the desert for the weekend.
>
> Don't desert me at the altar.
>
> My favorite dessert is strawberry shortcake.

forth—forward / **fourth**—next after third

> The settlers went forth into the wilderness.
>
> The fourth rule is this: Always study hard.

its—possessive form of *it* / **it's**—contraction of *it is*

> The cat licked its fur.
>
> It's too bad you have to go.

lose—to misplace or come to be without / **loose**—to be free from restraint

> Don't lose your keys.
> He tripped over his loose shoelace.

passed—went by / **past**—an earlier time; beyond

> We passed like ships in the night.
> That's all in the past.
> She walked past without saying a word.

piece—part of a whole / **peace**—opposite of war

> Give me a piece of that pie, please.
> We all want peace.

personal—private, intimate / **personnel**—employees

> That happens to be my personal business.
> He was hired by the personnel office.

principal—first in rank; the chief or head / **principle**—an accepted rule or belief

> Elmwood School has a new principal.
> Many arguments have been started over a principle.

quiet—making no noise; peaceable / **quite**—completely or entirely

> All's quiet on the street.
> Now I'm quite lost.

sole—only; the bottom of the foot / **soul**—the spirit

> She was the sole survivor.
> The shoemaker mended the sole of my shoe.
> She had a beautiful soul.

their—ownership / **there**—in that place / **they're**—contraction of *they are*

> Their coats are hanging in the closet.
> Put it over there.
> They're always very friendly.

to—a preposition; part of any infinitive / **too**—also, excessively / **two**—second

> I'm going to the mountains.
> I'm too tired to talk.
> You should go, too.
> That's too much whipped cream.
> She ate two hot dogs.

who's—contraction of *who is* / **whose**—the possessive case of *who*

Who's driving with me?

Whose scarf is this?

your—the possessive case of *you* / **you're**—contraction of *you are*

I found your notebook.

You're the boss.

Although these are, of course, not the only homophones—English is riddled with many others—these are some you are most likely to encounter.

PRACTICING 1

Underline the correct word choice for each sentence below.

1. You have (access/excess) to many computers.

2. It will have a severe (affect/effect) on my budget.

3. (Its, It's) too late to (altar/alter) my plans.

4. This is my (forth/fourth) trip to New York.

5. I drove (past/passed) her house with my heart pounding.

6. (There/their/they're) lies the problem.

7. She said that (its/it's) a matter of (principal/principle).

8. Are you (quite/quiet) finished?

9. He gave me a (piece/peace) of his mind.

10. (Whose/Who's) bringing the salad?

PRACTICING 2

Write a sentence for each of these pairs of homophones.

1. principal_____

   principle _____

2. capital_____

   capitol _____

3. personal _____

   personnel _____

4. course _____

    coarse _____

5. sole _____

    soul _____

Commonly Misspelled Words

Below is a list of words that are commonly misspelled. If you regularly have trouble with any words on this list, memorize the correct spelling.

LIST OF COMMONLY MISSPELLED WORDS

accidentally

acquaintance

acquire

address

already (not to be confused with *all ready*)

all right (always two words, just like *all wrong*)

answer

anxious

arithmetic

athletics

attendance

awful

awkward

believe (not to be confused with *belief*)

breathe (not to be confused with *breath*)

business

calendar

cemetery

changeable

chief

choose (not to be confused with *chose*)

conscience (not to be confused with *conscious*)

daily

definite

dependent

design

device (not to be confused with *devise*)

disappearance

embarrass

environment

especially

exaggerate

exercise

existence

familiar

fascinate

foreign

forty

fragrant

friend

fulfill

government

grammar

harass

height

hindrance

incredible

independent

interesting

irresistible

judgment

library

literature

maintenance

mathematics

medicine

million

miracle

miscellaneous

mischief

necessary

neighbor

noticeable

nuisance

occasion

occur/occurrence/occurred

offered

(cont.)

parallel	seize (not to be confused with *size*)
peculiar	separate
politics	several
possess	similar
practically	sincerely
precede	succeed
preferred	surprise
prejudice	temperature
preparation	than (not to be confused with *then*)
privilege	thorough
proceed	tragedy
receive	truly
recognize	unnecessary
referred/referring	until
relieve/relief	usually
resemblance	vegetable
restaurant	visitor
reverence	weird
ridiculous	writing
sandwich	

PRACTICING 3

Each of the following sentences contains a misspelled word from the list above. Write the corrected version in the blanks provided.

Example: Their existance was in doubt. _existence_

1. They met each other accidentaly. _____

2. My strong point is athaletics. _____

3. It was not easy to chose between them. _____

4. She can be very changable. _____

5. On this particular point, his judgement was flawed.

   _____

6. He has his own upholstery bisness. _____

7. I'm so dependant on her. _____

8. Maintenence said the problem was with the water heater.

   _____

9. Mathamatics has always been my worse subject.

   _____

10. It was not necessery to do more._____

PRACTICING 4

Circle the *correctly* spelled word in each of the following word-pairs.

1. miscellanous / miscellaneous

2. neighbor / naighbor

3. embarrass / embarress

4. conscience / conscence

5. ocasion / occasion

6. occurence / occurrence

7. poletics / politics

8. vegatable / vegetable

9. preparation / preperation

10. tragidy / tragedy

UNIT TEST

The paragraph that follows contains 20 of the spelling errors mentioned in this section. Correct each error.

When I was in grammer school, I made freinds with a foriegn exchange student. His name was Adam, and he was an intaresting kid. He came from England, and was very independant even though he was only eight years old. Early in our acquaintence, we decided to swap accents. So on a dayly basis, we would sit on the playground and try to talk like each other. I was from the South and had a southern accent, while he spoke like a Londoner, which I found irresestible. But much to our suprise, we found that we couldn't do it. Its very hard to capture another person's accent. Trying to do it makes you sound rediculus, or piculiar, to say the least. The other kids used to tease us, which embarassed us. It was hard enough allready for Adam to get adjusted without the nuisence of being teased for the way he sounded. We decided to stop the silly buseness of switching accents and just be ourselves. Many years later, on a social ocasion, I met Adam again. By then he was in his mid '20s and had remained in Atlanta. We talked about how the other kids used to harrass us and laughed about it. Not until later did I recanize a funny fact: Adam had ackwired a southern accent and now spoke exactly as I did!

Readings

The readings in this part are organized according to the writing strategies that you learned in Part III. They show how professional writers use the same techniques. The introduction, "Help for Your Reading," and the headnotes preceding each selection will help you get the most out of the readings. Use the questions that follow the readings to test your understanding of the material you've read.

Help for Your Reading

You can improve your reading with a few commonsense techniques. Here are some suggestions to help you read the selections in this book.

1. Scan the whole piece before you read.

Before you begin to actually read an essay, short story, or poem, casually look it over. Pay attention to the title—especially in the case of poems and short stories. The title is often a clue to the meaning of the piece. Turn the pages of an essay to see its major divisions, if any. Some essays are subdivided by heads; others appear as solid blocks of print. Scanning the heads as you turn the pages will tell you what an essay is about and what points it covers. Note the number of pages. What you are doing is looking over the essay as if it were a map for an upcoming trip. You are finding out how far you have to go and what kind of ground you have to cover.

2. Read the headnote first.

The **headnote** is the paragraph that precedes each writing selection. It gives you a general idea of what the reading is about and any surprises or twists you should look for. The headnote may also alert you to the work's main points. Through the headnote, the editors can whisper advice in your ear as you get ready to tackle the selection.

3. Write your reactions in the margins of the pages.

Get rid of the old-fashioned idea that writing in a book is a sin. If the book belongs to someone else or to the library, writing in it is *definitely* a sin. Otherwise, writing in a book is not sinful, but useful. Feel free to underline words or ideas. Scribble your reactions in the margin as you read. Writing down your reactions helps you become an active, rather than a passive, reader. When you react to a piece of writing, you involve yourself in it and are likely to get its point better than if you simply sit and read between snores. If a description is particularly sad, you might note: "This passage is gloomy." If the author's opinion annoys you, show your irritation by jotting down your reaction, whether it be, "That's a typical closed-minded opinion," or simply, "Rubbish." Another good use of marginal writing is to summarize in a phrase what the whole paragraph is about, so that when you reread, you can go straight to your summaries.

4. Underline key ideas.

All writing consists of two parts—a point and its proof. As shown in this text, most nonfiction paragraphs make a point and then try to prove it, using facts, examples, or reasons. To understand a paragraph, you must know its main point, usually found in the topic sentence. The topic sentence can be the opening sentence of a paragraph, or, less commonly, the closing sentence. An alert reader learns, therefore, to pay special attention to opening and closing sentences. Underlining the topic sentence is an excellent way to help you keep the main idea in mind as you read the rest of the paragraph. Consider this passage:

> <u>I have found over the years that the most effective way for me to write an essay is simply to begin writing.</u> Some friends of mine begin by doing research or by making an outline, but neither way works for me. What I do is sit down with a pen and pad and begin scribbling. At this point, I'm too shaky about what I want to say to use a computer. In fact, when I first start, I haven't the faintest idea what I'm going to say. My goal is simply to get something down on paper, anything. But once I have my first sentence, I'm ready to begin. It's a little bit like a diner sitting down to eat a meal, which does not really begin until the first bite. I may change that first sentence; I might not even use it in the final paper. But I have to have it to begin the writing. From there I might limp to a second sentence or even to a third. Or I might have a real outburst of creativity and draft an opening paragraph. Then I might go to the library or log on the Internet for information about my topic that I might use in the paper. But none of this can I do until I have that one sentence. I know this is a peculiar way of doing things, but that's how I write an essay, and I say "do what works for you."

The topic sentence is the key to the meaning of the paragraph. The rest of the paragraph supports and explains the topic sentence.

Also pay close attention to *signal words*, words that announce some important idea. Here are some examples, with the signal words underlined:

<u>The most significant reaction of all,</u> however, came from the eyewitnesses.

<u>One often overlooked fact</u> is that interest rates on personal loans are not tax deductible.

<u>Of particular significance</u> is the way the women themselves feel.

<u>Perhaps most important,</u> you must exercise to lose weight.

These signal words are clues to ideas the author considers particularly important.

5. Think about what you have read.

Every paragraph or so, stop and think about what you have just read. Make a mental summary—preferably aloud—to be sure you fully understand what you are reading. If you have trouble doing this, read the passage again, and perhaps even a third time, until you understand it.

6. Look up unfamiliar words in the dictionary.

Often **context**—surrounding words or sentences—will suggest a word's meaning. In the paragraph below, notice how context tells what the word *cacique* means:

> When Columbus first discovered the West Indies, he was greeted by a naked, peaceful people. His journals show that while he was slightly surprised at the lack of metal tools and weapons, he marveled that

everyone—men and women, as well as children—went around totally naked. Even the *caciques,* who were shown great respect by their people, were surrounded by advisers, and occasionally sported ornamental gold bracelets and necklaces that signified their high rank, were also stark naked, a fact Columbus found remarkable.

What is a *cacique?* Obviously, from the context of the paragraph, a cacique was a leader of these peaceful people.

Sometimes context tells us all we need to know about the meaning of a word. Consider this sentence: "The cows had to be herded back to their *byre* for milking." Although you may have no idea what the word *byre* means if you see it standing alone, in the context of this sentence, you are sure it must mean something like "barn," "stable," or "cowshed."

7. Reread.

Your first reading of an essay, short story, or poem will provide a general picture of the work. You will understand its broad outline, get its main idea, and absorb its general point of view. But in order to become a better writer, you must read, and reread, line by line and even word by word. Poems, especially, need rereading because so much meaning is contained in relatively few words. So rid yourself of the idea that five minutes before class starts you can skim the reading assignment and know it. Good writing requires careful rereading.

Narrating

Daddy Tucked the Blanket
Randall Williams

Looking back, most adults can remember being embarrassed about something in their backgrounds. The story that follows highlights the shame that comes from being poor. As you read, try to place yourself in the narrator's shoes; how would you have reacted under the same circumstances? Which details contribute most vividly to the portrait of a ramshackle house? What really matters in a home—a luxurious environment or a loving one?

1 About the time I turned 16, my folks began to wonder why I didn't stay home any more. I always had an excuse for them, but what I didn't say was that I had found my freedom and I was getting out.

2 I went through four years of high school in semirural Alabama and became active in clubs and sports; I made a lot of friends and became a regular guy, if you know what I mean. But one thing was irregular about me: I managed those four years without ever having a friend visit at my house.

3 I was ashamed of where I lived. I had been ashamed for as long as I had been conscious of class.

4 We had a big family. There were several of us sleeping in one room, but that's not so bad if you get along, and we always did. As you get older, though, it gets worse.

5 Being poor is a humiliating experience for a young person trying hard to be accepted. Even now—several years removed—it is hard to talk about. And I resent the weakness of these words to make you feel what it was really like.

6 We lived in a lot of old houses. We moved a lot because we were always looking for something just a little better than what we had. You have to understand that my folks worked harder than most people. My mother was always at home, but for her that was a full-time job—and no fun, either. But my father worked his head off from the time I can remember in construction and shops. It was hard, physical work.

7 I tell you this to show that we weren't shiftless. No matter how much money Daddy made, we never made much progress up the social ladder. I got out thanks to a college scholarship and because I was a little more articulate than the average.

8 I have seen my Daddy wrap copper wire through the soles of his boots to keep them together in the wintertime. He couldn't buy new boots because he had used the money for food and shoes for us. We lived like hell, but we went to school well-clothed and with a full stomach.

9 It really is hell to live in a house that was in bad shape 10 years before you moved in. And a big family puts a lot of wear and tear on a new house, too, so you can imagine how one goes downhill if it is teetering when you move in. But we lived in houses that were sweltering in summer and freezing in winter. I woke up every morning for a year and a half with plaster on my face where it had fallen out of the ceiling during the night.

This wasn't during the Depression; this was in the late 60's and early 70's. **10**

When we boys got old enough to learn trades in school, we would try to fix up the old houses we lived in. But have you ever tried to paint a wall that crumbled when the roller went across it? And bright paint emphasized the holes in the wall. You end up more frustrated than when you began, especially when you know that at best you might come up with only enough money to improve one of the six rooms in the house. And we might move out soon after, anyway. **11**

The same goes for keeping a house like that clean. If you have a house full of kids and the house is deteriorating, you'll never keep it clean. Daddy used to yell at Mama about that, but she couldn't do anything. I think Daddy knew it inside, but he had to have an outlet for his rage somewhere, and at least yelling isn't as bad as hitting, which they never did to each other. **12**

But you have a kitchen which has no counter space and no hot water, and you will have dirty dishes stacked up. That sounds like an excuse, but try it. You'll go mad from the sheer sense of futility. It's the same thing in a house with no closets. You can't keep clothes clean and rooms in order if they have to be stacked up with things. **13**

Living in a bad house is generally worse on girls. For one thing, they traditionally help their mother with the housework. We boys could get outside and work in the field or cut wood or even play ball and forget about living conditions. The sky was still pretty. **14**

But the girls got the pressure, and as they got older it became worse. Would they accept dates knowing they had to "receive" the young man in a dirty hallway with broken windows, peeling wallpaper and a cracked ceiling? You have to live it to understand it, but it creates a shame which drives the soul of a young person inward. **15**

I'm thankful none of us ever blamed our parents for this, because it would have crippled our relationships. As it worked out, only the relationship between our parents was damaged. And I think the harshness which they expressed to each other was just an outlet to get rid of their anger at the trap their lives were in. It ruined their marriage because they had no one to yell at but each other. I knew other families where the kids got the abuse, but we were too much loved for that. **16**

Once I was about 16 and Mama and Daddy had had a particularly violent argument about the washing machine, which had broken down. Daddy was on the back porch—that's where the only water faucet was—trying to fix it and Mama had a washtub out there washing school clothes for the next day and they were screaming at each other. **17**

Later that night everyone was in bed and I heard Daddy get up from the couch where he was reading. I looked out from my bed across the hall into their room. He was standing right over Mama and she was already asleep. He pulled the blanket up and tucked it around her shoulders and just stood there and tears were dropping off his cheeks and I thought I could faintly hear them splashing against the linoleum rug. **18**

Now they're divorced. **19**

I had courses in college where housing was discussed, but the sociologists never put enough emphasis on the impact living in substandard housing has on a person's psyche. Especially children's. **20**

Small children have a hard time understanding poverty. They want the same things children from more affluent families have. They want the same things they see advertised on television, and they don't understand why they can't have them. **21**

Other children can be incredibly cruel. I was in elementary school in Georgia—and this is interesting because it is the only thing I remember about that particular school—when I was about eight or nine. **22**

After Christmas vacation had ended, my teacher made each student 23 describe all his or her Christmas presents. I became more and more uncomfortable as the privilege passed around the room toward me. Other children were reciting the names of the dolls they had been given, the kinds of bicycles and the grandeur of their games and toys. Some had lists which seemed to go on and on for hours.

It took me only a few seconds to tell the class that I had gotten for 24 Christmas a belt and a pair of gloves. And then I was laughed at— because I cried—by a roomful of children and a teacher. I never forgave them, and that night I made my mother cry when I told her about it.

In retrospect, I am grateful for that moment, but I remember want- 25 ing to die at the time.

VOCABULARY

semirural (2)

class (3)

shiftless (7)

articulate (7)

teetering (9)

trades (11)

deteriorating (12)

impact (20)

substandard (20)

psyche (20)

affluent (21)

UNDERSTANDING WHAT YOU HAVE READ

Check the correct answer in the blank provided.

1. According to the narrator, it is difficult to keep an old house clean because

   _____ **a.** everything in it is deteriorating.

   _____ **b.** you have no sense of pride in it.

   _____ **c.** you don't have enough money to buy cleaning products.

   _____ **d.** the windows keep letting in dirt.

2. Having a shabby house because of being poor is more difficult on girls than on boys because

   _____ **a.** girls are more sensitive.

   _____ **b.** boys don't care about luxurious surroundings.

   _____ **c.** boys know they can make money once they finish school and start working.

   _____ **d.** girls spend more time doing house chores and they receive dates at home.

3. The parents in this story fought with each other but did not abuse their children because

   _____ **a.** the children would have ganged up on them.

   _____ **b.** the parents loved the children too much.

   _____ **c.** the uncles and aunts always protected the children.

   _____ **d.** the local social workers watched out for child abusers.

4. After the violent quarrel about the washing machine, what did the father do to the mother?

_____ **a.** He bought her a new washing machine.

_____ **b.** He apologized and promised to quit blaming her.

_____ **c.** He wept with shame.

_____ **d.** He went to her room and pulled the blanket over her shoulders.

5. What happened after Christmas to humiliate the narrator?

_____ **a.** He was told that his parents could not pay his tuition.

_____ **b.** A student accused him of living in a dirty shack.

_____ **c.** He had to tell the class that he received only a belt and a pair of gloves for Christmas.

_____ **d.** The church gave him some ugly, secondhand clothes.

THINKING ABOUT WHAT YOU HAVE READ

1. In paragraph 5, the narrator says that words are too weak to tell us what it was like to be poor. Do you think the narrator succeeded in conveying what it is like to be poor? Give reasons for your answer.

2. We are never told exactly why the parents got a divorce. What is your guess? Imagine the circumstances that led to the divorce.

3. In his final paragraph, the narrator writes, "I am grateful for that moment. . . ." What could have caused his gratitude for having felt so deeply embarrassed? Can you think of a painful moment in your own life for which you now feel grateful? Explain how the gratitude evolved.

4. What are some of the psychological effects of being poor, especially on children? How can some of these effects be avoided or lessened?

5. Despite the poverty described, how do you feel about the narrator's father? What kind of man is he? Does he possess characteristics that make him a good father? If so, what are they?

WRITING ASSIGNMENTS

1. Write a short narrative essay about something that happened to you in the past that embarrassed you. How would you react to that same incident today?

2. Support the following main idea, taken from paragraph 20 of the story: Substandard housing has an impact on a person's psyche, especially that of a child. If possible, narrate a personal experience to prove your point.

The Circuit

Francisco Jiminez

Most students consider school and learning a nuisance to endure between week-ends and holidays. But here is an entirely different take on going to school that you might not have thought of—by a migrant worker child who actually hungered for learning and felt deprived when his family's nomadic lifestyle kept him out of school. The narrator acquaints us with the harsh labor in the fields and the poverty and drudgery that is the farm laborers' lot. As you read the story, look for the techniques of a good narrative that you learned in Unit 7. Analyze the pacing of the story by focusing on which events are recreated in detail and which are glossed over to move the story along.

1 It was that time of year again. Ito, the strawberry sharecropper, did not smile. It was natural. The peak of the strawberry season was over and the last few days the workers, most of them braceros, were not picking as many boxes as they had during the months of June and July.

2 As the last days of August disappeared, so did the number of braceros. Sunday, only one—the best picker—came to work. I liked him. Sometimes we talked during our half-hour lunch break. That is how I found out he was from Jalisco, the same state in Mexico my family was from. That Sunday was the last time I saw him.

3 When the sun had tired and sunk behind the mountains, Ito signaled us that it was time to go home. "Ya esora," he yelled in his broken Spanish. Those were the words I waited for twelve hours a day, every day, seven days a week, week after week. And the thought of not hearing them again saddened me.

4 As we drove home Papá did not say a word. With both hands on the wheel, he stared at the dirt road. My older brother, Roberto, was also silent. He leaned his head back and closed his eyes. Once in a while he cleared from his throat the dust that blew in from outside.

5 Yes, it was that time of year. When I opened the front door to the shack, I stopped. Everything we owned was neatly packed in cardboard boxes. Suddenly I felt even more the weight of hours, days, weeks, and months of work. I sat down on a box. The thought of having to move to Fresno and knowing what was in store for me there brought tears to my eyes.

6 That night I could not sleep. I lay in bed thinking about how much I hated this move.

7 A little before five o'clock in the morning, Papá woke everyone up. A few minutes later, the yelling and screaming of my little brothers and sisters, for whom the move was a great adventure, broke the silence of dawn. Shortly, the barking of the dogs accompanied them.

8 While we packed the breakfast dishes, Papá went outside to start the "Carcanchita." That was the name Papá gave his old '38 black Plymouth. He bought it in a used-car lot in Santa Rosa in the winter of 1949. Papá was very proud of his little jalopy. He had a right to be proud of it. He spent a lot of time looking at other cars before buying this one. When he finally chose the "Carcanchita," he checked it thoroughly before driving it out of the car lot. He examined every inch of the car. He listened to the motor, tilting his head from side to side like a parrot, trying to detect any noises that spelled car trouble. After being satisfied with the looks and sounds of the car, Papá then insisted on knowing who the original owner was. He never did find out from the car salesman, but he bought the car anyway. Papá figured the original owner must have been

an important man because behind the rear seat of the car he found a blue necktie.

Papá parked the car out in front and left the motor running. "Listo," **9** he yelled. Without saying a word, Roberto and I began to carry the boxes out to the car. Roberto carried the two big boxes and I carried the two smaller ones. Papá then threw the mattress on top of the car roof and tied it with ropes to the front and rear bumpers.

Everything was packed except Mamá's pot. It was an old large gal- **10** vanized pot she had picked up at an army surplus store in Santa María the year I was born. The pot had many dents and nicks, and the more dents and nicks it acquired the more Mamá liked it. "Mi olla," she used to say proudly.

I held the front door open as Mamá carefully carried out her pot by **11** both handles, making sure not to spill the cooked beans. When she got to the car, Papá reached out to help her with it. Roberto opened the rear car door and Papá gently placed it on the floor behind the front seat. All of us then climbed in. Papá sighed, wiped the sweat off his forehead with his sleeve, and said wearily: "Es todo."

As we drove away, I felt a lump in my throat. I turned around and **12** looked at our little shack for the last time.

At sunset we drove into a labor camp near Fresno. Since Papá did not **13** speak English, Mamá asked the camp foreman if he needed any more workers. "We don't need no more," said the foreman, scratching his head. "Check with Sullivan down the road. Can't miss him. He lives in a big white house with a fence around it."

When we got there, Mamá walked up to the house. She went through **14** a white gate, past a row of rose bushes, up the stairs to the front door. She rang the doorbell. The porch light went on and a tall husky man came out. They exchanged a few words. After the man went in, Mamá clasped her hands and hurried back to the car. "We have work! Mr. Sullivan said we can stay there the whole season," she said, gasping and pointing to an old garage near the stables.

The garage was worn out by the years. It had no windows. The walls, **15** eaten by termites, strained to support the roof full of holes. The dirt floor, populated by earth worms, looked like a gray road map.

That night, by the light of a kerosene lamp, we unpacked and cleaned **16** our new home. Roberto swept away the loose dirt, leaving the hard ground. Papá plugged the holes in the walls with old newspapers and tin can tops. Mamá fed my little brothers and sisters. Papá and Roberto then brought in the mattress and placed it on the far corner of the garage. "Mamá, you and the little ones sleep on the mattress. Roberto, Panchito, and I will sleep outside under the trees," Papá said.

Early next morning Mr. Sullivan showed us where his crop was, and **17** after breakfast, Papá, Roberto, and I headed for the vineyard to pick.

Around nine o'clock the temperature had risen to almost one hundred **18** degrees. I was completely soaked in sweat and my mouth felt as if I had been chewing on a handkerchief. I walked over to the end of the row, picked up the jug of water we had brought, and began drinking. "Don't drink too much; you'll get sick," Roberto shouted. No sooner had he said that then I felt sick to my stomach. I dropped to my knees and let the jug roll off my hands. I remained motionless with my eyes glued on the hot sandy ground. All I could hear was the drone of insects. Slowly I began to recover. I poured water over my face and neck and watched the dirty water run down my arms to the ground.

I still felt a little dizzy when we took a break to eat lunch. It was past **19** two o'clock and we sat underneath a large walnut tree that was on the side of the road. While we ate, Papá jotted down the number of boxes we had picked. Roberto drew designs on the ground with a stick. Suddenly I noticed Papá's face turn pale as he looked down the road. "Here comes the school bus," he whispered loudly in alarm. Instinctively, Roberto and I ran and hid in the vineyards. We did not want to get in trouble for not going to school. The neatly dressed boys about my age got off. They carried books under their arms. After they crossed the street, the bus drove away. Roberto and I came out from hiding and joined Papá. "Tienen que tener cuidado," he warned us.

After lunch we went back to work. The sun kept beating down. The 20 buzzing insects, the wet sweat, and the hot dry dust made the afternoon seem to last forever. Finally the mountains around the valley reached out and swallowed the sun. Within an hour it was too dark to continue picking. The vines blanketed the grapes, making it difficult to see the bunches. "Vámonos," said Papá, signaling to us that it was time to quit work. Papá then took out a pencil and began to figure out how much we had earned our first day. He wrote down numbers, crossed some out, wrote down some more. "Quince," he murmured.

When we arrived home, we took a cold shower underneath a water- 21 hose. We then sat down to eat dinner around some wooden crates that served as a table. Mamá had cooked a special meal for us. We had rice and tortillas with "carne con chile," my favorite dish.

The next morning I could hardly move. My body ached all over. I felt 22 little control over my arms and legs.

This feeling went on every morning for days until my muscles finally 23 got used to the work.

It was Monday, the first week of November. The grape season was 24 over and I could now go to school. I woke up early that morning and lay in bed, looking at the stars and savoring the thought of not going to work and of starting sixth grade for the first time that year. Since I could not sleep, I decided to get up and join Papá and Roberto at breakfast. I sat at the table across from Roberto, but I kept my head down. I did not want to look up and face him. I knew he was sad. He was not going to school today. He was not going tomorrow, or next week, or next month. He would not go until the cotton season was over, and that was sometime in February. I rubbed my hands together and watched the dry, acid-stained skin fall to the floor in little rolls.

When Papá and Roberto left for work, I felt relief. I walked to the top 25 of a small grade next to the shack and watched the "Carcanchita" disappear in the distance in a cloud of dust.

Two hours later, around eight o'clock, I stood by the side of the road 26 waiting for school bus number twenty. When it arrived I climbed in. Everyone was busy either talking or yelling. I sat in an empty seat in the back.

When the bus stopped in front of the school, I felt very nervous. I looked out the bus window and saw boys and girls carrying books under 27 their arms. I put my hands in my pant pockets and walked to the principal's office. When I entered I heard a woman's voice say: "May I help you?" I was startled. I had not heard English for months. For a few seconds I remained speechless. I looked at the lady who waited for an answer. My first instinct was to answer her in Spanish, but I held back. Finally, after struggling for English words, I managed to tell her that I wanted to enroll in the sixth grade. After answering many questions, I was led to the classroom.

Mr. Lema, the sixth grade teacher, greeted me and assigned me a 28 desk. He then introduced me to the class. I was so nervous and scared at that moment when everyone's eyes were on me that I wished I were with Papá and Roberto picking cotton. After taking roll, Mr. Lema gave the class the assignment for the first hour. "The first thing we have to do this morning is finish reading the story we began yesterday," he said enthusiastically. He walked up to me, handed me an English book, and asked me to read. "We are on page 125," he said politely. When I heard this, I felt my blood rush to my head; I felt dizzy. "Would you like to read?" he asked hesitantly. I opened the book to page 125. My mouth was dry. My eyes began to water. I could not begin. "You can read later," Mr. Lema said understandingly.

For the rest of the reading period I kept getting angrier and angrier 29 with myself. I should have read, I thought to myself.

During recess I went into the restroom and opened my English book 30 to page 125. I began to read in a low voice, pretending I was in class. There were many words I did not know. I closed the book and headed back to the classroom.

Mr. Lema was sitting at his desk correcting papers. When I entered 31 he looked up at me and smiled. I felt better. I walked up to him and asked if he could help me with the new words. "Gladly," he said.

The rest of the month I spent my lunch hours working on English 32 with Mr. Lema, my best friend at school.

One Friday during lunch hour Mr. Lema asked me to take a walk 33 with him to the music room. "Do you like music?" he asked me as we entered the building.

"Yes, I like corridos," I answered. He then picked up a trumpet, blew 34 on it, and handed it to me. The sound gave me goose bumps. I knew that sound. I had heard it in many corridos. "How would you like to learn how to play it?" he asked. He must have read my face because before I could answer, he added, "I'll teach you how to play it during our lunch hours."

That day I could hardly wait to get home to tell Papá and Mamá the 35 great news. As I got off the bus, my little brothers and sisters ran up to meet me. They were yelling and screaming. I thought they were happy to see me, but when I opened the door to our shack, I saw that everything we owned was neatly packed in cardboard boxes.

VOCABULARY

sharecropper (1)	clasped (14)
signaled (3)	blanketed (20)
original (8)	hesitantly (27)
galvanized (10)	

UNDERSTANDING WHAT YOU HAVE READ

Check the correct answer in the blank provided.

1. What is the meaning of the opening sentence of the story—"It was that time of year again"?

   _____ **a.** It was time to move to the next farm.

   _____ **b.** It was time for the flu season to begin.

   _____ **c.** It was time to enjoy a summer vacation.

   _____ **d.** It was time to buy new clothes for work.

2. The father is very proud of

   _____ **a.** his children.

   _____ **b.** the living quarters in which the family lived.

_____ **c.** the family dog.

_____ **d.** his black '38 Plymouth.

3. Where had the mother found the pot she liked so much?

_____ **a.** At her grandmother's home in Mexico.

_____ **b.** At a Macy's sale.

_____ **c.** At an army surplus store.

_____ **d.** At a church rummage sale.

4. When the family worked for Mr. Sullivan, they stayed in

_____ **a.** a garage.

_____ **b.** the local Y.M.C.A.

_____ **c.** tents.

_____ **d.** barracks built for the help.

5. Who was Mr. Lema?

_____ **a.** The local sheriff.

_____ **b.** The owner of the vineyard.

_____ **c.** The narrator's teacher.

_____ **d.** The narrator's father.

THINKING ABOUT WHAT YOU HAVE READ

1. What were some of the conditions that made the work in the fields extremely difficult? List them.

2. Were there any causes for joy in the life described? If so, what were they?

3. Why did the boys run and hide when the school bus came down the road? What does this indicate about the lives of these migrant laborers?

4. Why does the narrator rejoice when the grape season is over? Why is he ashamed of facing his brother at the breakfast table (paragraph 23)?

5. What is the meaning of the sentence "I saw that everything we owned was neatly packed in cardboard boxes"?

WRITING ASSIGNMENTS

1. Narrate an incident in which you experienced a great disappointment.

2. Tell a story about a funny, sad, or nostalgic family dinner.

Describing

My Grandmother, the Bag Lady

Patsy Neal

The description that follows is heartrending in the honesty of its descriptive details. We cannot help but be moved by the author's view of her grandmother, whose world has shrunken to the dimensions of a bag, containing all of her possessions, attached to her walker. Those of us who have watched parents or grandparents deteriorate, as this grandmother has, recognize the symptoms and weep for the fate of anyone that lonely and that frightened. As you read, underline sensory details that you consider particularly vivid. Does the writer use any metaphors or similies?

Almost all of us have seen pictures of old, homeless ladies, moving about the streets of big cities with everything they own stuffed into a bag or a paper sack. 1

My grandmother is 89 years old, and a few weeks ago I realized with a jolt that she, too, had become one of them. Before I go any further, I had best explain that I did not see my grandmother's picture on TV. I discovered her plight during a face-to-face visit at my mother's house— in a beautiful, comfortable, safe, middle-class environment with good china on the table and turkey and chicken on the stove. 2

My grandmother's condition saddened me beyond words, for an 89-year-old should not have to carry around everything she owns in a bag. It's enough to be 89, without the added burden of packing the last fragments of your existence into a space big enough to accommodate only the minutest of treasures. 3

Becoming a bag lady was not something that happened to her overnight. My grandmother has been in a nursing home these last several years; at first going back to her own home for short visits, then less frequently as she became older and less mobile. 4

No matter how short these visits were, her greatest pleasure came from walking slowly around her home, touching every item lovingly and spending hours browsing through drawers and closets. Then, I did not understand her need to search out all her belongings. 5

As she spent longer days and months at the nursing home, I could not help noticing other things. She began to hide her possessions under the mattress, in her closet, under the cushion of her chair, in every conceivable, reachable space. And she began to think that people were "stealing" from her. 6

Unsteady. When a walker became necessary, my mother took time to make a bag that could be attached to it, so that my grandmother could carry things around while keeping her hands on the walker. I had not paid much attention to this bag until we went to the nursing home to take her home with us for our traditional Christmas Eve sharing of gifts. 7

As we left, my grandmother took her long, unsteady walk down the hallway, balancing herself with her walker, laboriously moving it ahead, one step at a time, until finally we were at the car outside. Once she 8 was safely seated, I picked up her walker to put it in the back. I could barely lift it. Then I noticed that the bag attached to it was bulging. Something clicked, but it still wasn't complete enough to grasp.

At home in my mother's house, I was asked to get some photographs from my grandmother's purse. Lifting her pocketbook, I was surprised again at the weight and bulk. I watched as my mother pulled out an alarm clock, a flashlight, a small radio, thread, needles, pieces of sewing, a book and other items that seemed to have no reason for being in a pocketbook. 9

I looked at my grandmother, sitting bent over in her chair, rummaging through the bag on the walker, slowly pulling out one item and then another, and lovingly putting it back. I looked down at her purse with all its disconnected contents and remembered her visits to her home, rummaging through drawers and through closets. 10

"Oh, Lord," I thought with sudden insight. "That walker and that purse are her home now." 11

I began to understand that over the years my grandmother's space of living had diminished like melting butter—from endless fields and miles of freedom as a child and young mother to, with age, the constrictions of a house, then a small room in a nursing home and finally to the tightly clutched handbag and the bag on her walker. 12

When the family sent her to a nursing home, it was the toughest decision it had ever had to make. We all thought she would be secure there; we would no longer have to worry about whether she had taken her medicine, or left her stove on, or was alone at night. 13

But we hadn't fully understood her needs. Security for my grandmother was not in the warm room at the nursing home, with 24-hour attendants to keep her safe and well fed, nor in the family who visited and took her to visit in their homes. In her mind her security was tied to those things she could call her own—and over the years those possessions had dwindled away like sand dropping through an hourglass: first her car, sold when her eyes became bad and she couldn't drive; then some furnishings she didn't really need. Later it was the dogs she had trouble taking care of. And finally it would be her home when it became evident that she could never leave the nursing home again. But as her space and mobility dwindled, so did her control over her life. 14

Dignity. I looked at my grandmother again, sitting so alone before me, hair totally gray, limbs and joints swollen by arthritis, at the hearing aid that could no longer help her hear, and the glasses too thick but so inadequate in helping her to see . . . and yet there was such dignity about her. A dignity I could not understand. 15

The next day, after my grandmother had been taken back to the nursing home and my mother was picking up in her room, she found a small scrap of paper my grandmother had scribbled these words on: 16

"It is 1:30 tonight and I had to get up and go to the bathroom. I cannot go back to sleep. But I looked in on Margaret and she is sleeping *so* good, and Patsy is sleeping too." 17

With that note, I finally understood, and my 89-year-old bag-lady grandmother changed from an almost helpless invalid to a courageous, caring individual still very much in control of her environment. 18

What intense loneliness she must have felt as she scribbled that small note on that small piece of paper with the small bag on her walker and her small purse next to her. Yet she chose to experience it alone rather than wake either of us from much-needed sleep. Out of her own great need, she chose to meet our needs. 19

As I held that tiny note, and cried inside, I wondered if she dreamed of younger years and more treasured possessions and a bigger world when she went back to sleep that night. I certainly hoped so. 20

VOCABULARY

plight (2)	rummaging (10)
minutest (3)	diminished (12)
mobile (4)	constrictions (12)
conceivable (6)	inadequate (15)
laboriously (8)	invalid (18)

UNDERSTANDING WHAT YOU HAVE READ

Check the correct answer in the blank provided.

1. Was the grandmother the kind of bag lady we expect to encounter on a city street?

   _____ **a.** Yes, except she had money.

   _____ **b.** No, because she was only 55 years old.

   _____ **c.** No, because she had a room in a good nursing home.

   _____ **d.** Yes—she wanted to live in the streets with other homeless women.

2. According to the author, becoming a bag lady was something that happened

   _____ **a.** after the grandmother had a stroke.

   _____ **b.** gradually over time.

   _____ **c.** overnight.

   _____ **d.** because no one loved her.

3. Who made the bag the grandmother could use to hang on her walker?

   _____ **a.** The author.

   _____ **b.** The grandmother's nursing home attendant.

   _____ **c.** Some women who belonged to a church organization.

   _____ **d.** The author's mother.

4. How did the family feel when they sent the grandmother to a nursing home?

   _____ **a.** They were happy they were no longer responsible for her.

   _____ **b.** It was the toughest decision they ever had to make.

   _____ **c.** They were unhappy because the nursing home was expensive.

   _____ **d.** They were too busy with other matters to care deeply.

5. At the end of the essay, the author describes her grandmother as a

   _____ **a.** courageous, caring individual.

   _____ **b.** childish, whimpering creature.

   _____ **c.** domineering, demanding patient.

   _____ **d.** senile woman who had lost all her faculties.

THINKING ABOUT WHAT YOU HAVE READ

1. Why do you think the bag and its contents became so precious to the grandmother?

2. The portrait of this grandmother is mostly sad, but the author does offer some beauty in her portrayal. Point to the paragraph in which this occurs.

3. How does the author feel about her grandmother's plight? How do the other members of the family feel?

4. In paragraph 11, the author has a sudden insight. What does she realize? Do you agree with her conclusion? Why or why not?

5. How does the author define security in her grandmother's life? Be specific in your answer.

WRITING ASSIGNMENTS

1. Describe the mental and physical state of an older person whom you know well. Try to be as understanding as possible of the person's attitudes and ways.

2. What will you like to be when you are 89? Describe the person you imagine yourself to be. Use specific details.

Black Cadillac

Bart Edelman

Except for the fact that this piece is written in stanzas with short lines, it is really more like an essay than a poem. If you read thoughtfully, you will get a clear image of what a Cadillac looked like in the fifties. Black was the color preferred by owners who wanted to drive a sleek, impressive car. As you read, also try to figure out the little drama that is developing. What is the conflict? How is it resolved? How do you feel about the ending?

The elongated fins,   1
A flying fish on wheels—
Grandpa's shiny new Cadillac
Floated down the block at twilight
And beached itself on the concrete sand.
Three toots of the horn
Brought us screaming from the house;
We swept around the immaculate sedan
And gazed in astonishment . . .
He'd really done it this time.   10

Grandpa stood in his pinstriped suit
With his back to us,
Whistling "Take Me Out To The Ballgame"
And smoking a Tareyton;
He jingled a pocketful of change,
Stroked a long string of keys
And turned towards us, grinning.
"So what do you think?
Anyone up for a ride?
It's only the shank of the evening.   20
I think we need to go nightlifin'.
Get inside and put your pajamas on.
We'll be out 'til the wee hours."

Past the frown on Mother's face we dashed,
Ready for adventure.
From our bedroom we heard
The exchange of raised voices,
Cross words,
A painful drawn out sigh,
Then nothing but silence   30
And an engine ignited.

By the time we reached the street,

He was gone;

We could barely make out

The slippery tail

Flipping in the wind,

Swimming far out to sea

As if it had never been there.

Mother told us calmly

That he had other stops to make,   40

But we knew the reason he didn't stay—

Why she always chased him away.

Months later,

When Grandpa came calling for us,

Willing to explain,

He was driving an old brown Chevrolet.

VOCABULARY

elongated (1)

immaculate (8)

shank (20)

ignited (31)

UNDERSTANDING WHAT YOU HAVE READ

Check the correct answer in the blank provided.

1. To what does the poet compare Grandpa's Cadillac?

   _____ **a.** A leopard.

   _____ **b.** A fish.

   _____ **c.** A black velvet blanket.

   _____ **d.** A pinstriped suit.

2. Grandpa wants to take his grandchildren

   _____ **a.** to the nearest coffee shop for ice cream.

   _____ **b.** to prayer meeting at church.

   _____ **c.** for a ride and some night life.

   _____ **d.** to hunt for night frogs at the pond.

3. Cross words are exchanged between

   _____ **a.** the grandfather and the mother.

   _____ **b.** the children and the mother.

   _____ **c.** the children and the grandfather.

   _____ **d.** the neighbor and the grandfather.

4. After the cross words, what happens?

_____ **a.** The children get into the car.

_____ **b.** The mother leaves in the car with the grandfather.

_____ **c.** The car can't start due to a dead battery.

_____ **d.** The grandfather drives off alone.

5. The next time the children see the grandfather, he is driving

_____ **a.** a Mercedes Benz.

_____ **b.** a Honda.

_____ **c.** a Chevrolet.

_____ **d.** a BMW.

THINKING ABOUT WHAT YOU HAVE READ

1. What is the conflict in this poem? Between which characters does it take place?

2. Why do you think the grandfather bought the black Cadillac?

3. Do you consider the grandfather lovable or not? How would you feel if he were your grandfather?

4. What kind of person is the mother? Why does she behave the way she does?

5. What do you think happened between the time of the incident narrated and the next time the grandfather came to visit?

WRITING ASSIGNMENTS

1. Describe your grandfather. What did he look like? What kind of personality did he have? How did you feel about him? If you do not remember your own grandfather, describe someone else's.

2. Describe the car of your dreams. Include the make, the style, the color—anything that will make this car seem real to your reader.

A View from Mount Ritter

Joseph T. O'Connor

Sometimes a harrowing experience can enhance your character, nudging you toward maturity and self-esteem. This is exactly what happened to the narrator of this essay who, as a high school student, joined an expedition to the top of Mount Ritter in northeast California. In recounting his frightening adventure, he focuses on the fury of a mountain storm to create a dominant impression. As you read, notice how his choice of words throughout provides concrete, vivid description that is rich in sensory detail.

"I hate this," I thought. We were on our way to the top of Mount Ritter in northeastern California. You would think everyone, near one of the tallest ridges in the Sierra Nevadas, would be in high spirits. But on this particular day the rain fell in torrents. Quarter-size hailstones pelted our protective helmets as thunder echoed through the canyons. 1

It was the second week of my mountain expedition in California. The first week there had not been a cloud in the sky, but on Tuesday of week two, a dark cover crept in from the west, painting the sunlit, blue sky black. The storm came in so fast we didn't even notice it until our shadows suddenly disappeared. 2

"Here it comes," our guide warned. As if God himself had given the order, the heavens opened, just a crack. Huge drops began falling but abruptly stopped, as if to say, "You know what's coming; here's a taste." As we began searching for shelter, a bolt of lightning ripped open the blackish clouds overhead and in unison thunder cracked, leaving everyone's ears ringing. We were in the midst of a huge July thunderstorm. Ethan, our guide, had said that during the summer in the high Sierras it might rain twice, but when it does, it's best not to be there. Suddenly lightning struck a tree not 20 feet from where I was standing. 3

"Lightning positions!" Ethan yelled frantically. A little too frantically for my taste. I thought he was used to this kind of thing. As scared as I was, squatting in a giant puddle of water and hailstones, with forks of lightning bouncing off the canyon walls around me, I couldn't help chuckling to myself at the sight of Ethan's dinner-plate-size eyeballs as he panicked like an amateur. Soon after the lightning died down some, we hiked to the shelter of nearby redwoods to put on rain gear. While we prayed for the rain to subside, I watched the stream we stood beside grow into a raging, white-water river. Another expeditioner, Mike, and I were under a full redwood donning our not-so-waterproof equipment when I realized we were standing on a small island. 4

"Mike! Let's go!" I yelled, my exclamation nearly drowned out by the roar of water surrounding us and another roll of thunder. 5

"I'm way ahead o' ya!" he screamed in his thick New York accent, and his goofy smile broke through the torrents. "Ya ready?" 6

"Yeah!" I yelled back, and jumped from our island into the knee-deep water. He followed as we slopped through the storm, losing our footing every few feet. 7

The unforgiving downpour lasted all day and into the night as we stumbled down the rocky cliffs seeking the driest place to set up camp. It was dusk before we found a small clearing in a pine forest, and began what was to be the worst night of my life. We constructed our tents in the dark, fumbling with the ropes with our frozen hands and finishing just as a stiffness like rigor mortis set in. We lay awake all night, shivering in 8 our wet sleeping bags while rain poured down and a small stream made its way through our tent.

It's funny how these memories keep coming back to me as if it was just yesterday. All this happened last summer, after my junior year in high school. I had decided to attend a mountaineering program in the Sierras. Two weeks in the back country with no sign of civilization. It sounded exciting and slightly dangerous, and I've always been up for a good adventure. I found out on that trip that nature is underestimated. The experience was the most invigorating, fulfilling, stimulating two weeks of my life. For the first time since I could remember, my head was crystal clear. I felt born again, only 2 weeks old. On top of Mount Ritter, 13,000 feet above sea level, I was entranced at the sight of the orange-red sun as it peeked over the glistening peaks far off in the east. Cumulous clouds appeared transparent as they glowed bright red in the morning glory. **9**

The wonder of all I'd experienced made me think seriously about what comes next. "Life after high school," I said to myself. "Uh-oh." What had I been doing for the last three years? I was so caught up in defying the advice of my parents and teachers to study and play by the rules that I hadn't considered the effects my actions would have on me. **10**

"Youth is wholly experimental," Robert Louis Stevenson wrote. Sure, there will be mistakes, but there will also be successes. I was a confused kid. Everyone—my parents, teachers and coaches—offered suggestions, but I chose to ignore them. I had "potential," they told me. As a typical teen, I thought I could make it on my own. I didn't want any help, and the more people tried to give it the more distant I grew. I was the kid who thought he could be perfect at anything without any preparation. I was lost in the daydream that I didn't need to study; I was going to play professional soccer. My game was good and I thought that practice, or getting good grades, for that matter, was unnecessary. Stubbornness and rebellion can be terrible things if they get out of control. **11**

"To get back one's youth one has merely to repeat one's follies." A day before my awakening on that fateful July sunrise, I would have disagreed with this quotation from Oscar Wilde. But after recognizing the results of my own follies for the first time, I thoroughly agree. **12**

This year, my final year in high school, I've at last cleared my head and buckled down. Judging by the past semester, I'm on the right track. My D average has U-turned into this report card's three B's and one A, landing me on my first Honor Roll. I intend to be on the Principal's List after this semester; then I hope to graduate and attend a community college in northern California, near the mountains, before transferring to a four-year school. **13**

Thanks to that morning's conversion, I am a new person. Now, I know I'll have to work hard. The sun streaming over the eastern Sierras wiped out the dark clouds that blurred my vision. Jonathan Harker in Bram Stoker's "Dracula" must have felt exactly the same way when he wrote in his journal: "No man knows 'till he has suffered from the night how sweet and how dear to his heart and eye the morning can be." **14**

VOCABULARY

torrents (1)

pelted (1)

abruptly (3)

subside (4)

donning (4)

rigor mortis (8)

stimulating (9)

entranced (9)

defying (10)

potential (11)

conversion (14)

UNDERSTANDING WHAT YOU HAVE READ

Check the correct answer in the blank provided.

1. The trip described took place

    _____ **a.** in a dream after having gone river rafting.

    _____ **b.** one summer after the narrator's junior year in high school.

    _____ **c.** when the narrator was 5 years old.

    _____ **d.** shortly before the narrator was married.

2. The expeditioners did not notice the storm coming until

    _____ **a.** their shadows suddenly disappeared.

    _____ **b.** the birds starting chirping frantically.

    _____ **c.** the leader yelled, "Put up the tents!"

    _____ **d.** lightening suddenly struck a camper.

3. While donning rain gear, the narrator suddenly noticed that

    _____ **a.** a deer was seeking shelter under the same tree.

    _____ **b.** a forest ranger appeared out of nowhere.

    _____ **c.** he was standing on a small island.

    _____ **d.** all the other campers were sleeping soundly.

4. The heavy rain

    _____ **a.** washed away the tents.

    _____ **b.** gradually turned into a warm summer drizzle.

    _____ **c.** caused a beautiful rainbow to appear.

    _____ **d.** lasted all day and into the night.

5. As a typical teen, the narrator

    _____ **a.** thought he could make it on his own.

    _____ **b.** grew more and more distant as people tried to help him.

    _____ **c.** believed he could be perfect without preparation.

    _____ **d.** all of the above.

THINKING ABOUT WHAT YOU HAVE READ

1. Why was this experience important in changing the narrator's outlook on life and his plans for the future?

2. How does the narrator make the storm seem real to the reader? Give specific examples of vivid language used.

3. The narrator also uses comparisons—similes and metaphors—to make his description vivid. Find examples and tell why each is effective.

4. Which paragraph, in your opinion, describes the most difficult part of the experience? Give reasons for your answer.

5. Would you have enjoyed the experience described in this essay? Why or why not?

WRITING ASSIGNMENTS

1. Using O'Connor's essay as a model, write an essay describing a striking aspect of nature you once experienced. Try to make the scene come to life for your reader.

2. Write an essay in which you narrate an incident in your past that contributed dramatically to your growth toward maturity.

Illustrating

So Who Makes Up All Those Signs that Tell Us What We Mustn't Do?

Bailey White

Perhaps, like the author, you have wondered who in the world thinks up all of the signs posted in public places to make people behave. If you have, then the essay that follows will speak familiarly to you. If you have not, then maybe the next time you encounter a sign that forbids you to do something, you will remember this essay. Notice how the author uses numerous examples—real and imaginary—to illustrate his point.

1   I was leaning over the little railing, looking down into the Devil's Millhopper, an interesting geological formation and the focal point of a Florida state park. Waterfalls plunge 120 feet into a bowl-shaped sinkhole, maidenhair ferns and moss grow in little crevices along the steep, sloping sides of the gorge, and a beautiful mist rises. I stood there feeling a reverence for those spectacles of the natural world. I felt the slow sweep of geologic time, I felt the remnants of the spiritual significance that place had had for the Indians who lived there for thousands of years; I felt the wonder and awe the European explorers experienced when they peered into that chasm for the first time.

2   Then another feeling crept over me, a deep, almost atavistic,* longing. It was the urge to throw something into the Devil's Millhopper. I looked around. A stone or a stick would do, but what I really wanted was a piece of food, the nibbled end of a hot-dog bun or a wedge of chocolate cake without icing. Then I noticed the sign, one of those tastefully unobtrusive state park signs: "Do Not Throw Food Or Trash In Gorge."

3   It was 4 A.M. and I was at the Los Angeles bus station, my next-to-last stop on a dreary transcontinental trip—three days and three nights on a Greyhound. My back ached, my knees ached, my head ached. Ever since El Paso, Texas, my seatmate had been an old man who chain-smoked Marlboro cigarettes and sucked and slobbered over a perpetual ham sandwich that kept oozing out of a greasy crumple of wax paper. I longed for a bath in my own bathtub at home, and then a deep sleep in my own bed, stretched out full length between clean sheets. But, I thought, pushing open the door of the bus station restroom, if I can just wash my feet and my hair I will be all right. I lined up my soap, my washrag and my little bottle of shampoo on the back of the sink and took off my shoes and socks. Aah, I thought. Then I saw the sign on the mirror: "Do Not Wash Hair Or Feet In the Sink."

---

*Throwback.

A few weeks ago I went into our little downtown restaurant and saw 4
that it had replaced its tired old salad bar with a gorgeous saltwater
aquarium with sea anemones, chunks of living coral and big, slow-
moving, colorful fish with faces I could almost recognize. I spent my
whole lunchtime staring into that tank, mesmerized by the fish as they
gracefully looped and glided, sending the tentacles of the sea anemones
into slow swirls and fanning out the tall grasses. When I finished my
sandwich I noticed that there were a couple of crumbs left on my plate,
just the size to pinch between thumb and finger.

Oh, I thought, to pinch up those crumbs and dip my fingers down into 5
the water, breaking through the smooth surface into the coolness and
silence of that peaceful world. A fish would make a looping turn, his
odd exophthalmic eyes would rotate slowly in their sockets and fix upon
the crumbs. Then he would angle up, and I would feel for just one exquis-
ite instant those raspy fish lips grating across my fingertips. With rising
delight and anticipation, I pinched up a crumb, two crumbs. I scrabbled
across to the plastic top of the tank, found the little door, lifted it open—
and then I saw the sign: "Do Not Feed The Fish."

"We Prohibit Climbing In Any Manner From Or Along the Canyon Rim." 6
"Do Not Pick Flowers." 7
"No Smoking, Eating Or Drinking." 8
"No Swinging From Vines In Trees." 9
"No Pedestrian Traffic In Woods." 10
"No Fishing." 11
"No Swimming." 12
"No Trespassing." 13

Don't get me wrong. I approve of these necessary and useful prohibi- 14
tions. But sometimes I wonder: Who makes them up and how does he know
so well the deep and touching urges of human beings to pick flowers, picnic
in unusual spots, walk in the woods, climb canyon walls, swing from vines
and feed already well-nourished animals? I imagine a sour, silent little
man skulking around in public places, watching us furtively with squinty
eyes and scribbling notes on his bulging pad with a gnawed pencil. In
national parks he disguises himself as a tourist in reflective sunglasses
and plaid Bermuda shorts. "Bryce Canyon," he notes with a smirk. "Uri-
nating on hoodoos and off cliffs." In zoos he wears khaki and lurks in the
shadows, hiding behind a bag of peanuts. "Touching the giraffe's tongue
through fence wire . . . feeling the camel's hump," he scribbles.

At night he goes home and, in his stark-white workshop illuminated 15
with fluorescent lights, he makes those forbidding signs. I imagine, one
night as he works late, the tendril of a grapevine creeping in his window
and, when his back is turned, gently nudging itself around him. "No
Touching!" he admonishes. But, with a clutch and a snatch, the vine
retracts, and he finds himself hurtling through the night sky above a
North Florida state park. "Do Not Swing From Vines!" he shrieks. And
with that the vine drops him into the vortex of a limpid spring. "No Swimming!" he sputters as the dark, icy water closes over his head. As he sinks,
pale-colored fish swim up and cock their eyes at him. "Do Not Feed The
Fish!" he squeaks. But slowly and precisely, the fish angle up, move in,
and then, all over, he feels the pick-pick-pick of those prickly lips.

VOCABULARY

focal (1)	exophthalmic (5)
gorge (1)	prohibitions (14)
reverence (1)	skulking (14)
geologic (1)	furtively (14)
remnants (1)	tendril (15)
chasm (1)	retracts (15)
unobtrusive (2)	vortex (15)
anemones (4)	limpid (15)

UNDERSTANDING WHAT YOU HAVE READ

Check the correct answer in the blank provided.

1. What is the first example of a sign the author gives?

   _____ **a.** "Do Not Feed the Fish or Birds."

   _____ **b.** "Do Not Throw Food Or Trash In Gorge."

   _____ **c.** "No Trespassing."

   _____ **d.** "No Swinging From Vines In Trees."

2. What did the writer try to do in the Los Angeles bus station?

   _____ **a.** Feed some homeless people.

   _____ **b.** Walk behind the cashier's window.

   _____ **c.** Drop a gum wrapper on the floor.

   _____ **d.** Wash his feet in the restroom sink.

3. What happened when the author tried to place some bread crumbs in a restaurant fish tank?

   _____ **a.** He noticed a sign stating, "Use Only Cracker Crumbs to Feed Fish."

   _____ **b.** Some children wanted to do the same.

   _____ **c.** A fish bit him.

   _____ **d.** He saw a sign stating, "Do Not Feed The Fish."

4. Does the author approve or disapprove of signs prohibiting certain actions?

   _____ **a.** He approves.

   _____ **b.** He disapproves.

   _____ **c.** He wishes they were not necessary.

   _____ **d.** He thinks they will lead to political dictatorship.

5. The author imagines that the one writing the signs is

   _____ **a.** an editor at the *Chicago Tribune*.

   _____ **b.** a little old lady from Boston.

   _____ **c.** a schoolteacher who hates children.

   _____ **d.** a sour little man skulking around in public places.

THINKING ABOUT WHAT YOU HAVE READ

1. The major question on the writer's mind is, "Who makes up all those signs that tell us what we must not do?" Why do you think this question intrigues him? Does it intrigue you? Why or why not?

2. Do you agree that human beings have a deep urge to break rules? What other rules do you see people breaking?

3. What penalty do you suggest for graffiti writers? ("Graffiti Forbidden" does not seem to work.)

4. Think of another possible imaginative creature whom you might describe as the sign creator. What kind of person would he or she be? Describe him or her as vividly as the author described his creature.

5. Do you believe it is necessary to have signs forbidding certain behaviors in public places? Why or why not?

WRITING ASSIGNMENTS

1. Write an essay on the importance of keeping public places clean. Use examples to support your point.

2. Write an essay about the way nature and beautiful monuments are destroyed by people. Illustrate your essay with examples.

Long Live High School Rebels

Thomas French

The essay that follows encourages high school students to think for themselves and disobey rules imposed only to keep them quiet and passive. This position is quite different from that of contemporary articles attacking high school students for laziness, irresponsibility, the way they speak, or the way they dress. What is your own opinion? Are high school students stifled by their principals and teachers? As you read, notice the author's use of examples to support his argument. Are his examples convincing?

Ten years ago I was in high school. It was the most absurd and savage place I have ever been. 1

To listen to the morning announcement, you'd have thought the most pressing crisis in the world was our student body's lack of school spirit. Seniors were grabbing freshmen, dragging them into the bathrooms and dunking their heads in the toilets—a ritual called "flushing." Basketball players were treated like royalty; smart kids were treated like peasants. And the administrators worshipped the word "immature." Inevitably, they pronounced it "imma-tour." Inevitably, they used it to describe us. 2

The principal and his assistants told us to act like adults, but they treated us like children. Stupid children. They told us what we could wear, when we could move, how close we could stand to our girlfriends, how fast we could walk to lunch and what topics were forbidden to write about in our school newspaper. 3

When I went out for the tennis team, I remember, the coach told me to cut my hair. It was down to my shoulders and looked terrible, but I loved it. I asked the coach what was the point. Just do it, he said. 4

If we were taught anything, it was that high school is not about learning but about keeping quiet. The easiest way to graduate was to do what you were told, all of what you were told, and nothing but what you were told. Most of us did just that. I smiled at the principal, stayed out of trouble, avoided writing articles critical of administration, asked only a few smart-alecky questions and cut my hair as ordered. I was so embarrassed afterwards that I wore a blue ski cap all day every day for weeks. 5

I admit to some lingering bitterness over the whole affair. I'd still like to know, for one thing, what the length of my hair had to do with my forehand. Maybe that's why, to this day, I almost always root for high school students when they clash intelligently with administrators. High school needs a good dose of dissension. If you've been there in recent years, and I have because I work with student newspapers around Pinellas County, you'd know it needs dissension more than ever. 6

A reminder of this came with the news that one day last month an assistant principal at St. Petersburg High was rummaging through a student's car in a school parking lot. When the assistant principal found three empty wine-cooler bottles and what was suspected to be some spiked eggnog inside the car, the student was suspended for five days. 7

Though the student has argued that the search was an unconstitutional violation of his rights, the incident should not have come as any huge surprise. High school officials around this county have been 8 searching through kids' cars and lockers for some time. One day a couple of years ago, a teacher tells me, officials at Lakewood High allowed police to search for drugs with dogs. At the time, students were gathered at an assembly on God and patriotism.

Searches tell students plainly enough what administrators think of them. But in this county, such incidents are only part of a larger tradition of control. Some memorable moments over the years: **9**

- In 1983, a group of boys at Lakewood High decided it was unfair that they weren't allowed to wear shorts to school but that girls were allowed to wear miniskirts. The rationale for the rule was that shorts—but not miniskirts—were too "distracting." To make fun of the rule, the boys began wearing miniskirts to school.

  Administrators laughed at first, but once the rebellion began attracting publicity, the principal suspended the ringleader. When dozens of students staged further protest in front of the school and refused to go to class, the principal suspended 37 of them, too. Later, although close to 1,400 signatures were gathered on a petition against the rule, the Pinellas County School Board bore down and decided to ban shorts from all middle and high schools. Miniskirts, however, were still allowed.

  "We need to set a moral standard for our children," explained board member Gerald Castellanos.
- Last year, William Grey, the principal of St. Petersburg High, suspended a ninth-grader who dyed her hair purple. "I just don't think school is the place for multi-colored heads," Grey said. He did acknowledge that he allowed students to dye their hair green for special events—the school's colors are green and white—but he insisted that was different because it was "promoting school spirit."
- Earlier this year at Pinellas Park High, two of the school's top students—they're number one and two in their class academically—were criticized by the principal when they wrote articles in the student newspaper pointing out that many of the school's students are sexually active and do not use birth control. I was working with the staff that year, and I know the two students wrote the articles in an effort to prevent teen-age pregnancies. But the principal called their work irresponsible—he disagreed with their methodology—and told the newspaper staff it should write more "positive" articles.
- This fall, says a teacher at Pinellas Park, the administration cracked down on cafeteria infractions by warning that anyone caught leaving a lunch tray on a table would be suspended.
- Last year, 16-year-old Manny Sferios and a group of other students from public and private high schools put together an underground magazine called *Not For Profit* and distributed several issues to students around the county. The magazine ridiculed apartheid, protested the proliferation of nuclear weapons and tried to prod students into thinking about something more than their next pair of designer jeans.

Not For Profit also contained a variety of swear words and ridiculed the small-mindedness of many school officials, and when administrators saw it, they began confiscating copies from kids and warning that those caught with the publication risked suspension. **10**

Though the officials said their main objection to *Not For Profit* was 11 its language, the magazine's activist stance also came under fire. Gerald Castellanos, the school board member, said he did not believe students were sophisticated enough to put together such a magazine.

"I sincerely sense the hand of some very anti-American, anti-free 12 enterprise types in here," he said. "And I don't believe they're students."

Castellanos' attitude was not surprising. Too often the people who 13 run our high schools and sit on our school boards are not prepared to accept or deal with students who think for themselves and stand up for themselves. It would mean a loss of some control, increased resistance to petty rules and a slew of hard questions for those official who'd rather present a "positive image" than openly confront the real problems in our schools.

There are plenty of real problems that need confronting. Alcohol. 14 Drugs. Broken families. Teen-age pregnancies. Not to mention what's happening in some of our classrooms.

While working on an article published earlier this year, I sat in a 15 couple of classes at St. Petersburg High—the school run by William Grey, the principal who took a stand on purple hair—and what I saw were rows and rows of kids who were bored beyond description. They were trading jokes while the teachers tried to speak. They were literally falling asleep at their desks. One boy who had no interest in the subject matter—it was American history, by the way—was allowed to get up and leave. Another sat in his seat, strumming his finger across his lips, making baby noises.

Dealing with apathy as deep as this is challenge enough for anyone. 16 It requires more teachers, more money, inspiration, real change—all of which are hard to come by. Throw that in with the other problems in our high schools, and the task becomes monumental.

I'm not saying that administrators aren't trying to cope with that 17 task. I know they are. But frequently they waste time and distance themselves from students by exerting their authority in other ways. Make sure the kids don't wear shorts. See to it they put away their lunch trays. Bring in the dogs every once in a while and let them sniff around the lockers. In the face of everything else, keep the school quiet. It's a way that adults tell themselves they're in charge. It's a way they tell themselves they're making a difference.

In the meantime, the ideas that our high schools should promote— 18 freedom of thought and expression, for one—get shoved aside. And the students whom we should be encouraging—the ones who have the brains and spirit to start their own magazine, to protest silly rules, to ask what the color of one's hair has to do with an education—are lectured, suspended and told to get back in line.

Kids know it stinks. Once in a while, they find the guts to step for- 19 ward and say so, even if it means getting in trouble. I think they should do it more often. Because if there's anything I regret about my own days in high school, it's that more of us didn't fight against the absurdity with every ounce of adolescent ingenuity and irreverence we had.

We should have commandeered the p.a. system one morning and read 20 aloud from Thoreau's *Civil Disobedience*. We should have boycotted the food in the cafeteria for a solid week. We should have sent a note home to the principal's parents informing them he was suspended until he grew up. We should have boned up on our rights in law library and published what we found in the school paper. And every time an adult said "imma-tour," we should have pulled kazoos out of our pockets and blown on them to our heart's content.

VOCABULARY

inevitably (2)

dissension (6)

methodology (9)

apartheid (9)

proliferation (9)

confiscating (10)

apathy (16)

ingenuity (19)

irreverence (19)

commandeered (20)

UNDERSTANDING WHAT YOU HAVE READ

Check the correct answer in the blank provided.

1. Ten years ago, when the author was in high school, he found it

    _____ **a.** a place where students learned about true democracy.

    _____ **b.** the most absurd and savage place he had ever been.

    _____ **c.** a campus with a modern building and good gym equipment.

    _____ **d.** an ideal spot to find your future wife.

2. The author objects to the fact that in his high school, the principal and assistants

    _____ **a.** cared only about getting salary raises for themselves.

    _____ **b.** would not allow students to have a senior prom.

    _____ **c.** told the students to act like adults but treated them like children.

    _____ **d.** expected too much from students who had not yet reached the age of 20.

3. When the boys at Lakewood High were not allowed to wear shorts to school while the girls could wear miniskirts, they

    _____ **a.** wrote to the local newspaper about how unfair the rule was.

    _____ **b.** staged a walkout and would not attend school for a week.

    _____ **c.** filled the principal's office with barrels of popcorn.

    _____ **d.** wore miniskirts to school.

4. Which of the following examples is not listed as an infraction in this essay?

    _____ **a.** Dyeing one's hair purple.

    _____ **b.** Locking the principal in his office.

    _____ **c.** Writing in the school paper that students were sexually active.

    _____ **d.** Putting together an underground magazine.

5. One of the great challenges of dealing with high school students is fighting their

    _____ **a.** apathy.

    _____ **b.** rudeness.

    _____ **c.** stupidity.

    _____ **d.** bad language.

THINKING ABOUT WHAT YOU HAVE READ

1. The author states (paragraphs 19, 20) that he regrets that more students in his day did not fight against the absurdity of high school discipline with all of the "adolescent ingenuity and irreverence" they had. Do you agree with his attitude? Give reasons for your answer.

2. What makes the author's task difficult as he sticks up for the rights of high school students? Do you think he manages to overcome the difficulty?

3. How would you counter the argument that high school students should rebel against all of the "absurd" regulations, such as dress codes and restrictions against freedom of speech?

4. Looking back on your own high school experience, how would you judge your high school principals or your teachers? What attitudes did they have toward you and the other students? Were you subjected to the kinds of regulations described in French's article?

5. Does French present both sides of the question? Why or why not? Do his examples strengthen his point of view? Why or why not?

WRITING ASSIGNMENTS

1. Do you agree with French? Write an essay in which you support or oppose his point of view, using convincing examples of your own.

2. Write about your high school experience, indicating whether or not it encouraged you to think on your own. Use examples that prove your point.

Explaining a Process

How I Was Bathed

Michael Ondaatje

This description of a process is a delightful peek into the life of the narrator. It captivates us because all of us have memories of special moments and people stored in our brains. We remember Grandpa taking us for ice cream, a teacher scolding us in front of the class, a scout hike up some glacier, or a quarrel with our best friend. This particular memory describes the process of being bathed at the age of five. Notice how the steps are described clearly and in logical order.

We are having a formal dinner. String hoppers, meat curry, egg 1
rulang, papadams, potato curry. Alice's date chutney, seeni sambol, mallung and brinjals and iced water. All the dishes are on the table and a good part of the meal is spent passing them around to each other. It is my favourite meal—anything that has string hoppers and egg rulang I eat with a lascivious hunger. For dessert there is buffalo curd and jaggery sauce—a sweet honey made from the coconut, like maple syrup but with a smoky taste.

In this formal setting Gillian begins to describe to everyone present how 2
I used to be bathed when I was five. She had heard the story in detail from Yasmine Gooneratne, who was a prefect with her at Bishop's College for Girls. I listen intently, making sure I get a good portion of the egg rulang.

The first school I went to was a girls' school in Colombo which 3
accepted young boys of five or six for a couple of years. The nurse or ayah in charge of our cleanliness was a small, muscular and vicious woman named Maratina. I roamed with my pack of school friends, usually filthy from morning to night, and every second evening we were given a bath. The bathroom was a sparse empty stone room with open drains in the floor and a tap to one side. We were marched in by Maratina and ordered to strip. She collected our clothes, threw them out of the room, and locked the door. The eight of us were herded terrified into one corner.

Maratina filled a bucket with water and flung the contents towards 4
our cowering screaming bodies. Another bucket was filled and hurled towards us hard as a police hose. Then she strode forward, grabbed a child by the hair, pulled him over to the centre, scrubbed him violently with carbolic soap and threw him towards the opposite side of the room. She plucked another and repeated the soaping. Totally in control of the squirming bodies she eventually scrubbed us all, then returned to the bucket and thrashed water over our soapy nakedness. Bleary-eyed, our bodies tingling and reeling, our hair curved back from the force of the throw, we stood there shining. She approached with a towel, dried us fast and brutally, and threw us out one by one to get into our sarongs and go to bed.

The guests, the children, everyone is laughing and Gillian is no doubt 5
exaggerating Yasmine's account in her usual style, her long arms miming the capture and scrub of five-year-olds. I am dreaming and wondering

why this was never to be traumatically remembered. It is the kind of event that should have surfaced as the first chapter of an anguished autobiographical novel. I am thinking also of Yasmine Gooneratne, now teaching at a university in Australia, whom I met just last year at an International Writers' Conference in New Dehli. We talked then mostly about Gillian who had also been at university with her. Why did *she* not tell me the story—this demure woman in a sari who was once "bath prefect" at Bishop's College Girl's School, who officiated over the cleansing of my lean five-year-old nakedness?

VOCABULARY

lascivious (1)
prefect (2)
sparse (3)
cowering (4)
carbolic (4)

sarongs (4)
miming (5)
traumatically (5)
demure (5)
sari (5)

UNDERSTANDING WHAT YOU HAVE READ

Check the correct answer in the blank provided.

1. According to certain details provided, where would you guess the narrative takes place?

_____ **a.** Africa.

_____ **b.** Russia.

_____ **c.** China.

_____ **d.** India.

2. Who is in charge of the boys' cleanliness?

_____ **a.** The cook, Alice.

_____ **b.** The author's older sister.

_____ **c.** The nurse, Maratina.

_____ **d.** Yasmine.

3. What is the first step in the bath process?

_____ **a.** To have the boys pick out some clean clothes.

_____ **b.** To have the boys strip.

_____ **c.** To recite a patriotic verse.

_____ **d.** To have each boy pick out a towel.

4. After the boys are brutally towel dried, what are they ordered to do?

_____ **a.** Say their prayers.

_____ **b.** Write letters to their parents.

_____ **c.** Read a book.

_____ **d.** Get into their sarongs and go to bed.

5. How do the guests react to Gillian's exaggerated account of the bath?

_____ **a.** They are bored.

_____ **b.** They laugh.

_____ **c.** They feel embarrassed.

_____ **d.** They are relieved that those days are over.

THINKING ABOUT WHAT YOU HAVE READ

1. The author wonders why the brutal bathing process never traumatized his life. In your view, why didn't it?

2. Why are the boys so terrified when they are herded into one corner to be bathed? Would you have been terrified at that age? Why or why not?

3. Does Maratina strike you as an evil woman? Why does she terrify the boys?

4. After Gillian has described the bath routine, the guests laugh in response. Do you consider the description humorous? If yes, what are the humorous details?

5. List the separate steps involved in the process of bathing the boys in order.

WRITING ASSIGNMENTS

1. Write about some routine process you remember from your childhood. Break it down into separate, clearly listed steps.

2. Write an essay about the process of getting up every morning. Describe each major step clearly and in the order in which it occurs.

How to Ace a Job Interview

Richard Koonce

The job interview is as close to being a universal experience as can be found in our society. Almost every one of us, at one time or other, has had a job interview. Until we retire, it is also an ordeal that is likely to be repeated. But, as the author tells us, it is an ordeal that we can prepare for and be better at if we know what to expect. Using the step-by-step approach that is typical of a process analysis, the author familiarizes us with what employers are typically looking for in a job seeker and teaches us how to make the best possible impression. As you read, pay particular attention to the step-by-step process the author uses in giving his advice.

1   Next to public speaking, most people think that enduring a job interview is one of the most stressful human experiences.

2   I wouldn't quibble with that. However, a lot of people not only manage to master the art of effective interviewing as they go about job searches, but actually grow to enjoy the interview experience.

3   Good thing! Job interviews are something we all have to deal with from time to time in our careers. So, it pays to know how to handle yourself effectively when you're sitting across the desk from a prospective employer. Indeed, knowing how to navigate the terrain of job interviews can pay off big time for your career, land you a better job than the one you initially interview for, and position you for the job success and satisfaction you deserve.

4   How do you ace a job interview? Here are some tips.

5   Recognize that when you interview for a job, employers are looking for evidence of four things: your ability to do the job, your motivation, your compatibility with the rest of the organization, and your self-confidence. If you understand how all those things play into an interviewer's questions (and an employer's hiring decisions), you'll have a better chance of getting hired.

6   Often the first thing an employer wants to know is, "Will you fit in?" Presuming a company has seen your resume ahead of time and invited you for an interview, it may assume you have certain skills. Now they want to know, "Will you be compatible with everyone else that works here?"

7   Fitting in is a real hot button for employers. That's because it's expensive to go through the rehiring process if someone doesn't work out.

8   Along with determining compatibility, employers want to know that you're motivated to do a job. And, they want to know why you want to work for their organization. So be ready with career highlights that illustrate why hiring you would be a good decision for the organization. Showcase your talents as an instructional designer for example, or tell the interviewer about the process improvement efforts you've put in place in your current job that ensure continuous refinement of training courses. Concise oral vignettes like these can make a great impression on interviewers.

9   Throughout the interview, breathe deeply, speak slowly, and focus on projecting yourself confidently. This is important. Employers want to see self-confidence in job seekers. A lot of job seekers are too modest. They downplay their accomplishments. Don't embellish or exaggerate, but don't be a shrinking violet either. Rehearse ahead of time the answers to key

questions that you expect to be asked, especially that all-time favorite: "Tell me about yourself."

    Some other points to keep in mind: 10

    Before the interview, do some research on the company you're inter- 11 viewing with. That will enable you to demonstrate knowledge of the company when you meet the interviewer. It may also prompt questions that you'll want to get answers to, even as questions are being asked of you.

    There are lots of research options. You can tap into the Internet and 12 pull down everything from company profiles to *Dun and Bradstreet* financial reports. You can talk to friends or coworkers that may know something about the organization. And don't forget to watch the paper for late-breaking developments about the company. (If you read in the paper the day of your interview that your prospective employer is about to file Chapter 11, you may want to think twice about working there!)

    Arrive for the interview early enough to go to the restroom to check 13 yourself out. The last thing you want is to arrive for your interview beaded with sweat, having just sprinted there from the subway stop two blocks away.

    Once in the interview, concentrate on making a pleasant and strong 14 first impression. Eighty percent of the first impression an interviewer gets of you is visual—and it's formed in the first two minutes of the meeting! So, men, wear a well-made suit, crisply starched white or blue shirt, and polished shoes. Women, you can get away with more color than men, but dress conservatively in dresses, or jacket and skirt combinations. Wearing a colorful scarf is a good way to weave in color, but keep jewelry to a minimum.

    As you answer questions, be sure to emphasize as often as you can 15 the reasons why your skills, background, and experience make you a good fit for the job that you're interviewing for.

    After the interview, immediately send a thank-you note to the inter- 16 viewer. This is a critical point of interview etiquette. Many job candidates eliminate themselves from competition for a job because they don't do this.

    Finally, learn from every job interview you have. Don't be hard on 17 yourself if things don't go your way. Even job interviews that don't go well can be great learning experiences. And in my own life, I can look back on interviews where I'm glad I didn't get the job!

VOCABULARY

quibble (2)	concise (8)
terrain (3)	vignettes (8)
compatibility (5)	embellish (9)
ensure (8)	prospective (12)
refinement (8)	etiquette (16)

UNDERSTANDING WHAT YOU HAVE READ

Check the correct answer in the blank provided.

1. What does the author call a "hot button" issue with employers?

    _____ **a.** The company's dress code.

    _____ **b.** Previous experience on the job.

    _____ **c.** A job seeker's political affiliation.

    _____ **d.** Whether or not an employee will fit in.

2. What should you be ready to provide at the interview?

_____ **a.** Career highlights.

_____ **b.** A pep talk about yourself.

_____ **c.** A salary demand.

_____ **d.** An organization chart of your present company.

3. What specific advice about your behavior at an interview does the author give?

_____ **a.** Boast about your accomplishments.

_____ **b.** Breathe deeply, speak slowly, and be self-confident.

_____ **c.** Mention your ability to network.

_____ **d.** Talk about your college accomplishments.

4. According to the author, many job seekers are

_____ **a.** too boastful.

_____ **b.** too gaudily dressed.

_____ **c.** too aggressive.

_____ **d.** too modest.

5. What should you do after the interview?

_____ **a.** Read up about the company.

_____ **b.** Send the interviewer a thank you note.

_____ **c.** Send the interviewer a questionnaire asking how you did.

_____ **d.** Tell your boss that you interviewed with a competitor.

THINKING ABOUT WHAT YOU HAVE READ

1. Which particular piece of advice in this article do you think is most valuable for future job interviews? Does any of the author's advice come as a surprise?

2. Every process writer uses transitions and other lead-ins to make the specific steps of the process clear. What are some of these that the author uses?

3. In paragraphs 5 through 8, the author concentrates on telling us what employers are looking for. What is his reason for doing this?

4. What is the worst job interview you've ever been on? Based upon what you've learned from this article, how do you think you could've made it better?

5. Based on job interviews that you've had, how important a part does physical appearance play in getting a job?

WRITING ASSIGNMENTS

1. Write a process essay telling another student how to study for a test.

2. Write an essay about any interview you've ever had. Use the process format, giving a step-by-step accounting of what happened.

Defining

Cheating

Dr. Laura Schlessinger

This article was written by a woman who writes a syndicated newspaper column but who is even better known as the host of the internationally syndicated talk radio program "Dr. Laura." In her column and on her talk show, she dispenses advice to troubled people who write or call in with various moral and ethical dilemmas. The particular problem discussed below, which leads to the definitions of "support" and "judgment," is probably more common than we might want to admit. Many of us have been tortured by the choice of either protecting a loved one who is doing wrong or sticking to a moral principle and telling. Dr. Laura has been criticized by some people as being too judgmental and moralistic in her advice, but at least she makes her position crystal clear through her twin definitions of support and judgment.

1 I recently received a letter from a very troubled young woman struggling with the concept of "support." Her married sister is fooling around despite her marital vows, despite the dependent children who love their dad, and despite this young woman's oh-so-careful admonitions.

2 The errant sister, obviously no stranger to expedience in definitions, criticized this young woman for not being supportive.

3 I guess in this case supportive would mean giving alibis for the adulterous sister's whereabouts, maybe even baby-sitting the children so more time would be available for trysts. It would also mean listening to the self-serving complaints that justify the adulterous behavior and generally maintaining a conspiracy of silence against the husband.

4 The young woman was torn between her values, her sense of loyalty to the husband, her fear for the welfare of the children, and her obligation to her sister.

5 One of the first dictionary definitions of "support" is "to sustain without giving way." How might that apply here? How can this woman sustain her relationship with her sister without having her own values give way?

6 Perhaps it would be to affirm the familial love while outlining the devastation being synthesized from her sister's selfish behavior. Perhaps it would be to offer specific resources (religious and/or psychotherapeutic) for the errant sister to use to face her fears, disappointments, personal limitations, frustrations, etc., in a more productive way.

7 Perhaps it would be to inform her sister that without efforts in these more positive directions, she would be obligated to force the issue by speaking the truth in front of the married couple.

8 To stay by people as they endure or struggle with difficult times in their lives is a blessing. To think that support necessarily means to accept, advocate or even cooperate in activities that are blatantly wrong is either weak or voyeuristic—and certainly not in the ultimate best interest of either person.

9 And that is where judgment must be brought in. Unfortunately, the term judgment has been distorted into an absolute negative by those who

wish to espouse a life philosophy of "anything goes"—that is, until they are the loser in someone else's self-centered life scenario.

Making judgments is a necessary part of the life of a creature with free will and a wide range of options. We must discern between choices that are decent and fair and those that are anything from inappropriate to evil and self-serving. By our judgments we forge our character; by the integrated judgments of a people we determine the level of decency of a society. **10**

That some people can run amok with "evil judgment" does not make judgment evil. Judgment is about opinion, evaluation, and discernment. It is an absolutely necessary quality for an individual who desires to live a decent, admirable, ethical life. Without a decision about right/wrong, noble/cowardly, charitable/selfish, we'd have no human civilization of merit. **11**

Therefore, it is quite proper for parents to express disappointment and even disdain for their adult child's significant lifestyle choices while keeping the door open for love, change, and growth. However, the parents may choose not to participate as a "family" with those whose commitment level precludes that title. **12**

Love does not mean you have to tolerate any behavior whatsoever. Love does mean that you have to offer direction, information, and hope. **13**

Love makes you responsible for conveying concepts such as "ethical," "right," "good," "moral," "decent," and "polite" because it demands of you that you take on the risks and challenges of supporting others in the very human struggle to be more than the animals. **14**

VOCABULARY

admonitions (1)	voyeuristic (8)
expedience (2)	espouse (9)
alibis (2)	scenario (9)
adulterous (3)	discern (10)
trysts (3)	forge (10)
conspiracy (3)	integrated (10)
sustain (5)	amok (11)
synthesized (6)	disdain (12)
errant (6)	precludes (12)

UNDERSTANDING WHAT YOU HAVE READ

Check the correct answer in the blank provided.

1. What was the subject of the letter written by the "troubled young woman"?

    _____ **a.** Cheating on income tax.

    _____ **b.** Cheating on a husband.

    _____ **c.** Cheating on a school exam.

    _____ **d.** Cheating at playing cards.

2. Which of the following did NOT cause the young woman to question her obligation to her sister?

    _____ **a.** Her own values.

    _____ **b.** Her sense of loyalty to the husband.

_____ **c.** The children's welfare.

_____ **d.** What people would think of her.

3. Which of the following does the author suggest as a solution?

_____ **a.** Avoiding the sister.

_____ **b.** Suggesting that the sister get a divorce.

_____ **c.** State her love for the sister but disapprove of her sister's behavior.

_____ **d.** Insist her sister quit cheating immediately.

4. What determines the level of decency in a society?

_____ **a.** The combined judgments of its people.

_____ **b.** The amount of money donated to good causes.

_____ **c.** How often the people go to church.

_____ **d.** The number of stay-at-home mothers.

5. When should parents express disapproval of their adult children's lifestyles?

_____ **a.** When these lifestyles are not good, moral, and decent.

_____ **b.** When these lifestyles are liberal rather than conservative.

_____ **c.** When these lifestyles depend on a high income.

_____ **d.** When these lifestyles are different from the parents' lifestyles.

THINKING ABOUT WHAT YOU HAVE READ

1. If a friend of yours were cheating on an exam and you knew about it, how would you handle the situation? Give reasons for your answer.

2. What is your definition of family loyalty? Give an example of your definition.

3. According to the author, we create our character from the individual judgments we make. Do you agree with her? Why or why not? Support your answer with evidence from your personal experience.

4. What does the author mean when she says that people "can run amok with evil judgment"?

5. What, if any, circumstance would cause you to withdraw from your family? Create a scenario that illustrates your point of view.

WRITING ASSIGNMENTS

1. Write an essay defining one of the following words from this article: love, cheat, loyalty, decent, opinion. First give its dictionary

definition, and then clarify the definition through example, anecdote, or other appropriate means. Your essay should answer the
question, "What does _____ mean?"

2. Write an essay defining one of the following pairs of words:
right/wrong, noble/cowardly, charitable/selfish. Use several of the
methods you learned in Unit 8.

"Both" or "Other"?
It's Not as Clear
as Black and White

Pamela Swanigan

This newspaper article uses definition as an organizing strategy, even though it begins on a different note—as a locker room interview following an NBA basketball game. The writer soon finds herself being pulled into a discussion of her racial heritage and ends up acknowledging that she belongs to the category of "other." The rest of the article tells what it feels like to be an interracial "other," neither black nor white but somewhere in between. Out of her discussion comes a definition of "other," the racial category that appears on many official forms. Note how the writer defines "other," even though she does so without using many of the techniques taught in the unit on defining a term (Unit 11).

1 I don't make a habit of arguing with semi-naked men who are taller sitting down than I am standing up, and I didn't go to the Chicago Bulls' exhibition game in Toronto last fall intending to do anything but watch the game and perhaps get a story for the newspaper I work for.

2 In talking with Bulls forward Horace Grant, the subject of my biracial heritage came up. When he asked me whether I consider myself black or white, I found myself having a very familiar debate in strange territory. As the daughter of a light-skinned black man and a white woman, I have been asked that question more often than I care to remember. After almost 29 years of experimenting with variations of the word "both," I have found that although this statement of fact is sometimes accepted in Canada, where I now live, most Americans I encounter reject it out of hand.

3 Horace Grant, a gentle and humorous man, proved remarkably stubborn in insisting that I couldn't say I was both, that I had to say one or the other (in his opinion, black, since that's what my birth certificate says—though my skin is actually white). But since "both" is the biological and cultural truth, I stuck to it until Michael Jordan gave me a better answer.

4 In the locker room after the game, after Grant, Bulls guard Scottie Pippen and I had been discussing the issue for several minutes, Jordan put his hands on my shoulders and said, "I'll tell you what you are. You're 'Other.' "

5 Jordan shrugged away my automatic protest and said matter-of-factly, "You can't put half a check mark in 'black' and half a check mark in 'white,' You have to check 'Other'—that means you're black and white."

6 I doubt he heard that equation as he spoke it, and certainly he didn't mean it as symbolically as I have since taken it.

7 But he was right. I am "Other" to a lot of people: To those who can't function unless they can apply their cultural assumptions; to those who see me as some sort of neutral point to be lobbied to one side or the other; to those who simply hate the other race too much to accept their co-existence in one person.

8 I am even "Other" to my step-grandmother, who once wrote to me, "Birds of a different feather may sit on the same branch but should not mate."

9 And yes, I'm "Other" to the people who make forms and created the category of "Other" instead of "Both" or "Mixed" or "Race Irrelevant."

Contrary to popular opinion, I do not have a choice of race; I have 10
what I was given, which is the genes, traits and prejudices of both. As a
child of the East Oakland, Calif., streets, I developed a lot of anger
toward whites. As a member of white society, I have absorbed some
stereotypes of black people. I have been called a nigger and a honky; for
anyone who's curious, they both hurt, equally.

Like most people, I crave a sense of belonging, but I can only make 11
the most of brief episodes of affinity before my "Otherness" drives me
back into internal exile. There are many glib conclusions and sweeping
judgments about racial issues; there are few easy answers. Maybe they
could start by changing the question. Until they do, I'll give the answer
Jordan gave me, in its logical inversion: I'm black and white—that means
I'm "Other."

VOCABULARY

affinity (11)
inversion (11)

UNDERSTANDING WHAT YOU HAVE READ

Check the correct answer in the blank provided.

1. Where does the article open?
   _____ **a.** New York.
   _____ **b.** Kingston, Jamaica.
   _____ **c.** Toronto.
   _____ **d.** Los Angeles.

2. Which NBA player kept pressing the author to declare her race?
   _____ **a.** Horace Grant.
   _____ **b.** Michael Jordan.
   _____ **c.** David Robinson.
   _____ **d.** Charles Barkley.

3. Which nationality rejects the author's identification of herself as "both"?
   _____ **a.** Canadian.
   _____ **b.** Finnish.
   _____ **c.** English.
   _____ **d.** American.

4. Which NBA player classified the writer's race as "other"?
   _____ **a.** Michael Jordan.
   _____ **b.** Scottie Pippen.
   _____ **c.** David Robinson.
   _____ **d.** Horace Grant.

5. How does the writer describe her complexion?

_____ **a.** Brown.

_____ **b.** Sepia.

_____ **c.** White.

_____ **d.** Black.

THINKING ABOUT WHAT YOU HAVE READ

1. Nowhere does the writer declare her intention to define, yet we are not surprised when she attempts a definition. How does she prepare us for the purpose of her article?

2. The author says that Canadians are willing to accept her calling herself "both" but that most Americans are not. Why? How do you explain the unwillingness of most Americans to accept "both" as her racial designation?

3. What technique does the author use in defining her racial heritage?

4. The author says she can "only make the most of brief episodes of affinity." What are "brief episodes of affinity"? Give an example.

5. Why do official forms generally ask for racial information about people? What purpose do you think such information serves?

WRITING ASSIGNMENTS

1. Define yourself in an essay.

2. Write an essay on interracial relations, using yourself and your friends as examples.

Classifying

Wait Divisions

Tom Bodett

*From the very beginning, the author makes it clear that this is an informal clas-
sification with made-up categories of his own invention. His aim is to entertain,
and his down-to-earth vocabulary and chatty sentences add to the folksiness of
the piece. Notice how early he tells us of his intent to classify. Notice also that
his categories are based on a single principle that he closely follows from beginning to end. As you read, try to find the writer's classifying principle.*

1 I read somewhere that we spend a full third of our lives waiting. I've
also read where we spend a third of our lives sleeping, a third working, and a third at our leisure. Now either somebody's lying, or we're
spending all our leisure time waiting to go to work or sleep. That can't
be true or league softball and Winnebagos never would have caught on.

2 So where are we doing all of this waiting and what does it mean to
an impatient society like ours? Could this unseen waiting be the source
of all our problems? A shrinking economy? The staggering deficit?
Declining mental health and moral apathy? Probably not, but let's take
a look at some of the more classic "waits" anyway.

3 The very purest form of waiting is what we'll call the *Watched-Pot
Wait*. This type of wait is without a doubt the most annoying of all. Take
filling up the kitchen sink. There is absolutely nothing you can do while
this is going on but keep both eyes glued to the sink until it's full. If you
try to cram in some extracurricular activity, you're asking for it. So you
stand there, your hands on the faucets, and wait. A temporary suspension
of duties. During these waits it's common for your eyes to lapse out of
focus. The brain disengages from the body and wanders around the imagination in search of distraction. It finds none and springs back into action
only when the water runs over the edge of the counter and onto your socks.

4 The phrase "A watched pot never boils" comes of this experience. Pots
don't care whether they are watched or not; the problem is that nobody
has ever seen a pot actually come to a boil. While they are waiting, their
brains turn off.

5 Other forms of the Watched-Pot Wait would include waiting for your drier
to quit at the laundromat, waiting for your toast to pop out of the toaster,
or waiting for a decent idea to come to mind at a typewriter. What they all
have in common is that they render the waiter helpless and mindless.

6 A cousin to the Watched-Pot Wait is the *Forced Wait*. Not for the weak
of will, this one requires a bit of discipline. The classic Forced Wait is starting your car in the winter and letting it slowly idle up to temperature before
engaging the clutch. This is every bit as uninteresting as watching a pot,
but with one big difference. You have a choice. There is nothing keeping you
from racing to work behind a stone-cold engine save the thought of the early
demise of several thousand dollars' worth of equipment you haven't paid for
yet. Thoughts like that will help you get through a Forced Wait.

7 Properly preparing packaged soup mixes also requires a Forced Wait.
Directions are very specific on these mixes. "Bring three cups water to

515

boil, add mix, simmer three minutes, remove from heat, let stand five minutes." I have my doubts that anyone has ever actually done this. I'm fairly spineless when it comes to instant soups and usually just boil the bejeezus out of them until the noodles sink. Some things just aren't worth a Forced Wait.

All in all Forced Waiting requires a lot of a thing called *patience*,   **8** which is a virtue. Once we get into virtues I'm out of my element, and can't expound on the virtues of virtue, or even lie about them. So let's move on to some of the more far-reaching varieties of waiting.

The *Payday Wait* is certainly a leader in the long-term anticipation   **9** field. The problem with waits that last more than a few minutes so that you have to actually do other things in the meantime. Like go to work. By far the most aggravating feature of the Payday Wait is that even though you must keep functioning in the interludes, there is less and less you are able to do as the big day draws near. For some of us the last few days are best spent alone in a dark room for fear we'll accidentally do something that costs money. With the Payday Wait comes a certain amount of hope that we'll make it, and faith that everything will be all right once we do.

With the introduction of faith and hope, I've ushered in the most   **10** potent wait class of all, the *Lucky-Break Wait*, or the *Wait for One's Ship to Come In*. This type of wait is unusual in that it is for the most part voluntary. Unlike the Forced Wait, which is also voluntary, waiting for your lucky break does not necessarily mean that it will happen.

Turning one's life into a waiting game of these proportions requires   **11** gobs of the aforementioned faith and hope, and is strictly for the optimists among us. For these people life is the thing that happens to them while they're waiting for something to happen to them. On the surface it seems as ridiculous as following the directions on soup mixes, but the Lucky-Break Wait performs an outstanding service to those who take it upon themselves to do it. As long as one doesn't come to rely on it, wishing for a few good things to happen never hurt anybody.

In the end it is obvious that we certainly do spend a good deal of our   **12** time waiting. The person who said we do it a third of the time may have been going easy on us. It makes a guy wonder how anything at all gets done around here. But things do get done, people grow old, and time boils on whether you watch it or not.

The next time you're standing at the sink waiting for it to fill while   **13** cooking soup mix that you'll have to eat until payday or until a large bag of cash falls out of the sky, don't despair. You're probably just as busy as the next guy.

VOCABULARY

apathy (2)   expound (8)
extracurricular (3)   interludes (9)
demise (6)

UNDERSTANDING WHAT YOU HAVE READ

Check the correct answer in the blank provided.

1. Why is the "Watched Pot Wait" so annoying?

   _____ **a.** Because it is long.

   _____ **b.** Because it is too steamy.

   _____ **c.** Because you have to do it every day.

   _____ **d.** Because there is absolutely nothing to do while it is going on.

2. What is an example of the classic "Forced Wait?"

_____ **a.** Waiting for your car to warm up.

_____ **b.** Waiting for the train.

_____ **c.** Waiting to use the bathroom.

_____ **d.** Waiting in line at a grocery store.

3. What kind of wait is a leader in the long-term anticipation field?

_____ **a.** The Watched-Pot Wait.

_____ **b.** The Payday Wait.

_____ **c.** The Lucky-Break Wait.

_____ **d.** The Forced Wait.

4. What virtue does forced waiting require?

_____ **a.** Luck.

_____ **b.** Love.

_____ **c.** Laziness.

_____ **d.** Patience.

5. According to the author, how much of our lives do we spend waiting?

_____ **a.** A third.

_____ **b.** A quarter.

_____ **c.** A half.

_____ **d.** A fifth.

THINKING ABOUT WHAT YOU HAVE READ

1. On what single principle is the author's wait classification based?

2. What example from campus life can you give of the "Forced Wait"?

3. What other principle can you think of that might be used to classify wait periods?

4. The author says that as the "Payday Wait" draws near, there is less and less we are able to do. Why?

5. How does the author end his essay? What makes this ending so effective?

WRITING ASSIGNMENTS

1. Write an essay that uses an organizing principle to classify the different kinds of waiting students must do.

2. Write an essay classifying any common student activity or task.

The Plot Against People

Russell Baker

This humorous essay is a tongue-in-cheek informal classification of inanimate objects. Baker tells us at the outset the basis of his classification and then pretends to quote the findings of science to back up his observations. Notice that once he has begun his classification, he sticks to it and does not waver or stray from his purpose. Pay attention to the transitions he uses as he moves from one category to another.

1   Inanimate objects are classified into three major categories—those that don't work, those that break down and those that get lost.

2   The goal of all inanimate objects is to resist man and ultimately to defeat him, and the three major classifications are based on the method each object uses to achieve its purpose. As a general rule, any object capable of breaking down at the moment when it is most needed will do so. The automobile is typical of the category.

3   With the cunning typical of its breed, the automobile never breaks down while entering a filling station with a large staff of idle mechanics. It waits until it reaches a downtown intersection in the middle of the rush hour, or until it is fully loaded with family and luggage on the Ohio Turnpike.

4   Thus it creates maximum misery, inconvenience, frustration and irritability among its human cargo, thereby reducing its owner's life span.

5   Washing machines, garbage disposals, lawn mowers, light bulbs, automatic laundry dryers, water pipes, furnaces, electrical fuses, television tubes, hose nozzles, tape recorders, slide projectors—all are in league with the automobile to take their turn at breaking down whenever life threatens to flow smoothly for their human enemies.

6   Many inanimate objects, of course, find it extremely difficult to break down. Pliers, for example, and gloves and keys are almost totally incapable of breaking down. Therefore, they have had to evolve a different technique for resisting man.

7   They get lost. Science has still not solved the mystery of how they do it, and no man has ever caught one of them in the act of getting lost. The most plausible theory is that they have developed a secret method of locomotion which they are able to conceal the instant a human eye falls upon them.

8   It is not uncommon for a pair of pliers to climb all the way from the cellar to the attic in its single-minded determination to raise its owner's blood pressure. Keys have been known to burrow three feet under mattresses. Women's purses, despite their great weight, frequently travel through six or seven rooms to find hiding space under a couch.

9   Scientists have been struck by the fact that things that break down virtually never get lost, while things that get lost hardly ever break down.

10   A furnace, for example, will invariably break down at the depth of the first winter cold wave, but it will never get lost. A woman's purse, which after all does have some inherent capacity for breaking down, hardly ever does; it almost invariably chooses to get lost.

11   Some persons believe this constitutes evidence that inanimate objects are not entirely hostile to man, and that a negotiated peace is possible. After all, they point out, a furnace could infuriate a man even more thoroughly by getting lost than by breaking down, just as a glove could upset him far more by breaking down than by getting lost.

Not everyone agrees, however, that this indicates a conciliatory atti- 12
tude among inanimate objects. Many say it merely proves that furnaces,
gloves and pliers are incredibly stupid.

The third class of objects—those that don't work—is the most curi- 13
ous of all. These include such objects as barometers, car clocks, cigarette lighters, flashlights and toy-train locomotives. It is inaccurate, of
course, to say that they never work. They work once, usually for the first
few hours after being brought home, and then quit. Thereafter, they
never work again.

In fact, it is widely assumed that they are built for the purpose of not 14
working. Some people have reached advanced ages without ever seeing
some of these objects—barometers, for example—in working order.

Science is utterly baffled by the entire category. There are many 15
theories about it. The most interesting holds that the things that don't
work have attained the highest state possible for an inanimate object,
the estate to which things that break down and things that get lost can
still only aspire.

They have truly defeated man by conditioning him never to expect 16
anything of them, and in return they have given man the only peace he
receives from inanimate society. He does not expect his barometer to
work, his electric locomotive to run, his cigarette lighter to light or his
flashlight to illuminate, and when they don't, it does not raise his blood
pressure.

He cannot attain that peace with furnaces and keys and cars and 17
women's purses as long as he demands that they work for their keep.

VOCABULARY

inanimate (1) inherent (10)
plausible (7) conciliatory (12)
virtually (9)

UNDERSTANDING WHAT YOU HAVE READ

Check the correct answer in the blank provided.

1. What three basic categories does this essay propose for inanimate
   objects?
   _____ a. Those that are solid, those that are liquid, and those
   that are gaseous.
   _____ b. Those that don't work, those that break down, and
   those that get lost.
   _____ c. Those we own, those we steal, and those we borrow.
   _____ d. Those that are male, those that are female, and those
   that are neither.

2. According to the author, what is the goal of all inanimate
   objects?
   _____ a. To resist and defeat man.
   _____ b. To work for man and please him.
   _____ c. To make man's life longer.
   _____ d. To tempt man to stray.

3. What are keys especially prone to do?

_____ **a.** Misfit.

_____ **b.** Jiggle in one's pocket.

_____ **c.** Stick in keyholes.

_____ **d.** Get lost.

4. What fact are scientists particularly struck by?

_____ **a.** That some objects never break down.

_____ **b.** That objects that break down never get lost.

_____ **c.** That objects are highly dependable.

_____ **d.** That objects have vibrations.

5. What particular object does the author single out as hardly ever working?

_____ **a.** A barometer.

_____ **b.** A bicycle.

_____ **c.** An ax.

_____ **d.** A spoon.

THINKING ABOUT WHAT YOU HAVE READ

1. How does the author achieve humor in this essay?

2. To support his classification of inanimate objects, what other strategy does Baker draw on extensively?

3. Where is the thesis statement of this essay? Why do you think the author chose to place it in this particular spot?

4. Read the thesis statement again. What is odd about the author's discussion of the categories, given this particular thesis statement?

5. Is this classification of objects complete? How do you know? Does its completeness matter? Why or why not?

WRITING ASSIGNMENTS

1. Write an essay classifying animals or pets.

2. Write an essay to entertain, using the classification strategy.

Comparing and Contrasting

Sadie and Maud
Gwendolyn Brooks

Poets do not usually use rhetorical strategies to develop their work, but sometimes a rhetorical pattern emerges naturally. In this poem, the comparison/contrast between Sadie and Maud is obvious. Look at the poem and try to find the bases of the comparisons. Ask yourself how the poet manages to create comparisons without using the usual comparison/contrast words and phrases such as in contrast to *or* whereas.

Maud went to college.   1
Sadie stayed at home.
Sadie scraped life
With a fine-tooth comb.

She didn't leave a tangle in.
Her comb found every strand.
Sadie was one of the livingest chits
In all the land.

Sadie bore two babies
Under her maiden name.   10
Maud and Ma and Papa
Nearly died of shame.

When Sadie said her last so-long
Her girls struck out from home.
(Sadie had left as heritage
Her fine-tooth comb.)

Maud, who went to college,
Is a thin brown mouse.
She is living all alone   20
In this old house.

UNDERSTANDING WHAT YOU HAVE READ

Check the correct answer in the blank provided.

1. Who went to college?

   _____ **a.** Sadie.

   _____ **b.** Maud.

   _____ **c.** Neither.

   _____ **d.** Both.

2. Who scraped life with a fine-tooth comb?

   _____ **a.** Maud.

   _____ **b.** Sadie.

   _____ **c.** Sadie's mother.

   _____ **d.** Maud's mother.

3. How many children did Maud have?

   _____ **a.** Three.

   _____ **b.** Four.

   _____ **c.** Two.

   _____ **d.** None.

4. What happened to Sadie?

   _____ **a.** She moved to California.

   _____ **b.** She died.

   _____ **c.** She went to prison.

   _____ **d.** She became a butcher.

5. What happened to Maud?

   _____ **a.** She eloped.

   _____ **b.** She ran away with a Fuller brush salesman.

   _____ **c.** She died.

   _____ **d.** She ended up all alone.

THINKING ABOUT WHAT YOU HAVE READ

1. What are some of the specific differences between Sadie and Maud mentioned in the poem?

2. What kind of person was Sadie? How would you sum her up?

3. What kind of heritage do you think Sadie left her daughters? What do the lines, "Sadie had left as heritage / Her fine-tooth comb" mean?

4. If you had to guess, what do you think was Maud's profession or occupation?

5. Which is the relationship between Sadie and Maud? Which of the two would you rather be?

WRITING ASSIGNMENTS

1. Write an essay comparing and contrasting any two people you know.

2. Using the poem as your guide, write an essay comparing and contrasting Sadie and Maud. Be specific about the bases of your contrasts. You may add additional details and examples.

Doctor-as-God Is Dead, or Dying

Ellen Goodman

Some comparison/contrasts are indirect and seem to emerge from an essay almost as an afterthought. For example, in this essay the writer presents an anecdote about a friend's discovery of a new kind of doctor; the discussion leads naturally to a comparison/contrast between doctors, new and old. Look for the transitions that guide you to the comparison/contrast as well as for the examples Goodman uses to clarify what the new doctors believe and how they think.

My friend went to the doctor's office expecting to find God. The doctors whom she knew always played God, except on Wednesday afternoon, when they played golf. 1

But what she discovered was that Doctor-God-Sir, the professional keeper of the Temple of the body, was not available. Instead, a new doctor sat down before her, opened up her chart, met her eyes sincerely and asked her to think of him as her "junior partner in health care." 2

This somewhat abrupt transfer from God to the junior partner had a startling effect on my friend's blood pressure. But she had discovered the latest trend of the medical profession: God is dead, or at least dying out. 3

The whole history of Doctor-as-God began way back when medicine men were merely priests. Eventually they got academic degrees and demanded a promotion, although there were some who thought that God was a little high. 4

Medicine still remained a profound mystery to the laity. Such is the way with all religions. It was conducted in Latin or Medicalese, which was Greek to the average person. The patient-supplicant was required to have faith, hope and a little something to put on the plate when it was passed. 5

We were expected to submit to such rituals as the knife and to such magic as pills. Few of us ever saw the appendix that was removed or understood how antibiotics work. But we took penicillin as a kind of oral penance for illness: four times a day for ten days, and bow to the east three times. 6

Somewhere along the way in this skeptical secular era the medical laity became less worshipful. The best and brightest of the young apprentices were also less willing to pretend omniscience. 7

And so we have now entered the era of the junior partner in health care. 8

What are the characteristics of a junior partner? First of all, an aura of humility. You can tell a junior partner by precisely how many times he or she uses the expression "We really don't know. . . ." Junior partners believe in sharing—especially in sharing doubts. 9

You can also identify junior partners by their passion for education. This friend called her J.P. recently when a bee sting had blown her arm up to the size of a large thigh. "What do I do"? she asked. He answered, "First let me tell you something about bee stings." 10

All junior partners have been educated by the full-disclosure, informed-consent school of medicine. Gods give out proclamations; J.P.s give odds. The odds that you will get better, the odds that you will get worse. Along with every prescription comes a description of side effects. If just one Manchurian lost an ear lobe or a belly button from this cream, you will hear about it. 11

Consider the true story of a woman who discussed the possibility of surgery with her J.P. After listening to his explanations she tried to recap 12 the pros and cons. "So," she said, "the worst that can happen. . . ." "Oh, no," he interrupted. "The worst that can happen is that you'll die from the anesthesia." After peeling her off the floor he admitted that this possibility was fairly remote—one in 30,000. This is called overinformed consent.

The most basic thing to remember for your next encounter with a J.P. is that he or she will not tell you what to do. Gods give commandments, but J.P.s only lay out options. It is up to you, the Senior Partner, to take responsibility for your health decisions. (This fact is on a poster in the J.P.s waiting room, near stacks of pamphlets on fiber in the diet.)   **13**

It is still possible, of course, to find God. But he is likely to be (1) he, (2) older or (3) a specialist in heart or brain surgery. The life-and-death stuff still seems to fall into the hands of you-know-Who.   **14**

Should we be surprised by the takeover of the junior partners? After all, isn't this what we all wanted? We wanted doctors to stop treating us like children. We wanted them to talk to us, tell us the whole story. We wanted them to stop acting like gods. We wanted them to admit their fallibility.   **15**

Isn't that right? Absolutely. Positively. I swear to God.   **16**

VOCABULARY

laity (5)	omniscience (7)
skeptical (7)	fallibility (15)
secular (7)	

UNDERSTANDING WHAT YOU HAVE READ

Check the correct answer in the blank provided.

1. With what other profession was early medicine identified?

     _____ **a.** Law.

     _____ **b.** Farming.

     _____ **c.** Clerical copying.

     _____ **d.** Priests.

2. What name does the author call the new kind of doctor?

     _____ **a.** The new god.

     _____ **b.** The junior partner.

     _____ **c.** The magistrate.

     _____ **d.** The pope.

3. What phrase is the new doctor fond of muttering?

     _____ **a.** We really don't know . . .

     _____ **b.** It's up to you . . .

     _____ **c.** You should stop smoking . . .

     _____ **d.** Walking is good for you . . .

4. What do the new doctors have a passion for?

     _____ **a.** Tennis.

     _____ **b.** Golf.

_____ **c.** Political parties.

_____ **d.** Education.

5. According to the author, what did we say we wanted from our doctors?

    _____ **a.** That they stop playing so much golf.

    _____ **b.** That they stop treating us like children.

    _____ **c.** That they be religious.

    _____ **d.** That they charge less.

THINKING ABOUT WHAT YOU HAVE READ

1. The author expands on the characteristics of the new doctor. By implication, what are the characteristics of the old doctor?

2. The author says that the old doctor is likely to be a male. What effect has the increased number of women in medicine had in bringing about the new type of doctor?

3. What pattern of comparison/contrast is used in this essay? Point to specific paragraphs to back up your answer.

4. What transitions does this writer use in this comparison/contrast?

5. Which of the two types of doctors would you rather have? Why?

WRITING ASSIGNMENTS

1. Write a comparison/contrast of any two medical people you know—doctors, nurses, dentists, medical receptionists.

2. Write an essay about your doctor.

They Stole Our Childhood

Lee Goldberg

Some comparison/contrasts are more complex than others. This one, for exam-ple, compares a generation of kids, as the writer sees them, and the media's image of those kids, especially as seen on television. What generation is he talk-ing about? Kids who grew up in the seventies or eighties? What's different between kids today and those described by the author? What does the title mean? Who stole the writer's childhood? What is so special about the kids portrayed in the television programs mentioned by the author?

We're the wonderful generation. 1

We are the kids who were "so adult" when our divorced parents read- 2
justed to the rigors of being suddenly single. We are the kids who discovered sex so early in our lives and were such overachievers in school.

We are looked on by our elders with admiration and awe. And yet, if 3
you wipe away the surface gloss, you will find that we are actually victims, casualties of our parents' need for us to grow up fast. That which
we are praised for is our biggest problem.

Day-to-day family life for us was a contradiction between what we 4
saw on the *Brady Bunch* and *Courtship of Eddie's Father* and what we
were actually living. We were supposed to be thinking about the big
dance, playing baseball, getting new handlebars on our bikes, gossiping
about our favorite TV stars and, when our parents weren't around, dressing up in their clothes and looking at ourselves in the mirror.

Instead we found ourselves not only dressing up in their clothes, but 5
adopting their state of mind as well. We worried about whether mom
would receive her child-support check, whether our parent's date for
tonight would become a breakfast guest tomorrow, whether our little sister
would ever remember what it was like to have two parents under one roof.

Our parents were always so proud of our capacity to make it on our 6
own, to "be adult." Parents were thinking of us less like children and more
like peers. Suddenly we kids weren't being treated like kids anymore.

Part of being adult was not indulging the child in us that hungered 7
for affection. Our generation, it seems, turned to sex for the affection we
lacked at home. As we saw it, needing a hug wasn't very adult. Sleeping
with someone was. It was an acceptable way to ask for the physical affirmation of self-worth that we weren't getting from our parents, who we
saw doing little hugging and a lot of sleeping around.

We found that spending more time at school or work was a welcome 8
alternative to going home in the afternoons. The media had taught us that
coming home from school meant milk and cookies, TV and playing with
friends, mom or a babysitter in the kitchen and dad back from work at 6.
Suddenly, going home meant confronting dad's new girlfriend, mom's
unpaid bills or playing parent to our younger siblings and our parents, too.

It's no wonder so many of us, barely into our 20s, feel as though 9
we've already been married and raised children. In divorce, parents seem
to become teen-agers, and the kids become the adults. Many of our
younger brothers and sisters see us more as their parents than their real
parents. As our parents pursued careers and re-entered the dating scene,
we children coped by forming our own little mini-families, with the older
kids parenting for the younger siblings. It was common for single mothers to joke about how their eldest son played doting father, checking out
her dates and offering sage advice. Or for parents to find their younger
kids wouldn't accept candy from them unless an older sister OK'd it first.

Our parents expected us to understand their problems and frustra- 10
tions, to grasp the complex machinations of divorce proceedings and the
emotional hazards they faced by dating again. More than understanding, they even solicited our advice and guidance in these delicate matters. Our parents sometimes pressured us into becoming participants in
their divorce proceedings, encouraging us to take sides. We found ourselves having to withdraw from them just to protect ourselves from the
potential pain that could be caused by mixed parental loyalties in the
midst of courtroom warfare.

We were rewarded with approval: "my kids are so grown-up," "my kids 11
can handle things," "my kids coped so well," "my kids can make it on
their own," "my kids are so together." What we missed was a chance to
be childish, immature and unafraid to admit we didn't have it all together.

We pay the price when we need parents to turn to and don't have 12
them—as we toil with our first serious relationships and when our long-
suppressed childish side rears its playful head.

Divorce didn't just split up our parents. It stole our childhood. 13

Our parents are paying, too. They ache for the closeness with us they 14
never had and may never get. They try to grasp memories of our childhood and come up nearly empty. They find themselves separated from
their children and wonder how the gap appeared. Some wake up to realize that they know their gas-station attendant better than their children.

The cure is not to curb divorce. We can start by realizing that this 15
generation, which may have it together intellectually, paid with its adolescence. What needs rethinking are the attitudes and expectations of
parents. Kids who are mature are fine. Kids who are "so adult" need help.

VOCABULARY

peers (6)   machinations (10)
indulging (7)   solicited (10)
affirmation (7)   long-suppressed (12)
siblings (9)

UNDERSTANDING WHAT YOU HAVE READ

Check the correct answer in the blank provided.

1. How, according to the author, was his generation looked on by
   their elders?

   _____ **a.** With horror.

   _____ **b.** With anger.

   _____ **c.** With pity.

   _____ **d.** With admiration and awe.

2. What two television programs contradicted the day-to-day family
   life of the author's generation?

   _____ **a.** *The Addams Family* and *The Munsters*.

   _____ **b.** *The Brady Bunch* and *Courtship of Eddie's Father*.

   _____ **c.** *Star Trek* and *Lost in Space*.

   _____ **d.** *Maude* and *Growing Pains*.

3. How did parents treat the author's generation?

_____ **a.** Like peers.

_____ **b.** Like children.

_____ **c.** Like scolding babysitters.

_____ **d.** Like jailers.

4. What does the author say his generation missed?

_____ **a.** Television.

_____ **b.** Outdoor sports.

_____ **c.** Participation in group activities.

_____ **d.** The chance to be childish.

5. What does the author claim his parents ache for?

_____ **a.** Closeness with their children.

_____ **b.** Money.

_____ **c.** Promotion at work.

_____ **d.** Responsibility.

THINKING ABOUT WHAT YOU HAVE READ

1. What paragraph can you point to that suggests a comparison/contrast will be drawn in this essay? What sentence states the purpose of this piece?

2. The writer begins by saying, "We're the wonderful generation." How do you think he means us to read that sentence?

3. What is the basis of the contrast drawn in paragraphs 3 and 4? Sum it up in one sentence.

4. How would you characterize the writer's tone? If he were talking to you face to face on this topic, how do you think he would sound?

5. The writer says the cure is not to curb divorce. What do you think the cure is?

WRITING ASSIGNMENTS

1. Write an essay comparing and contrasting the portrayal of family life on television and how it really is.

2. Compare and contrast your family with another family you know well.

Arguing

Tune In to TV, Tune Out to Language

Jack Smith

This essay from a weekly newspaper column presents an informal argument on the damage done by television viewing to the ability to read and write well. Note that the writer's dual purpose—to persuade and to entertain—is responsible for his light treatment of a serious subject. As you read, try to find the single sentence that sums up the writer's position. Ask yourself what combination of reasons and evidence the writer presents to support his opinion. Finally, determine whether he persuaded you to his point of view.

1   A recent nationwide survey shows that children 10 to 14 think television influences them to have sex before marriage, to regard money as the main goal in life, and to make them disrespectful of their parents.

2   It is thought-provoking to hear from children what everybody else already knows—that television is bad for you.

3   Movies on television such as "Indecent Proposal," in which multimillionaire Robert Redford offers a young married woman $1 million to spend one night with him (and she does), tend to support such conclusions.

4   I think television is not only corrupting our moral behavior, but also degrading our language. It is shocking that shows that have more obscene language than a Marine Corps barracks are hailed.

5   I have no doubt television is partly to blame for the plethora of teen pregnancies. If Michael Douglas and Sharon Stone can do it on the screen outside marriage, why not us?

6   But I am against censorship. TV movies are gamy because people like them that way. As I have often admitted, I myself like a good sexy movie, though I've had it with screen violence.

7   I certainly wouldn't like to see TV go back to the morality of the Hays Office, when a sexual encounter was suggested by wind blowing the curtains, but a little restraint wouldn't hurt.

8   The damage goes deeper than sexual morality. It's my opinion that TV movies are damaging our language. People used to read. Now they watch TV. If we learn the language by hearing it, and not by reading it, the language will suffer.

9   The Times itself, which should be a model of literacy, suffers from this fact. Although newspaper reporters are of necessity more literate than the average plumber, the younger ones may be losing their fine-tuning because of their addiction to television.

10   Hardly a day goes by that one can't find a misused homophone in the paper. A homophone is a word that sounds like another but is spelled differently and has a different meaning. *Plane* and *plain*, for example. Or *hair* and *hare*. Or *gnu* and *new*.

11   No one is likely to write *gnu* when he means *new*, or *hare* when he means *hair*. But the homophone error is so common that even more unlikely examples of it may be found.

Recently, a local newspaper (not The Times) wrote in a headline that   12
a certain *heir* (not *air*) apparent was giving up the *thrown*.

There is only one explanation for this kind of mistake. When the lan-   13
guage is learned by television, one never sees a word spelled.

Most of these errors are so outrageous that you can hardly believe   14
they got past a proofreader. But the old-fashioned proofreader, who wore
an eyeshade, chewed tobacco and was armed with a stubby pencil, is no
more. Those old curmudgeons may have been grumpy and cynical, but
they "gnu" the language. It isn't that we don't have proofreaders today,
but they probably aren't grumpy enough.

The Times is about to publish a new stylebook—a manual to guide   15
writers in the use of the language. It will be a miracle of research and
judgment. It will advise reporters that 18-year-old girls are not *girls*, but
women; that the F in *French fries* is capitalized; and that *graffiti* is both
singular and plural. It also advises that *forgo* and *forego* are not the same.

However, it does not furnish a list of homophones. As I say, there are   16
hundreds and a mere list would not fix them in a reporter's mind. One
must learn which is which by visual experience. By reading.

I used to be a great reader. I read *War and Peace* when I worked on the   17
night desk of the Honolulu Advertiser. I read *Les Miserables* in high school.

I have read hundreds of books. But today I am lucky if I read one a   18
month. I am a couch potato.

That is a phrase brought into the language by television. It means a   19
person who is so addicted to the tube he sits there on his couch, like a
potato, mindlessly watching TV, commercials and all.

I am also given to "channel surfing," which means using your hand   20
monitor to search through the channels for something sexy or violent, or
maybe the latest on O.J. Simpson.

I'm not saying television is all bad. For example, "The Three Tenors"   21
was great. I like old movies, even when sex is suggested by wind blowing the curtains. I love football and tennis.

However, I learned words by reading, so I know the difference between   22
hare and *hair* and between *hoarse* and *horse*. And I haven't given up.

Some day, I swear it, I'm going to read the Bible, top to bottom, find   23
out what it's all about.

VOCABULARY

plethora (5)
gamy (6)
curmudgeons (14)

UNDERSTANDING WHAT YOU HAVE READ
Check the correct answer in the blank provided.

1. Who were the subjects of the nationwide survey about television?

_____ **a.** Everyone.

_____ **b.** Women only.

_____ **c.** Men over 50.

_____ **d.** Children between 10 and 14.

2. What does the author say television is partly to blame for?

_____ **a.** The plethora of teen pregnancies.

_____ **b.** Low boy scout membership.

_____ **c.** The decline of Little League.

_____ **d.** Drive-by shootings.

3. What misused word type does the author blame on television viewing?

     _____ **a.** Nouns.

     _____ **b.** Verbs.

     _____ **c.** Interjections.

     _____ **d.** Homophones.

4. Which one of the novels listed below does the author claim to have read?

     _____ **a.** _Moby Dick_.

     _____ **b.** _War and Peace_.

     _____ **c.** _Gone With the Wind_.

     _____ **d.** _Ben Hur_.

5. What does the author call himself?

     _____ **a.** A fool.

     _____ **b.** A couch potato.

     _____ **c.** A dedicated reader.

     _____ **d.** A curmudgeon.

THINKING ABOUT WHAT YOU HAVE READ

1. What is the author's thesis statement? What about its phrasing might your teacher find objectionable?

2. What evidence does the author offer in support of his thesis statement? What is your opinion of his evidence?

3. This is an informal argument rather than a strictly formal one. If this were intended as a formal argument, how would you evaluate its effectiveness and the quality of its evidence and logic?

4. What effect, if any, do you think television has had on your own reading and writing skills ?

5. What is the primary example cited by the author in his argument on the effects of television on reading? Why do you think he chose to focus on this one example? How would you rate this example as evidence?

WRITING ASSIGNMENTS

1. Using yourself as your main example, write an essay arguing that television has had a negative effect on reading and writing skills.

2. Write an argument about the good aspects of television.

'Retaining' Schoolchildren Indicates Educators' Failure

Gerald W. Bracey

Nearly every school district has a policy for holding back students a grade or "retaining." Though the intention is well-meaning, the consequences are often harmful. In this article, the author takes aim at this widespread practice, arguing that it indicates a failure in educators rather than in the individual students who are held back. Notice the author's use of reasoning, statistics, and the time-honored practice of anticipating the opposition. As you read, ask yourself whether the author's proposed alternative offers a better solution to retaining.

1   Back to school means something a little different this year. With more and more states and school districts taking a hard line against social promotion, more and more students are finding themselves back for another year in the same grade. Most often it's first grade the kids are being required to repeat, and then there's a second peak in the eighth grade.

2   Given the increasing popularity of using failure as a pedagogical technique, it is important to know this about "retaining" children: It doesn't work.

3   Why do people think that failing kids works? Probably because they don't have much to compare it with. Usually all that teachers and parents get to see is how children struggle in their second year with the same material they did poorly on the first time around. Generally, the children do only a little better with it the second time, and teachers and parents then assume the children would have fared that much worse had they been promoted.

4   But that hunch isn't actually true. There have been situations in which some children who had low achievement-test scores were promoted while other children of the same low achievement were flunked, and the two strategies could be reliably compared. In those settings, the low-achieving children who were promoted showed as much and usually more academic growth than those who were left behind.

5   Retention is often presented as the only option. In fact, it is nothing more than a way of pretending to do something for a child without actually doing anything. Except making the kid pay with another year in school, surrounded by a group of strangers, all younger than the flunked child. Some teachers and administrators claim they need the threat of retention to make children work hard in school. They don't seem to realize that this is a stunning admission of incompetence, as if they had nothing else in their motivational arsenals.

6   No study has found that flunking children improves their self-esteem. Or makes them any more comfortable in school. On the contrary, it makes them want to leave as soon as they can. Children held back for a year are 50 percent more likely to drop out than other low-achieving students. Those held back twice are 90 percent more likely to drop out before graduating high school. And that greatly increases the chances that they'll end up on welfare, in sporadic minimum wage jobs, even in prison.

7   So what to do for low-achieving students? The answer gathered from research seems to be this: Provide these children extra assistance, summer school if need be (something that is a lot less expensive than having the child repeat the same grade the next year), and then promote

them. The best remedial programs have been able to increase achievement significantly, though on the whole these students still score well below grade level. And both that success and its limits are instructive. Plainly, what makes a difference is not the grade the students are in, but the quality and dynamics of the remedial teaching. Just as plainly, there are children who in any grade will achieve much less than average.

If the schools don't find ways to teach these children the most they   8
can learn in every grade, who exactly is failing whom?

VOCABULARY

promotion (1)   arsenals (5)
pedagogical (2)   self-esteem (6)
hunch (4   sporadic (6)
reliably (4)   instructive (7)
incompetence (5)   dynamics (7)
motivational (5)

QUESTIONS ABOUT UNDERSTANDING WHAT YOU HAVE READ

Check the correct answer in the blank provided.

1. Why is "back to school" different this year for many students?

    _____ **a.** Because schools are allowing all students to be promoted.

    _____ **b.** Because schools are doing away with social promotions.

    _____ **c.** Because parents are sending their children to private school.

    _____ **d.** Because too many classrooms will be overcrowded.

2. According to the author, retaining students

    _____ **a.** is necessary to save schools' reputations.

    _____ **b.** is necessary with large populations of poor students.

    _____ **c.** does not work.

    _____ **d.** works better than most parents think.

3. Studies have NOT found that retaining improves students'

    _____ **a.** love for learning.

    _____ **b.** self-esteem.

    _____ **c.** graduation rate.

    _____ **d.** all of the above.

4. What is the answer to students who don't do well in school?

    _____ **a.** Have them write a diary.

    _____ **b.** Tell their parents to turn off the TV.

    _____ **c.** Give them extra help in school.

    _____ **d.** Be more strict with them.

5. With what question does the article end?

_____ **a.** Why do we flunk kids?

_____ **b.** What can we do to help low-achieving students?

_____ **c.** How much money should we spend on low-achievers?

_____ **d.** Who exactly is failing whom?

THINKING ABOUT WHAT YOU HAVE READ

1. What do you think is meant by the question asked at the end of the article? State the meaning in your own words.

2. If you were doing poorly in school, what kind of help would you prefer? Give some specific examples.

3. Why is it that more students are held back in first and eighth grade than in any other grade? What could be done to lower the number of students retained in these grades?

4. Do you agree with the author's view of why people think failing kids works? (See paragraph 3.) What other reasons might there be?

5. If teachers were to give all failing students extra help, would they all then do well? Give reasons for your answer.

WRITING ASSIGNMENTS

1. Write an essay describing the class that you had the most trouble with in school. Say what the teacher could have done to help you.

2. Write an essay arguing for or against peer tutors in college.

Credits

PHOTO CREDITS

Index

D

"Daddy Tucked the Blanket" (Williams), 472–474
Dangling modifiers, 403–404
Definition:
  circular, 154–155
  essays in, 508–509, 512–513
  examples of, 149–150
  guidelines for when to use, 144–145
  incomplete, 156–157
Dependent clauses, 301–302
Description:
  dominant impression in, 104–105
  essays in, 481–482, 485–486, 488–489
  five senses in, 111
  organizing details in, 109–110
  using vivid supporting details in, 106–107
Dictionaries, 447
Discussible topic sentence, 51–52
Do/don't, was/wasn't, 333, 334–335
"Doctor-as-God Is Dead, or Dying" (Goodman), 524–525
Dominant impression, 104–105
Double comparisons, 396–397

E

Each/every, either/or, 333, 335–336, 339–340
Edelman, Bart, 485–486
Editing, 272–274
Entertainment, writing as, 17–18, 88
Essays:
  body of, 218–219, 225, 247, 253–254, 256–257
  conclusion of, 221, 225, 247–248, 258–260
  defined, 215
  editing, 272–274
  introduction of (*see* Introduction of essay)
  organizing, 247–263
  proofreading, 276
  repeating words and ideas in, 256
  revising, 267–271
  shell of, 261
  student example of, 223–224, 262–263, 276–280
  thesis statements (*see* Thesis statements)
  title of, 227–228

Evidence, for arguments, 199–200
Examples:
  in argument, 199
  common phrases in, 118
  false, 123
  in illustrating, 115–116
  introducing, 118
  number of, 121–122
  weak and strong, 119–120
Explaining a process, 129–138
  examples of, 130
  logical order of, 133–134
  topic sentence in, 132
  transitions in, 134–135
Extended examples, 121–122

F

Facts, 61–62, 250
  in argument, 199–200
Fallacies, 207–208
False examples, 123
Final consonant, doubling, 451–452
Final draft, 279–280
First draft, 276–279
Formal classification, 162
Formal definitions, 145, 147–148
Fragments:
  caused by a missing subject, 317
  due to added details, 323
  due to dependent words, 321–322
  due to -ing words, 318–319
  due to "to" clauses, 319–320
Freewriting, 31, 33–34
French, Thomas, 496–498
Fused sentences, 327

G

Gerunds, 292–293
Goldberg, Lee, 527–528
Goodman, Ellen, 524–525
Grabbers (opening sentences), 247–251

H

Headnote, 469
Helping verbs, 345, 346, 348–350
Homophones, 459–462
"How I Was Bathed" (Ondaatje), 501–502
"How to Ace a Job Interview" (Koonce), 504–505